PRAXIS
MIDDLE SCHOOL SCIENCE

By: Sharon Wynne, M.S.

XAMonline, INC.
Boston

To obtain permission(s) to use the material from this work for any purpose including workshops or seminars, please submit a written request to:

XAMonline, Inc.
25 First Street, Suite 106
Cambridge, MA 02141
Toll Free 1-800-301-4647
Email: info@xamonline.com
Web: www.xamonline.com
Fax: 1-617-583-5552

Library of Congress Cataloging-in-Publication Data

Wynne, Sharon A.
   PRAXIS Middle School Science 0439 / Sharon A. Wynne. 3rd ed
   ISBN 978-1-60787-343-3
   1. Middle School Science 0439
   2. Study Guides
   3. PRAXIS
   4. Teachers' Certification & Licensure
   5. Careers

Disclaimer:
The opinions expressed in this publication are the sole works of XAMonline and were created independently from the National Education Association, Educational Testing Service, or any State Department of Education, National Evaluation Systems or other testing affiliates.

Between the time of publication and printing, state specific standards as well as testing formats and Web site information may change and therefore would not be included in part or in whole within this product. Sample test questions are developed by XAMonline and reflect content similar to that on real tests; however, they are not former test questions. XAMonline assembles content that aligns with state standards but makes no claims nor guarantees teacher candidates a passing score. Numerical scores are determined by testing companies such as NES or ETS and then are compared with individual state standards. A passing score varies from state to state.

Printed in the United States of America   œ-1

PRAXIS Middle School Science 0439
ISBN: 978-1-60787-343-3

Table of Contents

DOMAIN I
SCIENTIFIC METHODOLOGY, TECHNIQUES, AND HISTORY 1

COMPETENCY 1
METHODOLOGY AND PHILOSOPHY 3

Skill 1.1: Demonstrate understanding of scientific methods of problem solving 3

Skill 1.2: Distinguish among scientific facts, models, theories, and laws 4

Skill 1.3: Use science process skills to experiment, to investigate, and to solve problems................................ 4

Skill 1.4: Demonstrate understanding of experimental design 5

Skill 1.5: Demonstrate knowledge of the historical roots of science 6

Skill 1.6: Demonstrate understanding of the unified, integrative nature of the various disciplines and concepts in science 7

COMPETENCY 2
MATHEMATICS, MEASUREMENT, AND DATA MANIPULATION 9

Skill 2.1: Demonstrate understanding of scientific measurement and notation systems..................................... 9

Skill 2.2: Demonstrate understanding of processes involved in manipulating, interpreting, and presenting scientific data 10

Skill 2.3: Interpret and draw conclusions from data, including those presented in tables, graphs, maps, and charts...................... 10

Skill 2.4: Identify and demonstrate an understanding of sources of error in data that is presented................................. 17

COMPETENCY 3
LABORATORY PROCEDURES AND SAFETY 17

Skill 3.1: Demonstrate understanding of procedures for safe preparation, storage, use, and disposal of laboratory and field materials.. 17

Skill 3.2: Identify laboratory and field equipment appropriate for scientific procedures 19

Skill 3.3: Demonstrate knowledge of safety and emergency procedures for the science classroom and laboratory 21

DOMAIN II
BASIC PRINCIPLES 25

COMPETENCY 4
MATTER AND ENERGY 27
Skill 4.1: Demonstrate understanding of the structure and properties of matter 27
Skill 4.2: Demonstrate understanding of the factors that influence the occurrence and abundance of the elements 28
Skill 4.3: Distinguish between physical and chemical changes of matter 30
Skill 4.4: Demonstrate understanding of the conservation of mass/energy 31
Skill 4.5: Demonstrate understanding of energy transformations 32

COMPETENCY 5
HEAT AND THERMODYNAMICS 33
Skill 5.1: Distinguish between heat and temperature 33
Skill 5.2: Demonstrate understanding of measurement, transfer, and effects of thermal energy 34
Skill 5.3: Solve quantitative problems dealing with the measurement and transfer of thermal energy 36
Skill 5.4: Demonstrate understanding of the First and Second Laws of thermodynamics 38

COMPETENCY 6
ATOMIC AND NUCLEAR STRUCTURE 39
Skill 6.1: Demonstrate understanding of atomic models and their experimental bases 39
Skill 6.2: Demonstrate understanding of atomic and nuclear structure and forces 42
Skill 6.3: Relate electron configuration to the chemical and physical properties of an atom 43
Skill 6.4: Demonstrate knowledge of characteristics of radioisotopes and radioactivity *(for example, half-life)* 45
Skill 6.5: Identify products of nuclear reactions 46

DOMAIN III
PHYSICAL SCIENCES 51

COMPETENCY 7
MECHANICS 55
Skill 7.1: Demonstrate understanding of straight-line, projectile, circular, and periodic motion 55
Skill 7.2: Demonstrate understanding of Newton's laws of motion 56
Skill 7.3: Distinguish between weight and mass 58

Skill 7.4: Demonstrate understanding of friction 58

Skill 7.5: Distinguish among work, energy, and power.. 59

Skill 7.6: Demonstrate understanding of simple machines and torque 60

Skill 7.7: Demonstrate understanding of linear momentum 61

Skill 7.8: Demonstrate understanding of the conservation of energy and the conservation of linear momentum 62

Skill 7.9: Demonstrate understanding of angular momentum and torque and angular momentum conservation............................. 63

Skill 7.10: Demonstrate understanding of the force of gravity 66

Skill 7.11: Demonstrate understanding of pressure and Pascal's principle of fluids 67

Skill 7.12: Demonstrate understanding of Archimedes' principle (buoyancy) 67

Skill 7.13: Demonstrate understanding of Bernoulli's principle for fluids 68

COMPETENCY 8
ELECTRICITY AND MAGNETISM 69

Skill 8.1: Demonstrate understanding of the repulsion and attraction of electric charges............................ 69

Skill 8.2: Demonstrate understanding of the characteristics of current electricity and simple circuits *(for example, resistance and Ohm's law, electromotive force, potential difference capacitance, current)*...................... 69

Skill 8.3: Compare and contrast series and parallel circuits 71

Skill 8.4: Compare and contrast conductors and insulators... 71

Skill 8.5: Apply Ohm's law to series and parallel circuits... 72

Skill 8.6: Compare and contrast direct current and alternating current 72

Skill 8.7: Identify sources of EMF *(for example, batteries, photo cells, generators)* 73

Skill 8.8: Demonstrate understanding of magnets, magnetic fields, and magnetic forces 73

Skill 8.9: Demonstrate understanding of how transformers and motors work 75

COMPETENCY 9
WAVES.. 76

Skill 9.1: Define and use the terms speed, amplitude, wavelength, and frequency 76

Skill 9.2: Distinguish between the characteristics of transverse and longitudinal waves........................... 76

Skill 9.3: Demonstrate understanding of reflection, refraction, dispersion, absorption, transmission, scattering, and superposition 77

Skill 9.4: Demonstrate understanding of diffraction and interference... 78

Skill 9.5: Demonstrate understanding of the Doppler Effect 79

Skill 9.6: Demonstrate understanding of polarization 80

Skill 9.7: Recognize the characteristics of sound waves *(for example, pitch, loudness, speed)* 80

Skill 9.8: Demonstrate understanding of how sound waves are produced by the vibrations of air columns and strings 81

Skill 9.9: Characterize the electromagnetic spectrum *(gamma rays to radio waves)*................................ 81

Skill 9.10: Demonstrate understanding of color and the visible spectrum *(for example, addition and subtraction, relationship to wave frequency)* 82

Skill 9.11: Demonstrate understanding of geometric optics *(mirrors, lenses, prisms, fiber optics)* **and of polarization** 82

COMPETENCY 10
PERIODICITY..83

Skill 10.1: Demonstrate understanding of the meaning of chemical periodicity 83

Skill 10.2: Demonstrate understanding of periodic trends in chemical and physical properties.................................84

COMPETENCY 11
THE MOLE AND CHEMICAL BONDING 88

Skill 11.1: Demonstrate understanding of the mole concept and chemical composition 88

Skill 11.2: Interpret and use chemical formulas 89

Skill 11.3: Demonstrate understanding of the systematic nomenclature of inorganic compounds 91

Skill 11.4: Demonstrate understanding of the nomenclature of simple organic compounds 94

Skill 11.5: Identify the various types of bonds 99

Skill 11.6: Interpret electron dot and structural formulas 100

COMPETENCY 12
THE KINETIC THEORY AND STATES OF MATTER 101

Skill 12.1: Demonstrate understanding of kinetic molecular theory..101

Skill 12.2: Demonstrate understanding of phase changes 103

Skill 12.3: Demonstrate understanding of the relationships among temperature, pressure, volume, and number of molecules of a gas 103

Skill 12.4: Demonstrate understanding of the characteristics of crystals 104

COMPETENCY 13
CHEMICAL REACTIONS 104

Skill 13.1: Demonstrate ability to balance chemical equations 104

Skill 13.2: Identify the various types of chemical reactions 105

Skill 13.3: Distinguish between endothermic and exothermic chemical reactions 105

Skill 13.4: Demonstrate understanding of the effects of temperature, pressure, concentration, and the presence of catalysts on chemical reactions 106

Skill 13.5: Demonstrate understanding of practical applications of electrochemistry.................................107

COMPETENCY 14
SOLUTIONS AND SOLUBILITY 108

Skill 14.1: Demonstrate understanding of solution terminology and distinguish among types of solutions 108

Skill 14.2: Demonstrate understanding of various types of solvents and factors affecting the dissolving process 109

Skill 14.3: Demonstrate understanding of the effect of temperature and pressure on the solubility of a solute 110

Skill 14.4: Demonstrate understanding of the physical and chemical properties of acids, bases, and salts 111

Skill 14.5: Demonstrate knowledge of the meaning of pH and the effects of buffers 112

DOMAIN IV
LIFE SCIENCES 115

COMPETENCY 15
THE CELL 119

Skill 15.1: Demonstrate knowledge of the structure and function of organelles, including membranes 119

Skill 15.2: Distinguish between prokaryotic and eukaryotic cells 121

Skill 15.3: Demonstrate understanding of the cell cycle and cytokinesis 122

Skill 15.4: Demonstrate understanding of chemical reactions in respiration and photosynthesis 123

Skill 15.5: Demonstrate understanding of mitosis and meiosis 127

COMPETENCY 16
GENETICS 129

Skill 16.1: Demonstrate understanding of DNA replication 129

Skill 16.2: Demonstrate understanding of the processes involved in protein synthesis 131

Skill 16.3: Demonstrate understanding of the causes and results of mutation 132

Skill 16.4: Demonstrate understanding of Mendelian inheritance *(monohybrid and dihybrid crosses)* 134

Skill 16.5: Demonstrate understanding of some aspects of non-Mendelian inheritance *(for example, multiple alleles, multiple genes)* 137

Skill 16.6: Demonstrate knowledge of how recombinant DNA is constructed 137

Skill 16.7: Identify uses of recombinant DNA *(for example, in the production of insulin)* 138

Skill 16.8: Demonstrate understanding of the interaction between heredity and environment 139

Skill 16.9: Identify chromosomal and gene aberrations that lead to common human genetic disorders *(for example, Down syndrome)* 142

COMPETENCY 17
EVOLUTION 143

Skill 17.1: Identify evidence that supports the theory of evolution 143

Skill 17.2: Demonstrate understanding of the mechanisms of evolution 144

Skill 17.3: Demonstrate knowledge of isolating mechanisms and speciation 146

Skill 17.4: Demonstrate understanding of the scientific hypotheses for the origin of life on Earth 147

COMPETENCY 18
DIVERSITY OF LIFE 148

Skill 18.1: Demonstrate understanding of the levels of organization and characteristics of life 148

Skill 18.2: Identify the elements of the hierarchical classification scheme into kingdom, phylum, class, order, family, genus, and species 149

Skill 18.3: Demonstrate knowledge of the characteristics of viruses, bacteria, protists, fungi, plants, and animals 150

COMPETENCY 19

PLANTS 155

Skill 19.1: Demonstrate understanding of the characteristics of vascular and nonvascular plants 155

Skill 19.2: Demonstrate understanding of the structure and function of roots, stems, and leaves 156

Skill 19.3: Demonstrate understanding of control mechanisms *(for example, hormones, photoperiods, and tropisms)* 157

Skill 19.4: Demonstrate understanding of water and nutrient uptake and transport systems 158

Skill 19.5: Demonstrate understanding of sexual and asexual reproduction in plants 158

COMPETENCY 20

ANIMALS 160

Skill 20.1: Demonstrate understanding of the anatomy and physiology of structures associated with life functions of organisms in the animal kingdom: digestion; circulation; respiration; excretion; nervous control; musculo-skeletal system; immunity; the endocrine system; reproduction; and development 160

Skill 20.2: Demonstrate knowledge of homeostasis and how it is maintained 167

Skill 20.3: Demonstrate knowledge of how animals respond to stimuli 168

COMPETENCY 21

ECOLOGY 169

Skill 21.1: Demonstrate understanding of population dynamics 169

Skill 21.2: Demonstrate knowledge of social behaviors *(for example, territoriality, dominance, altruism, threat display)* 170

Skill 21.3: Demonstrate understanding of intraspecific competition 170

Skill 21.4: Demonstrate understanding of interspecific relationships *(for example, commensalism, mutualism, parasitism)* 171

Skill 21.5: Demonstrate understanding of succession 172

Skill 21.6: Demonstrate understanding of the concepts of stability of ecosystems and the effects of disturbances 172

Skill 21.7: Demonstrate understanding of energy flow *(for example, trophic levels and food webs)* 174

Skill 21.8: Demonstrate understanding of biogeochemical cycles *(for example, nitrogen, carbon, water)* 175

Skill 21.9: Identify the types and characteristics of biomes 176

DOMAIN V

EARTH/SPACE SCIENCES 179

COMPETENCY 22

PHYSICAL GEOLOGY 183

Skill 22.1: Demonstrate understanding of the processes of mineral and rock formation 183

Skill 22.2: Demonstrate understanding of the methods used to identify and classify different types of minerals, rocks, and soils 184

Skill 22.3: Demonstrate knowledge of the structure of Earth and the physical characteristics of Earth's various layers 185

Skill 22.4: Demonstrate understanding of the internal processes and resulting features of Earth, including folding, faulting, earthquakes, and volcanoes 187

Skill 22.5: Demonstrate understanding of plate tectonic theory and the evidence that supports this theory 190

Skill 22.6: Demonstrate understanding of the hydrologic cycle and the processes by which water moves through the cycle 192

Skill 22.7: Demonstrate understanding of the processes of weathering, erosion, and deposition 193

COMPETENCY 23
HISTORICAL GEOLOGY

HISTORICAL GEOLOGY... 194

Skill 23.1: Demonstrate understanding of the principle of uniformitarianism 194

Skill 23.2: Demonstrate understanding of the basic principles of stratigraphy 195

Skill 23.3: Distinguish between relative and absolute time 196

Skill 23.4: Recognize the processes involved in the formation of fossils..196

Skill 23.5: Demonstrate understanding of the types of information fossils provide...198

Skill 23.6: Demonstrate understanding of the geologic timescale and how it was developed 200

Skill 23.7: Outline the sequence of important events in the Earth's history 201

COMPETENCY 24
OCEANOGRAPHY

OCEANOGRAPHY... 222

Skill 24.1: Demonstrate understanding of the geographic location of oceans and seas 222

Skill 24.2: Demonstrate understanding of the processes involved in the formation and movement of ocean waves.........224

Skill 24.3: Demonstrate understanding of the primary causes and factors that influence tides...............................224

Skill 24.4: Demonstrate knowledge of the major surface and deepwater currents in the oceans and the causes of these currents 225

Skill 24.5: Demonstrate understanding of the processes that influence the topography and landforms of the ocean floor and shorelines 227

Skill 24.6: Demonstrate understanding of the factors that influence the physical and chemical properties of seawater and nutrient cycles of the ocean...229

COMPETENCY 25
METEOROLOGY

METEOROLOGY 230

Skill 25.1: Demonstrate knowledge of the structure of the atmosphere and thermal and chemical properties of atmospheric layers 230

Skill 25.2: Demonstrate knowledge of the chemical composition of the atmosphere 233

Skill 25.3: Demonstrate understanding of the factors influencing seasonal and latitudinal variation of solar radiation...................233

Skill 25.4: Demonstrate understanding of the causes of global wind belts 234

Skill 25.5: Identify the factors that contribute to small-scale atmospheric circulation 235

Skill 25.6: Distinguish among the terms relative humidity, absolute humidity, dew point, and frost point...................237

Skill 25.7: Demonstrate knowledge of various cloud and precipitation types and their formation 238

Skill 25.8: Characterize major types of air masses in terms of temperature, moisture content, and source areas........241

Skill 25.9: Demonstrate understanding of high- and low-pressure systems 242

Skill 25.10: Demonstrate understanding of the structure and movement of frontal systems (cold, warm, stationary, occluded) and the air circulation around and weather associated with frontal systems............................243

Skill 25.11: Interpret information on weather maps 246

Skill 25.12: Demonstrate understanding of the analyses needed to perform short-term weather forecasting and recognize some of the methods used to perform long-term weather forecasting 247

Skill 25.13: Demonstrate understanding of the regional and local natural factors that affect climate......................250

Skill 25.14: Demonstrate understanding of how humans affect and are affected by climate *(for example, desertification, greenhouse effect, volcanic ash effect, El Niño)* 252

COMPETENCY 26
ASTRONOMY 255

Skill 26.1: Demonstrate knowledge of the major theories of origin and structure of the universe 255

Skill 26.2: Define and use large units of distance *(for example, astronomical unit, lightyear, parsec)* 256

Skill 26.3: Demonstrate understanding of the origin and life cycle of stars..257

Skill 26.4: Demonstrate understanding of the major theories involving the origin of the solar system 259

Skill 26.5: Identify the major features and characteristics of the Sun and the source of the Sun's energy..............260

Skill 26.6: Identify the components of the solar system and characterize the physical features and movements of the planets, asteroids, comets, and other solar system components 261

Skill 26.7: Demonstrate understanding of the geometry of the Earth-moon-Sun system and the causes of lunar and solar eclipses 263

Skill 26.8: Demonstrate understanding of the causes of moon phases 264

Skill 26.9: Demonstrate understanding of the causes of Earth's seasons 265

Skill 26.10: Demonstrate knowledge of how units of time *(for example, year, day, hour)* are based on Earth's motions 265

Skill 26.11: Demonstrate understanding of time zones on Earth 266

Skill 26.12: Demonstrate understanding of geosynchronous orbits and recognize how satellites have contributed to science and technology...266

Skill 26.13: Recognize the contributions of manned and unmanned space missions and the present limitations of space exploration..267

Skill 26.14: Recognize the scientific contribution of remote sensing 268

DOMAIN VI
SCIENCE, TECHNOLOGY, AND SOCIETY 269

COMPETENCY 27
SCIENCE, TECHNOLOGY, AND SOCIETY 271

Skill 27.1: Demonstrate an understanding of the uses and applications of science and technology in daily life *(e.g., production, transmission, and use of energy; production, storage, use, management, and disposal of consumer products; management of natural resources; nutrition and public health issues, agricultural practices, etc.)* 271

Skill 27.2: Demonstrate understanding of the social, political, ethical, and economic issues arising from the use of certain technologies *(e.g., cloning, prolonging life, prenatal testing, etc.)* and the impact of science and technology on the environment and human affairs...275

DOMAIN VII
SHORT CONTENT ESSAYS

SHORT CONTENT ESSAYS 277

SAMPLE TEST

Sample Test 285

Answer Key 301

Rigor Table 301

Sample Test with Rationales..302

PRAXIS
MIDDLE SCHOOL
SCIENCE

SECTION 1
ABOUT XAMONLINE

XAMonline—A Specialty Teacher Certification Company

Created in 1996, XAMonline was the first company to publish study guides for state-specific teacher certification examinations. Founder Sharon Wynne found it frustrating that materials were not available for teacher certification preparation and decided to create the first single, state-specific guide. XAMonline has grown into a company of over 1,800 contributors and writers and offers over 300 titles for the entire PRAXIS series and every state examination. No matter what state you plan on teaching in, XAMonline has a unique teacher certification study guide just for you.

XAMonline—Value and Innovation

We are committed to providing value and innovation. Our print-on-demand technology allows us to be the first in the market to reflect changes in test standards and user feedback as they occur. Our guides are written by experienced teachers who are experts in their fields. And our content reflects the highest standards of quality. Comprehensive practice tests with varied levels of rigor means that your study experience will closely match the actual in-test experience.

To date, XAMonline has helped nearly 600,000 teachers pass their certification or licensing exams. Our commitment to preparation exceeds simply providing the proper material for study—it extends to helping teachers **gain mastery** of the subject matter, giving them the **tools** to become the most effective classroom leaders possible, and ushering today's students toward a **successful future**.

SECTION 2
ABOUT THIS STUDY GUIDE

Purpose of This Guide

Is there a little voice inside of you saying, "Am I ready?" Our goal is to replace that little voice and remove all doubt with a new voice that says, "I AM READY. **Bring it on!**" by offering the highest quality of teacher certification study guides.

Organization of Content

You will see that while every test may start with overlapping general topics, each is very unique in the skills they wish to test. Only XAMonline presents custom content that analyzes deeper than a title, a subarea, or an objective. Only XAMonline presents content and sample test assessments along with **focus statements**, the deepest-level rationale and interpretation of the skills that are unique to the exam.

Title and field number of test

→Each exam has its own name and number. XAMonline's guides are written to give you the content you need to know for the specific exam you are taking. You can be confident when you buy our guide that it contains the information you need to study for the specific test you are taking.

Subareas

→These are the major content categories found on the exam. XAMonline's guides are written to cover all of the subareas found in the test frameworks developed for the exam.

Objectives

→These are standards that are unique to the exam and represent the main subcategories of the subareas/content categories. XAMonline's guides are written to address every specific objective required to pass the exam.

Focus statements

→These are examples and interpretations of the objectives. You find them in parenthesis directly following the objective. They provide detailed examples of the range, type, and level of content that appear on the test questions. **Only XAMonline's guides drill down to this level.**

How Do We Compare with Our Competitors?

XAMonline—drills down to the focus statement level.
CliffsNotes and REA—organized at the objective level
Kaplan—provides only links to content
MoMedia—content not specific to the state test

Each subarea is divided into manageable sections that cover the specific skill areas. Explanations are easy to understand and thorough. You'll find that every test answer contains a rejoinder so if you need a refresher or further review after taking the test, you'll know exactly to which section you must return.

How to Use This Book

Our informal polls show that most people begin studying up to eight weeks prior to the test date, so start early. Then ask yourself some questions: How much do you really know? Are you coming to the test straight from your teacher-education program or are you having to review subjects you haven't considered in ten years? Either way, take a **diagnostic or assessment test** first. Also, spend time on sample tests so that you become accustomed to the way the actual test will appear.

This guide comes with an online diagnostic test of 30 questions found online at *www.XAMonline.com*. It is a little boot camp to get you up for the task and reveal things about your compendium of knowledge in general. Although this guide is structured to follow the order of the test, you are not required to study in that order. By finding a time-management and study plan that fits your life you will be more effective. The results of your diagnostic or self-assessment test can be a guide for how to manage your time and point you toward an area that needs more attention.

After taking the diagnostic exam, fill out the **Personalized Study Plan** page at the beginning of each chapter. Review the competencies and skills covered in that chapter and check the boxes that apply to your study needs. If there are sections you already know you can skip, check the "skip it" box. Taking this step will give you a study plan for each chapter.

Week	Activity
8 weeks prior to test	Take a diagnostic test found at www.XAMonline.com
7 weeks prior to test	Build your Personalized Study Plan for each chapter. Check the "skip it" box for sections you feel you are already strong in. ✗ SKIP IT ☐
6-3 weeks prior to test	For each of these four weeks, choose a content area to study. You don't have to go in the order of the book. It may be that you start with the content that needs the most review. Alternately, you may want to ease yourself into plan by starting with the most familiar material.
2 weeks prior to test	Take the sample test, score it, and create a review plan for the final week before the test.
1 week prior to test	Following your plan (which will likely be aligned with the areas that need the most review) go back and study the sections that align with the questions you may have gotten wrong. Then go back and study the sections related to the questions you answered correctly. If need be, create flashcards and drill yourself on any area that you makes you anxious.

SECTION 3
ABOUT THE PRAXIS EXAMS

What Is PRAXIS?

PRAXIS II tests measure the knowledge of specific content areas in K-12 education. The test is a way of insuring that educators are prepared to not only teach in a particular subject area, but also have the necessary teaching skills to be effective. The Educational Testing Service administers the test in most states and has worked with the states to develop the material so that it is appropriate for state standards.

PRAXIS Points

1. The PRAXIS Series comprises more than 140 different tests in over 70 different subject areas.

2. Over 90% of the PRAXIS tests measure subject area knowledge.

3. The purpose of the test is to measure whether the teacher candidate possesses a sufficient level of knowledge and skills to perform job duties effectively and responsibly.

4. Your state sets the acceptable passing score.

5. Any candidate, whether from a traditional teaching-preparation path or an alternative route, can seek to enter the teaching profession by taking a PRAXIS test.

6. PRAXIS tests are updated regularly to ensure current content.

Often **your own state's requirements** determine whether or not you should take any particular test. The most reliable source of information regarding this is your state's Department of Education. This resource should have a complete list of testing centers and dates. Test dates vary by subject area and not all test dates necessarily include your particular test, so be sure to check carefully.

If you are in a teacher-education program, check with the Education Department or the Certification Officer for specific information for testing and testing timelines. The Certification Office should have most of the information you need.

If you choose an alternative route to certification you can either rely on our website at *www.XAMonline.com* or on the resources provided by an alternative certification program. Many states now have specific agencies devoted to alternative certification and there are some national organizations as well, for example:

National Association for Alternative Certification

http://www.alt-teachercert.org/index.asp

Interpreting Test Results

Contrary to what you may have heard, the results of a PRAXIS test are not based on time. More accurately, you will be scored on the raw number of points you earn in relation to the raw number of points available. Each question is worth one raw point. It is likely to your benefit to complete as many questions in the time allotted, but it will not necessarily work to your advantage if you hurry through the test.

Follow the guidelines provided by ETS for interpreting your score. The web site offers a sample test score sheet and clearly explains how the scores are scaled and what to expect if you have an essay portion on your test.

Scores are usually available by phone within a month of the test date and scores will be sent to your chosen institution(s) within six weeks. Additionally, ETS now makes online, downloadable reports available for 45 days from the reporting date.

It is **critical** that you be aware of your own state's passing score. Your raw score may qualify you to teach in some states, but not all. ETS administers the test and assigns a score, but the states make their own interpretations and, in some cases, consider combined scores if you are testing in more than one area.

What's on the Test?

The Praxis Middle School Science 0439 exam lasts 2 hours and consists of two sections: one with 90 multiple-choice questions and one with 3 constructed-response questions. The breakdown of the questions is as follows:

Category	Approximate Number of Questions	Approximate Percentage of the Test
I: Scientific Methodology, Techniques, and History	9	8%
II: Basic Principles	14	11%

Continued on next page

III: Physical Sciences	22	18%
IV: Life Sciences	18	15%
V: Earth/Space Sciences	18	15%
VI: Science, Technology, and Society	9	8%
VII: Short Content Essays (Physical Sciences, Life Sciences, Earth/Space Sciences)	3	25%

Question Types

You're probably thinking, enough already, I want to study! Indulge us a little longer while we explain that there is actually more than one type of multiple-choice question. You can thank us later after you realize how well prepared you are for your exam.

1. **Complete the Statement.** The name says it all. In this question type you'll be asked to choose the correct completion of a given statement. For example:

> **The Dolch Basic Sight Words consist of a relatively short list of words that children should be able to:**
>
> A. Sound out
>
> B. Know the meaning of
>
> C. Recognize on sight
>
> D. Use in a sentence

The correct answer is C. In order to check your answer, test out the statement by adding the choices to the end of it.

2. **Which of the Following.** One way to test your answer choice for this type of question is to replace the phrase "which of the following" with your selection. Use this example:

> **Which of the following words is one of the twelve most frequently used in children's reading texts:**
>
> A. There
>
> B. This
>
> C. The
>
> D. An

Don't look! Test your answer. _____ is one of the twelve most frequently used in children's reading texts. Did you guess C? Then you guessed correctly.

3. Roman Numeral Choices. This question type is used when there is more than one possible correct answer. For example:

> **Which of the following two arguments accurately supports the use of cooperative learning as an effective method of instruction?**
> I.   Cooperative learning groups facilitate healthy competition between individuals in the group.
> II. Cooperative learning groups allow academic achievers to carry or cover for academic underachievers.
> III. Cooperative learning groups make each student in the group accountable for the success of the group.
> IV. Cooperative learning groups make it possible for students to reward other group members for achieving.
>
> A. I and II
> B. II and III
> C. I and III
> D. III and IV

Notice that the question states there are **two** possible answers. It's best to read all the possibilities first before looking at the answer choices. In this case, the correct answer is D.

4. Negative Questions. This type of question contains words such as "not," "least," and "except." Each correct answer will be the statement that does **not** fit the situation described in the question. Such as:

> **Multicultural education is not**
>
> A. An idea or concept
> B. A "tack-on" to the school curriculum
> C. An educational reform movement
> D. A process

Think to yourself that the statement could be anything but the correct answer. This question form is more open to interpretation than other types, so read carefully and don't forget that you're answering a negative statement.

5. **Questions that Include Graphs, Tables, or Reading Passages.** As always, read the question carefully. It likely asks for a very specific answer and not a broad interpretation of the visual. Here is a simple (though not statistically accurate) example of a graph question:

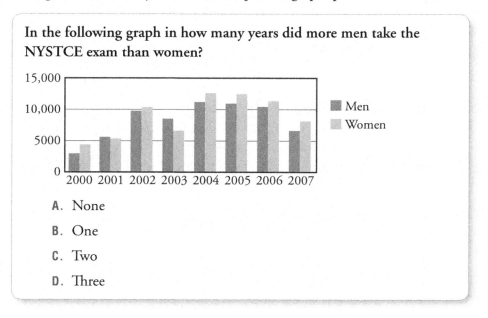

In the following graph in how many years did more men take the NYSTCE exam than women?

A. None

B. One

C. Two

D. Three

It may help you to simply circle the two years that answer the question. Make sure you've read the question thoroughly and once you've made your determination, double check your work. The correct answer is C.

SECTION 4
HELPFUL HINTS

Study Tips

1. **You are what you eat.** Certain foods aid the learning process by releasing natural memory enhancers called CCKs (cholecystokinin) composed of tryptophan, choline, and phenylalanine. All of these chemicals enhance the neurotransmitters associated with memory and certain foods release memory

enhancing chemicals. A light meal or snacks of one of the following foods fall into this category:

- Milk
- Rice
- Eggs
- Fish
- Nuts and seeds
- Oats
- Turkey

The better the connections, the more you comprehend!

2. See the forest for the trees. In other words, get the concept before you look at the details. One way to do this is to take notes as you read, paraphrasing or summarizing in your own words. Putting the concept in terms that are comfortable and familiar may increase retention.

3. Question authority. Ask why, why, why? Pull apart written material paragraph by paragraph and don't forget the captions under the illustrations. For example, if a heading reads *Stream Erosion* put it in the form of a question (Why do streams erode? What is stream erosion?) then find the answer within the material. If you train your mind to think in this manner you will learn more and prepare yourself for answering test questions.

4. Play mind games. Using your brain for reading or puzzles keeps it flexible. Even with a limited amount of time your brain can take in data (much like a computer) and store it for later use. In ten minutes you can: read two paragraphs (at least), quiz yourself with flash cards, or review notes. Even if you don't fully understand something on the first pass, your mind stores it for recall, which is why frequent reading or review increases chances of retention and comprehension.

5. Get pointed in the right direction. Use arrows to point to important passages or pieces of information. It's easier to read than a page full of yellow highlights. Highlighting can be used sparingly, but add an arrow to the margin to call attention to it.

6. Place yourself in exile and set the mood. Set aside a particular place and time to study that best suits your personal needs and biorhythms. If you're a night person, burn the midnight oil. If you're a morning person set yourself up with some coffee and get to it. Make your study time and place as free from distraction as possible and surround yourself with what you need, be it silence or music. Studies have shown that music can aid in concentration, absorption, and retrieval of information. Not all music, though. Classical music is said to work best

7. **The pen is mightier than the sword.** Learn to take great notes. A by-product of our modern culture is that we have grown accustomed to getting our information in short doses. We've subconsciously trained ourselves to assimilate information into neat little packages. Messy notes fragment the flow of information. Your notes can be much clearer with proper formatting. *The Cornell Method* is one such format. This method was popularized in *How to Study in College*, Ninth Edition, by Walter Pauk. You can benefit from the method without purchasing an additional book by simply looking up the method online. Below is a sample of how *The Cornell Method* can be adapted for use with this guide.

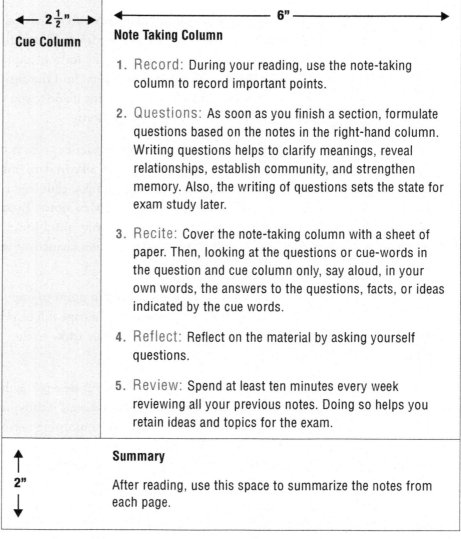

← 2½" →
Cue Column

← 6" →
Note Taking Column

1. Record: During your reading, use the note-taking column to record important points.

2. Questions: As soon as you finish a section, formulate questions based on the notes in the right-hand column. Writing questions helps to clarify meanings, reveal relationships, establish community, and strengthen memory. Also, the writing of questions sets the state for exam study later.

3. Recite: Cover the note-taking column with a sheet of paper. Then, looking at the questions or cue-words in the question and cue column only, say aloud, in your own words, the answers to the questions, facts, or ideas indicated by the cue words.

4. Reflect: Reflect on the material by asking yourself questions.

5. Review: Spend at least ten minutes every week reviewing all your previous notes. Doing so helps you retain ideas and topics for the exam.

↑
2"
↓
Summary

After reading, use this space to summarize the notes from each page.

*Adapted from How to Study in College, Ninth Edition, by Walter Pauk, ©2008 Wadsworth

8. **Check your budget.** You should at least review all the content material before your test, but allocate the most amount of time to the areas that need the most refreshing. It sounds obvious, but it's easy to forget. You can use the study rubric above to balance your study budget.

Testing Tips

1. **Get smart, play dumb.** Sometimes a question is just a question. No one is out to trick you, so don't assume that the test writer is looking for something other than what was asked. Stick to the question as written and don't overanalyze.

2. **Do a double take.** Read test questions and answer choices at least twice because it's easy to miss something, to transpose a word or some letters. If you have no idea what the correct answer is, skip it and come back later if there's time. If you're still clueless, it's okay to guess. Remember, you're scored on the number of questions you answer correctly and you're not penalized for wrong answers. The worst case scenario is that you miss a point from a good guess.

3. **Turn it on its ear.** The syntax of a question can often provide a clue, so make things interesting and turn the question into a statement to see if it changes the meaning or relates better (or worse) to the answer choices.

4. **Get out your magnifying glass.** Look for hidden clues in the questions because it's difficult to write a multiple-choice question without giving away part of the answer in the options presented. In most questions you can readily eliminate one or two potential answers, increasing your chances of answering correctly to 50/50, which will help out if you've skipped a question and gone back to it (see tip #2).

5. **Call it intuition.** Often your first instinct is correct. If you've been studying the content you've likely absorbed something and have subconsciously retained the knowledge. On questions you're not sure about trust your instincts because a first impression is usually correct.

6. **Graffiti.** Sometimes it's a good idea to mark your answers directly on the test booklet and go back to fill in the optical scan sheet later. You don't get extra points for perfectly blackened ovals. If you choose to manage your test this way, be sure not to mismark your answers when you transcribe to the scan sheet.

The proctor will write the start time where it can be seen and then, later, provide the time remaining, typically fifteen minutes before the end of the test.

7. Become a clock-watcher. You have a set amount of time to answer the questions. Don't get bogged down laboring over a question you're not sure about when there are ten others you could answer more readily. If you choose to follow the advice of tip #6, be sure you leave time near the end to go back and fill in the scan sheet.

Do the Drill

No matter how prepared you feel it's sometimes a good idea to apply Murphy's Law. So the following tips might seem silly, mundane, or obvious, but we're including them anyway.

1. Remember, you are what you eat, so bring a snack. Choose from the list of energizing foods that appear earlier in the introduction.

2. You're not too sexy for your test. Wear comfortable clothes. You'll be distracted if your belt is too tight or if you're too cold or too hot.

3. Lie to yourself. Even if you think you're a prompt person, pretend you're not and leave plenty of time to get to the testing center. Map it out ahead of time and do a dry run if you have to. There's no need to add road rage to your list of anxieties.

4. Bring sharp number 2 pencils. It may seem impossible to forget this need from your school days, but you might. And make sure the erasers are intact, too.

5. No ticket, no test. Bring your admission ticket as well as **two** forms of identification, including one with a picture and signature. You will not be admitted to the test without these things.

6. You can't take it with you. Leave any study aids, dictionaries, notebooks, computers, and the like at home. Certain tests **do** allow a scientific or four-function calculator, so check ahead of time to see if your test does.

7. Prepare for the desert. Any time spent on a bathroom break **cannot** be made up later, so use your judgment on the amount you eat or drink.

8. Quiet, Please! Keeping your own time is a good idea, but not with a timepiece that has a loud ticker. If you use a watch, take it off and place it nearby but not so that it distracts you. And **silence your cell phone**.

To the best of our ability, we have compiled the content you need to know in this book and in the accompanying online resources. The rest is up to you. You can use the study and testing tips or you can follow your own methods. Either way, you can be confident that there aren't any missing pieces of information and there shouldn't be any surprises in the content on the test.

If you have questions about test fees, registration, electronic testing, or other content verification issues please visit *www.ets.org*.

Good luck!

Sharon Wynne
Founder, XAMonline

DOMAIN I
SCIENTIFIC METHODOLOGY, TECHNIQUES, AND HISTORY

PERSONALIZED STUDY PLAN

KNOWN MATERIAL/ SKIP IT

PAGE	COMPETENCY AND SKILL	
3	**1:**	**Methodology and philosophy**	☐
	1.1:	Demonstrate understanding of scientific methods of problem solving	☐
	1.2:	Distinguish among scientific facts, models, theories, and laws	☐
	1.3:	Use science process skills to experiment, to investigate, and to solve problems	☐
	1.4:	Demonstrate understanding of experimental design	☐
	1.5:	Demonstrate knowledge of the historical roots of science	☐
	1.6:	Demonstrate understanding of the unified, integrative nature of the various disciplines and concepts in science	☐
9	**2:**	**Mathematics, measurement, and data manipulation**	☐
	2.1:	Demonstrate understanding of scientific measurement and notation systems	☐
	2.2:	Demonstrate understanding of processes involved in manipulating, interpreting, and presenting scientific data	☐
	2.3:	Interpret and draw conclusions from data	☐
	2.4:	Identify and demonstrate an understanding of sources of error in data that is presented	☐
17	**3:**	**Laboratory procedures and safety**	☐
	3.1:	Demonstrate understanding of procedures for safe preparation, storage, use, and disposal of laboratory and field materials	☐
	3.2:	Identify laboratory and field equipment appropriate for scientific procedures	☐
	3.3:	Demonstrate knowledge of safety and emergency procedures	☐

COMPETENCY 1
METHODOLOGY AND PHILOSOPHY

SKILL 1.1 Demonstrate understanding of scientific methods of problem solving

The **SCIENTIFIC METHOD** is the basic process that drives scientific discovery. It involves several steps, from formulating a hypothesis to making a conclusion.

> **SCIENTIFIC METHOD:** the basic process that drives scientific discovery

1. **Pose a question:** Although many discoveries happen by chance, the standard thought process of a scientist begins with forming a question to research. The more limited the question, the easier it is to set up an experiment to answer it.

2. **Form a hypothesis:** Once the question is formulated, take an educated guess about the answer to the problem or question.

3. **Conduct the test:** To make a test fair, data from an experiment must have a variable or a condition that can be changed such as temperature or mass. A good test will try to manipulate as few variables as possible to see which variable is responsible for the result. This requires a second example of a control. A control is an extra setup in which all the conditions are the same except for the variable being tested.

4. **Observe and record the data:** Reporting of the data should state specifics of how the measurements were calculated. For instance, a graduated cylinder needs to be read with proper procedures. For beginning students, technique must be part of the instructional process to give validity to the data.

5. **Draw a conclusion:** Compare the data collected with that from other sets. A conclusion is the judgment derived from the data results.

6. **Graph data:** Graphing data takes numbers and demonstrates patterns that might otherwise be harder to see or make conclusions from. This increases the ease of communicating data to an audience.

SKILL 1.2 Distinguish among scientific facts, models, theories, and laws

Scientific theory and experimentation must be repeatable, provable, and changeable. Science depends on communication, agreement, and disagreement among scientists. It is composed of theories, laws, and hypotheses.

A **HYPOTHESIS** is an unproved theory or educated guess to best explain a phenomenon. Research and testing prove or disprove a hypothesis.

A **SCIENTIFIC THEORY** is a proven hypothesis that explains a set of related observations or relationships.

A **LAW** predicts events that occur with uniformity under the same conditions (laws of nature, law of gravity).

A **MODEL** is a simplification or substitute for what we are actually studying, understanding, or predicting and is a basic element of the scientific method. A model is a substitute, but it is similar to what it represents. We encounter models at every step of our daily living. The Periodic Table of the elements is a model chemists use for predicting the properties of the elements. Physicists use Newton's laws to predict how objects will interact, such as planets and spaceships. In geology, the continental drift model predicts the past positions of continents. Samples, ideas, and methods are all examples of models. The primary activity of the hundreds of thousands of US scientists is to produce new models, resulting in tens of thousands of scientific papers published per year.

Science is limited by the available technology. For instance, the invention of the microscope made possible the discovery of the cell. As our technology improves, we gain more avenues to test hypotheses. The discoveries of science also are limited by the amount and quality of data that we can collect and varying methods of interpreting it. These limitations change explanations as new technologies emerge.

HYPOTHESIS: an unproved theory or educated guess to best explain a phenomenon

SCIENTIFIC THEORY: a proven hypothesis that explains a set of related observations or relationships

LAW: predicts events that occur with uniformity under the same conditions

MODEL: a simplification or substitute for what we are actually studying

SKILL 1.3 Use science process skills to experiment, to investigate, and to solve problems

The steps in scientific inquiry are:

1. Pose a question

2. Form a hypothesis to provide a plausible explanation

3. Propose and perform an experiment to test this hypothesis

4. Compare the predicted and observed results

5. Form conclusions and determine whether the hypothesis is correct or incorrect

6. If incorrect, form a new hypothesis and repeat the process

Normally, knowledge is integrated in the form of a lab report, with a title specifying the topic of study. The abstract is a summary of the report written at the beginning of the paper. The purpose should always be defined and will state the problem and include the hypothesis (educated guess) of what is expected from the outcome of the experiment. The entire experiment should relate to this problem. It is important to describe exactly what was done to prove or disprove a hypothesis.

A control is necessary to prove that the outcome resulted from the changed conditions and would not just happen normally. Only one variable should be manipulated at one time. Observations and results of the experiment should be recorded, including all results from data. Drawings, graphs, and illustrations should be included to support information. Observations are objective, whereas analysis and interpretation is subjective. A conclusion should explain why the results of the experiment either proved or disproved the hypothesis.

Science attempts to investigate and explain the natural world. Its related field, technology, attempts to solve human adaptation problems. Technology often results from the application of scientific discoveries, and advances in technology can increase the impact of scientific discoveries. For example, Watson and Crick used science to discover the structure of DNA, and their discovery led to many biotechnological advances in the manipulation of DNA. These technological advances greatly influenced the medical and pharmaceutical fields. The success of Watson and Crick's experiments, however, was dependent on the technology available. Without the necessary technology, the experiments would have failed.

SKILL 1.4 Demonstrate understanding of experimental design

The procedure used to obtain data is important to the outcome. Experiments consist of controls and variables. A **CONTROL** is the experiment run under normal conditions. The **VARIABLE** is the factor that is changed. In biology, the variable may be light, temperature, pH, time, etc. The differences in tested variables may be used to make a prediction or form a hypothesis. Only one variable should

> **CONTROL:** an experiment run under normal conditions

> **VARIABLE:** an experiment that is run with one factor that is changed

be tested at a time, so one would not alter both the temperature and pH of the experimental subject at the same time.

INDEPENDENT VARIABLE: one that is changed or manipulated by the researcher

An **INDEPENDENT VARIABLE** is one that is changed or manipulated by the researcher, such as the amount of light a plant receives or the temperature at which bacteria is grown. A **DEPENDENT VARIABLE** is one that is influenced by the independent variable.

DEPENDENT VARIABLE: one that is influenced by the independent variable

When designing an experiment, it is important to limit bias as much as possible. Scientific research can be biased in the choice of which data to consider, in the reporting or recording of the data, and/or in how the data are interpreted. The scientist's emphasis may be influenced by his/her nationality, sex, ethnic origin, age, or political convictions. Awareness of potential biases will aid you in planning your experiment.

SKILL 1.5 Demonstrate knowledge of the historical roots of science

ANTON VAN LEEUWENHOEK: the father of microscopy who made magnifying lenses that allowed him to see and describe microscopic life

ANTON VAN LEEUWENHOEK is known as the father of microscopy. In the 1650s, Leeuwenhoek began making tiny lenses that gave magnifications up to 300x. He was the first to see and describe bacteria, yeast plants, and the microscopic life found in water. Over the years, light microscopes have advanced to produce greater clarity and magnification. The scanning electron microscope (SEM) was developed in the 1950s. Instead of light, a beam of electrons passes through the specimen. Scanning electron microscopes have a resolution about one thousand times greater than light microscopes. The disadvantage of the SEM is that the chemical and physical methods used to prepare the sample result in the death of the specimen.

LOUIS PASTEUR: discovered the role of microorganisms in the cause of disease, pasteurization, and the rabies vaccine

ROBERT KOCH: discovered that specific diseases were caused by specific pathogens

In the late 1800s, **LOUIS PASTEUR** discovered the role of microorganisms in the cause of disease, pasteurization, and the rabies vaccine. **ROBERT KOCH** took this observation one step further by formulating that specific diseases were caused by specific pathogens. Koch's postulates are still used as guidelines in the field of microbiology: the same pathogen must be found in every diseased person, the pathogen must be isolated and grown in culture, the disease must be induced in experimental animals from the culture, and the same pathogen must be isolated from the experimental animal.

JAMES WATSON AND FRANCIS CRICK: discovered that the structure of a DNA molecule is a double helix

In the 1950s, **JAMES WATSON** and **FRANCIS CRICK** discovered that the structure of a DNA molecule is a double helix. This structure made it possible to explain DNA's ability to replicate and to control the synthesis of proteins.

The use of animals in biological research has expedited many scientific discoveries, including the workings of the circulatory and reproductive systems. One significant use of animals is for the testing of drugs, vaccines, and other products (such as perfumes and shampoos) before use or consumption by humans. Along with the pros of animal research, the cons are also very significant. The debate about the ethical treatment of animals has been ongoing since the introduction of animals in research. Many people believe the use of animals in research is cruel and unnecessary. Animal use is federally and locally regulated. The purpose of the Institutional Animal Care and Use Committee (IACUC) is to oversee and evaluate all aspects of an institution's animal care and use program.

SKILL 1.6 Demonstrate understanding of the unified, integrative nature of the various disciplines and concepts in science

MATH, SCIENCE, and TECHNOLOGY have common themes in how they are applied and understood. All three use models, diagrams, and graphs to simplify a concept for analysis and interpretation. Patterns observed in these systems lead to predictions based on these observations.

> **MATH, SCIENCE, AND TECHNOLOGY:** use models, diagrams, and graphs to simplify a concept for analysis and interpretation

Over the course of Earth's history, living organisms have been greatly affected by Earth processes. Volcanic eruptions, plate tectonics, and climate change have affected whether living things have survived or how they have adapted to survive.

Earth's processes also have affected how humans live. The most fertile land for farming is at the base of volcanoes. We have developed technologies to irrigate farmland, build "safe" buildings in earthquake-prone areas, and prevent low-lying areas from flooding. Currently, humans' impact on the environment and on the Earth's temperature is being widely felt. All in all, biology has been greatly affected by Earth processes.

Science and chemistry are tightly woven. The chemical composition of the rocks and the temperature and pressure at which crystals form are an obvious connection between chemistry and Earth science (geology). Chemistry and oceanography are connected inherently because the salinity of Earth's oceans is affected by the temperature at which water freezes, the density of water, and the solubility of certain chemical compounds. Chemistry and meteorology are connected through the chemical makeup of the atmosphere and the effects that human-released chemicals have on the atmosphere (i.e., CFC's effect on the ozone layer and carbon dioxide's role in climate change).

Earthquakes, plate tectonics, and meteorology are all related to physics. Fault production and earthquakes are caused by the processes of plate tectonics forming zones of weakness in the crust. The pressure builds up along fault lines until it exceeds the static frictional force of the fault line, releasing seismic waves. The frictional force and the dynamics of the Earth's motion during earthquakes are all related to physics.

Meteorology and physics are closely related. Changes in atmospheric pressure cause winds, updrafts, and storms. These pressure changes are caused by changes in temperature. Warm, moist air rises because it is less dense than the air surrounding it. As air rises and cools, it condenses, forming cloud systems. When meteorologists predict the weather, they study the physics of the interaction between volume, humidity, temperature, and pressure.

Mathematics can be used to solve many problems in science. Examples include finding the relative humidity, the residence time of materials in the soil, discharge of water, and genetic probabilities. Algebra and trigonometry are extensively used in physics.

The following are the concepts and processes generally recognized as common to all scientific disciplines:

SYSTEMS: items organized into small groups based on interaction or interdependence

ORDER: explains the behavior and measurability of organisms and events in nature

MODELS: a miniaturized representation of a larger event or system

EVIDENCE: anything that furnishes proof

EVOLUTION: the process of change over a long period of time

- Because the natural world is so complex, the study of science involves the organization of items into smaller groups based on interaction or interdependence. These groups are called **SYSTEMS**. Examples of organization are the periodic table of elements and the five-kingdom classification scheme for living organisms. Examples of systems are the solar system, cardiovascular system, Newton's laws of force and motion, and the laws of conservation of matter. **ORDER** refers to the behavior and measurability of organisms and events in nature. The arrangement of planets in the solar system and the life cycle of bacterial cells are examples of order.

- Scientists use evidence and models to form explanations of natural events. **MODELS** are miniaturized representations of a larger event or system. **EVIDENCE** is anything that furnishes proof.

- Constancy and change describe the observable properties of natural organisms and events. Scientists use different systems of measurement to observe change and constancy. For example, the freezing and melting points of given substances and the speed of sound are constant under constant conditions. Growth, decay, and erosion are all examples of natural change.

- **EVOLUTION** is the process of change over a long period of time. While biological evolution is the most common example, one can also classify technological advancement, changes in the universe, and changes in the environment as evolution. **EQUILIBRIUM** is the state of balance between opposing forces of change. Homeostasis and ecological balance are examples of equilibrium.

- Form and function are properties of organisms and systems that are closely related. The function of an object usually dictates its form, and the form of an object usually facilitates its function. For example, the form of the heart (e.g. muscle, valves) allows it to perform its function of circulating blood through the body.

> **EQUILIBRIUM:** the state of balance between opposing forces of change, such as homeostasis and ecological balance

COMPETENCY 2
MATHEMATICS, MEASUREMENT, AND DATA MANIPULATION

SKILL 2.1 Demonstrate understanding of scientific measurement and notation systems

Science uses the **METRIC SYSTEM**. It is accepted worldwide and allows easier comparison among experiments done by scientists around the world.

- The meter is the basic unit of length. One meter is 1.1 yards.

- The liter is the basic metric unit of volume. 1 gallon is 3.846 liters.

- The gram is the basic metric unit of mass. 1000 grams is 2.2 pounds.

> **METRIC SYSTEM:** the global standard for scientific measurement and notation

The following prefixes are used to describe the multiples of the basic metric units.

deca-	10X the base unit	deci-	1/10 the base unit
hecto-	100X the base unit	centi-	1/100 the base unit
kilo-	1,000X the base unit	milli-	1/1,000 the base unit
mega-	1,000,000X the base unit	micro-	1/1,000,000 the base unit
giga-	1,000,000,000X the base unit	nano-	1/1,000,000,000 the base unit
tera-	1,000,000,000,000X the base unit	pico-	1/1,000,000,000,000 the base unit

Appropriate Measuring Devices

There is an appropriate measuring device for each aspect of science and an appropriate way to measure each variable. A microscope is used to view microscopic objects. A centrifuge is used to separate two or more parts in a liquid sample. The Internet and teaching guides offer resources for laboratory ideas.

The common instrument used for measuring volume is the graduated cylinder. The unit of measurement is usually in milliliters (mL), read for accuracy at the bottom of the meniscus, the curved surface of the liquid.

The common instrument used for measuring mass is the triple beam balance. The triple beam balance is measured in tenths of a gram and can be estimated to hundredths of a gram.

The ruler or meter sticks are the most commonly used instruments for measuring length.

LINE GRAPHS: compares different sets of related data or predicts data that have not yet been measured

---

SKILL 2.2 **Demonstrate understanding of processes involved in manipulating, interpreting, and presenting scientific data**

BAR GRAPH or **HISTOGRAM:** compares different items by representing them as bars or rectangles

PIE CHART: organizes data as part of a whole circle

The type of graphic representation used to display observations depends on the data that is collected. **LINE GRAPHS** compare different sets of related data or predict data that have not yet been measured. For example, a line graph could compare the rate of activity of different enzymes at varying temperatures. A **BAR GRAPH** or **HISTOGRAM** compares different items and makes comparisons based on these data. For example, a bar graph could compare the ages of children in a classroom. A **PIE CHART** organizes data as part of a whole. A pie chart could display the percent of time students spend on various after-school activities.

SKILL 2.3 **Interpret and draw conclusions from data, including those presented in tables, graphs, maps, and charts**

When first collected, data initially are organized into tables, spreadsheets, or databases. For example, the table below presents carbon dioxide concentrations taken over many years from the observatory atop the Mauna Loa volcano.

ATMOSPHERIC CO2 CONCENTRATIONS AT MAUNA LOA													
Year	Jan.	Feb.	March	April	May	June	July	Aug.	Sept.	Oct.	Nov.	Dec.	Annual
1958	--	--	315.71	317.45	317.50	--	315.86	314.93	313.19	--	313.34	314.67	--
1959	315.58	316.47	316.65	317.71	318.29	318.16	316.55	314.80	313.84	313.34	314.81	315.59	315.98
1960	316.43	316.97	317.58	319.03	320.03	319.59	318.18	315.91	314.16	313.83	315.00	316.19	316.91
1961	316.89	317.70	318.54	319.48	320.58	319.78	318.58	316.79	314.99	315.31	316.10	317.01	317.65
1962	317.94	318.56	319.69	320.58	321.01	320.61	319.61	317.40	316.26	315.42	316.69	317.69	318.45
1963	318.74	319.08	319.86	321.39	322.24	321.47	319.74	317.77	316.21	315.99	317.07	318.36	318.99
1964	319.57	--	--	--	322.23	321.89	320.44	318.70	316.70	316.87	317.68	318.71	--
1965	319.44	320.44	320.89	322.13	322.16	321.87	321.21	318.87	317.81	317.30	318.87	319.42	320.03
1966	320.62	321.59	322.39	323.70	324.07	323.75	322.40	320.37	318.64	318.10	319.79	321.03	321.37
1967	322.33	322.50	323.04	324.42	325.00	324.09	322.55	320.92	319.26	319.39	320.72	321.96	322.18
1968	322.57	323.15	323.89	325.02	325.57	325.36	324.14	322.11	320.33	320.25	321.32	322.90	323.05
1969	324.00	324.42	325.64	326.66	327.38	326.70	325.89	323.67	322.38	321.78	322.85	324.12	324.62
1970	325.06	325.98	326.93	328.13	328.07	327.66	326.35	324.69	323.10	323.07	324.01	325.13	325.68
1971	326.17	326.68	327.18	327.78	328.92	328.57	327.37	325.43	323.36	323.56	324.80	326.01	326.32
1972	326.77	327.63	327.75	329.72	330.07	329.09	328.05	326.32	324.84	325.20	326.50	327.55	327.46
1973	328.54	329.56	330.30	331.50	332.48	332.07	330.87	329.31	327.51	327.18	328.16	328.64	329.68
1974	329.35	330.71	331.48	332.65	333.09	332.25	331.18	329.40	327.44	327.37	328.46	329.58	330.25
1975	330.40	331.41	332.04	333.31	333.96	333.59	331.91	330.06	328.56	328.34	329.49	330.76	331.15
1976	331.74	332.56	333.50	334.58	334.87	334.34	333.05	330.94	329.30	328.94	330.31	331.68	332.15
1977	332.92	333.42	334.70	336.07	336.74	336.27	334.93	332.75	331.58	331.16	332.40	333.85	333.90
1978	334.97	335.39	336.64	337.76	338.01	337.89	336.54	334.68	332.76	332.54	333.92	334.95	335.50

Continued on next page

1979	336.23	336.76	337.96	338.89	339.47	339.29	337.73	336.09	333.91	333.86	335.29	336.73	336.85
1980	338.01	338.36	340.08	340.77	341.46	341.17	339.56	337.60	335.88	336.01	337.10	338.21	338.69
1981	339.23	340.47	341.38	342.51	342.91	342.25	340.49	338.43	336.69	336.85	338.36	339.61	339.93
1982	340.75	341.61	342.70	343.56	344.13	343.35	342.06	339.82	337.97	337.86	339.26	340.49	341.13
1983	341.37	342.52	343.10	344.94	345.75	345.32	343.99	342.39	339.86	339.99	341.16	342.99	342.78
1984	343.70	344.51	345.28	347.08	347.43	346.79	345.40	343.28	341.07	341.35	342.98	344.22	344.42
1985	344.97	346.00	347.43	348.35	348.93	348.25	346.56	344.69	343.09	342.80	344.24	345.56	345.90
1986	346.29	346.96	347.86	349.55	350.21	349.54	347.94	345.91	344.86	344.17	345.66	346.90	347.15
1987	348.02	348.47	349.42	350.99	351.84	351.25	349.52	348.10	346.44	346.36	347.81	348.96	348.93
1988	350.43	351.72	352.22	353.59	354.22	353.79	352.39	350.44	348.72	348.88	350.07	351.34	351.48
1989	352.76	353.07	353.68	355.42	355.67	355.13	353.90	351.67	349.80	349.99	351.30	352.53	352.91
1990	353.66	354.70	355.39	356.20	357.16	356.22	354.82	352.91	350.96	351.18	352.83	354.21	354.19
1991	354.72	355.75	357.16	358.60	359.34	358.24	356.17	354.03	352.16	352.21	353.75	354.99	355.59
1992	355.98	356.72	357.81	359.15	359.66	359.25	357.03	355.00	353.01	353.31	354.16	355.40	356.37
1993	356.70	357.16	358.38	359.46	360.28	359.60	357.57	355.52	353.70	353.98	355.33	356.80	357.04
1994	358.36	358.91	359.97	361.26	361.68	360.95	359.55	357.49	355.84	355.99	357.58	359.04	358.88
1995	359.96	361.00	361.64	363.45	363.79	363.26	361.90	359.46	358.06	357.75	359.56	360.70	360.88
1996	362.05	363.25	364.03	364.72	365.41	364.97	363.65	361.49	359.46	359.60	360.76	362.33	362.64
1997	363.18	364.00	364.57	366.35	366.79	365.62	364.47	362.51	360.19	360.77	362.43	364.28	363.76
1998	365.32	366.15	367.31	368.61	369.30	368.87	367.64	365.77	363.90	364.23	365.46	366.97	366.63
1999	368.15	368.86	369.58	371.12	370.97	370.33	369.25	366.91	364.60	365.09	366.63	367.96	368.29
2000	369.08	369.40	370.45	371.59	371.75	371.62	370.04	368.04	366.54	366.63	368.20	369.43	369.40
2001	370.17	371.39	372.00	372.75	373.88	373.17	371.48	369.42	367.83	367.96	369.55	371.10	370.89
2002	372.29	372.94	373.38	374.71	375.40	375.26	373.87	371.35	370.57	370.10	371.93	373.63	372.95

(Carbon Dioxide Information Analysis Center [CDIAC])

Looking at this table of data in various ways we can make several observations, with the help of a calculator:

- Data Completeness: There are some gaps in the data between 1958 and 1964. From 1965 on, observations of CO_2 levels in the atmosphere have been made consistently every month.

- Seasonal Effects: Looking across the rows of data, we can identify seasonal trends within years. For example, we can see that the highest concentrations tend to be in April, May, and June, and the lowest concentrations tend to be in September and October. The difference appears to be about 4–5 ppm.

- Long-Term Trends: Looking down the columns of data, we can evaluate long-term trends over the years shown. In every month, concentrations of CO2 have risen approximately 58 ppm over 45 years, or about 1.3 ppm/yr.

Line Graphs

While these trends can be observed from tables of data, the data are then compiled into graphs or charts. Graphs help scientists visualize and interpret variations and patterns in data. The following is the same set of data presented as a line graph:

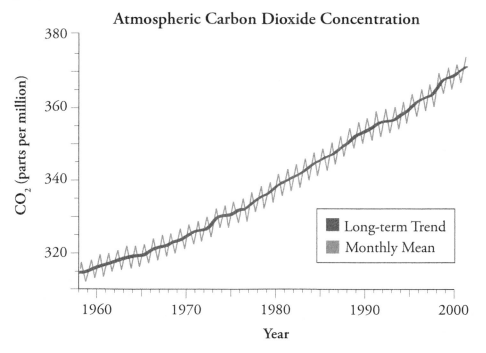

Atmospheric CO_2 measured at Mauna Loa. This is a famous graph called the Keeling Curve (courtesy NASA)

Bar Graphs

To use a bar graph, first determine the scale used for the graph. Then note the length of each bar on the graph to determine the amount or number of each category of data.

Example: From the bar graph below, determine the percentage of students eligible for athletic programs that require that students maintain a C or better average.

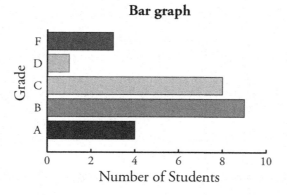

Bar graph

Solution: From the bar graph, we can see that 4 students received an A, 9 received a B, 8 received a C, 1 received a D, and 3 students received an F. The total number of students is $4 + 9 + 8 + 1 + 3 = 25$ students. Of these, $4 + 9 + 8 = 21$ received A, B, or C grades. The percentage of students eligible for athletic programs is 21/25, or 84%.

Circle or Pie Graphs

To make a circle or pie graph, total all the information that is to be included on the graph. Determine the central angle to be used for each sector of the graph using the following formula:

percent of total × 360º = degrees in central angle

Lay out the central angles to these sizes, label each section, and include its percent of the total.

Example: Graph the following information on a circle graph and identify the percentage of monthly expenses going to basic living expenses (rent, food, and utilities).

MONTHLY EXPENSES	
Rent	$400
Food	$150
Utilities	$75
Clothes	$75
Church	$100
Misc.	$200

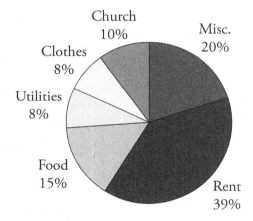

Solution: The percentage of expenses going to rent, food, and utilities can be easily added up from the graph: 39% + 15% + 8% = 62%. In addition, a rapid visual assessment of these three sections of the graph indicates that the proportion is roughly $\frac{2}{3}$.

Scatter Plots

Scatter plots compare two characteristics of the same group of things or people and usually consist of a large body of data. They show how much one variable is affected by another. The relationship between the two variables is their correlation. The closer the data points come to making a straight line when plotted, the closer the correlation.

Example: What conclusions can be drawn from the graph below, correlating salaries of geologists with years of experience?

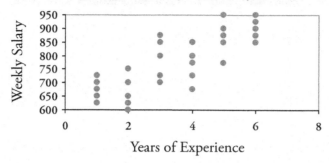

Solution: The weekly salary of geologists is partially correlated with years of experience, since the overall range of salaries paid rises with years of experience. However, other factors are also important, because the ranges overlap substantially among years.

Histograms

Histograms are used to summarize information from large sets of data that can be naturally grouped into intervals. The vertical axis indicates frequency (the number of times any particular data value occurs), and the horizontal axis indicates data values or ranges of data values. The number of data values in any interval is the frequency of the interval.

Example: The starting salaries of 13 geologists are shown in the histogram below. What is the most frequent salary offered, and what is the median salary?

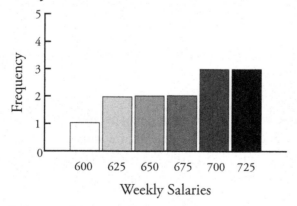

Solution: The most frequent salaries offered are $700/week and $725/week, which occur with equal frequency. To find the median starting salary, translate the above data into a data set for all 13 geologists, ordered from least to most money as follows: {600, 625, 625, 650, 650, 675, 675, 700, 700, 700, 725, 725, 725}. The median is the middle value from this set, or $675.

SKILL 2.4 Identify and demonstrate an understanding of sources of error in data that is presented

There are many ways in which errors can creep into measurements because of

- Improper use of the instruments used for measuring, weighing, and so on

- Parallax error (incorrectly positioning the eyes during reading of measurements)

- Using different instruments and methods of measurement during an experiment

- Using different sources of materials, resulting in variations of the content of certain compounds used for experimentation

Besides these mentioned above, there can be other possible sources of error as well. When reviewing data that is presented, it is important to be mindful of the possibility of error. An experiment is valid only when all the constants such as time, place, method of measurement, and so on are strictly controlled.

COMPETENCY 3
LABORATORY PROCEDURES AND SAFETY

SKILL 3.1 Demonstrate understanding of procedures for safe preparation, storage, use, and disposal of laboratory and field materials

All laboratory solutions should be prepared as directed in the lab manual. Care should be taken to avoid contamination. All glassware should be rinsed thoroughly with distilled water before using and cleaned well after use. All solutions should be made with distilled water as tap water contains dissolved particles that may affect the results of an experiment. Unused solutions should be disposed of according to local disposal procedures.

The "**RIGHT TO KNOW LAW**" covers science teachers who work with potentially hazardous chemicals. Briefly, the law states that employees must be informed of potentially toxic chemicals. If requested, an inventory must be made available

RIGHT TO KNOW LAW: covers science teachers who work with potentially hazardous chemicals and requires that employees be informed of potentially toxic chemicals

of the kind, hazards, and properties of the chemicals and checked against the "Substance List." Training must be provided on the safe handling and interpretation of the Material Safety Data Sheet.

The following chemicals are potential carcinogens and are not allowed in school facilities:

- Acrylonitrile
- Arsenic compounds
- Asbestos
- Benzidine
- Benzene
- Cadmium compounds
- Chloroform
- Chromium compounds
- Ethylene oxide
- Ortho-toluidine
- Nickel powder
- Mercury

Chemicals should not be stored on bench tops or heat sources. They should be stored in groups based on their reactivity with one another and in protective storage cabinets in a secured, dry area. All containers within the lab must be labeled. Acids are to be locked in a separate area. Suspect and known carcinogens must be labeled as such and segregated within trays to contain leaks and spills.

Waste should be separated based on its reactivity with other chemicals. Chemical waste should be disposed of in properly labeled containers according to local disposal procedures. Any questions regarding safe disposal or chemical safety may be directed to the local fire department.

Biological material should never be stored near food or water used for human consumption. All biological material should be appropriately labeled. All blood and body fluids should be put in a secure container with a lid to prevent leaking. All biological waste should be disposed of in biological hazardous waste bags.

Material safety data sheets are available—either directly from the company of acquisition or the Internet—for every chemical and biological substance. The manuals for equipment used in the lab should be read and understood before using them. Safety goggles should be worn while working with glassware in case of an accident.

Lab materials are readily available from the many school suppliers that routinely send their catalogues to schools. Many times, common materials are available at the local grocery store. The use of locally available flora and fauna both reduces cost and familiarizes students with local organisms.

SKILL 3.2 Identify laboratory and field equipment appropriate for scientific procedures

Bunsen burners: Hot plates should be used whenever possible to avoid the risk of burns or fire. If Bunsen burners are used, the following precautions should be followed:

1. Know the location of fire extinguishers and safety blankets, and train students in their use. Long hair and long sleeves should be secured and out of the way.

2. Turn the gas all the way on and make a spark with the striker.

3. Adjust the air valve at the bottom of the Bunsen burner until the flame shows an inner cone.

4. Adjust the flow of gas to the desired flame height by using the adjustment valve.

5. Do not touch the barrel of the burner since it is hot.

6. The preferred method to light burners is to use strikers rather than matches.

Graduated Cylinder: Used for precise measurements, graduated cylinders should always be placed on a flat surface. The surface of the liquid will form a meniscus (a lens-shaped curve). The measurement is read at the bottom of this curve.

Balance: Electronic balances are easy to use, but can be expensive. An electronic balance should always be tared before measuring and should be used on a flat surface. Substances should always be placed on a piece of paper to avoid messes and damage to the instrument.

Triple beam balances must be used on a level surface. Use the screws located at the bottom of the balance to make adjustments. To measure a sample's weight, start with the largest counterweight first, and set it to the last notch that does not tip the balance. Do the same with the next largest, etc., until the pointer remains at zero. The total mass is the total of all the readings on the beams. Again, use paper under the substance to protect the equipment.

Buret: A **BURET** is used to dispense precisely measured volumes of liquid. A stopcock controls the volume of liquid being dispensed.

> **BURET:** uses a stopcock to dispense precisely measured volumes of liquid

Light microscope: Light microscopes are commonly used in laboratory experiments. Several procedures should be followed to properly care for this equipment:

- Clean all lenses with lens paper only.
- Carry the microscope with two hands; one on the arm and one on the base.
- Always begin focusing on low power, then switch to high power.
- Store microscopes with the low-power objective down.
- Always use a coverslip when viewing wet mount slides.
- Bring the objective down to its lowest position, then focus, moving up to avoid breaking the slide or scratching the lens.

Wet mount slides should be made by placing a drop of water on the specimen and then putting a glass coverslip on top of the drop of water. Dropping the coverslip at a forty-five degree angle will help in avoiding air bubbles.

Total magnification is determined by multiplying the ocular (usually 10X) and the objective (usually 10X on low, 40X on high).

- **Chromatography:** Chromatography uses the principles of capillarity to separate substances such as plant pigments. Molecules of a larger size will move more slowly up the paper, whereas smaller molecules will move more quickly, producing corresponding lines of pigment.

- **Indicator:** Any substance used to assist in the classification of another substance. An example of an indicator is litmus paper that measures whether a substance is acidic or basic. Blue litmus turns pink when placed in an acid, and pink litmus turns blue when dipped in a base. pH paper is a more accurate measure of pH, with the paper turning different colors depending on the pH value.

- **Centrifuge:** A centrifuge spins substances at a high speed to separate the denser from the lighter portions of a solution. The denser part of a solution settles to the bottom of the test tube, while the lighter material stays on top. Centrifugation separates blood into blood cells and plasma, with the heavier blood cells settling to the bottom.

- **Electrophoresis:** Electrophoresis uses electrical charges of molecules to separate them according to their size. The molecules, such as DNA or proteins, are pulled through a gel toward either the positive end of the gel box (if the material has a negative charge) or the negative end of the gel box (if the material has a positive charge). DNA is negatively charged and moves toward the positive charge.

- Spectrophotometry: Spectrophotometry measures percent of light at different wavelengths absorbed and transmitted by a pigment solution.

SKILL 3.3 Demonstrate knowledge of safety and emergency procedures for the science classroom and laboratory

All science labs should contain the following items of safety equipment. Those marked with an asterisk are required by state laws.

- Fire blanket that is visible and accessible*

- Ground Fault Circuit Interrupters (GFCI) within two feet of water supplies

- Signs designating room exits*

- Emergency shower providing a continuous flow of water*

- Emergency eyewash station that can be activated by the foot or forearm*

- Eye protection for every student and a means of sanitizing equipment*

- Emergency exhaust fans providing ventilation to the outside of the building*

- Master cut-off switches for gas, electricity, and compressed air (switches must have permanently attached handles, and cut-off switches must be clearly labeled)*

- An ABC fire extinguisher*

- Storage cabinets for flammable materials*

- Chemical spill control kit

- Fume hood with a motor that is spark proof

- Protective laboratory aprons made of flame retardant material

- Signs that alert to potential hazardous conditions

- Containers for broken glassware, flammables, corrosives, and waste

- Containers should be labeled

Students should wear safety goggles when performing dissections, heating, or while using acids and bases. Hair should always be tied back, and objects should never be placed in the mouth. Food should not be consumed while in the laboratory. Hands should always be washed before and after laboratory experiments.

The Teacher's Responsibility

It is the responsibility of the teacher to provide a safe environment for his or her students. Proper supervision greatly reduces the risk of injury. A teacher should never leave a class for any reason without providing alternate supervision.

All students and staff should be trained in first aid in the science classroom and laboratory and reminded always to report all accidents, however minor, to the lab instructor immediately. In most situations, you should immediately call 911. Please refer to your school's specific safety plan for accidents in the classroom and laboratory.

The classroom/laboratory should have a complete first-aid kit with supplies that are up-to-date and checked frequently for expiration. Know the location and use of fire extinguishers, eye-wash stations, and safety showers in the lab.

Accident Procedures

In case of an accident, eye washes and showers should be used for eye contamination or for a chemical spill that covers the student's body. Small chemical spills should be contained and cleaned by the teacher with kitty litter or a chemical spill kit. For large spills, the school administration and the local fire department should be notified. Biological spills should also be handled only by the teacher. When appropriate, contamination with biological waste can be cleaned by using bleach.

Do not attempt to smother a fire in a beaker or flask with a fire extinguisher. The force of the stream of material from it will turn over the vessel and result in a larger fire. Just place a watch glass or a wet towel over the container to cut off the supply of oxygen.

If your clothing is on fire, **do not run** because this only increases the burning. It is normally best to fall on the floor and roll over to smother the fire. If necessary, use the fire blanket or safety shower in the lab to smother the fire. Below are common accidents that everyone who uses the laboratory should be trained to respond to.

- Burns (Chemical or Fire): Use deluge shower for 15 minutes.
- Burns (Clothing on fire): Use safety shower immediately. Keep victim immersed 15 minutes to wash away both heat and chemicals. All burns should be examined by medical personnel.
- Chemical spills: Chemical spills on hands or arms should be washed immediately with soap and water. Spills that cover clothing and other parts of the body should be drenched under the safety shower. If strong acids or bases are spilled on clothing, the clothing should be removed.

- If a large area is affected, remove clothing and immerse victim in the safety shower. If a small area is affected, remove article of clothing and use deluge shower for 15 minutes.

- Eyes (chemical contamination): Hold the eye wide open and flush with water from the eye wash for about 15 minutes. Seek medical attention.

- Ingestion of chemicals or poisoning: See antidote chart on wall of lab for general first-aid directions. The victim should drink large amounts of water. All chemical poisonings should receive medical attention.

After an accident, two factors are considered; foreseeability and negligence. **FORESEEABILITY** is the anticipation that an event may occur under certain circumstances. **NEGLIGENCE** is the failure to exercise ordinary or reasonable care.

FORESEEABILITY: the anticipation that an event may occur under certain circumstances

NEGLIGENCE: the failure to exercise ordinary or reasonable care

DOMAIN II
BASIC PRINCIPLES

PERSONALIZED STUDY PLAN

KNOWN MATERIAL/ SKIP IT

PAGE	COMPETENCY AND SKILL	
27	**4: Matter and energy**	☐
	4.1: Demonstrate understanding of the structure and properties of matter	☐
	4.2: Demonstrate understanding of the factors that influence the occurrence and abundance of the elements	☐
	4.3: Distinguish between physical and chemical changes of matter	☐
	4.4: Demonstrate understanding of the conservation of mass/energy	☐
	4.5: Demonstrate understanding of energy transformations	☐
33	**5: Heat and thermodynamics**	☐
	5.1: Distinguish between heat and temperature	☐
	5.2: Demonstrate understanding of measurement, transfer, and effects of thermal energy	☐
	5.3: Solve quantitative problems dealing with the measurement and transfer of thermal energy	☐
	5.4: Demonstrate understanding of the First and Second Laws of thermodynamics	☐
39	**6: Atomic and nuclear structure**	☐
	6.1: Demonstrate understanding of atomic models and their experimental bases	☐
	6.2: Demonstrate understanding of atomic and nuclear structure and forces	☐
	6.3: Relate electron configuration to the chemical and physical properties of an atom	☐
	6.4: Demonstrate knowledge of characteristics of radioisotopes and radioactivity	☐
	6.5: Identify products of nuclear reactions	☐

COMPETENCY 4
MATTER AND ENERGY

SKILL 4.1 **Demonstrate understanding of the structure and properties of matter**

Everything in our world is made up of **MATTER**, whether it is a rock, a building, an animal, or a person. Matter is defined by its characteristics: it takes up space and it has mass.

MASS is a measure of the amount of matter in an object. Two objects of equal mass will balance each other on a simple balance scale no matter where the scale is located. For instance, two rocks with the same amount of mass that are in balance on Earth will also be in balance on the moon. They will feel heavier on Earth than on the moon because of the gravitational pull of the Earth. So, although the two rocks have the same mass, they will have different weights at the two different sites.

WEIGHT is the measure of the Earth's pull of gravity on an object. It can also be defined as the pull of gravity between other bodies. The units of weight measure that we commonly use are the pound in English measure and the kilogram in metric measure.

In addition to mass, matter also has the property of volume. **VOLUME** is the amount of cubic space that an object occupies. Volume and mass together give a more exact description of the object. Two objects may have the same volume but different mass, or the same mass but different volumes, etc. For instance, consider two cubes that are each one cubic centimeter, one made from plastic, one from lead. They have the same volume, but the lead cube has more mass. The measure that we use to describe the cubes takes into consideration both the mass and the volume. **DENSITY** is the mass of a substance contained per unit of volume. If the density of an object is less than the density of a liquid, the object will float in the liquid. If the object is denser than the liquid, then the object will sink.

> **MATTER:** makes up everything in the world; takes up space and it has mass
>
> **MASS:** the measure of the amount of matter in an object
>
> **WEIGHT:** the measure of the earth's pull of gravity on an object; also the pull of gravity between other bodies
>
> **VOLUME:** the amount of cubic space that an object occupies
>
> **DENSITY:** the mass of a substance contained per unit of volume

Determining Density

Density is stated in grams per cubic centimeter (g / cm^3) where the gram is the standard unit of mass. To find an object's density, you must measure its mass and its volume. Then divide the mass by the volume ($D = m / V$).

To find an object's density, first use a balance to find its mass. Then calculate its volume. If the object is a regular shape, you can find the volume by multiplying the length, width, and height together. If it is an irregular shape, however, you can find the volume by seeing how much water it displaces. Measure the water in the container before and after the object is submerged. The difference will be the volume of the object.

Determining Specific Gravity

Specific gravity is the ratio of the density of a substance to the density of water. For instance, the specific density of one liter of alcohol is calculated by comparing its mass (0.81 kg) to the mass of one liter of water (1 kg):

$$\frac{\text{mass of 1 L alcohol}}{\text{mass of 1 L water}} = \frac{0.81 \text{ kg}}{1.00 \text{ kg}} = 0.81$$

PHYSICAL PROPERTY: a characteristic that can be observed without changing the identity of a substance

CHEMICAL PROPERTIES: describes the capacity of a substance to be changed into new substances

Properties of Matter

Physical properties and chemical properties of matter describe the appearance or behavior of a substance. A **PHYSICAL PROPERTY** can be observed without changing the identity of a substance. For instance, you can describe the color, mass, shape, and volume of a book. **CHEMICAL PROPERTIES** describe the ability of a substance to be changed into new substances. Baking powder goes through a chemical change as it changes into carbon dioxide gas during the baking process.

SKILL 4.2 **Demonstrate understanding of the factors that influence the occurrence and abundance of the elements**

The stars manufactured every chemical element heavier than hydrogen.

Most cosmologists believe that the Earth is the indirect result of a supernova. The thin cloud (planetary nebula) of gas and dust, from which the Sun and its planets are formed, was struck by the shock wave and remnant matter from an exploded star(s) outside of our galaxy. In fact, the stars manufactured every chemical element heavier than hydrogen.

The solar system is divided into two sections: the inner and outer planets. The inner planets' composition reflects the Sun's attraction of the heavier elements. The outer planets' composition reflects the lighter, less dense elements attracted less by the Sun's gravitational mass. On each planet, heavier elements sink inward to form the core. Lighter elements form the atmosphere.

Our planet's earliest history was quite violent. Besides being repeatedly struck by meteorites, the Earth's birthing process produced frequent eruptions that caused water—primarily in the form of water vapor from gaseous hydrous minerals—to rise to the surface. The solar system contributed additional water as the Earth acquired its basic form. Comets—primarily composed of water and other light, hydrous materials—bombarded the Earth's surface, and their melting added to the water volume. The primordial seas were initially very acidic, but as the hydrologic cycle of evaporation and precipitation took hold, soluble minerals dissolved and were carried to the seas, gradually easing the degree of acidity. The exchange of minerals though the hydrologic cycle further modified the water's chemistry. Sodium, being extremely soluble, remained in the water longer than the other common elements, and the percentage of sodium in the Earth's oceans has not varied appreciably for at least 600 million years.

The Earth's birthing process produced frequent eruptions that caused water to rise to the surface, and the solar system contributed additional water to the primoridial seas.

Scientists have deduced that the Earth's core is composed of iron and nickel. We know that the Earth's crust is rich in silica, and that the atmosphere is composed of approximately 78% Nitrogen and 21% Oxygen.

The percentage of sodium in the Earth's oceans has not varied appreciably for at least 600 million years.

There are 92 naturally occurring chemical elements in the universe. It is the continual reaction of these molecules that contributes to the diversity of molecular arrangements. In the Earth Sciences, the atomic structure of the elements and how they combine to form new substances is of critical importance. Either combining or dissolving energy bonds, both electrical and chemical, forms most minerals.

Of the 92 naturally occurring elements, just eight make up 99% of Earth's mass. 20 of the elements are relatively common while the other 72 elements are rare to very rare.

Of the 92 naturally occurring elements, just eight make up 99% of Earth's mass.

LIST OF THE MOST COMMON ELEMENTS ON EARTH BY WEIGHT	
Oxygen 46.6%	Calcium 3.6%
Silicon 27.7%	Sodium 2.8%
Aluminum 8.1%	Potassium 2.6%
Iron 5.0%	Magnesium 2.1%

SKILL 4.3 Distinguish between physical and chemical changes of matter

PHYSICAL CHANGE: does not create a new substance and does not rearrange atoms into different compounds.

CHEMICAL CHANGE: a chemical reaction that converts one substance into another by rearranging atoms to form a different compound

SOLID: matter that has a definite shape and volume

LIQUID: matter that has a definite volume, but no shape

GAS: matter that has no shape or volume and spreads out to occupy the entire space of whatever container it is in

ENERGY: the ability to cause change in matter

EVAPORATION: the process of changing a liquid to a gas

CONDENSATION: the process of changing a gas to a liquid

COMPOSITION REACTION: two or more substances combine to form a compound

Matter constantly changes. A **PHYSICAL CHANGE** does not create a new substance. Atoms are not rearranged into different compounds. The material has the same chemical composition as it had before the change. Changes of state are physical changes. Frozen water or gaseous water is still H_2O. Taking a piece of paper and tearing it up is a physical change. You simply have smaller pieces of paper.

Iron Nail

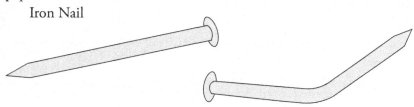

Bent Iron Nail: Physical change—still an iron nail

A **CHEMICAL CHANGE** is a chemical reaction. It converts one substance into another because atoms are rearranged to form a different compound. Paper undergoes a chemical change when you burn it. You no longer have paper. A chemical change to a pure substance alters its properties.

Rusty Iron Nail: Chemical Change—iron oxide (rust) is present

The phase of matter (solid, liquid, or gas) is identified by its shape and volume. A **SOLID** has a definite shape and volume. A **LIQUID** has a definite volume, but no shape. A **GAS** has no shape or volume because it will spread out to occupy the entire space of whatever container it is in.

ENERGY is the ability to cause change in matter. Applying heat to a frozen liquid changes it from solid back to liquid. Continue heating it and it will boil and give off steam, a gas.

EVAPORATION is the change in phase from liquid to gas. **CONDENSATION** is the change in phase from gas to liquid.

In a **COMPOSITION REACTION**, two or more substances combine to form a compound.

$$A + B \rightarrow AB$$

i.e., sulfur and oxygen gives sulfur dioxide

In a **DECOMPOSITION REACTION**, a compound breaks down into two or more simpler substances.

$$AB \rightarrow A + B$$

i.e., water breaks down into hydrogen and oxygen

In a **SINGLE REPLACEMENT REACTION**, a free element replaces an element that is part of a compound.

$$A + BX \rightarrow AX + B$$

i.e., iron plus copper sulfate yields iron sulfate plus copper

In a **DOUBLE REPLACEMENT REACTION**, parts of two compounds replace each other. In this case, the compounds seem to switch partners.

$$AX + BY \rightarrow AY + BX$$

i.e., sodium chloride plus mercury nitrate yields sodium nitrate plus mercury chloride

SKILL 4.4 Demonstrate understanding of the conservation of mass/energy

The principle of conservation states that certain measurable properties of an isolated system remain constant despite changes in the system. Two important principles of conservation are the conservation of mass and charge.

The **PRINCIPLE OF CONSERVATION OF MASS** states that the total mass of a system is constant. Examples of conservation in mass in nature include the burning of wood, rusting of iron, and phase changes of matter. When wood burns, the total mass of the products, such as soot, ash, and gases, equals the mass of the wood and the oxygen that reacts with it. When iron reacts with oxygen, rust forms. The total mass of the iron-rust complex does not change. Finally, when matter changes phase, mass remains constant. Thus, when a glacier melts due to atmospheric warming, the mass of liquid water formed is equal to the mass of the glacier.

The **PRINCIPLE OF CONSERVATION OF CHARGE** states that the total electrical charge of a closed system is constant. Thus, in chemical reactions and interactions of charged objects, the total charge does not change. Chemical reactions and the interaction of charged molecules are essential and common processes in living organisms and systems.

LAW OF CONSERVATION OF ENERGY states that matter is neither created nor destroyed. The corollary to this tenet is that matter merely changes state. Thus, as matter undergoes a phase change, energy is either given off or absorbed.

DECOMPOSITION REACTION: a compound breaks down into two or more simpler substances

SINGLE REPLACEMENT REACTION: decomposition reaction: a compound breaks down into two or more simpler substances

DOUBLE REPLACEMENT REACTION: parts of two compounds replace each other, seeming to switch partners

PRINCIPLE OF CONSERVATION OF MASS: the total mass of a system is constant

When matter changes phase, mass remains constant.

PRINCIPLE OF CONSERVATION OF CHARGE: the total electrical charge of a closed system is constant

LAW OF CONSERVATION OF ENERGY: matter is neither created nor destroyed but merely changes state, either giving off or absorbing energy in the process

The first law of thermodynamics is a restatement of conservation of energy: In a closed system, the total amount of energy always stays the same. It can change from one form to another, but the total amount of energy never changes.

SKILL 4.5 Demonstrate understanding of energy transformations

Energy: The ability to do work (to cause change).

Work: The energy expended when the position or speed of an object is moved against an opposing force. Measured in **JOULES**, work is the product of the force on an object and the distance through which the object is moved.

JOULES: measurement of work as the product of the force on an object and the distance through which the object is moved

Energy is neither created nor destroyed. Any time something happens, energy is simply changing from one form to another.

FORMS OF ENERGY	
Thermal energy (heat)	The energy of moving atoms and molecules
Chemical energy	The energy that bonds atoms and molecules together
Nuclear energy	The energy of moving the nucleus of an atom
Mechanical energy	The energy of moving objects
Potential energy	The energy stored in an object due to its position
Elastic potential energy	The energy stored in elastic (stretchable) objects such as rubber bands or springs
Gravitational potential energy	The energy an object has when it is in an elevated position
Kinetic Energy	The energy an object has due to its mass and motion

Thermodynamics and the States of Matter

There are four states of matter: Liquid, Solid, Gas, and Plasma.

Matter can change state if the temperature of the substance is increased or lowered. When we apply heat from a source to a substance, we are actually transferring energy from the heat source to the substance. The molecules absorb the energy and move faster, causing the temperature of the substance to rise.

It takes more heat transfer to cause a change from a liquid to a vapor, or a vapor to a liquid (evaporation), than it does to change a solid to a liquid, or a liquid to a solid (fusion).

See also Skill 5.2

> *There are four states of matter: Liquid, Solid, Gas, and Plasma.*

> *Note: Plasma is essentially a superheated, molten gas, and not all physicists or textbooks agree that it is a separate state of matter.*

COMPETENCY 5
HEAT AND THERMODYNAMICS

SKILL 5.1 **Distinguish between heat and temperature**

Heat and temperature are different physical quantities. **HEAT** is a measure of energy. **TEMPERATURE** is the measure of how hot (or cold) a body is with respect to a standard object.

Two concepts are important in the discussion of temperature changes. Objects are in thermal contact if they can affect each other's temperatures. If you set a hot cup of coffee on a desk top, the two objects are in thermal contact with each other and will begin affecting each other's temperatures. Heat flows from the hotter object to the cooler: The coffee will become cooler and the desktop warmer. Eventually, they will have the same temperature. When this happens, they are in **THERMAL EQUILIBRIUM**.

> **HEAT:** a measure of energy

> **TEMPERATURE:** the measure of how hot (or cold) a body is with respect to a standard object

> **THERMAL EQUILIBRIUM:** state in which two objects have the same temperature

HEAT CAPACITY: the amount of heat energy that it takes to raise the temperature of an object by one degree

HEAT CAPACITY of an object is the amount of heat energy that it takes to raise the temperature of the object by one degree.

Heat capacity (C) per unit mass (m) is called specific heat (c):

$$c = \frac{C}{m} = \frac{Q / \Delta}{m}$$

Specific heats for many materials have been calculated and can be found in tables.

There are a number of ways to measure specific heat, each requiring raising the temperature of a specific amount of water by a specific amount. These conversions of heat energy and work are called the mechanical equivalent of heat.

CALORIE: the amount of energy that it takes to raise one gram of water one degree Celsius

The CALORIE is the amount of energy that it takes to raise one gram of water one degree Celsius.

KILOCALORIE: is the amount of energy that it takes to raise one kilogram of water by one degree Celsius

The KILOCALORIE is the amount of energy that it takes to raise one kilogram of water by one degree Celsius. Food calories are kilocalories.

In the International System of Units (SI), the calorie is equal to 4.184 joules.

British thermal units (BTU) = 252 calories = 1.054 kJ

SKILL 5.2 **Demonstrate understanding of measurement, transfer, and effects of thermal energy**

We cannot rely on our sense of touch to determine temperature because the heat from a hand may be conducted more efficiently by certain objects, making them feel colder. Thermometers are used to measure temperature. A small amount of mercury in a capillary tube will expand when heated. The thermometer and the object whose temperature it is measuring are put in contact long enough for them to reach thermal equilibrium. Then the temperature can be read from the thermometer scale.

Three Temperature Scales

Celsius: The freezing point of water is set at 0 and the steam (boiling) point is set at 100. The interval between the two is divided into 100 equal parts called degrees Celsius.

Fahrenheit: The freezing point of water is 32 degrees and the boiling point is 212. The interval between is divided into 180 equal parts called degrees Fahrenheit.

Temperature readings can be converted from one to the other as follows.

Fahrenheit to Celsius **Celsius to Fahrenheit**
C = 5/9 (F − 32) F = (9/5) C + 32

Kelvin: The degrees are set just like the Celsius scale, but the zero point is moved to the triple point of water: Inside a closed vessel, water is in thermal equilibrium in all three states (ice, water, and vapor) at 273.15 degrees Kelvin. This temperature is equivalent to .01 degrees Celsius. Because the degrees are the same in the two scales, temperature changes are the same in Celsius and Kelvin. Temperature readings can be converted from Celsius to Kelvin units.

Celsius to Kelvin **Kelvin to Celsius**
K = C + 273.15 C = K − 273.15

Changes in Heat Energy

Heat energy that is transferred into or out of a system is **HEAT TRANSFER**. The temperature change is positive for a gain in heat energy and negative when heat is lost from the object or system.

The formula for heat transfer is $Q = mc\Delta T$ where Q is the amount of heat energy transferred, m is the amount of substance (in kilograms), c is the specific heat of the substance, and ΔT is the change in temperature of the substance. It is important to assume that the objects in thermal contact are isolated and insulated from their surroundings.

A calorimeter uses the transfer of heat from one substance to another to determine the specific heat of the substance.

When an object undergoes a change of phase it goes from one physical state (solid, liquid, or gas) to another. For instance, water can go from liquid to solid (freezing) or from liquid to gas (boiling). The heat that is required to change matter from one state to the other is called **LATENT HEAT**.

The **HEAT OF FUSION** is the amount of heat that it takes to change from a solid to a liquid or the amount of heat released during the change from liquid to solid. The heat of fusion is measured in calories required to change 1 gram of water from a solid to a liquid, or back, equal to 80 cal/gram.

The **HEAT OF VAPORIZATION** is the amount of heat that it takes to change from a liquid to a gaseous state. The heat of vaporization is measured in calories required to change 1 gram of water from a liquid to a vapor, or back, equal to 540 cal/gram.

HEAT TRANSFER: heat energy that is transferred into or out of a system

If a substance in a closed container loses heat, then another substance in the container must gain heat.

LATENT HEAT: the heat that is required to change matter from one state to another

HEAT OF FUSION: the amount of heat that it takes to change from a solid to a liquid or the amount of heat released during the change from liquid to solid

HEAT OF VAPORIZA-TION: the amount of heat that it takes to change from a liquid to a gaseous state

Methods of Heat Transfer

- Conduction: The transfer of heat energy through a substance or from one substance to another by direct contact of atoms and molecules. For example: electricity through a wire.

- Convection: The transfer of heat in liquids and gases as groups of molecules move in currents. For example: a toaster oven, or home heating systems that employ a fan to circulate warmer air.

- Radiation: The transfer of energy by electromagnetic waves. For example: a microwave oven.

An example of all three methods of heat transfer occurs in the thermos bottle or Dewar flask. The bottle is constructed of double walls of Pyrex glass with space in between. Air is evacuated from the space between the walls, and the inner wall is silvered. The lack of air between the walls lessens heat loss by convection and conduction. The heat inside is reflected by the silver, cutting down heat transfer by radiation. Hot liquids remain hotter and cold liquids remain colder longer.

SKILL 5.3 **Solve quantitative problems dealing with the measurement and transfer of thermal energy**

All heat transfer is the movement of thermal energy from hot to cold matter. This movement down a thermal gradient is a consequence of the second law of thermodynamics. The three methods of heat transfer are listed and explained below.

Conduction depends on electron diffusion or photo vibration. The bodies of matter themselves do not move; the heat is transferred because adjacent atoms vibrate against each other or electrons flow between atoms. This type of heat transfer is most common when two solids come in direct contact with each other because molecules in a solid are in close contact with one another and so the electrons can flow freely. It stands to reason, then, that metals are good conductors of thermal energy because their metallic bonds allow the freest movement of electrons. Similarly, conduction is better in denser solids, for example, copper-bottomed pots quickly convey heat, and a hot water bottle readily conducts heat to a person's body.

The amount of heat transferred by conduction through a material depends on several factors. It is directly proportional to the temperature difference ΔT between the surface from which the heat is flowing and the surface to which it is transferred. Heat flow H increases with the area A through which the flow occurs and also with the time duration t. The thickness of the material reduces the flow of heat. The relationship between all these variables is expressed as

$$H = \frac{k.t.A.\Delta T}{d}$$

where the proportionality constant k is known as the thermal conductivity, a property of the material. Thermal conductivity of a good conductor is close to 1 (0.97 cal/cm.s. $°C$ for silver) while good insulators have thermal conductivity that is nearly zero (0.0005 cal/cm.s.$°C$ for wood).

Problem: A glass window pane is 50 cm long and 30 cm wide. The glass is 1 cm thick. If the temperature indoors is 15°C higher than it is outside, how much heat will be lost through the window in 30 minutes? The thermal conductivity of glass is 0.0025 cal/cm.s.°C.

Solution: The window has area A = 1500 sq. cm and thickness d = 1 cm. Duration of heat flow is 1800 s and the temperature difference ΔT = 15°C. Therefore heat loss through the window is given by

$$H = (0.0025 \times 1800 \times 1500 \times 15)/1 = 101250 \text{ calories}$$

Convection involves the movement in currents of warm particles to cooler areas. Convection may be either natural or forced, depending on how the current of warm particles develops. Natural convection occurs when molecules near a heat source absorb thermal energy (typically via conduction), become less dense, and rise. Cooler molecules then take their place and a natural current is formed. Forced convection, as the name suggests, occurs when pumps, fans, or other means bring liquids or gases into contact with warmer or cooler masses. Because the free motion of particles with different thermal energy is key to this mode of heat transfer, convection is most common in liquid and gases. Convection, however, can transfer heat between a liquid or a gas and a solid.

Forced convection is used in "forced air" home heating systems and is common in industrial manufacturing processes. Natural convection is responsible for ocean currents and many atmospheric events and often arises in association with conduction, for instance, in the air near a radiator or the water in a pot heating on the stove. The mathematical analysis of heat transfer by convection is far more complicated than for conduction or radiation and will not be addressed here.

Radiation occurs via electromagnetic (EM) radiation. All matter warmer than absolute zero (that is, all known matter) radiates heat, regardless of the presence of any medium. Thus, it occurs even in a vacuum. Since light and radiant heat are both part of the EM spectrum, we can easily visualize how heat is transferred via radiation. For instance, just like light, radiant heat is reflected by shiny materials and absorbed by dark materials. Common examples of radiant heat include the way sunlight travels from the Sun to warm the Earth, heating homes with radiators, and the warmth of incandescent light bulbs.

The amount of energy radiated by a body at temperature T and having a surface area A is given by the Stefan-Boltzmann law expressed as

$$I = e\sigma A T^4$$

where I is the radiated power in watts, e (a number between 0 and 1) is the emissivity of the body and σ is a universal constant known as Stefan's constant that has a value of $5.6703 \times 10^{-8} W / m^2 . K^4$ Black objects absorb and radiate energy very well and have emissivity close to 1. Shiny objects that reflect energy are not good absorbers or radiators and have emissivity close to 0.

A body not only radiates thermal energy but also absorbs thermal energy from its surroundings. The net power radiation from a body at temperature T in an environment at temperature T_0 is given by

$$I = e\sigma A(T^4 - T_0^4)$$

Problem: Calculate the net power radiated by a body of surface area 2 sq. m, temperature 30°C and emissivity 0.5 placed in a room at a temperature of 15°C.

Solution: $I = 0.5 \times 5.67 \times 10^{-8} \times 2(303^4 - 288^4) = 88W$

SKILL 5.4 Demonstrate understanding of the First and Second Laws of thermodynamics

> **LAWS OF THERMODYNAMICS:** the relationship between heat and forms of energy and work (mechanical, electrical, etc.) in systems in thermal equilibrium

The relationship between heat and forms of energy and work (mechanical, electrical, etc.) are the **LAWS OF THERMODYNAMICS**. These laws deal strictly with systems in thermal equilibrium—not those in the process of gradual or rapid transition. Systems that are nearly always in a state of equilibrium are called **REVERSIBLE SYSTEMS**.

> **REVERSIBLE SYSTEMS:** systems that nearly always are in a state of equilibrium

The first law of thermodynamics is a restatement of conservation of energy. The change in heat energy supplied to a system (Q) is equal to the sum of the change in the internal energy (U) and the change in the work done by the system against internal forces (W). $\Delta Q = \Delta U + \Delta W$.

The second law of thermodynamics is stated in two parts:

1. No machine is 100% efficient. It is impossible to construct a machine that only absorbs heat from a heat source and performs an equal amount of work because some heat will always be lost to the environment.

2. Heat cannot spontaneously pass from a colder to a hotter object. An ice cube sitting on a hot sidewalk will melt into a little puddle, but it will never spontaneously cool and form the same ice cube. Certain events have a preferred direction called the arrow of time.

ENTROPY is the measure of how much energy or heat is available for work. Work occurs only when heat is transferred from hotter to cooler objects, and, once done, no more work can be extracted. The energy is still being conserved, but is not available for work as long as the objects are the same temperature. Theory has it that, eventually, all things in the universe will reach the same temperature, and then, energy will no longer be usable.

> **ENTROPY:** the measure of how much energy or heat is available for work

COMPETENCY 6
ATOMIC AND NUCLEAR STRUCTURE

> **SKILL Demonstrate understanding of atomic models and their**
> **6.1 experimental bases**

The atomic theory of matter suggests that

1. All matter consists of atoms

2. All atoms of an element are identical

3. Different elements have different atoms

4. Atoms maintain their properties in a chemical reaction

The atomic theory of matter was first suggested by the Greek Democritus. The atomic theory of matter states that matter is made up of tiny, rapidly moving particles. These particles move more quickly when warmer, because temperature is a measure of average kinetic energy of the particles. Warmer molecules therefore move farther away from each other, with enough energy to separate from each other more often and for greater distances.

In the 1780s, a scientist and schoolteacher John Dalton expanded on Democritus's idea with observations about air:

- Air is a mixture of different kinds of gases

- These gases do not separate on their own

- It is possible to compress gases into a smaller volume

- Particles of different substances must be different from each other and must maintain their own mass when combined with other substances

Dalton's Model of the Atom suggested that:

- Matter is made up of atoms

- Atoms of an element are similar to each other

- Atoms of different elements are different from each other

- Atoms combine with each other to form new kinds of compounds

The present model of the atom is much different from Dalton's model.

In the late 1800s, British scientist William Thompson investigated how electric current flowed through a vacuum tube and hypothesized that:

- If rays are made of charged particles, then an electric field would attract them

- If a particle is charged, then a magnet will affect its motion

From his work, Thompson proved that the rays were made of negative particles, later called electrons.

THOMPSON'S MODEL:
The atom is made of negative particles equally mixed in a sphere of positive material

The results of his experimentation produced THOMPSON'S MODEL: The atom is made of negative particles equally mixed in a sphere of positive material.

In 1896 it was discovered that some elements give off particles with a positive charge. These elements have 7,000 times the mass of electrons. The British scientist Ernest Rutherford called these alpha particles and in 1909 used them to test Thompson's model. He hammered gold foil until it was less than 1mm thick, then fired alpha particles at the foil, and then used a telescope and a screen to locate the alpha particles. His hypothesis was that if Thompson's theory was right, then the alpha particles would pass through the foil in a straight line. He found that most particles passed through as expected, but some appeared to bounce off in another direction, which Thompson's model could not explain. The result of his experiment gave rise to Rutherford's Model:

- Most of the atom is empty space, which allows most of the alpha particles to pass directly through it

- The center of the atom is composed of a nucleus containing most of the mass and all of the positively charged particles of the atom

- The scattering of particles occurs when they collide with the nucleus

- Electrons occupy the space outside the nucleus

- The atom is neutral because the protons in the nucleus equal the electrons in the space outside the nucleus

Based on Rutherford's model, scientists thought that the electrons of an atom might orbit the nucleus much like the planets orbit the Sun. If this was true, they could expect two things:

1. As electrons orbit, they give off light energy continuously. If this light energy is passed through a prism, it would produce a band of color.

2. As the orbiting electrons gave off light, they would lose energy and spiral into the nucleus of the atom, causing the atom to collapse; therefore, the atom would take up no space.

Scientists observed lines of color and dark lines, but no color bands. Also, because matter in fact does take up space, then the orbiting atoms cannot collapse into nothing. Danish scientist Neils Bohr created another model to explain these observations in 1913:

- Electrons orbit the nucleus, but only certain allowed orbits

- An electron in an allowed orbit will not lose energy

- When an electron moves from an outer orbit to an inner orbit, it gives off energy

- When an electron moves from an inner orbit to an outer orbit, it absorbs energy

Bohr's model explains only the very simplest atoms, such as hydrogen. Today's more sophisticated atomic model is based upon how waves react.

SKILL 6.2 Demonstrate understanding of atomic and nuclear structure and forces

ATOM: a nucleus surrounded by a cloud with moving electrons

An **ATOM** is a nucleus surrounded by a cloud with moving electrons. The electrons do not actually follow a fixed circular path as in Bohr's model. Instead, they swirl around the nucleus in a large region called the Electron Cloud.

NUCLEONS: nucleic particles that when electrically charged are protons and when electrically neutral are neutrons

The nucleus, the center of the atom, is composed of **NUCLEONS**, which when electrically charged are protons and when electrically neutral are neutrons. **PROTONS** are positively charged particles. The mass of a proton is about 2,000 times that of the mass of an electron. The number of protons in the nucleus of an atom is called its **ATOMIC NUMBER**. All atoms of the same element have the same atomic number.

PROTON: a positively charged particle

Neutrons and protons have about the same mass, but neutrons have no charge. Neutrons were discovered because scientists observed that not all atoms in neon gas have the same mass. They had identified isotopes. **ISOTOPES** of an element have the same number of protons in the nucleus, but have different numbers of neutrons, hence have different masses.

ATOMIC NUMBER: the number of protons in the nucleus of an atom

Recent discoveries have also challenged the fundamental tenet that the atom was the smallest division possible. Quantum physicists have discovered subatomic particles called neutrinos and quarks. Although the implications and mechanics of the newly discovered particles are still not fully understood, quarks are now believed to be the fundamental building blocks of all nucleons.

ISOTOPES: an atom of an element that has the same number of protons as other atoms of the same element but with a different number of neutrons.

Neutrinos, on the other hand, are extremely light particles that belong to a class of six particles called Leptons, which many scientists believe are the true elementary particles, the building blocks of which all matter is composed.

Quarks are now believed to be the fundamental building blocks of all nucleons.

Atomic Mass

The mass of matter is measured against a standard mass such as the gram. Scientists measure the relative mass of an atom by comparing it to that of a standard atom: the isotope of the element carbon with six (6) neutrons. It is called carbon-12 and assigned a mass of 12 atomic mass units (amu). Therefore, the **ATOMIC MASS UNIT (AMU)** is the standard unit for measuring the mass of an atom, equal to the mass of a carbon atom.

ATOMIC MASS UNIT (AMU): the standard unit for measuring the mass of an atom, equal to the mass of a carbon atom.

The **MASS NUMBER** of an atom is the sum of its protons and neutrons. In any element, there is a mixture of isotopes, some having slightly more or slightly fewer protons and neutrons. The **ATOMIC MASS** of an element is an average of the mass numbers of its atoms.

TERMS USED TO DESCRIBE ATOMIC NUCLEI			
Term	**Example**	**Meaning**	**Characteristic**
Atomic number	# protons (p)	same for all atoms of a given element	Carbon (C) atomic number = 6 (6p)
Mass number	# protons + # neutrons (p + n)	changes for different isotopes of an element	C − 12 (6p + 6n) C − 13 (6p + 7n)
Atomic mass	average mass of the atoms of the element	usually not a whole number	atomic mass of Carbon equals 12.011

See also Skill 6.3

MASS NUMBER: the sum of an atom's protons and neutrons

ATOMIC MASS: an average of the mass numbers of an element's atoms

SKILL 6.3 Relate electron configuration to the chemical and physical properties of an atom

Each atom has an equal number of electrons (negative) and protons (positive). Therefore, atoms are neutral. Electrons orbiting the nucleus occupy energy levels that are arranged in order and the electrons tend to occupy the lowest energy level available. A **STABLE ELECTRON ARRANGEMENT** is an atom that has all of its electrons in the lowest possible energy levels.

STABLE ELECTRON ARRANGEMENT: an atom that has all of its electrons in the lowest possible energy levels

Energy Levels in Atoms

Each energy level holds a maximum number of electrons. However, an atom with more than one level does not hold more than eight electrons in its outermost shell.

Level	Name	Max. # of Electrons
First	K shell	2
Second	L shell	8
Third	M shell	18
Fourth	N shell	32

This can help explain why chemical reactions occur. Atoms react with each other when their outer levels are unfilled. When atoms either exchange or share electrons with each other, these energy levels become filled and the atom becomes more stable.

As an electron gains energy, it moves from one energy level to a higher energy level. The electron cannot leave one level until it has enough energy to reach the next level. **EXCITED ELECTRONS** are electrons that have absorbed energy and have moved farther from the nucleus.

Electrons can also lose energy. When they do, they fall to a lower level. However, they can only fall to the lowest level that has room for them. This explains why atoms do not collapse.

The outermost electrons in the atoms are called **VALENCE ELECTRONS**. Because they are the ones involved in the bonding process, they determine the properties of the element.

Atomic Bonds

A **CHEMICAL BOND** is a force of attraction that holds atoms together. When atoms are bonded chemically, they cease to have their individual properties. For instance, hydrogen and oxygen combine into water and no longer look like hydrogen and oxygen.

A **COVALENT BOND** is formed when two atoms share electrons. Atoms whose outer shells are not filled with electrons are unstable and readily combine with other unstable atoms. By combining and sharing electrons, they act as a single unit. Covalent bonding happens among nonmetals. When covalent bonds occur between two nonidentical atoms, they are always polar.

COVALENT COMPOUNDS are compounds whose atoms are joined by covalent bonds. Table sugar, methane, and ammonia are examples of covalent compounds.

An **IONIC BOND** is a bond formed by the transfer of electrons. It happens when metals and nonmetals bond. Before chlorine and sodium combine, for instance, the sodium has one valence electron and chlorine has seven. Neither valence shell is filled, but the chlorine's valence shell is almost full. During the reaction, the sodium gives one electron to the chlorine atom so both atoms then have filled shells and are stable.

Before the bonding, both atoms were neutral, but when one electron was transferred, it upset the balance of protons and electrons in each atom. The chlorine atom took on one extra electron and the sodium atom released one electron. The atoms have now become **IONS**—atoms with an unequal number of protons and

EXCITED ELECTRONS: electrons that have absorbed energy and have moved farther from the nucleus

VALENCE ELECTRONS: the outermost electrons in an atom

CHEMICAL BOND: the force of attraction that holds atoms together

COVALENT BOND: formed when two atoms share electrons

COVALENT COMPOUNDS: compounds whose atoms are joined by covalent bonds

IONIC BOND: a bond formed by the transfer of electrons

IONS: an atom with an unequal number of protons and electrons

electrons. To determine whether the ion is positive or negative, compare the number of protons (+ charge) to the electrons (− charge). If there are more electrons the ion will be negative. If there are more protons, the ion will be positive.

Compounds that result from the transfer of metal atoms to nonmetal atoms are called IONIC COMPOUNDS. Sodium chloride (table salt), sodium hydroxide (drain cleaner), and potassium chloride (salt substitute) are examples of ionic compounds.

IONIC COMPOUNDS: compounds that result from the transfer of metal atoms to nonmetal atoms

Properties

A physical property of matter can be observed with one of the five senses—usually sight, smell, or sometimes taste—or measured on a scale such as a thermometer. A physical property belongs to a substance because of what it is, for example, the wetness of water. (Warning: Do NOT taste anything in a laboratory!) Physical properties include state (liquid, solid, gas, or plasma), hardness, color, taste, odor, freezing point, melting point, boiling point, density, electrical conductivity, thermal conductivity, luster, and malleability. Physical properties do not change unless the matter is chemically changed. Gold that is mined in the United States will have the same physical properties as gold mined in South Africa.

A CHEMICAL PROPERTY of matter depends upon how the substance reacts with other substances. For example, when exposed to or combined with oxygen, does it rust, does it burn, or is it unaffected? Measuring these properties will change the chemical and physical nature of the substance. Examples of chemical properties are combustibility, rusting, pH and pOH, reactivity with water and various acids and bases, electromotive force, electronegativity, ionization potential, and preference for various types of bonding. To test these, one has to change the substance chemically.

CHEMICAL PROPERTY: a property of matter that depends upon how the substance reacts with other substances

In Skill 10.2 groups of elements are explained along with their associated physical and chemical properties.

SKILL 6.4 Demonstrate knowledge of characteristics of radioisotopes and radioactivity *(for example, half-life)*

Isotopes are atoms that have like numbers of protons, but unlike numbers of neutrons. Most elements have two to ten stable isotopes, each of which may cause a modification of the element's physical properties. Only 20 of the 83 elements present in significant quantities on the Earth have a single, stable isotope. Writing the element's name followed by its mass number, such as U-235, denotes an isotope.

RADIOMETRIC DATING: the most accurate method of absolute dating that measures the decay of naturally occurring radioactive isotopes

RADIOMETRIC DATING, the most accurate method of absolute dating, measures the decay of naturally occurring radioactive isotopes. These isotopes are great timekeepers because their rate of decay is constant. Elements decay because of the inherent structure of the nucleus of the atoms. Neutrons hold the positively charged protons together, but the protons attempt to repel each other. In some heavy elements, the protons repel each other to such a degree that the proton tears itself apart (decays). By losing protons, the atom becomes another element. The decay starts the moment an isotope crystallizes in a rock unit, and chemicals, weathering, environment, or temperature do not affect it.

The radioactive decay causes the (mother) element to change into a (daughter) element, and this relationship during the series of isotope decay is the basis for radiometric dating. Although many isotopes are used in radiometric dating, the most widely known method is **CARBON-14 DATING**. Carbon-14 is unstable and decays, decomposes, and transmutes to Nitrogen-14. The dating process compares the ratio of Carbon-14 to Nitrogen-14 in an object. Since the decay occurs at a known rate, it is predictable and serves as a clock standard. Carbon-14 decays quickly, however, and can be used to date only organic compounds less than 40,000 years old.

CARBON-14 DATING: the most widely known method of radiometric dating

Knowing the half-life of the isotopes is the key factor in the radiometric dating process.

Knowing the half-life of the isotopes is the key factor in the radiometric dating process. If we know the half-life, we can compare the ratio of isotopes found in the object, and count backward to get an accurate date. The most common element checked is the ratio of Uranium to Lead.

Example: 1 gram of 238Uranium. After 100 million years, you have 0.013g of 206Pb (lead) and 0.989 of 238U. After 4.5 billion years, you have 0.433g 206Pb and .500g of 238U. Therefore, the half-life of 238U is roughly 4.5 billion years.

Note: Only Carbon-14 can be used to date organic compounds. The other isotopes are not found in organic compounds.

SKILL 6.5 Identify products of nuclear reactions

NUCLEAR REACTION: a reaction that involves the nucleus of an atom and thus changes the element into a different element

Chemical reactions involve the breaking and forming of bonds between atoms. Bonds involve only the outer electrons and do not affect the nucleus. When a reaction involves a nucleus, elements are changed into different elements. This is called a **NUCLEAR REACTION**.

The binding energy released when the nuclei of atoms are split apart in a nuclear reaction is called NUCLEAR ENERGY.

Types of Nuclear Reactions

NUCLEAR FISSION occurs when the nuclei are split apart, forming smaller nuclei and releasing energy. The fission of many atoms in a short time period releases a large amount of energy. "Heavy water" is used in a nuclear reactor to slow down neutrons, controlling and moderating nuclear reactions. Controlling the release so that energy is released slowly gives us nuclear submarines and nuclear power plants.

NUCLEAR FUSION, the opposite, occurs when small nuclei combine to form a larger nucleus. It begins with the hydrogen atom, which has the smallest nucleus. During one type of fusion, four hydrogen nuclei are fused at very high pressures and temperatures to form one helium atom. The Sun and stars are made mostly of hydrogen that is constantly fusing. As the hydrogen forms helium, it releases an energy that we see as light. When all of the hydrogen is used, the star will no longer shine. Scientists estimate that the Sun has enough hydrogen to keep it glowing for another four billion years.

During a nuclear reaction, elements change into other, RADIOACTIVE ELEMENTS. Uranium is a radioactive element. The element uranium breaks down and changes into the element lead. Most natural radioactive elements break down slowly, so energy is released over a long period of time.

The Basics of Nuclear Reactions

The basic principle behind a nuclear reaction is simple; in the process of fission (splitting an atom), if you bombard the nucleus of an atom with a neutron, you cause the nucleus to split into two nuclei.

Example: When a neutron strikes an atom of U-235, the uranium atom splits to form an atom of Krypton-92, and an atom of Barium-141. The product of this reactive split is a release of energy and three neutrons.

In turn, each of the newly released neutrons can react with another atom of U-235, producing three atoms of Krypton-92, three atoms of Barium-141, more energy, and nine more neutrons. The reactive process repeats itself over and over, releasing yet more energy and more neutrons. This process is called a CHAIN REACTION: a process in which an action causes a reaction that causes subsequent cycles of action and reaction.

NUCLEAR ENERGY: the binding energy released when the nuclei of atoms are split apart in a nuclear reaction

NUCLEAR FISSION: a nuclear reaction in which the nuclei are split apart, forming smaller nuclei and releasing energy

NUCLEAR FUSION: a nuclear reaction in which small nuclei combine to form a larger nucleus, releasing energy

RADIOACTIVE ELEMENTS: elements that are the result of a nuclear reaction

CHAIN REACTION: a process in which an action causes a reaction that causes subsequent cycles of action and reaction

ALBERT EINSTEIN'S EQUATION: E = mc², or the energy released during fission is directly proportional to the mass of the substance times the speed of light squared

Based upon **ALBERT EINSTEIN'S EQUATION** of $E = mc^2$, the energy released during fission is directly proportional to the mass of the substance times the speed of light squared. Considering that the speed of light is 2.99792458 m/s, in layman terms, this equation simply illustrates the tremendous amount of energy available for release by a fission reaction.

Put another way, we can compare a chain reaction to a landslide. Small pieces of rock rolling down a hillside strike other rocks in their path. Those rocks move, hitting other rocks, and the process grows exponentially, eventually carrying down the hillside a massive amount of material with great energy that sweeps up everything in its path.

Left uncontrolled, a fission chain reaction releases an almost unbelievable amount of energy in seconds, as was demonstrated in 1945 by the uncontrolled chain reaction of U-235 in the form of an atomic bomb.

Nuclear Power

Our world is energy dependent, and the primary purpose of nuclear reactors is to supply that energy. Fortunately, we can control the fission process by limiting the number of neutrons available for reactions.

Nuclear power plants

Control rods of boron, graphite, and cadmium are inserted between the radioactive fuel rods in a nuclear reactor. These control rods absorb neutrons and are designed to limit the number of neutrons to one per fission reaction.

In a highly simplified explanation, nuclear power plants generate electricity by surrounding the reactor core located in the reactor chamber with a series of pipes called the primary system, which circulates water around and through the chamber.

The energy released during fission heats the water to the point of vaporization. The pipes of the primary system in turn are routed—outside of the chamber—near a second set of water-circulating pipes called the secondary system.

When the heat carried away from the reactor core by the primary system is released into the secondary system by convection, the water in the secondary system water also evaporates, flashing to steam that is used to drive steam turbines that are geared to electrical generators.

Both the primary and secondary system waters are recycled in a closed-loop system, since the steam eventually cools and condenses, returning to a liquid state.

Safety considerations for nuclear reactors

The inherent potential weakness of a nuclear reactor is safely controlling the reaction. The rods are critical to controlling the reaction. If there is more than one neutron released, the reaction can speed up to a dangerous level. With the rods fully inserted, less than one neutron is released, stopping the reaction. The mechanisms that insert and remove the control rods must function correctly on demand. The continued circulation of water to remove excess heat is absolutely critical to the safe operation of the reactor. Likewise, ensuring that radioactive steam from the primary system isn't vented to the atmosphere is another key safety concern.

A breeder reactor produces electricity and also produces plutonium or uranium fuel as a byproduct. When nonfissionable U-238 is mixed with fissionable isotopes in a breeder reactor, the liberated neutrons convert the U-238 into Pu-239. When nonfissionable Th-232, an isotope of Thorium—a member of the Actinide Series of elements—is mixed with fissionable materials, it's converted to fissionable U-233.

A breeder reactor creates more fissionable fuel than it consumes. Unfortunately, plutonium, while useful as a nuclear fuel, has an extremely long half-life and is known to be one of the most toxic substances to living organisms. Unlike radioactive elements such as uranium, which damage cellular structure causing cancer, plutonium kills cells outright. Another major problem is disposing of the plutonium-fueled breeder reactors' wastes, as plutonium takes hundreds of thousands of years to decay.

DOMAIN III
PHYSICAL SCIENCES

PERSONALIZED STUDY PLAN

KNOWN MATERIAL/ SKIP IT

PAGE	COMPETENCY AND SKILL	
55	**7: Mechanics**	☐
	7.1: Demonstrate understanding of straight-line, projectile, circular, and periodic motion	☐
	7.2: Demonstrate understanding of Newton's laws of motion	☐
	7.3: Distinguish between weight and mass	☐
	7.4: Demonstrate understanding of friction	☐
	7.5: Distinguish among work, energy, and power	☐
	7.6: Demonstrate understanding of simple machines and torque	☐
	7.7: Demonstrate understanding of linear momentum	☐
	7.8: Demonstrate understanding of the conservation of energy and the conservation of linear momentum	☐
	7.9: Demonstrate understanding of angular momentum and torque and angular momentum conservation	☐
	7.10: Demonstrate understanding of the force of gravity	☐
	7.11: Demonstrate understanding of pressure and Pascal's principle of fluids	☐
	7.12: Demonstrate understanding of Archimedes' principle (buoyancy)	☐
	7.13: Demonstrate understanding of Bernoulli's principle for fluids	☐
69	**8: Electricity and magnetism**	☐
	8.1: Demonstrate understanding of the repulsion and attraction of electric charges	☐
	8.2: Demonstrate understanding of the characteristics of current electricity and simple circuits	☐
	8.3: Compare and contrast series and parallel circuits	☐
	8.4: Compare and contrast conductors and insulators	☐
	8.5: Apply Ohm's law to series and parallel circuits	☐
	8.6: Compare and contrast direct current and alternating current	☐
	8.7: Identify sources of EMF	☐
	8.8: Demonstrate understanding of magnets, magnetic fields, and magnetic forces	☐
	8.9: Demonstrate understanding of how transformers and motors work	☐

PERSONALIZED STUDY PLAN

✘✔

KNOWN MATERIAL/ SKIP IT

PAGE	COMPETENCY AND SKILL	
76	**9: Waves**	☐
	9.1: Define and use the terms speed, amplitude, wavelength, and frequency	☐
	9.2: Distinguish between transverse and longitudinal waves	☐
	9.3: Demonstrate understanding of reflection, refraction, dispersion, absorption, transmission, scattering, and superposition	☐
	9.4: Demonstrate understanding of diffraction and interference	☐
	9.5: Demonstrate understanding of the Doppler Effect	☐
	9.6: Demonstrate understanding of polarization	☐
	9.7: Recognize the characteristics of sound waves	☐
	9.8: Demonstrate understanding of how sound waves are produced	☐
	9.9: Characterize the electromagnetic spectrum	☐
	9.10: Demonstrate understanding of color and the visible spectrum	☐
	9.11: Demonstrate understanding of geometric optics and of polarization	☐
83	**10: Periodicity**	☐
	10.1: Demonstrate understanding of the meaning of chemical periodicity	☐
	10.2: Demonstrate understanding of periodic trends in chemical and physical properties	☐
88	**11: The mole and chemical bonding**	☐
	11.1: Demonstrate understanding of the mole concept and chemical composition	☐
	11.2: Interpret and use chemical formulas	☐
	11.3: Demonstrate understanding of the systematic nomenclature of inorganic compounds	☐
	11.4: Demonstrate understanding of the nomenclature of simple organic compounds	☐
	11.5: Identify the various types of bonds	☐
	11.6: Interpret electron dot and structural formulas	☐
101	**12: The kinetic theory and states of matter**	☐
	12.1: Demonstrate understanding of kinetic molecular theory	☐
	12.2: Demonstrate understanding of phase changes	☐
	12.3: Demonstrate understanding of the relationships among temperature, pressure, volume, and number of molecules of a gas	☐
	12.4: Demonstrate understanding of the characteristics of crystals	☐

PERSONALIZED STUDY PLAN

PAGE	COMPETENCY AND SKILL	KNOWN MATERIAL/ SKIP IT
104	**13: Chemical reactions**	☐
	13.1: Demonstrate ability to balance chemical equations	☐
	13.2: Identify the various types of chemical reactions	☐
	13.3: Distinguish between endothermic and exothermic chemical reactions	☐
	13.4: Demonstrate understanding of the effects of temperature, pressure, concentration, and the presence of catalysts on chemical reactions	☐
	13.5: Demonstrate understanding of practical applications of electrochemistry	☐
108	**14: Solutions and solubility**	☐
	14.1: Demonstrate understanding of solution terminology and distinguish among types of solutions	☐
	14.2: Demonstrate understanding of various types of solvents and factors affecting the dissolving process	☐
	14.3: Demonstrate understanding of the effect of temperature and pressure on the solubility of a solute	☐
	14.4: Demonstrate understanding of the physical and chemical properties of acids, bases, and salts	☐
	14.5: Demonstrate knowledge of the meaning of pH and the effects of buffers	☐

A. PHYSICS

COMPETENCY 7
MECHANICS

Straight-Line Motion

To make an object move, initially a force has to be applied, since force has the capacity to move an object. We also need to take into account friction, which makes moving objects slow down, a characteristic that Galileo first noted. Newton's first law of motion states that an object at rest remains at rest unless acted upon by force. When force is applied to an object it moves in a straight line. A moving object has speed, velocity, and acceleration. Force can influence moving objects in many ways: make them move, slow down, stop, increase speed, decrease speed, etc.

Projectile Motion

By definition, a projectile has only one force acting on it—the force of gravity. The horizontal motion of the projectile is the result of the tendency of any object in motion to remain in motion at constant velocity. Projectiles travel with a parabolic trajectory because the downward force of gravity accelerates them downward from their otherwise straight-line trajectory. Gravity affects the vertical motion, not the horizontal motion, of the projectile. Gravity causes a downward displacement from the position that the object would be in if there were no gravity.

Circular Motion

Circular motion is defined as rotation along a circle: in a circular path or in a circular orbit. The rotation around a fixed axis of a three-dimensional body involves circular motion of its parts. Circular motion involves acceleration of the moving object by a centripetal force that pulls the moving object toward the center of the circular orbit. According to Newton's first law of motion, without this acceleration, the object would move slowly in a straight line, Circular motion is accelerated even though the speed is constant, because the object's velocity is constantly changing direction.

A special kind of circular motion—called a spinning (or rotational) motion—occurs when an object rotates around its own center of mass.

Examples of circular motion are artificial satellites orbiting the Earth in a geo-synchronous orbit, a stone tied to a rope and being swung in circles, a race car turning through a curve on a racetrack, an electron moving perpendicular to a uniform magnetic field, and a gear turning inside a mechanism.

Periodic Motion

Periodic motion occurs when an object moves back and forth in regular motion, for example, a weight on a string swinging back and forth (pendulum) and a ball bouncing up and down. Periodic motion is characterized by three things:

1. Velocity: Each object—the bouncing ball, the weight on a pendulum—has velocity.

2. Period or frequency: You can measure the time it takes for the object to go back and forth.

3. Amplitude: Amplitude is half the distance the object goes in the period. For an object in rotation, the amplitude is the radius of the circle (half the diameter).

There are many devices that use the characteristics of periodic motion. A clock is the most common device. Another use of periodic motion is in the study of wave motion, including light, sound, and music.

SKILL 7.2 Demonstrate understanding of Newton's laws of motion

---

Classical physics is primarily aimed at explaining the observable phenomena that surround us. It is often referred to as Newtonian physics in honor of Sir Isaac Newton, the preeminent physicist of his time.

NEWTON'S FIRST LAW OF MOTION (THE LAW OF INERTIA): objects at rest tend to stay at rest, and objects in motion tend to stay in motion, unless something causes them to change

Inertia

If you simply look at this book without touching it or changing its position, you are demonstrating **NEWTON'S FIRST LAW OF MOTION (THE LAW OF INERTIA):** every body continues in its state of rest, or of motion in a straight line at constant speed, unless it is compelled to change that state by forces exerted upon it.

In simplified form, this law can be stated as: objects at rest tend to stay at rest, and objects in motion tend to stay in motion, unless something causes them to change.

The book remained at rest and did not spontaneously change position. This is because no force was applied to cause it to change its INERTIA—the tendency of an object to resist a change in its motion.

> **INERTIA:** the tendency of an object to resist a change in its motion

Mass Resists Acceleration

If you push the book along the desktop with your hand, the book changes position in a gradual manner. However, if you drop kick the book into the corner, the change is abrupt, and the book flies toward the corner at a faster speed.

These actions both illustrate NEWTON'S SECOND LAW—the acceleration produced by a net force on a body is directly proportional to the magnitude of the net force, in the same direction of the net force, and inversely proportional to the mass of the body.

Essentially, Sir Isaac conveyed through his law that the reaction of an object—its acceleration away from the force—is the result of the amount of force applied, as modified by the mass (weight) of the object the force is applied to, expressed in the equation $F = ma$.

> **NEWTON'S SECOND LAW:** the acceleration produced by a net force on a body is directly proportional to the magnitude of the net force, in the same direction of the net force, and inversely proportional to the mass of the body

It was easy to push or drop kick the book. It had little mass (weight) in comparison to the force you exerted on it. Consequently the gentle push made it move a little and slowly. But the kick applied a much higher level of force, and, consequently, the book rocketed away from you.

The results would have been far different, however, if you had tried to make a 100-pound block fly across the room at the same rate as the book did. You would have had to apply a significantly larger amount of force. In simple terms, mass resists acceleration.

Opposite and Equal Reaction

NEWTON'S THIRD LAW states that whenever one body exerts a force on a second body, the second body exerts an equal and opposite force on the first.

Most people have heard of this law, often summed up as "opposite and equal reaction." One of the best illustrations of this concept is trying to get out of a small boat. As you step forward toward the dock, you are applying a force to the boat. If it isn't tied up, it moves backward as you move forward. Most people don't realize that the reason that you moved forward was that as you pushed on the boat, the boat pushed back!

> **NEWTON'S THIRD LAW:** whenever one body exerts a force on a second body, the second body exerts an equal and opposite force on the first

Once again, the relative masses of the objects applying the force come into play. If you push on a wall, the wall pushes back. But did the wall move? Not unless it was quite flimsy or you happen to have superpowers. Because of the wall's mass, it was unaffected by the much weaker force you applied. It pushed back with an opposite and equal force, essentially canceling out your efforts to topple it. Consequently, neither you nor the wall changed position.

Nothing Falls Upward

Newton also turned his immense talents toward explaining why things don't fall upward by developing the **LAW OF UNIVERSAL GRAVITATION** that states that every object attracts every other object with a force that for any two objects is directly proportional to the mass of each object.

Gravity, the attractive force between objects, is at work when you toss this book into the air. The body attracting the book back to you is the immense mass of the Earth. In relation to the mass of the book, it's not surprising that the book comes down.

But what if you shot the book into outer space? Would it come down? The answer depends on the amount of force applied to the book and the distance it reaches from the center of the Earth. Remember, the law says that the attractive force of gravity depends on the distance of the center of mass of the objects involved.

> **LAW OF UNIVERSAL GRAVITATION:** every object attracts every other object with a force directly proportional to the mass of each object

> *Mass is an integral part of most physical processes.*

SKILL 7.3 **Distinguish between weight and mass**

See Skill 4.1

SKILL 7.4 **Demonstrate understanding of friction**

Surfaces that touch each other have a certain resistance to motion. This resistance is **FRICTION**.

1. The materials that make up the surfaces will determine the magnitude of the frictional force

> **FRICTION:** the resistance to motion exhibited by surfaces that touch each other

2. The frictional force is independent of the area of contact between the two surfaces

3. The direction of the frictional force is opposite to the direction of motion

4. The frictional force is proportional to the normal force between the two surfaces in contact

STATIC FRICTION describes the force of friction of two surfaces that are in contact but do not have any motion relative to each other, such as a block sitting on an inclined plane. KINETIC FRICTION describes the force of friction of two surfaces in contact with each other when there is relative motion between the surfaces.

> **STATIC FRICTION:** the force of friction of two surfaces that are in contact without any motion relative to each other
>
> **KINETIC FRICTION:** the force of friction of two surfaces in contact with each other with relative motion between the surfaces

SKILL 7.5 Distinguish among work, energy, and power

WORK	Done on an object when an applied force moves through a distance
ENERGY	The ability to cause change in matter
POWER	The work done divided by the amount of time that it took to do it, in other words, the rate at which work is done (Power = Work ÷ Time)
AMOUNT OF WORK DONE	Equal to the force applied over the distance it is applied. (Work = Force × Distance)

If you apply more force (i.e., kicking the book), you do more work. If you move the book farther, again, you do more work. The critical point is distinguishing on which object work is being done. Example: If you hold this book over your head, no work is being done on the book. Some work was done initially to place it in that position, but once it is there, no further work is accomplished. After a while, you will get tired of holding the book, your shoulder muscles will cramp. As the muscles contract, they do work on a biological scale. But no work is done on the book unless you move its position.

Work falls into two general categories:

• Work done to change the speed of something

• Work done against an opposing force

You do work on something when you force it to move.

NEWTON-METER: the unit of measurement for work—a combination of the unit of force, Newtons (N), and a unit of distance, meter (m), also known as a Joule

JOULE: measurement for work; 1J = 1 N of force exerted over 1 m of distance

POWER: the rate at which work is done, equal to the amount of work done divided by the time it took to do it, or P = w/t

WATT: a measure of power, in joules per second or a watt. One watt (W) of power = one joule of work done in one second

The unit of measurement for work is a combination of the unit of force, Newton (N), and a unit of distance, meter (m), known as a **NEWTON-METER**. However this combination more often is referred to by its other name, a Joule (J). A **JOULE** of work is done when 1 N of force is exerted over 1 m of distance.

Note that the examples given to illustrate work didn't mention anything about how long it took to accomplish the work. That's because when you introduce a time factor, you are actually talking about **POWER**, the rate at which work is done. Power is equal to the amount of work done divided by the amount of time during which the work was done. This can be shown as: P=w/t.

Power conveys an implication of force. If the power is doubled, the same amount of work is done, but in half the time it originally took.

Look at power from this viewpoint: a gallon of gas can do a specified amount of work, but the power produced when we burn it can be any amount, depending on how fast it's burned.

Example: An automobile engine produces 50 units of power for a half-hour; a jet engine produces 90,000 units of power for one second. Which of the two engines is more powerful?

Power is measured in joules per second, more familiarly known as a **WATT**. One watt (W) of power is expended when one joule of work is done in one second. Usually, however, we deal with watts on a larger scale when we talk about power. Your electricity bill is based on kilowatts (kW); one kW is equal to 1000 watts.

SKILL **Demonstrate understanding of simple machines and torque**
7.6

Simple machines make work easier. Simple machines include:

- Inclined plane
- Lever
- Wheel and axle
- Pulley

Complex machines are two or more simple machines working together. A wheelbarrow is an example of a complex machine. It uses a lever and a wheel and axle. Machines of all types ease workload by changing the size or direction of an applied force. The amount of effort saved when using simple or complex machines is called the MECHANICAL ADVANTAGE or MA.

TORQUE is the force that results in a change in rotational motion. This force is defined by linear force multiplied by a radius. It can be directly related to the lever, a simple machine.

MECHANICAL ADVANTAGE: the amount of effort saved when using simple or complex machines

TORQUE: the force that results in a change in rotational motion

SKILL 7.7 Demonstrate understanding of linear momentum

Our world is not static; it moves, and things on it move. To describe movement, physicists and, by extension, Earth scientists, use specific terms to show how an object moves. If a moving object is not moving in a circle, the movement is called linear motion.

- Speed: A measure of how fast an object is moving. It is the rate at which distance is covered and is measured in terms of distance divided by time.

  Example: The reading (for instance, 55 mph) on the speedometer in your car.

- Instantaneous Speed: The speed that an object has at any given instant.

  Example: You get a ticket for driving 65 mph in a 55-mph zone. The speed that is shown on the ticket is an instantaneous speed.

- Average Speed: The average of the speeds obtained by an object in its movement over a total distance, divided by the time it took to cover the distance.

- Velocity: A measure of how fast and in which direction an object is moving. Note how closely this definition is to that of speed. Although we normally treat the words speed and velocity as having the same meaning, in actuality, they are quite different.

We calculate velocity exactly the same as we do for speed:—distance divided by time, but we must describe the direction to express velocity, and direction isn't confined to mean only a compass point such as north or south, but also includes up, down, right, left, forward, and backward.

- Constant Velocity: An object moving with a constant speed with no change in direction.

  Example: If you walk forward in a straight line with no turns or change in speed, you have constant velocity. But if you slow down or turn a corner, you do not have constant velocity.

- Acceleration: The rate of change in velocity. It is velocity divided by time. The term also applies to a decrease in velocity. We often refer to this as

- Deceleration: Strictly speaking however, an increase or decrease in velocity is simply acceleration.

- Momentum: Inertia in motion. Although this definition may seem contradictory, as most people think of inertia as a static situation, recall the definition of inertia: the tendency of an object to resist a change in motion. Thus, an object sitting still has inertia; its motion is actually no motion. Momentum is based upon the **FORMULA OF MOMENTUM**, which is mass × velocity. This means that if you change either the mass of the object involved or the velocity of its motion, you will change its momentum.

FORMULA OF MOMENTUM: mass × velocity

  Example: You are driving a car, see an accident up ahead, and apply your brakes. By applying your brakes you changed the momentum of your car. It still has the same mass, but you reduced velocity by braking.

IMPULSE: a force exerted over a time period

To change the momentum you are applied an **IMPULSE**, a force exerted over a time period. This time period can either be long or short, and each produces a different change in momentum.

  Example: If you simply tapped your brakes, the force acting on the brake pads was slight, producing a small change in velocity, and by extension, momentum. If you continuously braked (almost standing on the pedal in an emergency situation), however, you caused a long impulse transfer to the brake pads, and thereby produced a large change in momentum (you stopped).

SKILL 7.8 Demonstrate understanding of the conservation of energy and the conservation of linear momentum

Many chemical reactions give off energy. Like matter, energy can change form but it can neither be created nor destroyed during a chemical reaction. This is the law of conservation of energy (*See also Skill 4.5*). In other words, energy can be transformed into various forms such as kinetic, potential, electric, or heat energy, but the total amount of energy remains constant. Energy often changes from kinetic (motion) to potential (stored) or in the opposite direction from potential to kinetic, as when you toss a ball or pebbles fall off a cliff.

The law of conservation of momentum states that the total momentum of a closed system of objects with no external interactions is constant. By extension, the object being studied will always continue with the same velocity unless acted on by a force outside the system.

> *Example: A car in motion will travel at the same velocity unless acted upon by your tapping the gas or brake, or over the course of time by friction.*

SKILL 7.9 Demonstrate understanding of angular momentum and torque and angular momentum conservation

Linear motion is measured in rectangular coordinates. Rotational motion is measured differently, in terms of the angle of displacement. There are three common ways to measure rotational displacement: by degrees, revolutions, and radians. The relationship between degrees and revolutions is easy to understand: one revolution is 360°. Radians are slightly less well known and are defined as: $\frac{\text{arc length}}{\text{radius}}$. Therefore $360° = 2\pi$ radians, and 1 radian $= 57.3°$.

The major concepts of linear motion are duplicated in rotational motion with linear displacement replaced by angular displacement.

Angular velocity ω = rate of change of angular displacement

Angular acceleration α = rate of change of angular velocity

Also, the linear velocity v of a rolling object can be written as $v = r\omega$ and the linear acceleration as $a = r\alpha$.

One important difference in the equations relates to the use of mass in rotational systems. In rotational problems, not only is the mass of an object important but also its location. In order to include the spatial distribution of the mass of the object, a term called moment of inertia is used, $I = m_1 r_1^2 + m_2 r_2^2 + \cdots + m_n r_n^2$. The moment of inertia is always defined with respect to a particular axis of rotation.

Example: If the radius of the wheel on the left is 0.75m, what is its moment of inertia about an axis running through its center perpendicular to the plane of the wheel?

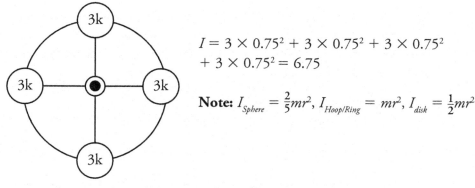

$$I = 3 \times 0.75^2 + 3 \times 0.75^2 + 3 \times 0.75^2 + 3 \times 0.75^2 = 6.75$$

Note: $I_{Sphere} = \frac{2}{5}mr^2$, $I_{Hoop/Ring} = mr^2$, $I_{disk} = \frac{1}{2}mr^2$

The rotational analog of Newton's second law of motion is given in terms of torque τ, moment of inertia I, and angular acceleration α:

$$\tau = I\alpha$$

where the torque τ is the rotational force on the body. The torque τ produced by a force F acting at a distance r from the point of rotation is given by the product of r and the component of the force that is perpendicular to the line joining the point of rotation to the point of action of the force.

A concept related to the moment of inertia is the radius of gyration (k), which is the average distance of the mass of an object from its axis of rotation, i.e., the distance from the axis where a point mass m would have the same moment of inertia.

$k_{Sphere} = \sqrt{\frac{2}{5}}r$, $k_{Hoop/Ring} = r$, $k_{disk} = \frac{r}{\sqrt{2}}$. As you can see $I = mk^2$

This is analogous to the concept of center of mass, the point where an equivalent mass of infinitely small size would be located, in the case of linear motion.

Angular momentum (L), and rotational kinetic energy (KEr), are therefore defined as follows: $L = I\omega$, $KE_r = \frac{1}{2}I\omega^2$

As with all systems, energy is conserved unless the system is acted on by an external force. This can be used to solve problems such as the one below.

Example: A uniform ball of radius r and mass m starts from rest and rolls down a frictionless incline of height h. When the ball reaches the ground, how fast is it going?

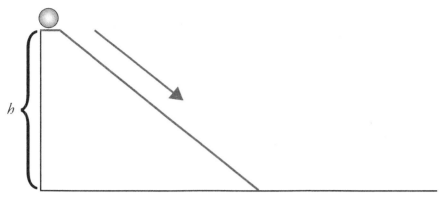

$$PE_{initial} + KE_{rotational/initial} + KE_{linear/initial} = PE_{final} + KE_{rotational/final} + KE_{linear/final}$$

$$mgh + 0 + 0 = 0 + \frac{1}{2}I\omega_{final}^2 + \frac{1}{2}mv_{final}^2 \rightarrow mgh = \frac{1}{2} \times \frac{2}{5} mr^2 \omega_{final}^2 + \frac{1}{2}mv_{final}^2$$

$$mgh = \frac{1}{5}mr^2 (\frac{v_{final}}{r})^2 + \frac{1}{2}mv_{final}^2 \rightarrow mgh = \frac{1}{5}mv_{final}^2 + \frac{1}{2}mv_{final}^2$$

$$gh = \frac{7}{10}v_{final}^2 \rightarrow v_{final} = \sqrt{\frac{10}{7}gh}$$

Similarly, unless a net torque acts on a system, the angular momentum remains constant in both magnitude and direction. This can be used to solve many different types of problems including ones involving satellite motion.

Conservation of momentum requires vector math.

Example: Imagine a pool table like the one below. Both balls are 0.5 kg in mass. Before the collision, the white ball is moving with the velocity indicated by the solid line and the black ball is at rest. After the collision, the black ball is moving with the velocity indicated by the dashed line (a 135° angle from the direction of the white ball). With what speed, and in what direction, is the white ball moving after the collision?

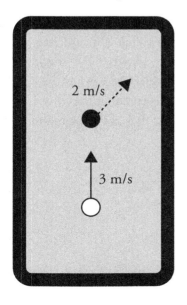

$$P_{white/before} = .5 \times (0, 3) = (0, 1.5) \; P_{black/before} = 0 \; P_{total/before} = (0,1.5)$$
$$P_{black/after} = .5 \, (2 \cos45, 2 \sin 45) = (0.71, 0.71)$$
$$P_{white/after} = (-0.71, 0.79)$$

i.e., the white ball has a velocity of $v = \sqrt{(-.71)^2 + (0.79)^2} = 1.06 m/s$ and is moving at an angle of $\theta = \tan^{-1}\left(\frac{0.79}{-0.71}\right) = -48°$ from the horizontal

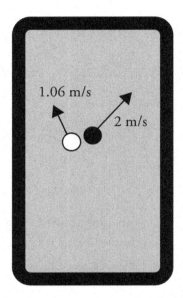

SKILL 7.10 Demonstrate understanding of the force of gravity

Gravity is the force that results in bodies being attracted to one another or gravitation. Gravitation is most commonly associated with weight and the orbits of celestial bodies. The force that the earth's gravity exerts on an object with a specific mass is called the object's weight on Earth. Weight is a force that is measured in Newtons. Weight (W) = mass times acceleration due to gravity (W = mg). When an object moves in a circular path, a force must be directed toward the center of the circle in order to keep the motion going. This constraining force is called CENTRIPETAL FORCE. Gravity is the centripetal force that keeps a satellite circling the Earth.

CENTRIPETAL FORCE: the constraining force directed toward the center of a circle to keep an object moving in a circular path

SKILL 7.11 Demonstrate understanding of pressure and Pascal's principle of fluids

As a substance is heated, the molecules begin moving faster within the container. As the substance becomes a gas and those molecules hit the sides of the container, pressure builds. **PRESSURE** is the force exerted on each unit of area of a surface. Pressure is measured in a unit called the **PASCAL**. One Pascal (pa) is equal to one Newton of force pushing on one square meter of area. **PASCAL'S PRINCIPLE** states that pressure applied to an enclosed fluid is transmitted undiminished to every part of the fluid, as well as to the walls of the container.

Volume, Temperature, and Pressure of Gas are Related

Temperature and pressure: As the temperature of a gas increases, its pressure increases. When you drive a car, the friction between the road and the tire heats up the air inside the tire. Because the temperature increases, so does the pressure of the air on the inside of the tire.

Temperature and volume: At a constant pressure, an increase in temperature causes an increase in the volume of a gas. If you apply heat to an enclosed container of gas, the pressure inside the bottle will increase as the heat increases. This is called **CHARLES' LAW**.

These relations (pressure and temperature, and temperature and volume) are direct variations. As one component increases (decreases), the other also increases (decreases). However, pressure and volume vary inversely.

Pressure and volume: At a constant temperature, a decrease in the volume of a gas causes an increase in its pressure. The gas pressure inside a tire pump increases as you press down on the pump handle because you are compressing the gas, or forcing it to exist in a smaller volume. This relationship between pressure and volume is called **BOYLE'S LAW**.

SKILL 7.12 Demonstrate understanding of Archimedes' principle (buoyancy)

The law of buoyancy is named after Archimedes of Syracuse, the Greek who first discovered it. **ARCHIMEDES' PRINCIPLE** states that the buoyant force is equal to the weight of the displaced fluid. The weight of the displaced fluid is directly

PRESSURE: the force exerted on each unit of area of a surface

PASCAL: unit for measuring pressure; one Pascal (pa) = one Newton of force pushing on one square meter of area

PASCAL'S PRINCIPLE: pressure applied to an enclosed fluid is transmitted undiminished to every part of the fluid, as well as to the walls of the container

CHARLES' LAW: pressure inside an enclosed container will increase as applied heat increases

BOYLE'S LAW: pressure and volume vary inversely; at a constant temperature, a decrease in the volume of a gas causes an increase in its pressure

ARCHIMEDES' PRINCIPLE: the buoyant force is equal to the weight of the displaced fluid, or the weight of the displaced fluid is directly proportional to its volume

proportional to the volume of the displaced fluid (specifically, if the surrounding fluid is of uniform density). Thus, among objects with equal masses, the one with greater volume has greater buoyancy.

Suppose a rock's weight is measured as 10 Newtons, when suspended by a string in a vacuum. Suppose that when the rock is lowered by the string into the water, it displaces water weighing 3 Newtons. The buoyant force is $10 - 3 = 7$ Newtons. The density of the immersed object relative to the density of the fluid is easily calculated without measuring any volumes in the following equation:

Relative density = Weight divided by (Weight − Apparent Immersed Weight)

The applications of Archimedes' principle are many and important:

- Submarines
- Diving weighting system
- Naval architecture
- Flotation
- Buoyancy compensator, and many more

SKILL 7.13 Demonstrate understanding of Bernoulli's principle for fluids

BERNOULLI'S PRINCIPLE: as the speed of a fluid, gas, or liquid increases, the pressure it exerts decreases

VENTURI EFFECT: the decrease in pressure that results from passing a gas, fluid, or liquid through a constricted tube that causes its velocity to increase

BERNOULLI'S PRINCIPLE states that as the speed of a fluid, gas, or liquid increases, the pressure it exerts decreases. This principle is named for the mathematician/scientist, Daniel Bernoulli, though it was previously understood by Leonhard Euler and others. In a fluid flow with no viscosity, and therefore one in which pressure difference is the only accelerating force, it is equivalent to Newton's laws of motion.

Bernoulli's principle also describes the **VENTURI EFFECT** that is used in carburetors and elsewhere. In a carburetor, air is passed through a venturi tube in order to decrease its pressure. This happens because the air velocity increases as it flows through the constricted tube. Thus, Bernoulli's principle is of great practical application in aircraft flight and carburetors.

COMPETENCY 8
ELECTRICITY AND MAGNETISM

SKILL **Demonstrate understanding of the repulsion and attraction of**
8.1 **electric charges**

See Skill 8.8

SKILL **Demonstrate understanding of the characteristics of current**
8.2 **electricity and simple circuits** *(for example, resistance and Ohm's law, electromotive force, potential difference capacitance, current)*

An **ELECTRIC CIRCUIT** is a path along which electrons flow. A simple circuit can be created with a dry cell, wire, and a bell, or light bulb. When all are connected, the electrons flow from the negative terminal, through the wire to the device and back to the positive terminal of the dry cell. If there are no breaks in the circuit, the device will work. The circuit is closed. Any break in the flow will create an open circuit and cause the device to shut off.

The device (bell, bulb) is an example of a **LOAD**. A load is a device that uses energy. Suppose that you also add a buzzer so that the bell rings when you press the buzzer button. The buzzer is acting as a **SWITCH**. A switch is a device that opens or closes a circuit. Pressing the buzzer makes the connection complete and the bell rings. When the buzzer is not engaged, the circuit is open and the bell is silent.

When an electron goes through a load, it does work and therefore loses some of its energy. The measure of how much energy is lost is called the **POTENTIAL DIFFER-ENCE**. The potential difference between two points is the work needed to move a charge from one point to another.

Potential difference is measured in a unit called the **VOLT**. **VOLTAGE** is potential difference. The higher the voltage, the more energy the electrons have. This energy is measured by a device called a voltmeter. To use a voltmeter, place it in a circuit parallel with the load you are measuring.

ELECTRIC CIRCUIT: a path along which electrons flow

LOAD: a device that uses energy

SWITCH: a device that opens or closes a circuit

POTENTIAL DIFFER-ENCE: the measure of how much energy is lost when electrons go through a load; also, the work needed to move a charge from one point to another

VOLT: unit for measuring potential difference

VOLTAGE: amount of potential difference; the higher the voltage, the more energy the electrons have

CURRENT: the number of electrons per second that flow past a point in a circuit

RESISTANCE: the ability of the material to oppose the flow of electrons through it

OHMS: unit for measuring resistance

OHM'S LAW: current (I) is equal to potential difference (V) divided by resistance (R)

CAPACITANCE: a measure of the stored electric charge per unit electric potential

The function of capacitors is to store electrical energy.

CURRENT is the number of electrons per second that flow past a point in a circuit. Current is measured with a device called an ammeter. To use an ammeter, put it in series with the load you are measuring.

As electrons flow through a wire, they lose potential energy. Some is changed into heat energy because of resistance. **RESISTANCE** is the ability of the material to oppose the flow of electrons through it. All substances have some resistance, even if they are good conductors such as copper. This resistance is measured in units called **OHMS**. A thin wire will have more resistance than a thick one because it will have less room for electrons to travel. A thicker wire offers more possible paths for the electrons to flow. Resistance also depends on the length of the wire. The longer the wire, the more resistance it will have.

Potential difference, resistance, and current form a relationship know as **OHM'S LAW**. Current (I) is equal to potential difference (V) divided by resistance (R).

$$I = V \div R$$

See also Skill 8.5

If you have a wire with resistance of 5 ohms and a potential difference of 75 volts, you can calculate the current by

$I = 75$ volts $\div$ 5 ohms

$I = 15$ amperes

A current of 10 or more amperes will cause a wire to get hot. 22 amperes is about the maximum for a house circuit. Anything above 25 amperes can start a fire.

CAPACITANCE (C) is a measure of the stored electric charge per unit electric potential. The mathematical definition is:

$$C = \frac{Q}{V}$$

It follows from the definition above that the units of capacitance are coulombs per volt, a unit known as a farad (F=C/V). In circuits, devices called parallel plate capacitors are formed by two closely spaced conductors. The function of capacitors is to store electrical energy. When a voltage is applied, electrical charges build up in both the conductors (typically referred to as plates). These charges on the two plates have equal magnitude but opposite sign.

In summary, a capacitor is "charged" as electrical energy is delivered to it and opposite charges accumulate on the two plates. The two plates generate electric fields and a voltage develops across the dielectric. The energy stored in the capacitor, then, is equal to the amount of work necessary to create this voltage.

SKILL 8.3 Compare and contrast series and parallel circuits

A **SERIES CIRCUIT** is one where the electrons have only one path along which they can move. When one load in a series circuit goes out, the circuit is open. An example of this is a set of Christmas tree lights that is missing a bulb. None of the bulbs will work.

A **PARALLEL CIRCUIT** is one where the electrons have more than one path to move along. If a load goes out in a parallel circuit, the other load will still work because the electrons can still find a way to continue moving along the path.

SERIES CIRCUIT: one where the electrons have only one path along which they can move

PARALLEL CIRCUIT: one where the electrons have more than one path to move along

SKILL 8.4 Compare and contrast conductors and insulators

Electrical current requires the free flow of electrons. Various materials allow different degrees of electron movement and are classified as conductors, insulators, or semiconductors (in certain, typically man-made environments, superconductors also exist). When charge is transferred to a mass of material, the response is highly dependent on whether that material is a conductor or insulator.

CONDUCTORS are materials that allow for free and easy movement of electrons. Some of the best conductors are metal, especially copper and silver because these materials are held together with metallic bonds, which involve delocalized electrons shared by atoms in a lattice. If a charge is transferred to a conductor, the electrons will flow freely and the charge will quickly distribute itself across the material in a manner dictated by the conductor's shape.

INSULATORS are materials that do not allow conduction. Good insulators include glass, rubber, and wood. These materials have chemical structures in which the electrons are closely localized to the individual atoms. In contrast to a conductor, a charge transferred to an insulator will remain localized at the point where it was introduced because the movement of electrons will be highly impeded.

Electrical current requires the free flow of electrons.

CONDUCTORS: materials that allow for free and easy movement of electrons

INSULATORS: materials that do not allow conduction

SKILL 8.5 Apply Ohm's law to series and parallel circuits

OHM'S LAW: the current passing through a conductor is directly proportional to the voltage drop and inversely proportional to the resistance of the conductor, or *V = IR*

Ohm's law is the most important tool we possess to analyze electrical circuits. **OHM'S LAW** states that the current passing through a conductor is directly proportional to the voltage drop and inversely proportional to the resistance of the conductor. Stated mathematically, this is:

$$V = IR$$

Problem: The circuit diagram below shows three resistors connected to a battery in series. A current of 1.0A flows through the circuit in the direction shown. It is known that the equivalent resistance of this circuit is 25 Ω. What is the total voltage supplied by the battery?

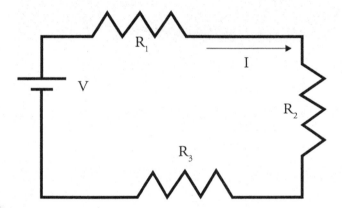

ALTERNATING CURRENT (AC): a type of electrical current with cyclically varying magnitude and direction

Solution: To determine the battery's voltage, we simply apply Ohm's Law:
$$V = IR = 1.0A \times 25\Omega = 25V$$

SKILL 8.6 Compare and contrast direct current and alternating current

AC is the type of current delivered to businesses and residences.

ALTERNATING CURRENT (AC) is a type of electrical current with cyclically varying magnitude and direction. This is differentiated from **DIRECT CURRENT (DC)**, which has constant direction. Though other waveforms are sometimes used, the vast majority of AC current is sinusoidal (wavelike). Thus we use wave terminology to help us describe AC current.

DIRECT CURRENT (DC): a type of electrical current with constant scirection

SKILL 8.7 Identify sources of EMF *(for example, batteries, photo cells, generators)*

A **BATTERY** consists of one or more electrochemical cells connected together. Electron transfer from the oxidation to the reduction reaction may take place only through an external circuit.

Electrochemical systems provide a source of **ELECTROMOTIVE FORCE**, also called voltage or cell potential and measured in volts *(also see Skill 8.2)*. Electrons are allowed to leave the chemical process at the anode and permitted to enter at the cathode. The result is a negatively charged anode and a positively charged cathode.

GENERATORS are devices that are the opposite of motors in that they convert mechanical energy into electrical energy. The mechanical energy can come from a variety of sources: combustion engines, blowing wind, falling water, or even a hand crank or bicycle wheel. Most generators rely on electromagnetic induction to create an electrical current. These generators consist of magnets and a coil. The magnets create a magnetic field, and the coil is located within this field. Mechanical energy, from whatever source, is used to spin the coil within this field. As stated by Faraday's Law, this produces a voltage.

> **BATTERY:** consists of one or more electrochemical cells connected together with electron transfer taking place only through an external circuit

> **ELECTROMOTIVE FORCE:** also called voltage or cell potential and measured in volts

> **GENERATORS:** devices that are the opposite of motors in that they convert mechanical energy into electrical energy

SKILL 8.8 Demonstrate understanding of magnets, magnetic fields, and magnetic forces

Magnets have a north pole and a south pole. Like poles repel and different poles attract. A **MAGNETIC FIELD** is the space around a magnet where its force will affect objects. The closer you are to a magnet, the stronger the force. As you move away, the force becomes weaker.

Some materials act as magnets and some do not because magnetism is a result of electrons in motion. The most important motion in this case is the spinning of the individual electrons. Electrons spin in pairs in opposite directions in most atoms. The magnetic field that each spinning electron creates is canceled out by the electron that is spinning in the opposite direction.

In an atom of iron, however, there are four unpaired electrons, and the magnetic fields of these electrons are not canceled out. Their fields add up to make a tiny magnet. Their fields exert forces on each other, setting up small areas in the iron

> **MAGNETIC FIELD:** the space around a magnet where its force will affect objects

MAGNETIC DOMAINS: small areas in a magnetic substance where atomic magnetic fields line up in the same direction

called **MAGNETIC DOMAINS** where atomic magnetic fields line up in the same direction.

You can make a magnet out of an iron nail by stroking the nail in the same direction repeatedly with a magnet, which causes poles in the atomic magnets in the nail to be attracted to the magnet. The tiny magnetic fields in the nail line up in the direction of the magnet, increasing the domains pointing in the direction of the magnet. Eventually, one large domain results and the nail becomes a magnet.

A bar magnet has a north pole and a south pole. If you break the magnet in half, each piece will have a north and south pole.

The earth has a magnetic field. In a compass, a tiny, lightweight magnet is suspended and will line its south pole up with the North Pole magnet of the earth.

You can make a magnet out of a coil of wire by connecting the ends of the coil to a battery. When the current goes through the wire, the wire acts in the same way that a magnet does: it is called an **ELECTROMAGNET**.

ELECTROMAGNET: a magnet made by running a current through a coil of wire whose ends are connected to a battery

The poles of the electromagnet will depend upon which way the electric current runs. An electromagnet can be made more powerful in three ways:

1. Make more coils

2. Put an iron core (nail) inside the coils

3. Use more battery power

Telegraphs use electromagnets to send messages around the world. When a telegraph key is pushed, current flows through a circuit, turning on an electromagnet that attracts an iron bar. The iron bar hits a sounding board that responds with a click. Release the key and the electromagnet turns off.

Scrap metal can be removed from waste materials by using a large electromagnet suspended from a crane. When the electromagnet is turned on, only the metal in the pile of waste will be attracted to it. All other materials will stay on the ground.

Air conditioners, vacuum cleaners, and washing machines use electric motors. An electric motor uses an electromagnet to change electric energy into mechanical energy.

Electromagnetic induction is used in a **TRANSFORMER**, a device that magnetically couples two circuits together to allow the transfer of energy between the two circuits without requiring motion. Typically, a transformer consists of a couple of coils and a magnetic core. A changing voltage applied to one coil (the primary) creates a flux in the magnetic core, which induces voltage in the other coil (the secondary). All transformers operate on this simple principle though they range in size and function from those in tiny microphones to those that connect the components of the United States power grid.

ELECTRIC MOTORS are found in many common appliances such as fans and washing machines. The operation of a motor is based on the principle that a magnetic field exerts a force on a current-carrying conductor because the current-carrying conductor itself generates a magnetic field, the basic principle that governs the behavior of an electromagnet. In a motor, this idea is used to convert electrical energy into mechanical energy, most commonly rotational energy. Thus the components of the simplest motors must include a strong magnet and a current-carrying coil placed in the magnetic field in such a way that the force on it causes it to rotate.

Motors may be run using DC or AC current and may be designed in a number of ways with varying levels of complexity. A very basic DC motor consists of the following components:

- A field magnet

- An armature with a coil around it that rotates between the poles of the field magnet

- A power supply that supplies current to the armature

- An axle that transfers the rotational energy of the armature to the working parts of the motor

- A set of commutators and brushes that reverse the direction of power flow every half rotation so that the armature continues to rotate

TRANSFORMER: a device that magnetically couples two circuits together to allow the transfer of energy between the two circuits without requiring motion

One of the most important functions of transformers is that they allow us to "step-up" and "step-down" between vastly different voltages.

ELECTRIC MOTOR: uses a strong magnet and a current-carrying coil placed in the magnetic field in such a way that the force on it causes it to rotate, converting electrical energy into mechanical energy

COMPETENCY 9

WAVES

SKILL Define and use the terms speed, amplitude, wavelength, and
9.1 frequency

SPEED OF LIGHT (C):
3×10^8 m/sec

FREQUENCY: the number of complete waveform cycles that pass a fixed point in one second and is measured in hertz $(Hz = 1/f)$

WAVELENGTH: the distance between the start and the end of one full cycle of the waveform (wave top to wave top)

AMPLITUDE: the distance between the top and midpoint of a waveform

WAVE PERIOD: the time between the passing of two successive waves

The **SPEED OF LIGHT (C)** is 3×10^8 m/sec.

The speed of a waveform is expressed in units of Hertz (Hz), as a function of wavelength (λ) times the frequency (f).

FREQUENCY (f) is the number of complete waveform cycles that pass a fixed point in one second and is measured in hertz $(Hz = 1/f)$.

WAVELENGTH is the distance between the start and the end of one full cycle of the waveform (wave top to wave top). The symbol for wavelength is the Greek letter (λ) Lambda. Wavelength and frequency have an inverse relationship. If frequency goes up, the wavelength goes down. If wavelength goes up, the frequency goes down.

Light is actually a waveform that travels by electromagnetic fields. Unlike sound, light can travel through a vacuum. Sound travels due to an increase or decrease of particle vibrations through the air so cannot travel in a vacuum. We measure light in wavelengths.

AMPLITUDE is the distance between the top and midpoint of a waveform. The **WAVE PERIOD** is the time between the passing of two successive waves.

SKILL Distinguish between the characteristics of transverse and
9.2 longitudinal waves

Transverse waves are characterized by the particle motion being perpendicular to the wave motion; longitudinal waves are characterized by the particle motion being parallel to the wave motion. Transverse waves cannot spread in a gas or liquid. Sound waves are a good example of longitudinal waves.

SKILL 9.3 Demonstrate understanding of reflection, refraction, dispersion, absorption, transmission, scattering, and superposition

See also Skill 9.2

Light interacts with matter by refraction, dispersion, absorption, transmission, scattering, and superposition. In a transparent material such as a lens, most of the light is transmitted through. Opaque objects such as rocks or cars partially absorb and partially reflect light.

Shadows illustrate one of the basic properties of light. Light travels in a straight line. If you put your hand between a light source and a wall, you will interrupt the light and produce a shadow.

When light hits a surface, it is reflected. The angle of the incoming light—the angle of incidence—is the same as the angle of the reflected light—the angle of reflection. It is this reflected light that allows you to see objects. You see the objects when the reflected light reaches your eyes. Different surfaces reflect light differently. Rough surfaces scatter light in many different directions. A smooth surface reflects the light in one direction. If it is smooth and shiny (like a mirror), reflection allows you to see your image in the surface.

When light enters a different medium, it bends. This bending, or change of speed, is called REFRACTION.

SCATTERING is the dispersion of light according to the size of the particulate matter it encounters in the sky. The particulate matter encountered includes ice, water, dust, aerosols, and temperature gradients. Outer space appears black to us because these particulates are not present to scatter the light.

- MIE Scattering: This occurs when light encounters particles greater than 0.5 μm (microns). These particles scatter everything and cause a white appearance of objects such as seen in clouds and fog.

- Rayleigh Scattering: This occurs when light encounters particles less than 0.5 μm (microns). In this situation, differential scattering occurs and the shorter wavelengths are scattered more. Rayleigh Scattering gives off colors, and since the shorter wavelengths are more prevalent, we see the colors at that end of the visible spectrum. This is why the sky appears blue.

Scattering Effects

Blue skies: Our atmosphere is full of small particles that cause Rayleigh Scattering in the blue–violet range. Our eyes are most sensitive to blue. While other colors are present in Rayleigh Scattering, we normally don't see them.

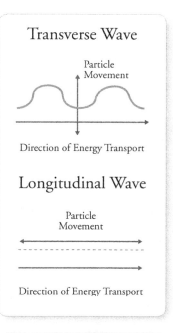

Transverse Wave

Particle Movement

Direction of Energy Transport

Longitudinal Wave

Particle Movement

Direction of Energy Transport

Reflected light allows you to see objects.

REFRACTION: the bending, or change of speed, caused when light enters a different medium

SCATTERING: the dispersion of light according to the size of the particulate matter it encounters in the sky

Red sunsets: As the earth moves, sunlight goes through more of the atmosphere and the colors get more scattered. Sunsets occur because the light is passing through a thicker wedge of the atmosphere, so the blues are scattered away and the reds are more visible.

Refractive Effects

Refraction gives the sun a flattened appearance. The most common refractive effect, however, is to create mirages.

MIRAGE: an image that originates in the lower layers of the troposphere (created by differences in temperature of the air layers near the ground) but is reflected onto the ground

MIRAGES are created by differences in temperature of the air layers near the ground. Although the images actually originate in the lower layers of the troposphere, they are reflected onto the ground. There are two types of mirages classified by the relative position of their temperature differentials:

1. Inferior Mirage: When a cold layer is positioned over a warm layer, it produces a mirage with a shimmering appearance, appearing lower to the ground.

2. Superior Mirage: When a warm layer is positioned over a cold layer, it produces a mirage that does not shimmer and appears higher off the ground.

NOVAYA ZEMLYA EFFECT: an optical effect in the Arctic region that makes the sun appear to rise earlier than expected

NOVAYA ZEMLYA EFFECT is an optical effect created only under specific atmospheric conditions in the Arctic regions. This long-distance optical phenomenon occurs when a layer of very cold air is trapped between a layer of warm air and a layer of cold air, refracting light from far away through the trapped layer. The result is that the Sun appears to rise earlier than expected.

RAINBOWS: an event in which tiny water drops selectively refract reflected light in the form of an arch

RAINBOWS appear only if two conditions are present: the sun must be at your back, and water drops less than 0.5 μm (microns) are in the air. The small size of the water drops causes them to selectively refract, and the reflected colors appear to form an arch with the reds on the outside (bent the most), and the violets on the inside (bent the least).

SKILL 9.4 **Demonstrate understanding of diffraction and interference**

Light can be diffracted, or bent around the edges of an object; the light gets split and is refracted differentially as in a prism. **DIFFRACTION** occurs when light goes through a narrow slit and the light bends slightly around the edges of the slit. You can demonstrate this by pressing your thumb and forefinger together, making a very thin slit between them. Hold them about 8 cm from your eye and look at a distant source of light. The pattern you observe is caused by the diffraction of light.

Ice crystals are the driving factor in most diffractive effects.

Halo: The ice crystals diffract the light, creating either a 22° or 46° ring around the moon or the sun. The distance of the halo from the moon or sun depends on the orientation of the ice crystals.

Sundogs: These are relatively uncommon effects that occur when light passes through the face of the ice crystals and creates the optical illusion of three suns.

Coronas: This effect is similar to that of a halo, but water droplets, not ice crystals, create the ring around the sun.

INTERFERENCE is the interaction of two or more waves that meet. Constructive interference occurs when the crests of the two waves meet at the same point in time. Conversely, destructive interference occurs when the crest of one wave and the trough of the other meet at the same point in time. It follows, then, that constructive interference increases amplitude, and destructive interference decreases it. We can also consider interference in terms of wave phase: waves that are out of phase with one another will interfere destructively, while waves that are in phase with one another will interfere constructively.

> **DIFFRACTION:** occurs as light passes through a narrow slit and bends slightly around the edges of the slit; a form of differential refraction as in a prism

> *Ice crystals are the driving factor in most diffractive effects.*

> **INTERFERENCE:** the interaction of two or more waves that meet

SKILL 9.5 Demonstrate understanding of the Doppler Effect

Change in experienced frequency due to relative motion of the source of the sound is called the DOPPLER EFFECT. When a siren approaches, the pitch is high. When it passes, the pitch drops. As a moving sound source approaches a listener, the sound waves are closer together, causing an increase in wave frequency in the sound that is heard. As the source passes the listener, the waves spread out and the wave frequency experienced by the listener is lower. The Doppler effect can be used to measure the motion of an object both on Earth and in space.

> **DOPPLER EFFECT:** change in experienced frequency due to relative motion of the sound source

SKILL 9.6 Demonstrate understanding of polarization

POLARIZED LIGHT: has vibrations confined to a single plane that is perpendicular to the direction of motion

Light and other electromagnetic radiation can be polarized because the waves are transverse. **POLARIZED LIGHT** has vibrations confined to a single plane that is perpendicular to the direction of motion. Light can be polarized by passing it through special filters that block all vibrations except those in a single plane. By blocking out all but one place of vibration, polarized sunglasses cut down on glare.

SKILL 9.7 Recognize the characteristics of sound waves *(for example, pitch, loudness, speed)*

PITCH: depends on and correlates to the frequency of the sound that the ear receives

The **PITCH** of a sound depends on the frequency that the ear receives. High-pitched sound waves have high frequencies. High notes are produced by an object that is vibrating at a greater number of times per second than one that produces a low note.

INTENSITY: the amount of sound energy that crosses a unit of area in a given unit of time

The **INTENSITY** of a sound is the amount of energy that crosses a unit of area in a given unit of time. The loudness of the sound is subjective and depends upon the effect on the human ear. Two tones of the same intensity but different pitches may appear to have different loudness. The intensity level of sound is measured in decibels. Normal conversation is about 60 decibels. A power saw is about 110 decibels.

The amplitude of a sound wave determines its loudness.

The amplitude of a sound wave determines its loudness. Loud sound waves have large amplitudes. The larger the sound wave, the more energy is needed to create the wave.

BEATS: a series of loud and soft sounds generated when the waves meet; when the crests combine, they produce loud sounds, and when they don't, they nearly cancel each other out and produce soft sounds

If you have two tuning forks that produce different pitches, then one will produce sounds of a slightly higher frequency. When you strike the two forks simultaneously, you may hear beats. **BEATS** are a series of loud and soft sounds. This is because when the waves meet, the crests combine at some points and produce loud sounds. At other points, they nearly cancel each other out and produce soft sounds.

Demonstrate understanding of how sound waves are produced by the vibrations of air columns and strings

SOUND WAVES are produced by a vibrating body. The vibrating object moves forward and compresses the air in front of it, then reverses direction, lessening pressure on the air and allowing expansion of the air molecules. One compression and expansion creates one longitudinal wave. Sound can be transmitted through any gas, liquid, or solid but cannot be transmitted through a vacuum because there are no particles present to vibrate and bump into adjacent particles to transmit the waves. The vibrating air molecules move back and forth, parallel to the direction of motion of the wave as they pass the energy from adjacent air molecules closer to the source to air molecules farther away from the source.

SOUND WAVES: produced by a vibrating body that moves forward, compressing the air in front of it, then moves backward, lessening pressure on the air

Characterize the electromagnetic spectrum *(gamma rays to radio waves)*

The electromagnetic spectrum's frequency (f) is measured in hertz and wavelength (λ) is measured in meters. The frequency times the wavelength of every electromagnetic wave equals the speed of light (3×10^8 m/sec.).

COMMON WAVELENGTHS OF THE ELECTROMAGNETIC SPECTRUM		
	λ	f
Radio waves	$10^5 - 10^{-1}$ meters	$10^3 - 10^9$ hertz
Microwaves	$10^{-1} - 10^{-3}$ meters	$10^9 - 10^{11}$ hertz
Infrared radiation	$10^{-3} - 10^{-6}$ meters	$10^{11.2} - 10^{14.3}$ hertz
Visible light	$10^{-6.2} - 10^{-6.9}$ meters	$10^{14.3} - 10^{15}$ hertz
Ultraviolet radiation	$10^{-7} - 10^{-9}$ meters	$10^{15} - 10^{17.2}$ hertz
X-rays	$10^{-9} - 10^{-11}$ meters	$10^{17.2} - 10^{19}$ hertz
Gamma rays	$10^{-11} - 10^{-15}$ meters	$10^{19} - 10^{23.25}$ hert

SKILL
9.10 **Demonstrate understanding of color and the visible spectrum** *(for example, addition and subtraction, relationship to wave frequency)*

SPECTRUM: white light separated by wavelengths into a series different colors

White light can be separated by wavelengths into a series different colors called a **SPECTRUM**. A spectrograph can photograph a spectrum. Wavelengths of light have distinctive colors. The color red has the longest wavelength and violet has the shortest wavelength. Wavelengths are arranged to form an electromagnetic spectrum (see previous figure) that ranges from very long radio waves to very short gamma rays. Visible light covers a small portion of the electromagnetic spectrum.

Color perception is a complex subject involving many disciplines. When you look at an object and perceive a distinct color, you are not necessarily seeing a single frequency of light. Consider, for instance, that you are looking at a shirt, and it appears green to your eye. In such an instance, there may be several frequencies of light striking your eye, yet your eye-brain system interprets the frequencies as being green.

WHITE: not a color but rather the presence of all of the frequencies of visible light

ROYGBIV: the entire spectrum of visible light

Color perception can be simplified if we think in terms of primary colors of light. **WHITE** is not a color but rather the presence of all of the frequencies of visible light. When we speak of white light, we are referring to red, orange, yellow, green, blue, indigo, violet (**ROYGBIV**)—the entire spectrum of visible light. Any three colors (or frequencies) of light that produce white light when combined with the correct intensity are called primary colors of light. There is a variety of sets of primary colors but the most common are red (R), green (G) and blue (B). Mixing two or three of these three primary colors in varying degrees of intensity can produce a wide range of other colors.

COLOR SUBTRACTION: identifying which color or colors of light are subtracted (absorbed) and which are reflected from the original set

Atoms are capable of selectively absorbing one or more frequencies of light. A shirt made of a material that absorbs blue light will do so and it will reflect the other frequencies of the visible spectrum. The apparent color of the shirt is determined by identifying which color or colors of light are subtracted (absorbed) and which are reflected from the original set, a process is called **COLOR SUBTRACTION**.

SKILL
9.11 **Demonstrate understanding of geometric optics** *(mirrors, lenses, prisms, fiber optics)* **and of polarization**

Light can travel through thin fibers of glass or plastic without escaping the sides. Light on the inside of these fibers is reflected so that it stays inside the fiber until it reaches the other end. Such **FIBER OPTICS** are being used to carry telephone messages. Sound waves are converted to electric signals that are coded into a series of light pulses that move through the optical fiber until they reach the other end. At that time, they are converted back into sound.

FIBER OPTICS: thin fibers of glass or plastic through which light pulses (converted from sound waves) travel without escaping the sides and thus can carry telephone messages

The image that you see in a bathroom **MIRROR** is a virtual image because it only seems to be where it is. However, a curved mirror can produce a real image. A real image is produced when light passes through the point where the image appears. A real image can be projected onto a screen.

MIRROR: typically produces a virtual image

Cameras use a convex lens to produce an image on film. A convex lens is thicker in the middle than at the edges. The image size depends upon the focal length (distance from the focal point] to the lens). The longer the focal length, the larger the image. A converging lens produces a real image whenever the object is far enough from the lens so that the rays of light from the object can hit the lens and be focused into a real image on the other side of the lens.

Eyeglasses can help correct sight defects by changing where an image seen is focused on the retina of the eye. If a person is nearsighted, the lens of his eye focuses images in front of the retina. In this case, the corrective lens for eyeglasses will be concave so that the image will reach the retina. In the case of farsighted-ness, the lens of the eye focuses the image behind the retina. The correction will call for a convex lens so that the image is brought forward into sharper focus.

Eyeglasses can help correct sight defects by changing where an image seen is focused on the retina of the eye.

See also Skill 9.6

B. CHEMISTRY

COMPETENCY 10
PERIODICITY

| SKILL 10.1 | Demonstrate understanding of the meaning of chemical periodicity |

PERIODIC TABLE OF ELEMENTS: a tabular arrangement of elements in rows and columns, highlighting the regular repetition of properties of the elements

The **PERIODIC TABLE OF ELEMENTS** is a tabular arrangement of elements in rows and columns, highlighting the regular repetition of properties of the elements.

In 1869, Russian chemist Dmitri Mendeleev and German chemist J. Lothar Meyer independently discovered that if the elements were arranged in order of atomic weight, they could be placed in horizontal rows, layered one under the other, so that the elements in each vertical column had similar properties.

Subsequent experimentation with arrangement later in the century showed that if the elements were arranged by atomic number, rather than weight, a more cohesive, comprehensive, and orderly arrangement of elements would result. This arrangement by atomic number is still in use today and forms the baseline for our modern periodic table.

> *If the elements are arranged in rows and columns by atomic number, the elements in each vertical column have similar properties*

The basic arrangement of rows and columns actually represents periods and groups.

A **PERIOD** comprises the elements in any one horizontal row of the periodic table.

A **GROUP** comprises the elements in any one column of the periodic table.

> **PERIOD:** the elements in any one horizontal row of the periodic table

> **GROUP:** the elements in any one column of the periodic table

Interpreting the periodic table

If you examine the table, you can see that the first period (the uppermost row, starting on the left) consists of only two elements, Hydrogen (H) and Helium (He). This period number sequence continues down the page, with each subsequent row having a sequential number and a varying number of elements. The sixth period actually has 32 elements assigned, but to ensure that the chart remains orderly, they are shown as separate insert rows at the bottom of the chart.

The groups are arrayed in vertical columns with the numbering scheme posted at the top of each group. The numbers designate either representative elements (the main group), or transition elements. The two rows mentioned earlier at the bottom of the chart are the inner-transition elements.

SKILL 10.2 Demonstrate understanding of periodic trends in chemical and physical properties

---

The periodic table of elements makes it is easy to locate elements with similar properties. There are three types of elements that are grouped by color: metals, nonmetals, and metalloids.

Element Key

The individual boxes that comprise the elements shown on the table contain a great deal of information about the element. Besides the placement of the box in the table to show its period and group, the box also provides the element's atomic number, symbol, and atomic weight (given in amu—atomic mass units).

Element Key

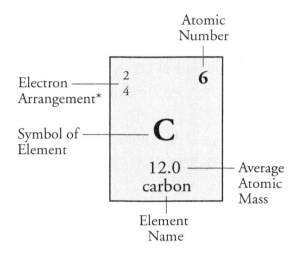

* Number of electrons on each level.
Top number represents the innermost level.

Principles of Organization

To aid identification, most charts are color-coded, with metals, metalloids, and nonmetals each having their own specific color. Depending on the manufacturer, the box may also show the full name of the element, its state (solid, gas, liquid), and possibly its subenergy-level orbital designation. Traditionally, the periodic table has its columns marked IA through VIIIA. The Union of Physicists and Chemists suggested arabic numbers 1 through 18, and these are the ones used in this text.

A METAL is a substance or mixture that has a characteristic luster, or shine, and is generally a good conductor of heat and electricity. Except for Mercury, metals are solid at room temperature and are more or less MALLEABLE (can be hammered into sheets) and DUCTILE (can be drawn into wire).

By contrast, a NONMETAL is an element that does not exhibit the characteristics of a metal. Most of the nonmetals are gases, and the ones that are solids are generally hard and brittle. Bromine is the only liquid nonmetal.

Caught in the middle are the METALLOIDS, elements having both metallic and nonmetallic properties.

METAL: a substance or mixture that has a characteristic luster, or shine, and is generally a good conductor of heat and electricity

MALLEABLE: can be hammered into sheets

DUCTILE: can be drawn into wire

NONMETAL: an element that does not exhibit the characteristics of a metal; most are gases, and the ones that are solids are generally hard and brittle

METALLOIDS: elements having both metallic and nonmetallic properties

Metals

With the exception of hydrogen, all elements in group 1 are alkali metals. These metals are shiny, softer, and less dense, and the most chemically active of all metals. They react easily with water. Group 2 metals are the alkaline earth metals. They are harder, denser, have higher melting points, and also are chemically active.

The transition elements (groups 3 to 12) are metals that include silver, gold, and mercury. These elements are hard and have high melting points; their compounds often are colorful.

The Lanthanide series on one of the bottom rows are metals that are predominantly used in making alloys, and the Actinide series are all radioactive elements.

Elements can be combined to make metallic objects. An **ALLOY** is a mixture of two or more elements having properties of metals, but are not necessarily all metals. For instance, steel is made up of the metal iron and the nonmetal carbon.

> **ALLOY:** a mixture of two or more elements having properties of metals, but are not necessarily all metals

Nonmetals

Nonmetals are not as easy to recognize as metals because they do not always share physical properties. In general, however, the properties of nonmetals are the opposite of metals: They are not shiny, are brittle, and are not good conductors of heat and electricity. Nonmetals are solids, gases, and one liquid (bromine).

Nonmetals have four to eight electrons in their outermost energy levels and tend to attract electrons to their outer energy levels. As a result, the outer levels usually are filled with eight electrons. This difference in the number of electrons is what sets nonmetals apart from metals. The outstanding chemical property of nonmetals is that they react with metals.

Halogens (group 17) combine readily with metals to form salts. Table salt, fluoride toothpaste, and bleach all contain an element from the halogen family.

The Noble Gases (group 18) are so named because they do not react chemically with other elements, much like the nobility did not mix with the masses. As a general rule, these gases are inert (inactive) and will combine with other elements only under very specific conditions. In recent years, chemists have been able to prepare compounds of krypton and xenon.

Metalloids

Metalloids (groups 13 to 16) have properties in between those of metals and nonmetals. They are arranged in stair steps across the groups.

Physical properties:

- All are solids having the appearance of metals

- All are white or gray, but not shiny

- All will conduct electricity but not as well as a metal

Chemical properties:

- They have some characteristics of metals and of nonmetals

- Their properties do not follow patterns like metals and nonmetals; each must be studied individually

For example, boron, the first element in group 13, is a poor conductor of electricity at low temperatures, but becomes a good conductor if you increase its temperature. By contrast, metals, which are good conductors, lose this ability as they are heated. It is because of this property that boron is so useful as a semiconductor. SEMICONDUCTORS are used in electrical devices that have to function at temperatures too high for metals.

Silicon, the second element in group 14, also is a semiconductor and is found in great abundance in the earth's crust. Sand is made of a silicon compound, silicon dioxide. Silicon is also used in the manufacture of glass and cement.

SEMICONDUCTORS: typically a metalloid used in electrical devices that have to function at temperatures too high for metals

Electron Configuration Determines Reactivity

The sections of the periodic table reflect the electron configurations of the elements and the suborbital levels occupied by the electrons. As you move across any period on the table, you soon see that the electron configuration of the atom determines its chemical reactivity.

Each element in the table has one more electron in its outer energy level than the element that precedes it. Because of their structure, alkali metals have one more electron in an outer orbital position. Consequently, little energy is needed to remove the electron and ionize the atom (*see also Skill 6.3*).

The further you move down the table, the less energy is required to achieve ionization. Thus, the alkali metals exist in the realm of the $1+$ ion. The alkaline earth metals, (group 2), are also very reactive and it takes only a little more energy to ionize them. They are in the realm of the $2+$ ions.

The number placement and energy level of an atom's electrons determines how that atom will react with other atoms.

As you move across groups 13 through 18, the ionization energies increase and consequently, the compounds made of the elements in those groups are more covalent than ionic.

Groups 16 and 17, however, have a high enough **ELECTRON AFFINITY**—the readiness of an element to attract and hold an extra electron—to attract and hold one or two electrons, so the oxygen group and the halogens are reactive. Fluorine (F) is the most active of the halogens and activity decreases down the group.

> **ELECTRON AFFINITY:** the readiness of an element to attract and hold an extra electron

COMPETENCY 11
THE MOLE AND CHEMICAL BONDING

> **SKILL 11.1** Demonstrate understanding of the mole concept and chemical composition

> **MOLE:** that number whose mass in grams is numerically equal to the atomic mass, molecular mass, or formula mass of the substance

A single atom or molecule weighs so little it cannot be measured using a balance in the lab. It's useful to have a system that permits a large number of chemical particles to be described as one unit, analogous to a dozen of 12 of something, or 144, as one gross. A useful number of atoms, molecules, or formula units is that number whose mass in grams is numerically equal to the atomic mass, molecular mass, or formula mass of the substance. This quantity is called the **MOLE**, abbreviated mol. Because the ^{12}C isotope is assigned an exact value of 12 atomic mass units, there are exactly 12 g of ^{12}C in one mole of ^{12}C. The atomic mass unit is also called a Dalton, and either "u" (for "unified atomic mass unit") or "Da" may be used as an abbreviation. Older texts use "amu." To find the molar mass of a substance, use the periodic table to determine the molecular weight of each atom in the substance, and multiply by the number of each atom present. For example: It's been found experimentally that the number of atoms, ions, molecules, or anything else in one mole is 6.022045×10^{23}. For most purposes, three significant digits are sufficient, and 6.02×10^{23} will be used. This value was named in honor of Amedeo Avogadro and is called **AVOGADRO'S NUMBER**.

> **AVOGADRO'S NUMBER:** the number of atoms, ions, molecules, or anything else in one mole, or 6.02×10^{23}

> **LAW OF DEFINITE PROPORTIONS (LAW OF CONSTANT COMPOSITION):** a pure compound, whatever its source, always contains definite or constant proportions of the elements by mass

LAW OF DEFINITE PROPORTIONS (LAW OF CONSTANT COMPOSITION): a pure compound, whatever its source, always contains definite or constant proportions of the elements by mass. It has a fixed composition.

MIXTURE: a material that can be separated by physical means into two or more substances. Most materials around us are mixtures, and a mixture has a variable composition. Mixtures are classified into two types:

HETEROGENEOUS MIXTURE: a mixture that consists of physically distinct parts, each with different properties. Example: Sugar and salt stirred together.

HOMOGENEOUS MIXTURE (SOLUTION): a mixture that is uniform in its properties throughout a given sample.

> **MIXTURE:** a material that can be separated by physical means into two or more substances

> **HETEROGENEOUS MIXTURE:** a mixture that consists of physically distinct parts, each with different properties

> **HOMOGENEOUS MIXTURE (SOLUTION):** a mixture that is uniform in its properties throughout a given sample

SKILL 11.2 Interpret and use chemical formulas

A formula is a shorthand that uses symbols and subscripts to show what is in a compound. The letter symbols tell us the elements that are involved and the number subscripts tell us how many atoms of each element are involved. No subscript is used if there is only one atom involved. For example, the compound methane gas is CH_4, has one carbon atom and 4 hydrogen atoms.

Let us look at aerobic respiration. Our tissues need energy for growth, repair, movement, excretion, and so on. This energy is obtained from glucose supplied to the tissues by our blood. In aerobic respiration, glucose is broken down in the presence of oxygen into carbon dioxide and water, and energy is released, which is used for our metabolic processes. The above reaction can be written in the form of a word reaction.

glucose + oxygen = carbon dioxide + water + energy

By using chemical symbols and subscripts we can rewrite the above word equation into a proper chemical equation:

$$C_6H_{12}O_6 + 6O_2 = 6CO_2 + 6H_2O + Energy$$

The compounds on the left side of the equation are called reactants and the compounds on the right side of the reaction are called products. The reactants in the above equation have to combine in a fixed proportion for a chemical reaction to take place.

One or more substances are formed during a CHEMICAL REACTION. Also, energy is released during some chemical reactions. Sometimes the energy release is slow and sometimes it is rapid. In a fireworks display, energy is released very rapidly, but the chemical reaction that produces tarnish on a silver spoon happens very slowly.

> **CHEMICAL REACTION:** a chemical event in which one or more substances are formed

**CHEMICAL EQUILIB-
RIUM:** state reached when
the quantities of reactants
and products are no longer
shifting, but the reaction
may still proceed with
equal forward and back-
ward reaction

CHEMICAL EQUILIBRIUM is reached when the quantities of reactants and products are at a "steady state" and no longer shifting, but the reaction may still proceed forward and backward. The rate of forward reaction must equal the rate of backward reaction.

In one kind of chemical reaction, two elements combine to form a new substance. We can represent the reaction and the results in a chemical equation.

Carbon and oxygen form carbon dioxide. The equation can be written:

$$C \quad + \quad O_2 \quad \rightarrow \quad CO_2$$

| 1 atom of | + | 1 atom of | → | 1 molecule of |
| carbon | | oxygen | | carbon dioxide |

No matter is ever gained or lost during a chemical reaction; therefore the chemical equation must be *balanced*. This means that there must be the same number of molecules on both sides of the equation. Remember that the subscript numbers indicate the number of atoms in the elements. The number of molecules is shown by the number in front of an element or compound. If no number appears, assume that it is 1 molecule.

In a second kind of chemical reaction, the molecules of a substance split, forming two or more new substances. An electric current can split water molecules into hydrogen and oxygen gas.

$$2H_2O \quad \rightarrow \quad 2H_2 \quad + \quad O_2$$

| 2 molecules | → | 2 molecules | + | 1 molecule |
| of water | | of hydrogen | | of oxygen |

In a third kind of chemical reaction, elements change places with each other, as when iron changes places with copper in the compound copper sulfate:

$$CuSo_4 \quad + \quad Fe \quad \rightarrow \quad FeSO_4 \quad + \quad Cu$$

| copper sulfate | + | iron (steel wool) | → | iron sulfate | + | Copper |

Sometimes two sets of elements change places. In this example, an acid and a base are combined:

$$HCl \quad + \quad NaOH \quad \rightarrow \quad NaCl \quad + \quad H_2O$$

| hydrochloric acid | + | sodium hydroxide | → | sodium chloride (table salt) | + | water |

Demonstrate understanding of the systematic nomenclature of inorganic compounds

Naming rules for inorganics depend on whether the chemical is an ionic compound or a molecular compound containing only covalent bonds. There are special rules for naming acids. The rules below describe a group of traditional "semi-systematic" names accepted by the International Union of Pure and Applied Chemistry (IUPAC).

Ionic Compounds

Ionic compounds are named with the **CATION** (positive ion) first. Nearly all cations in inorganic chemistry are monatomic, meaning they consist of just one atom (like Ca^{2+}, the calcium ion.) and are formed from a metal ion. For common ionic compounds, the alkali metals always have a $1+$ charge, and the alkali earth metals always have a $2+$ charge.

> **CATION:** positive ion

Many metals may form cations of more than one charge. In this case, a roman numeral in parentheses after the name of the element is used to indicate the ion's charge in a particular compound.

This Roman numeral method is known as the Stock system. An older nomenclature used the suffix *–ous* for the lower charge and *–ic* for the higher charge and is still used occasionally.

> Example: Fe^{2+} is the iron(II) ion and Fe^{3+} is the iron(III) ion.

The only common inorganic polyatomic cation is ammonium: NH_4.

The **ANION** (negative ion) is named and written last. Monatomic anions are formed from nonmetallic elements and are named by replacing the end of the element's name with the suffix *–ide*.

> **ANION:** negative ion

> Examples: Cl^- is the chloride ion, S^{2-} is the sulfide ion, and N^{3-} is the nitride ion.

OXOANIONS (also called oxyanions) contain one element in combination with oxygen. Many common polyatomic anions are oxoanions that end with the suffix *–ate*. If an element has two possible oxoanions, the one with the element at a lower oxidation state ends with *–ite*. This anion will also usually have less oxygen per atom. Additional oxoanions are named with the prefix *hypo–* if they have a lower oxidation number than the *–ite* form, and the prefix *per–* if they have a higher oxidation number than the *–ate* form.

> **OXOANIONS:** contain one element in combination with oxygen

COMMON EXAMPLES OF OXOANIONS			
		CO_3^{2-}	carbonate
SO_3^{2-}	sulfite	SO_4^{2-}	sulfate
PO_3^{3-}	phosphite	PO_4^{3-}	phosphate

If an H atom is added to a polyatomic anion with a negative charge greater than one, the word *hydrogen* or the prefix *bi-* are used for the resulting anion. If two H atoms are added, *dihydrogen* is used.

Examples: bicarbonate or hydrogen carbonate ion: HCO_3^- dihydrogen phosphate ion: $H_2PO_4^-$

Ionic compounds: hydrates

Water molecules often occupy positions within the lattice of an ionic crystal. These compounds are called hydrates, and the water molecules are known as water of hydration. The water of hydration is added after a centered dot in a formula. In a name, a number-prefix (listed below for molecular compounds) indicating the number of water molecules is followed by the root –hydrate.

Ionic compounds: putting it all together

We now have the tools to name most common salts, given a formula, and to write a formula for them, given a name. To determine a formula given a name, we must find the number of anions and cations that are needed to achieve a neutral charge.

Example: Determine the formula of cobalt(II) phosphite octahydrate.

Solution: For the cation, find the symbol for cobalt (Co) and recognize that it is present as Co^{2+} ions from the roman numerals. For the anion, remember the phosphite ion is PO_3^{3-}. A neutral charge is achieved with 3 Co^{2+} ions for every 2 PO_3^{3-} ions. Add eight H_2O for water of hydration for the answer:
$CO_3 (PO_3)_2 \times 8H_2O$.

Molecular compounds

MOLECULAR COMPOUNDS (compounds making up molecules with a neutral charge) usually are composed entirely of nonmetals and are named by placing the less electronegative atom first. The suffix –ide is added to the second, more electronegative atom, and prefixes indicating numbers are added to one or both names if needed.

MOLECULAR COMPOUNDS: compounds (usually composed entirely of nonmetals) making up molecules with a neutral charge

PREFIXES INDICATING NUMBERS									
Prefix	mono-	di-	tri-	tetra-	penta-	hexa-	hepta-	octa-	nona-	deca-
Meaning	1	2	3	4	5	6	7	8	9	10

The final "o" or "a" may be left off these prefixes for oxides.

The electronegativity requirement (placing the less electronegative atom first) is the reason the compound with two oxygen atoms and one nitrogen atom is called nitrogen dioxide, NO_2 and *not* dioxygen nitride O_2N. The hydride of sodium is NaH, sodium hydride, but the hydride of bromine is HBr, hydrogen bromide (or hydrobromic acid if it's in aqueous solution). Oxygen is only named first in compounds with fluorine such as oxygen difluoride, OF_2, and fluorine is never placed first because it is the most electronegative element.

> *Examples:* N_2O_4, *dinitrogen tetroxide (or tetraoxide)*
> Cl_2O_7, *dichlorine heptoxide (or heptaoxide)*
> ClF_5 *chlorine pentafluoride*

Acids

There are special naming rules for acids that correspond with the suffix of their corresponding anion if hydrogen were removed from the acid. Anions ending with *–ide* correspond to acids with the prefix *hydro–* and the suffix *–ic*. Anions ending with *–ate* correspond to acids with no prefix that end with *–ic*. Oxoanions ending with *–ite* have associated acids with no prefix and the suffix *–ous*. The *hypo–* and *per–* prefixes are maintained.

RELATED ANION AND ACID NAMES			
anion	**anion name**	**acid**	**acid name**
Cl^-	chloride	HCl(aq)	hydrochloric acid
CN^-	cyanide	HCN(aq)	hydrocyanic acid
CO_3^{2-}	carbonate	H_2CO_3(aq)	carbonic acid
SO_3^{2-}	sulfite	H_2SO_3(aq)	sulfurous acid
SO_4^{2-}	sulfate	H_2SO_4(aq)	sulfuric acid

Continued on next page

For additional resources, see:

chemistry.alanearhart.org /Tutorials/Nomen /nomen-part7.html has thousands of sample questions. Don't do them all in one sitting.

www.iupac.org/reports /provisional/abstract04 /connelly_310804.html is IUPAC's latest report on inorganic nomenclature

anion	anion name	acid	acid name
ClO^-	hypochlorite	$HClO(aq)$	hypochlorous acid
ClO_2^-	chlorite	$HClO_2(aq)$	chlorous acid
ClO_3^-	chlorate	$HClO_3(aq)$	chloric acid
ClO_4^-	perchlorate	$HClO_4(aq)$	perchloric acid

SKILL 11.4 Demonstrate understanding of the nomenclature of simple organic compounds

HYDROCARBONS: the simplest organic compounds, containing only carbon and hydrogen

ALKANES: a hydrocarbon compound containing only single bonds

SATURATED: describing a hydrocarbon like an alkane that has the maximum number of hydrogen atoms possible for its carbon backbone

UNSATURATED: describing a hydrocarbon like an alkene that has fewer than the maximum number of hydrogen atoms possible

Organic compounds contain carbon, and have their own branch of chemistry because of the huge number of carbon compounds in nature, including nearly all the molecules in living things. The 1979 IUPAC organic nomenclature is used and taught most often today, and it is the nomenclature described here.

The simplest organic compounds are called **HYDROCARBONS** because they contain only carbon and hydrogen. Hydrocarbon molecules may be divided into the classes of cyclic and open-chain depending on whether they contain a ring of carbon atoms. Open-chain molecules may be divided into branched or straight-chain categories.

ALKANES contain only single bonds. Alkanes have the maximum number of hydrogen atoms possible for their carbon backbone, so they are called **SATURATED**. Alkenes, alkynes, and aromatics are **UNSATURATED** because they have fewer hydrogens.

Straight-chain alkanes, also called normal alkanes, are the simplest hydrocarbons. They consist of a linear chain of carbon atoms. The names of these molecules contain the suffix –*ane* and a root based on the number of carbons in the chain. A single molecule may be represented in multiple ways.

If one hydrogen is removed from an alkane, the residue is called an alkyl group. The –*ane* suffix is replaced by –*yl* when this residue is used as a functional group. Functional groups are used to systematically build up the names of organic molecules.

Branched alkanes are named using a four-step process:

1. Find the longest continuous carbon chain. This is the parent hydrocarbon.

2. Number the atoms on this chain beginning at the end near the first branch point, so the lowest locant numbers are used. Locant numbers describe the position of a functional group within a molecule. Number functional groups from the attachment point.

3. Determine the numbered locations and names of the substituted alkyl groups. Use *di–*, *tri–*, and similar prefixes for alkyl groups represented more than once. Separate numbers by commas and groups by dashes.

4. List the locations and names of alkyl groups in alphabetical order by their name (ignoring the di–, tri– prefixes) and end the name with the parent hydrocarbon.

BRANCHED ALKANES WITH IUPAC-ACCEPTED COMMON NAMES		
Structure	Systematic name	Common name
H_3C — CH — CH_3 ; H_3C	2-methylpropane	isobutane
CH_3 — CH ; H_3C — $C H_2$ — ... — CH_3	2-methylbutane	isopentane
CH_3 ; H_3C — C — CH_3 ; CH_3	2,2-dimethylpropane	neopentane

ALKYL GROUPS WITH IUPAC-ACCEPTED COMMON NAMES		
Structure	**Systematic name**	**Common name**
H_3C CH_3 CH	1-methylethyl	isopropyl
H_3C CH—CH_2 H_3C	2-methylpropyl	isobutyl
C_{H_2} CH_3 H_3C CH	1-methylpropyl	*sec*-butyl

Note: The systematic names assign a locant number of 1 to the attachment point.

ALKENES: also called olefins, are hydrocarbons that contain one or more double bonds

ALKENES, also called olefins, are hydrocarbons that contain one or more double bonds. The suffix used in the naming of alkenes is –*ene*, and the number roots are those used for alkanes of the same length. A number preceding the name shows the location of the double bond for alkenes of length four and above. Alkenes with one double bond have the general formula C_nH_{2n}. Multiple double bonds are named using –*diene*, –*triene*, etc. The suffix –*enyl* is used for functional groups after a hydrogen is removed from an alkene. Ethene and propene have the common names ethylene and propylene. The ethenyl group has the common name vinyl and the 2-propenyl group has the common name allyl. *Cis-trans isomerism* is often part of the complete name for an alkene.

Examples:

$H_2C═CH_2$ *is ethylene or ethene.* $H_2C═CH$ *is a vinyl or ethenyl group.*

is propylene or propene.

is 2-hexene.

ALKYNES are hydrocarbons that contain one or more triple bonds. They are named in a similar way to alkenes. The suffix used for alkynes is *–yne*. Ethyne is often called acetylene. Alkynes with one triple bond have the general formula C_nH_{2n-2}. Multiple triple bonds are named using *–diyne*, *–triyne*, etc. Add *–ynyl–* for functional groups composed of alkynes after the removal of a hydrogen atom.

Hydrocarbons with both double and triple bonds are known as **ALKENYNES**. The locant number for the double bond precedes the name, and the locant for the triple bond follows the suffix *–en* and precedes the suffix *–yne*.

> **ALKYNES:** hydrocarbons that contain one or more triple bonds

> **ALKENYNES:** hydrocarbons with both double and triple bonds

Examples:

$HC≡CH$ *is acetylene or ethyne.*

CH_3 *is 1-butyne.*

$HC≡C—CH_2$

ALICYCLIC HYDROCARBONS use the prefix *cyclo–* before the number root for the molecule. The structures for these molecules are often written as if the molecule lay entirely within the plane of the paper even though in reality, these rings dip above and below a single plane. When there is more than one substitution on the ring, numbering begins with the first substitution listed in alphabetical order. *Cis-trans isomerism* is often part of the complete name for a cycloalkane.

> **ALICYCLIC HYDRO-CARBONS:** an alicyclic compound is cyclic but not aromatic

Examples:

H_2C is cyclopropane

H_2C — CH_2

H_2C — CH_2 is methylcyclohexane.

H_3C — CH CH_2

H_2C — CH_2

AROMATIC HYDROCARBONS are hydrocarbons that structurally are related to benzene or made up of benzene molecules fused together. These molecules are called arenes to distinguish them from alkanes, alkenes, and alkynes. All atoms in arenes lie in the same plane. In other words, aromatic hydrocarbons are flat. Aromatic molecules have electrons that are free to migrate throughout the molecule.

Substitutions onto the benzene ring are named in alphabetical order using the lowest possible locant numbers. The prefix *phenyl*–may be used for C_6H_5– (benzene less a hydrogen) attached as a functional group to a larger hydrocarbon residue. Arenes in general form aryl functional groups. A phenyl group may be represented in a structure by the symbol θ. The prefix *benzyl*–may be used for $C_6H_5CH_2$– (methylbenzene with a hydrogen removed from the methyl group) attached as a functional group.

Examples:

or   is benzene.

Substitutive and Functional Class Names

Hydrocarbons consist entirely of nonpolar C-H bonds with no unpaired electrons. These compounds are relatively unreactive. The substitution of one or more atoms with unpaired electrons into the hydrocarbon backbone creates a hydrocarbon derivative. The unpaired electrons result in polar or charged portions of these molecules. These atoms fall into categories known as functional groups, and they create local regions of reactivity. Alkyl, alkenyl, alkynyl, and aryl groups may also be considered functional groups in some circumstances, as described in the previous skill.

Two types of names are often used for the same hydrocarbon derivative. For substitutive names, the hydrocarbon name is written out and the correct prefix or suffix is added for the derivative group. For functional class names, the hydrocarbon is written as a functional group and the derivative is added as a second word.

> *Examples:* CH_3Br *may be called bromomethane (substitutive name) or methyl bromide (functional class name).* CH_3CH_2OH *is ethanol (substitutive name) or ethyl alcohol (functional class name).*

The acyl group is shown below. There are nonsystematic number roots for hydrocarbon derivatives containing acyl groups or derived from acyl groups. These are the ketones, carboxylic acids, esters, nitriles, and amides.

A final word about IUPAC organic nomenclature

"IUPAC nomenclature" has become a synonym for "correct nomenclature," but the most recent IUPAC recommendations for organic nomenclature are ignored in most textbooks and curricula in the United States. This situation is similar to the nomenclature for inorganic chemistry in that the older nomenclature is "systematic enough" to be taught and to avoid most errors but is a poor choice to name new compounds in an unambiguous way.

SKILL 11.5 Identify the various types of bonds

The outermost electrons in the atoms are called valence electrons. Because they are the ones involved in the bonding process, they determine the properties of the element.

Chemical bonds are formed when atoms with incomplete valence shells share or completely transfer their valence electrons (*also see Skill 6.3*). There are three types of chemical bonds, covalent and ionic bonds being stronger than hydrogen bonds.

The weakest of the three bonds is the **HYDROGEN BOND**. A hydrogen bond is formed when one electronegative atom shares a hydrogen atom with another

HYDROGEN BOND: the weakest of the three types of chemical bonds, formed when one electronegative atom shares a hydrogen atom with another electronegative atom electronegative atom. An example of a hydrogen bond is water (H_2O) bonding with ammonia (NH_3). The H^+ attracts the negatively charged nitrogen in a weak bond. Weak hydrogen bonds are beneficial because they can briefly form, the atoms can respond to one another, and then break apart to bond to another. This is a very important role in the chemistry of life.

SKILL 11.6	Interpret electron dot and structural formulas

The structural formula of a chemical compound is a graphic representation of the molecular structure. It demonstrates how the atoms are arranged and shows the chemical bonding within the molecule. There are three common representations: condensed, Lewis type, and line-angle formulae.

CONDENSED STRUCTURAL FORMULAS include the elemental atoms and their sub/superscripts. An example for ethanol would be:

$$CH_3CH_2OH$$

CONDENSED STRUCTURAL FORMULAS: the elemental atoms and their sub/superscripts

LINE ANGLE DRAWINGS use angled lines that intersect and terminate with the designated elements. For organic compounds, carbon is assumed and not entered (if you see a line terminating in a blank space assume carbon is present there and has enough hydrogen atoms to give the carbon atom four bonds).

$$H_2C =\!=\!= CH$$

LINE ANGLE DRAWINGS: angled lines that intersect and terminate with the designated elements

LEWIS DOT STRUCTURES provide a method for keeping track of each atom's valence electrons in a molecule. Drawing Lewis structures is a three-step process:

1. Add the number of valence shell electrons for each atom. If the compound is an anion, add the charge of the ion to the total electron count because anions have "extra" electrons. If the compound is a cation, subtract the charge of the ion.

2. Write the symbols for each atom showing how the atoms connect to each other.

3. Draw a single bond (one pair of electron dots or a line) between each pair of connected atoms. Place the remaining electrons around the atoms as unshared pairs. If every atom has an octet of electrons except H atoms with two electrons, the Lewis structure is complete. Shared electrons count toward both atoms. If there are too few electron pairs to do this, draw multiple

LEWIS DOT STRUCTURE: a method for keeping track of each atom's valence electrons in a molecule

bonds (two or three pairs of electron dots between the atoms) until an octet is around each atom (except H atoms with two). If there are too many electron pairs to complete the octets with single bonds, then the octet rule is broken for this compound.

COMPETENCY 12
THE KINETIC THEORY AND STATES OF MATTER

Demonstrate understanding of kinetic molecular theory

Gas **PRESSURE** results from molecular collisions with container walls. The number of molecules striking an area on the walls and the average kinetic energy per molecule are the only factors that contribute to pressure. A higher temperature increases speed and kinetic energy. There are more collisions at higher temperatures, but the average distance between molecules does not change, and thus density does not change in a sealed container.

KINETIC MOLECULAR THEORY (KMT) explains how pressure and temperature influence the behavior of gases by making a few assumptions, namely:

1. The energies of intermolecular attractive and repulsive forces may be neglected

2. The average kinetic energy of the molecules is proportional to absolute temperature

3. Energy can be transferred between molecules during collisions, and the collisions are elastic, so the average kinetic energy of the molecules doesn't change due to collisions

4. The volume of all molecules in a gas is negligible compared with the total volume of the container

Strictly speaking, molecules also contain some kinetic energy by rotating or experiencing other motions. The motion of a molecule from one place to another is called **TRANSLATION**. Translational kinetic energy is the form that is transferred

> **PRESSURE:** results from molecular collisions with container walls

> *A higher temperature increases speed and kinetic energy.*

> **KINETIC MOLECULAR THEORY (KMT):** explains how pressure and temperature influence the behavior of gases

> **TRANSLATION:** the motion of a molecule from one place to another

by collisions, and kinetic molecular theory ignores other forms of kinetic energy, because they are not proportional to temperature.

Molecules have kinetic energy (they move around), and they also have intermolecular attractive forces (they stick to each other). The relationship between these two determines whether a collection of molecules will be a gas, liquid, or solid.

A GAS has an indefinite shape and an indefinite volume. The kinetic model for a gas is a collection of widely separated molecules, each moving in a random and free fashion, with negligible attractive or repulsive forces between them. Gases will expand to occupy a larger container so there is more space between the molecules. Gases can also be compressed to fit into a small container so the molecules are less separated. Diffusion occurs when one material spreads into or through another. Gases diffuse rapidly and move from one place to another.

A LIQUID assumes the shape of the portion of any container that it occupies and has a specific volume. The kinetic model for a liquid is a collection of molecules attracted to each other with sufficient strength to keep them close to each other but with insufficient strength to prevent them from moving around randomly. Liquids have a higher density and are much less compressible than gases, because the molecules in a liquid are closer together. Diffusion occurs more slowly in liquids than in gases, because the molecules in a liquid stick to each other and are not completely free to move.

A SOLID has a definite volume and a definite shape. The kinetic model for a solid is a collection of molecules attracted to each other with sufficient strength to essentially lock them in place. Each molecule may vibrate, but it has an average position relative to its neighbors. If these positions form an ordered pattern, the solid is called CRYSTALLINE. Otherwise, it is called AMORPHOUS. Solids have a high density and are almost incompressible because the molecules are close together. Diffusion occurs extremely slowly because the molecules almost never alter their position.

In a solid, the energy of intermolecular attractive forces is much stronger than the kinetic energy of the molecules, so kinetic energy and kinetic molecular theory are not very important. As temperature increases in a solid, the vibrations of individual molecules grow more intense and the molecules spread slightly farther apart, decreasing the density of the solid.

The relationship between kinetic energy and molecular attractive forces determines whether a collection of molecules will be a gas, liquid, or solid.

GAS: has an indefinite shape and an indefinite volume

LIQUID: assumes the shape of the portion of any container that it occupies and has a specific volume

SOLID: has a definite volume and a definite shape

CRYSTALLINE: describes the ordered pattern of molecules in some solids

AMORPHOUS: describes the random but tight pattern of molecules in some solids

In a liquid, the energy of intermolecular attractive forces is about as strong as the kinetic energy of the molecules, and both play a role in the properties of liquids.

In a gas, the energy of intermolecular forces is much weaker than the kinetic energy of the molecules. Kinetic molecular theory is usually applied to gases and is best described by imagining ourselves shrinking down to become a molecule and picturing what happens when we bump into other molecules and into container walls.

SKILL Demonstrate understanding of phase changes
12.2

The **PHASE OF MATTER** (solid, liquid, or gas) is identified by its shape and volume. A solid has a definite shape and volume. A liquid has a definite volume, but no shape. A gas has no shape or volume because it will spread out to occupy the entire space of whatever container it is in.

Energy is the ability to cause change in matter. Applying heat to a frozen liquid changes it from solid back to liquid. Continue heating it and it will boil and give off steam, a gas.

Evaporation is the change in phase from liquid to gas. Condensation is the change in phase from gas to liquid.

The law of conservation of energy states that matter is neither created nor destroyed, and the corollary to this tenet is that matter merely changes state. Thus, as matter undergoes a phase change, energy is either given off or absorbed. *See also Skill 4.4*

PHASE OF MATTER: (solid, liquid, or gas) is identified by its shape and volume

As matter undergoes a phase change, energy is either given off or absorbed.

SKILL Demonstrate understanding of the relationships among
12.3 temperature, pressure, volume, and number of molecules of a gas

See Skill 7.11

SKILL 12.4 Demonstrate understanding of the characteristics of crystals

Crystalline structure, form or shape—not chemical composition—is the key defining factor in identifying minerals. **CRYSTALLINE STRUCTURE** is defined as the most efficient arrangement of atoms that form a crystal shape.

MINERALS are crystalline solids whose structure reflects the repetitive, periodic array of atoms. This array—the **LATTICE**—forms the basis for the **UNIT CELL**, the basic repeating unit in a crystal that possesses the symmetry and properties of the mineral. The angles present at the bonding points of the atoms determine the fundamental geometric shape of the crystal. These shapes are classified as either isometric (cubic), tetragonal, orthorhombic, hexagonal, monoclinic, triclinic, or rhobohedral.

COMPETENCY 13
CHEMICAL REACTIONS

SKILL 13.1 Demonstrate ability to balance chemical equations

Chemists use a set of rules to properly balance equations:

1. Determine the correct formulas for all reactants and products, using subscripts to balance ionic charges.

2. Write formulas for reactants on the left of the arrow and predict the products and write their formulas to the right of the arrow.

3. Under the reactants, list all the elements in the reactants, starting with metals, then nonmetals, listing oxygen last and hydrogen next to last. Under the products, list all the elements in the same order as those under the reactants (straight across from them).

4. Count the atoms of each element on the left side and list the numbers next to the elements. Repeat for products. Don't forget that subscripts outside parentheses multiply everything inside the parentheses, including subscripts inside the parentheses.

5. For the first element in the list that has unequal numbers of atoms, use a coefficient (large numeral to the left of the compound or element) to give the correct number of atoms. Never change the subscripts to balance an equation.

6. Go to the next unbalanced element and balance it, moving down the list until all are balanced.

7. Start back at the beginning of the list and actually count the atoms of each element on each side of the arrow to make sure the number listed is the actual number. Rebalance and recheck as needed.

Example: $Al(OH)_3 + NaOH \rightarrow NaAlO_2 + 2\,H_2O$

Al = 1	Al = 1
Na = 1	Na = 1
H = 3 + 1 = 4	H = ~~2~~ 4
O = 3 + 1 = 4	O = ~~2 + 1 = 3~~ 2 + 2 = 4
	Put a 2 in front of H_2O

SKILL 13.2 Identify the various types of chemical reactions

See Skill 4.3

SKILL 13.3 Distinguish between endothermic and exothermic chemical reactions

If during a chemical reaction, more energy is needed to break the reactant bonds than is released when product bonds form, the reaction is **ENDOTHERMIC** and heat is absorbed from the environment, and the environment becomes colder.

> **ENDOTHERMIC CHEMICAL REACTION:** one in which more energy is needed to break the reactant bonds than is released when product bonds form, so heat is absorbed

On the other hand, if more energy is released through the formation of product bonds than is needed to break reactant bonds, the reaction is **EXOTHERMIC** and the excess energy is released to the environment as heat. The temperature of the environment goes up.

The total energy absorbed or released in the reaction can be determined by using bond energies. The total energy change of the reaction is equal to the total energy of all of the bonds of the products minus the total energy of all of the bonds of the reactants.

> **EXOTHERMIC CHEMICAL REACTION:** one in which more energy is released through product bond formation than is needed to break reactant bonds, so heat is released

SKILL 13.4 Demonstrate understanding of the effects of temperature, pressure, concentration, and the presence of catalysts on chemical reactions

The rate of most simple reactions increases with temperature because a greater fraction of molecules have the kinetic energy required to overcome the reaction's **ACTIVATION ENERGY**. The chart below shows the effect of temperature on the distribution of kinetic energies in a sample of molecules. These curves are called **MAXWELL-BOLTZMANN DISTRIBUTIONS**. The shaded areas represent the fraction of molecules containing sufficient kinetic energy for a reaction to occur. This area is larger at a higher temperature so more molecules are above the activation energy threshold, and more molecules react per second.

> **ACTIVATION ENERGY:** the amount of energy needed for the reaction to start

> **MAXWELL-BOLTZMANN DISTRIBUTIONS:** graphed curves showing the effect of temperature on the distribution of kinetic energies in a sample of molecules

> *For an animated audio tutorial on energy diagrams, see:*
>
> www.mhhe.com/physsci /chemistry /essentialchemistry/flash /activa2.swf

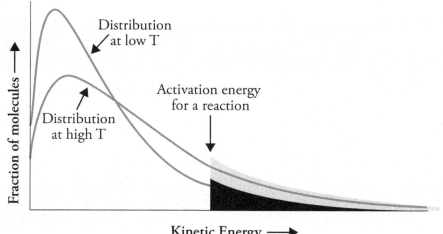

Distribution at low T

Distribution at high T

Activation energy for a reaction

Fraction of molecules →

Kinetic Energy →

> *Reaction rates increase with reactant concentration.*

Kinetic molecular theory may be applied to reaction rates as well as to physical constants like pressure. Reaction rates increase with reactant concentration because more reactant molecules are present and more are likely to collide with one another in a certain volume at higher concentrations. The nature of these relationships determines the rate law for the reaction. For ideal gases, the concentration of a reactant is its molar density, and this varies with pressure and temperature.

Kinetic molecular theory also predicts that reaction rate constants (values for k) increase with temperature because of two reasons:

1. More reactant molecules will collide with each other per second

2. These collisions will each occur at a higher energy that is more likely to overcome the activation energy of the reaction

A **CATALYST** is a material that increases the rate of a chemical reaction without changing itself permanently in the process. Catalysts provide an alternate reaction mechanism for the reaction to proceed in the forward and in the reverse direction. Therefore, catalysts have no impact on the chemical equilibrium of a reaction. They will not make a less favorable reaction more favorable.

Catalysts reduce the activation energy of a reaction. Molecules with such low energies that they would take a long time to react will react more rapidly if a catalyst is present.

The impact of a catalyst may also be represented on an energy diagram. A catalyst increases the rate of both the forward and reverse reactions by lowering the activation energy for the reaction. Catalysts provide a different activated complex for the reaction at a lower energy state.

Biological catalysts are called **ENZYMES**.

> **CATALYST:** a material that increases the rate of a chemical reaction without changing itself permanently in the process

> *Catalysts have no impact on the chemical equilibrium of a reaction.*

> *A catalyst increases the rate of both the forward and reverse reactions by lowering the activation energy for the reaction.*

> **ENZYMES:** a biological catalyst

SKILL 13.5 Demonstrate understanding of practical applications of electrochemistry

Chemistry is important to the earth sciences because the joining and dissolution of elements form the basic structures of the various minerals that make up Earth materials.

If elements combine by sharing electrons, the interactions can result in materials that are extremely resistant to weathering (i.e., granite), or conversely, are highly susceptible to erosive processes (i.e., sandstone).

Likewise, the joining of two familiar elements, sodium and chlorine, produce salt (NaCl), and the presence of NaCl in the continental material is ultimately responsible for the salinity of the oceans.

We also depend heavily on chemical combinations for basic building materials. Limestone, $CaCO_3$, is the most widely used building material in the United States. Without the processes by which elements join together, a vast array of medical, structural, and recreational products would not exist.

COMPETENCY 14
SOLUTIONS AND SOLUBILITY

> ### SKILL 14.1 Demonstrate understanding of solution terminology and distinguish among types of solutions

Colloids, solutions, and suspensions are types of mixtures consisting of two or more components. Solutions are homogenous mixtures because they are uniform throughout. In other words, the individual components are evenly distributed throughout the mixture. Colloids and suspensions are heterogeneous mixtures. Heterogeneous mixtures are not uniform. Rather, they consist of clumps or pockets of the individual components.

Solutions are homogenous mixtures of two or more components. The components of solutions are atoms and molecules; thus the particles are 1 **NANOMETER** (nm) or less in diameter. Solutions are transparent and do not usually absorb visible light. An example of a solution is sugar and water.

NANOMETER: one billionth of a meter (1×10^{-9} meter)

Suspensions are heterogeneous mixtures consisting of particles larger than those found in solutions. The diameter of particles found in suspensions is greater than 1000 nm. Thus, these particles are visible to the naked eye. Suspensions are murky or opaque and not transparent. Machine shaking can evenly distribute suspensions, but the components will settle out in time. Examples of suspensions include blood and a mixture of oil and water.

Colloids are heterogeneous mixtures consisting of particles intermediate in size between those found in solutions and suspensions. The diameter of particles found in colloids is between 1 and 1000 nm. Colloids appear homogenous to the naked eye and do not settle out into components. Colloids scatter light and are opaque. Milk is an example of a colloid.

See also Skill 11.1

SKILL 14.2 Demonstrate understanding of various types of solvents and factors affecting the dissolving process

Liquid solutions are the most common, but any two phases may form a solution. When a pure liquid and a gas or solid form a liquid solution, the pure liquid is called the SOLVENT, and the nonliquids are called SOLUTES. When all components in the solution originally were liquids, then the one present in the greatest amount is called the solvent, and the others are called solutes. Solutions with water as the solvent are called aqueous solutions. The amount of solute in a solvent is called its concentration. A solution with a small concentration of solute is called dilute, and a solution with a large concentration of solute is called concentrated.

Particles in solution are free to move about and collide with each other, vastly increasing the likelihood that a reaction will occur compared with particles in a solid phase. Aqueous solutions may react to produce an insoluble substance that will fall out of solution as a solid or gas PRECIPITATE in a precipitation reaction. Aqueous solutions may also react to form additional water, or a different chemical in aqueous solution.

As more solid solute particles dissolve in a liquid solvent, the concentration of solute increases, and the chance that dissolved solute will collide with the remaining undissolved solid also increases. A collision may result in a solute particle reattaching itself to the solid. This process is called CRYSTALLIZATION, and is the opposite of the solution process. EQUILIBRIUM occurs when no additional solute will dissolve because the rates of crystallization and solution are equal.

A solution at equilibrium with undissolved solute is a saturated solution. The amount of solute required to form a saturated solution in a given amount of solvent is called the solubility of that solute. If less solute is present, the solution is called unsaturated. It is also possible to have more solute than the equilibrium amount, resulting in a solution that is termed supersaturated.

Pairs of liquids that mix in all proportions are called miscible. Liquids that don't mix are called immiscible.

SOLVENT: the pure liquid in a liquid solution

SOLUTES: the nonliquids in a liquid solution

PRECIPITATE: an insoluble substance that falls out of an aqueous solution as a solid or gas as a result of a reaction

CRYSTALLIZATION: when collision results in a solute particle reattaching itself to the solid, it reverses the solution process

EQUILIBRIUM: occurs when no additional solute will dissolve because the rates of crystallization and solution are equal

SKILL 14.3 Demonstrate understanding of the effect of temperature and pressure on the solubility of a solute

Increasing the partial pressure of a gas will increase the solubility of the gas in a liquid.

Temperature and pressure greatly affect the solubility of a solute. Pressure does not dramatically alter the solubility of solids or liquids, but kinetic molecular theory predicts that increasing the partial pressure of a gas will increase the solubility of the gas in a liquid. If a substance is distributed between gas and solution phases and pressure is exerted, more gas molecules will impact the gas/liquid interface per second, so more will dissolve until a new equilibrium is reached at a higher solubility.

Increasing temperature will decrease the solubility of a gas in a liquid.

Increasing temperature will decrease the solubility of a gas in a liquid because kinetic energy opposes intermolecular attractions and permits more molecules to escape from the liquid phase. The vapor pressure of a pure liquid increases with temperature for the same reason. Greater kinetic energy will favor material in the gas phase.

For solid and liquid solutes, the impact of temperature depends on whether the solution process requires or releases heat. The following brief analysis is applicable for the effect of temperature on solutions.

Three processes occur when a solution is formed:

1. Solute particles are separated from each other, and heat is required to break these bonds

2. Solvent particles are separated from each other to create space for solute particles, and heat is required to break these bonds also

3. Solute and solvent particles interact with each other forming new bonds, and releasing heat

LE CHATELIER'S PRINCIPLE: solubility will increase with increasing temperature for an endothermic solution process

If the heat required for the first two processes is greater than the heat released by the third, then the entire reaction may be written as an endothermic process, and according to **LE CHATELIER'S PRINCIPLE**, solubility will increase with increasing temperature for an endothermic solution process. This occurs for most salts in water, including NaCl. There is a large increase for potassium nitrate—KNO_3.

Solubility will decrease with increasing temperature for an exothermic solution process.

However, heat is released when many solutes enter solution, and the entire reaction is exothermic. Solubility will decrease with increasing temperature for an exothermic solution process.

SKILL 14.4 Demonstrate understanding of the physical and chemical properties of acids, bases, and salts

ACID: a substance that releases a hydrogen ion in solution. An acidic solution has an excess of (H⁺) ions.

BASE: a substance that combines with a hydrogen ion in solution. A base (alkaline) solution has an excess of hydroxide (OH⁻) ions.

An acid contains one element of hydrogen (H). Although it is never wise to taste a substance to identify it, acids have a sour taste. Vinegar and lemon juice are both acids, and acids occur in many foods in a weak state. Strong acids can burn skin and destroy materials.

COMMON ACIDS		
Sulfuric acid	H_2SO_4	Used in medicines, alcohol, dyes, and car batteries
Nitric acid	HNO_3	Used in fertilizers, explosives, cleaning materials
Carbonic acid	H_2CO_3	Used in soft drinks
Acetic acid	$HC_2H_3O_2$	Used in making plastics, rubber, photographic film, and as a solvent

Bases have a bitter taste, and the stronger ones feel slippery. Like acids, strong bases can be dangerous and should be handled carefully. All bases contain the elements oxygen and hydrogen (OH). Many household cleaning products contain bases.

COMMON BASES		
Sodium hydroxide	NaOH	Used in making soap, paper, vegetable oils, and refining petroleum
Ammonium hydroxide	NH_4OH	Used in making deodorants, bleaching compounds, cleaning compounds
Potassium hydroxide	KOH	Used in making soaps, drugs, dyes, alkaline batteries, and purifying industrial gases
Calcium hydroxide	$Ca(OH)_2$	Used in making cement and plaster

ACID: a substance that releases a hydrogen ion in solution; an acidic solution has an excess of (H⁺) ions

BASE: a substance that combines with a hydrogen ion in solution; a base (alkaline) solution has an excess of hydroxide (OH⁻) ions

INDICATOR: a substance that changes color when it comes in contact with an acid or a base

SALT: one product of combining a base and an acid

NEUTRALIZATION: the result of combining a base and an acid, producing a salt and water

An **INDICATOR** is a substance that changes color when it comes in contact with an acid or a base. Litmus paper is an indicator. Blue litmus paper turns red in an acid. Red litmus paper turns blue in a base. A substance that is neither acid nor base is neutral. Neutral substances do not change the color of litmus paper.

When an acid and a base combine chemically, they form a **SALT** and water, a process called **NEUTRALIZATION**. Table salt (NaCl) is an example of this process. Salts are used in toothpaste, epsom salts, and cream of tartar. Calcium chloride ($CaCl_2$) is used on frozen streets and walkways to melt ice.

OXIDES are compounds that are formed when oxygen combines with another element. Rust is an oxide formed when oxygen combines with iron.

SKILL 14.5 Demonstrate knowledge of the meaning of pH and the effects of buffers

OXIDES: compounds that are formed when oxygen combines with another element

Maintaining a proper balance between acids and bases is critical to sustaining life.

PH SCALE: measures the concentration of hydrogen ions (acidity) of a solution

Pure water is considered neutral and is pegged at a pH of 7.0.

Maintaining a proper balance between acids and bases is critical to sustaining life. This balance is measured on the **PH SCALE**, which measures the concentration of hydrogen ions in a solution.

Pure water is considered neutral and is pegged at a pH of 7.0. As the numbers drop, the acidity increases. As the numbers rise, the alkaline (base) properties increase. *See also Skill 14.4*

The increase or decrease from a neutral pH is based upon the interactions of the hydrogen and hydroxide ions in the water. Hydrogen ions (H^+) and hydroxide ions (OH^-) are found in equal concentrations in pure water.

Seawater is not pure water. It actually is slightly alkaline with a pH of 7.4 to 8.4 with a median acidity around 8.0-8.1.

This alkalinity is maintained despite the high concentrations of carbon dioxide because of the forms the CO_2 takes in the seawater. Although the CO_2 does combine with the water to make carbonic acid (H_2CO_3), some of this acid breaks down to produce hydrogen ions (H^+), bicarbonate ions (HCO_3^-), and carbonate ions (CO_3^{2-}). This breakdown results in maintaining the alkalinity, because as the pH of the ocean drops (increases in acidity), a reaction occurs which removes more H^+ ions, returning the water to the proper balance.

Likewise, if the pH level increases (becomes more alkaline), more H^+ ions are added to the water, once again maintaining the proper balance. This self-correcting feature of the seawater is called **BUFFERING**.

Buffers usually are composed of weak acids and their salts, or weak bases and their salts. An appropriate acid or base/salt combination will buffer a solution only when it is at sufficient concentration and has a pKa close to the desired pH of the solution. Thus, a buffered solution can be created as follows:

1. Select a compound with a pKa close the desired pH.

2. Determine what the buffer concentration must be; typical concentrations are between 1mM and 200 mM.

3. Using the pKa, calculate the number of moles of acid/salt or base/salt that must be present at the desired pH.

4. Covert moles to grams and weigh out the components.

5. If both salt and acid (or base) are available, use the appropriate amount of each.

6. If only the acid is available, add the entire needed compound in acid form; then use enough base (NaOH) to convert the proper portion to salt.

7. Dissolve all components in slightly less water than is needed to reach the final volume.

8. Check the pH and adjust if necessary. Add water to reach the final volume.

> **BUFFERING:** the self-correcting feature of substances like seawater that allows them to maintain an acidity level within a constant narrow range

DOMAIN IV
LIFE SCIENCES

PERSONALIZED STUDY PLAN

KNOWN MATERIAL/ SKIP IT

PAGE	COMPETENCY AND SKILL	
119	**15: The cell**	☐
	15.1: Demonstrate knowledge of the structure and function of organelles, including membranes	☐
	15.2: Distinguish between prokaryotic and eukaryotic cells	☐
	15.3: Demonstrate understanding of the cell cycle and cytokinesis	☐
	15.4: Demonstrate understanding of chemical reactions in respiration and photosynthesis	☐
	15.5: Demonstrate understanding of mitosis and meiosis	☐
129	**16: Genetics**	☐
	16.1: Demonstrate understanding of DNA replication	☐
	16.2: Demonstrate understanding of the processes involved in protein synthesis	☐
	16.3: Demonstrate understanding of the causes and results of mutation	☐
	16.4: Demonstrate understanding of Mendelian inheritance	☐
	16.5: Demonstrate understanding of some aspects of non-Mendelian inheritance	☐
	16.6: Demonstrate knowledge of how recombinant DNA is constructed	☐
	16.7: Identify uses of recombinant DNA	☐
	16.8: Demonstrate understanding of the interaction between heredity and environment	☐
	16.9: Identify chromosomal and gene aberrations that lead to common human genetic disorders	☐
143	**17: Evolution**	☐
	17.1: Identify evidence that supports the theory of evolution	☐
	17.2: Demonstrate understanding of the mechanisms of evolution	☐
	17.3: Demonstrate knowledge of isolating mechanisms and speciation	☐
	17.4: Demonstrate understanding of the scientific hypotheses for the origin of life on Earth	☐
148	**18: Diversity of life**	☐
	18.1: Demonstrate understanding of the levels of organization and characteristics of life	☐
	18.2: Identify the elements of the hierarchical classification scheme into kingdom, phylum, class, order, family, genus, and species	☐
	18.3: Demonstrate knowledge of the characteristics of viruses, bacteria, protists, fungi, plants, and animals	☐

PERSONALIZED STUDY PLAN

KNOWN MATERIAL/ SKIP IT

PAGE	COMPETENCY AND SKILL	
155	**19: Plants**	☐
	19.1: Demonstrate understanding of the characteristics of vascular and nonvascular plants	☐
	19.2: Demonstrate understanding of the structure and function of roots, stems, and leaves	☐
	19.3: Demonstrate understanding of control mechanisms	☐
	19.4: Demonstrate understanding of water and nutrient uptake and transport systems	☐
	19.5: Demonstrate understanding of sexual and asexual reproduction in plants	☐
160	**20: Animals**	☐
	20.1: Demonstrate understanding of the anatomy and physiology of structures associated with life functions of organisms in the animal kingdom: digestion; circulation; respiration; excretion; nervous control; musculo-skeletal system; immunity; the endocrine system; reproduction; and development	☐
	20.2: Demonstrate knowledge of homeostasis and how it is maintained	☐
	20.3: Demonstrate knowledge of how animals respond to stimuli	☐
169	**21: Ecology**	☐
	21.1: Demonstrate understanding of population dynamics	☐
	21.2: Demonstrate knowledge of social behaviors	☐
	21.3: Demonstrate understanding of intraspecific competition	☐
	21.4: Demonstrate understanding of interspecific relationships	☐
	21.5: Demonstrate understanding of succession	☐
	21.6: Demonstrate understanding of the concepts of stability of ecosystems and the effects of disturbances	☐
	21.7: Demonstrate understanding of energy flow	☐
	21.8: Demonstrate understanding of biogeochemical cycles	☐
	21.9: Identify the types and characteristics of biomes	☐

COMPETENCY 15
THE CELL

SKILL Demonstrate knowledge of the structure and function of organelles, 15.1 including membranes

Parts of Eukaryotic Cells

1. Nucleus: The brain of the cell. The nucleus contains:

   – Chromosomes: DNA, RNA, and proteins tightly coiled to conserve space while providing a large surface area.

   – Chromatin: Loose structure of chromosomes, called chromatin when the cell is not dividing.

   – Nucleoli: The site where ribosomes are made, seen as dark spots in the nucleus.

   – Nuclear membrane: Contains pores which let RNA out of the nucleus. The nuclear membrane is continuous with the endoplasmic reticulum, which allows the membrane to expand or shrink if needed.

2. Ribosomes: The site of protein synthesis. Ribosomes may be free floating in the cytoplasm (the nonnucleic interior of the cell) or attached to the endoplasmic reticulum. There may be up to a half a million ribosomes in a cell, depending on how much protein the cell makes.

3. Endoplasmic reticulum: The "roadway" of the cell that allows for transport of materials throughout and out of the cell. The endoplasmic reticulum (ER) is folded and provides a large surface area. The lumen of the endoplasmic reticulum helps keep materials out of the cytoplasm and headed in the right direction. The endoplasmic reticulum is capable of building new membrane material.

   There are two types: Smooth endoplasmic reticulum contains no ribosomes on its surface. Rough endoplasmic reticulum contains ribosomes on its surface. This form of ER is abundant in cells that make many proteins, as in the pancreas, which produces many digestive enzymes.

4. **Golgi complex or Golgi apparatus:** A stacked structure that increases surface area and sorts, modifies, and packages molecules that are made in other parts of the cell. These molecules are either sent out of the cell or to other organelles within the cell.

5. **Lysosomes:** Found mainly in animal cells. They contain digestive enzymes that break down food, waste substances, viruses, damaged cell components, and eventually the cell itself. It is believed that lysosomes are responsible for the aging process.

6. **Mitochondria:** Large organelles that make adenosine triphosphate (ATP) to supply energy to the cell. Muscle cells have many mitochondria because they use a great deal of energy. The folds inside the mitochondria, called **cristae**, provide a large surface area for the reactions of cellular respiration to occur. Mitochondria have their own DNA and are capable of reproducing themselves if a demand is made for additional energy. Mitochondria are found only in animal cells.

7. **Plastids:** Found only in photosynthetic organisms. They are similar to mitochondria because of their double-membrane structure. They also have their own DNA and can reproduce as needed for the increased capture of sunlight. There are several types of plastids:

   – **Chloroplasts:** Green, function in photosynthesis; capable of trapping sunlight.

   – **Chromoplasts:** Make and store yellow and orange pigments; provide color to leaves, flowers and fruits.

   – **Amyloplasts:** Store starch and are used as a food reserve; abundant in tubers like potatoes.

8. **Cell wall:** Found only in plant cells. Composed of cellulose and fibers, it is thick enough for support and protection, yet porous enough to allow water and dissolved substances to enter. Cell walls are cemented to each other.

9. **Vacuoles:** Hold stored food and pigments. Vacuoles' large size in plants allow them to fill with water in order to provide **turgor** pressure. Lack of turgor pressure causes a plant to wilt.

10. **Cytoskeleton:** Composed of protein filaments attached to the plasma membrane and organelles. They provide a framework for the cell and aid in cell movement. The protein filaments constantly change shape and move about. Three types of fibers make up the cytoskeleton:

   – **Microtubules:** The largest of the three. They make up cilia and flagella for locomotion. Flagella grow from a basal body. Some examples are sperm cells and tracheal cilia. Centrioles, also composed of microtubules, form the spindle fibers that pull the cell apart during cell division. Centrioles are not found in the cells of higher plants.

- Intermediate filaments: Smaller than microtubules but larger than microfilaments. They help the cell keep its shape.

- Microfilaments: Smallest of the three. Made of actin and small amounts of myosin (as in muscle cells), they function in cell movement such as cytoplasmic streaming, endocytosis, and ameboid movement. Microfilaments also pinch the two new cells apart after cell division.

SKILL 15.2 Distinguish between prokaryotic and eukaryotic cells

The cell is the basic unit of all living things. There are two types of cells. Prokaryotic cells include only the bacteria and blue-green algae. Bacteria were most likely the first cells and date back in the fossil record to 3.5 billion years ago.

PROKARYOTIC CELLS are distinct because:

1. They have no defined nucleus or nuclear membrane. The DNA and ribosomes float freely within the cell.

2. They have a thick cell wall to protect the cell, to give it shape, and to keep the cell from bursting.

3. The cell walls contain amino sugars (glycoproteins).

4. Some have a capsule made of polysaccharides, which make the bacteria sticky (as plaque on your teeth).

5. Some have pili, which are protein strands that allow for attachment of the bacteria and may be used for sexual reproduction called conjugation.

6. Some have flagella for movement.

EUKARYOTIC CELLS are found in protists, fungi, plants, and animals. Some features of eukaryotic cells include:

1. They are usually larger than prokaryotic cells.

2. They contain many organelles, which are membrane-bound areas for specific cell functions.

The cell is the basic unit of all living things.

PROKARYOTIC CELLS: Prokaryotic cells: include only the bacteria and blue-green algae, have no defined nucleus, but do have a thick cell wall containing amino sugars

EUKARYOTIC CELLS: found in protists, fungi, plants, and animals, have cytoplasm, a cytoskeleton, and more complex structures like organelles

3. They contain a cytoskeleton that provides a protein framework for the cell.

4. They contain cytoplasm to support the organelles and contain the ions and molecules necessary for cell function.

> The purpose of cell division is to provide growth and repair in body (somatic) cells and to replenish or create sex cells for reproduction.

SKILL 15.3 **Demonstrate understanding of the cell cycle and cytokinesis**

MITOSIS: the division of somatic (body) cells

MEIOSIS: the division of sex cells (eggs and sperm)

CYTOKINESIS: the process whereby the cytoplasm of a single cell is divided to produce two daughter cells

MITOTIC (M) PHASE: the shortest phase of the cell cycle, in which mitosis and cytokinesis divide the nucleus and cytoplasm, respectively

INTERPHASE: the stage where the cell grows and copies the chromosomes in preparation for the mitotic phase

> Cancer cells do not respond to density-dependent inhibition. They divide excessively and invade other tissues.

The purpose of cell division is to provide growth and repair in body (somatic) cells and to replenish or create sex cells for reproduction. There are two forms of cell division. **MITOSIS** is the division of somatic (body) cells and **MEIOSIS** is the division of sex cells (eggs and sperm). **CYTOKINESIS** is the process whereby the cytoplasm of a single cell is divided to produce two daughter cells. It usually initiates during the late stages of mitosis, and sometimes meiosis, splitting the cell into two to ensure that chromosome number is maintained from one generation to the next.

Mitosis is divided into two parts: the **MITOTIC (M) PHASE** and **INTERPHASE**. In the mitotic phase, mitosis and cytokinesis divide the nucleus and cytoplasm, respectively. This phase is the shortest phase of the cell cycle. Interphase is the stage where the cell grows and copies the chromosomes in preparation for the mitotic phase. Interphase occurs in three stages of growth: $G1$ (growth) period is when the cell is growing and metabolizing, the S period (synthesis) is where new DNA is being made and the $G2$ phase (growth) is where new proteins and organelles are being made to prepare for cell division.

To Divide or Not to Divide

The restriction point occurs late in the G1 phase of the cell cycle when the decision for the cell to divide is made. If all the internal and external cell systems are working properly, the cell proceeds to replicate. Cells may also decide not to proceed past the restriction point. This nondividing cell state is called the $G0$ phase. Many specialized cells remain in this state.

The density of cells also regulates cell division. Density-dependent inhibition occurs when the cells crowd one another and consume all the nutrients, thereby halting cell division. Cancer cells do not respond to density-dependent inhibition. They divide excessively and invade other tissues. As long as there are nutrients, cancer cells are "immortal."

Respiration

CELLULAR RESPIRATION is the metabolic pathway in which food (glucose, etc.) is broken down to produce energy in the form of ATP. Both plants and animals use respiration to create energy for metabolism. In respiration, energy is released by the transfer of electrons in a process known as an **OXIDATION-REDUCTION (REDOX) REACTION**. The oxidation phase of this reaction is the loss of an electron and the reduction phase is the gain of an electron. Redox reactions are important for the stages of respiration.

Step 1: Glycolysis

Glycolysis is the first step in respiration, which occurs in the cytoplasm of the cell and does not require oxygen. Each of the ten stages of glycolysis is catalyzed by a specific enzyme. The following is a summary of those stages.

In the first stage the reactant is glucose. For energy to be released from glucose, it must be converted to a reactive compound. This conversion occurs through the phosphorylation of a molecule of glucose by the use of two molecules of ATP. This is an investment of energy by the cell. A total of four ATP molecules are made in four stages. Since two molecules of ATP were needed to start the reaction in stage 1, there is a net gain of two ATP molecules at the end of glycolysis. This accounts for only two percent of the total energy in a molecule of glucose.

Beginning with pyruvate, which was the end product of glycolysis, the following steps occur before entering the Krebs cycle:

1. Pyruvic acid is changed to acetyl-CoA (coenzyme A). This is a three carbon pyruvic acid molecule which has lost one molecule of carbon dioxide (CO_2) to become a two carbon acetyl group. Pyruvic acid loses a hydrogen to NAD^+ which is reduced to NADH.

2. Acetyl CoA enters the Krebs cycle. For each molecule of glucose it started with, two molecules of Acetyl CoA enter the Krebs cycle (one for each molecule of pyruvic acid formed in glycolysis).

Step 2: The Krebs cycle

The Krebs cycle (also known as the citric acid cycle) occurs in four major steps.

First, the two-carbon acetyl CoA combines with a four-carbon molecule to form a six-carbon molecule of citric acid. Next, two carbons are lost as carbon dioxide

CELLULAR RESPIRA-TION: the metabolic pathway in which food (glucose, etc.) is broken down to produce energy in the form of ATP

Both plants and animals use respiration to create energy for metabolism.

OXIDATION-REDUCTION (REDOX) REACTION: the process in respiration that releases energy through the sequential loss and gain of electrons

Since two molecules of ATP were needed to start the reaction in stage 1, there is a net gain of two ATP molecules at the end of glycolysis.

(CO_2) and a four-carbon molecule is formed to become available to join with CoA to form citric acid again. Because we started with two molecules of CoA, two turns of the Krebs cycle are necessary to process the original molecule of glucose. In the third step, eight hydrogen atoms are released and picked up by FAD and NAD (vitamins and electron carriers).

Finally, for each molecule of CoA (remember, there were two to start with) you get:

- 3 molecules of NADH $\times$ 2 cycles
- 1 molecule of $FADH_2$ $\times$ 2 cycles
- 1 molecule of ATP $\times$ 2 cycles

> The Krebs cycle in itself does not produce much ATP, but functions mostly in the transfer of electrons to be used in the electron transport chain where the most ATP is made.

Therefore, this completes the breakdown of glucose. At this point, a total of four molecules of ATP have been made; two from glycolysis and one from each of the two turns of the Krebs cycle. Six molecules of carbon dioxide have been released; two prior to entering the Krebs cycle, and two for each of the two turns of the Krebs cycle. Twelve carrier molecules have been made; ten NADH and two $FADH_2$. These carrier molecules will carry electrons to the electron transport chain. ATP is made by substrate level phosphorylation in the Krebs cycle. Notice that the Krebs cycle in itself does not produce much ATP, but functions mostly in the transfer of electrons to be used in the electron transport chain where the most ATP is made.

Step 3: The electron transport chain

ELECTRON TRANSPORT CHAIN: the final step in respiration that creates 34 molecules of ATP through oxidative phosphorylation

In the **ELECTRON TRANSPORT CHAIN**, NADH transfers electrons from glycolysis and the Kreb's cycle to the first molecule in the chain of molecules embedded in the inner membrane of the mitochondrion. The electron transport chain does not make ATP directly. Instead, it breaks up a large free energy drop into a more manageable amount. The chain uses electrons to pump H^+ across the mitochondrion membrane. The H^+ gradient is used to form ATP synthesis in a process called chemiosmosis (oxidative phosphorylation). The electron transport chain and oxidative phosphorylation produces 34 ATP.

> The electron transport chain does not make ATP directly. Instead, the chain uses electrons to pump H^+ across the mitochondrion membrane, where most ATP production takes place.

So, the net gain from the whole process of respiration is 36 molecules of ATP:

- Glycolysis: 4 ATP made, 2 ATP spent = net gain of 2 ATP
- Acetyl CoA: 2 ATP used
- Krebs cycle: 1 ATP made for each turn of the cycle = net gain of 2 ATP
- Electron transport chain: 34 ATP gained

Photosynthesis

PHOTOSYNTHESIS is an anabolic process that stores energy in the form of a three-carbon sugar. We will use glucose as an example for this section. Only organisms that contain chloroplasts (plants, some bacteria, some protists) perform photosynthesis. There are a few terms to be familiar with when discussing photosynthesis.

An **AUTOTROPH** (self-feeder) is an organism that makes its own food from the energy of the sun or other elements. Autotrophs include:

- Photoautotroph: makes food from light and carbon dioxide, releasing oxygen that can be used for respiration
- Chemoautotroph: oxidizes sulfur and ammonia, as some bacteria

The **CHLOROPLAST** is the site of photosynthesis. It is similar to the mitochondria due to the increased surface area of the thylakoid membrane. The thylakoid membrane contains pigments (chlorophyll) that are capable of capturing light energy. A chloroplast also contains a fluid called stroma between the stacks of thylakoids.

Photosynthesis reverses the electron flow. Water is split by the chloroplast into hydrogen and oxygen. The oxygen is given off as a waste product as carbon dioxide is reduced to sugar (glucose). This requires the input of energy, which comes from the sun.

Stage 1: Light reactions

Photosynthesis occurs in two stages: the **LIGHT REACTIONS** and the Calvin cycle (dark reactions). The conversion of solar energy to chemical energy occurs in the light reactions. Electrons are transferred by the absorption of light by chlorophyll and cause the water to split, releasing oxygen as a waste product. The chemical energy that is created in the light reaction is in the form of NADPH. ATP is also produced by a process called photophosphorylation. These forms of energy are produced in the thylakoids and are used in the Calvin cycle to produce sugar.

Stage 2: The Calvin cycle

The second stage of photosynthesis is the **CALVIN CYCLE**. Carbon dioxide in the air is incorporated into organic molecules already in the chloroplast. The NADPH produced in the light reaction is used as reducing power for the reduction of the carbon to carbohydrate. ATP from the light reaction is also needed to convert carbon dioxide to carbohydrate (sugar).

PHOTOSYNTHESIS: an anabolic process that stores energy in the form of a three- carbon sugar

AUTOTROPH: an organism that makes its own food from the energy of the sun or other elements

CHLOROPLAST: the site of photosynthesis

Photosynthesis reverses the electron flow, using the sun's energy to split water into hydrogen and oxygen and reduce carbon dioxide to glucose.

LIGHT REACTIONS: the first stage in photosynthesis, in which solar energy is converted to chemical energy

CALVIN CYCLE: the second stage in photosynthesis in which energy from the light reactions is used to reduce carbon to sugar

Sun, chlorophyll, and excited electrons

The process of photosynthesis is made possible by the presence of the sun. Visible light ranges in wavelengths of 750 nanometers (red light) to 380 nanometers (violet light). As wavelength decreases, the amount of energy available increases. Light is carried as photons; a photon is a fixed quantity of energy. Light is reflected (what we see), transmitted, or absorbed (what the plant uses). The plant's pigments capture light of specific wavelengths. Remember that the light that is reflected is what we see as color. Plant pigments include:

- Chlorophyll a: reflects green/blue light; absorbs red light

- Chlorophyll b: reflects yellow/green light; absorbs red light

- Carotenoids: reflects yellow/orange; absorbs violet/blue

The pigments absorb photons. The energy from the light excites electrons in the chlorophyll that jump to orbitals with more potential energy and reach an "excited," or unstable, state.

The formula for photosynthesis is:
$$CO_2 + H_2O + energy\ (from\ sunlight) \rightarrow C_6H_{12}O_6 + O_2$$

The high-energy electrons are trapped by primary electron acceptors which are located on the thylakoid membrane. These electron acceptors and the pigments form reaction centers called photosystems that are capable of capturing light energy. Photosystems contain a reaction-center chlorophyll that releases an electron to the primary electron acceptor. This transfer is the first step of the light reactions.

- Photosystem I is composed of a pair of chlorophyll a molecules. Photosystem I is also called P700 because it absorbs light of 700 nanometers. Photosystem I makes ATP whose energy is needed to build glucose.

- Photosystem II is also called P680 because it absorbs light of 680 nanometers. Photosystem II produces ATP + $NADPH_2$ and the waste gas oxygen.

Both photosystems are bound to the thylakoid membrane, close to the electron acceptors.

The production of ATP is termed photophosphorylation due to the use of light. Photosystem I uses cyclic photophosphorylation because the pathway occurs in a cycle. It can also use noncyclic photophosphorylation, which starts with light and ends with glucose. Photosystem II uses noncyclic photophosphorylation only.

The Relationship Between Cellular Respiration and Photosynthesis

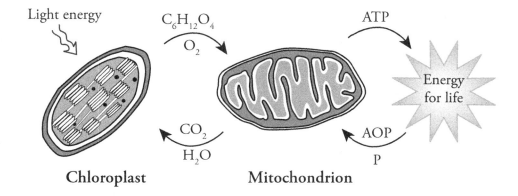

SKILL 15.5 Demonstrate understanding of mitosis and meiosis

Mitosis is the division of somatic cells and meiosis is the division of sex cells (eggs and sperm). The table below summarizes the major differences between the two processes.

MITOSIS	MEIOSIS
Division of somatic cell	Division of sex cells
Two cells result from each division	Four cells or polar bodies result from each division
Chromosome number is identical	Chromosome number is half of the two parent cells
For cell growth and repair	Recombinations provide genetic diversity

CELL DIVISION GLOSSARY	
Gamete	Sex cell or germ cell; eggs and sperm
Chromatin	Loose chromosomes; the state of chromosomes when the cell is not dividing

Continued on next page

Chromosome	Tightly coiled, visible chromatin; this state is found when the cell is dividing
Homologues	Chromosomes that contain the same information, are of equal length, and contain the same genes
Diploid	2n number; diploid chromosomes are a pair of chromosomes (in somatic cells)
Haploid	1n number; haploid chromosomes are a half of a pair (in sex cells)

The Stages of Mitosis ("IPMAT")

1. Interphase: Chromatin is loose, chromosomes are replicated, cell metabolism is occurring. Technically, Interphase is not a stage of mitosis.

2. Prophase: Once the cell enters prophase, it proceeds through the following steps continuously, with no stopping. The chromatin condenses to become visible chromosomes. The nucleolus disappears, and the nuclear membrane breaks apart. Mitotic spindles form, which will eventually pull the chromosomes apart. They are composed of microtubules. The cytoskeleton breaks down, and the spindles are pushed to the poles or opposite ends of the cell by the action of centrioles.

3. Metaphase: Kinetechore fibers attach to the chromosomes, which cause the chromosomes to line up in the center of the cell (think "middle" for metaphase).

4. Anaphase: Centromeres split in half and homologous chromosomes separate. The chromosomes are pulled to the poles of the cell, with identical sets at either end.

5. Telophase: Two nuclei are formed, each with a full set of DNA that is identical to that of the parent cell. The nucleoli become visible, and the nuclear membrane reassembles. A cell plate is visible in plant cells, whereas a cleavage furrow is formed in animal cells. The cell is pinched into two cells. Cytokinesis, or division, of the cytoplasm and organelles occurs.

The Stages of Meiosis

Meiosis contains the same five stages as mitosis but is repeated in order to reduce the chromosome number by one half. This way, when the sperm and egg join during fertilization, the haploid number is reached. There are two steps to meiosis.

Meiosis I: chromosomes are replicated; cells remain diploid

Prophase I: Replicated chromosomes condense and pair with homologues to form a tetrad. Crossing over (the exchange of genetic material between homologues to further increase diversity) occurs during Prophase I.

Metaphase I: Homologous sets attach to spindle fibers after lining up in the middle of the cell.

Anaphase I: Sister chromatids remain joined and move to the poles of the cell.

Telophase I: Two new cells are formed; chromosome number is still diploid.

Meiosis II: reduces the chromosome number in half

Prophase II: Chromosomes condense.

Metaphase II: Spindle fibers form again, sister chromatids line up in center of cell, centromeres divide, and sister chromatids separate.

Anaphase II: Separated chromosomes move to opposite ends of cell.

Telophase II: Four haploid cells form for each original sperm germ cell. One viable egg cell gets all the genetic information, and three polar bodies form with no DNA. The nuclear membrane reforms and cytokinesis occurs.

COMPETENCY 16
GENETICS

SKILL 16.1 Demonstrate understanding of DNA replication

A **GENE** is a unit of genetic information. DNA (Deoxyribonucleic acid) makes up genes that in turn make up the chromosomes. DNA is wound tightly around proteins in order to conserve space. The DNA/protein combination makes up the chromosome. **DNA** controls the synthesis of proteins, thereby controlling total cell activity. DNA is capable of making copies of itself.

GENE: a unit of genetic information

<table>
<tr><td colspan="1">STRUCTURE OF DNA</td></tr>
<tr><td>Made of nucleotides; a five-carbon sugar/phosphate group and nitrogen base (either adenine, guanine, cytosine, or thymine, known as amino acids).</td></tr>
<tr><td>Consist of a sugar/phosphate backbone that is covalently bonded. The bases are joined down the center of the molecule and are attached by hydrogen bonds, which are easily broken during replication.</td></tr>
<tr><td>The amount of adenine equals the amount of thymine, and the amount of cytosine equals the amount of guanine.</td></tr>
<tr><td>The shape is that of a twisted ladder called a double helix. The sugar/phosphates make up the sides of the ladder and the base pairs make up the rungs of the ladder.</td></tr>
</table>

DNA: controls the synthesis of proteins, thereby controlling total cell activity. DNA is capable of making copies of itself

DNA (Deoxyribonucleic acid) makes up genes that in turn make up the chromosomes.

Enzymes control each step of the replication of DNA.

DNA Replication

Enzymes control each step of the replication of DNA. The molecule untwists. The hydrogen bonds between the bases break and serve as a pattern for replication. Free nucleotides found inside the nucleus join on to form a new strand. Two new pieces of DNA are formed which are identical. This is a very accurate process. There is only one mistake for every billion nucleotides added. This is because there are enzymes (polymerases) present that proofread the molecule. In eukaryotes, replication occurs in many places along the DNA at once. The molecule may open up at many places like a broken zipper. In prokaryotic circular plasmids, replication begins at a point on the plasmid and goes in both directions until it meets itself.

Base pairing rules are important in determining a new strand of DNA sequence. For example, if our original strand of DNA had the sequence

ATCGGCAATAGC

This may be called our sense strand since it contains a sequence that makes sense or codes for something. The complementary strand (or other side of the ladder) would follow base pairing rules (A bonds with T and C bonds with G and would read:

TAGCCGTTATCG

When the molecule opens up and nucleotides join on, the base pairing rules create two new identical strands of DNA:

ATCGGCAATAGC   and   ATCGGCAATAGC
TAGCCGTTATCG   TAGCCGTTATCG

SKILL 16.2 Demonstrate understanding of the processes involved in protein synthesis

It is necessary for cells to manufacture new proteins for growth and repair of the organism. **PROTEIN SYNTHESIS** is the process that allows the DNA code to be read and carried out of the nucleus into the cytoplasm in the form of RNA (ribonucleic acid). This is where the **RIBOSOMES** are found, which are the sites of protein synthesis. The protein is then assembled according to the instructions on the DNA. There are several types of RNA.

- **Messenger RNA (mRNA):** Copies the code from DNA in the nucleus and takes it to the ribosomes in the cytoplasm.

- **Transfer RNA (tRNA):** Free floating in the cytoplasm, its job is to carry and position amino acids for assembly on the ribosome.

- **Ribosomal RNA (rRNA):** Found in the ribosomes. It makes a place for the proteins to be made and is believed to have many important functions.

Along with enzymes and amino acids, the RNA assists in the building of proteins. There are two stages of protein synthesis:

TRANSCRIPTION: This phase allows for the assembly of mRNA and occurs in the nucleus where the DNA is found. The DNA splits open and the mRNA reads the code and "transcribes" the sequence onto a single strand of mRNA. For example, if the code on the DNA is T A C C T C G T A C G A, the mRNA will make a complementary strand reading: A U G G A G C A U G C U (uracil replaces thymine in RNA).

Each group of three bases (nucleotide sequences) is called a codon. The codon eventually will code for a specific amino acid to be carried to the ribosome. "Start" codons begin the building of the protein, and "stop" codons end transcription. When the stop codon is reached, the mRNA separates from the DNA and leaves the nucleus for the cytoplasm.

TRANSLATION: This is the assembly of the amino acids to build the protein and occurs in the cytoplasm. The nucleotide sequence is translated to choose the correct amino acid sequence. As the rRNA translates the code at the ribosome, tRNAs that contain an anticodon seek out the correct amino acid and bring it back to the ribosome. For example, using the codon sequence from the example above:

The mRNA reads A U G / G A G / C A U / G C U
The anticodons are U A C / C U C / G U A / C G A

The amino acid sequence would be:
Methionine (start): Glu – His – Ala.

PROTEIN SYNTHESIS: the process that allows the DNA code to be read and carried out of the nucleus into the cytoplasm in the form of RNA

RIBOSOMES: the sites of protein synthesis

TRANSCRIPTION: the first phase of protein synthesis that allows for the assembly of mRNA and occurs in the nucleus where the DNA is found; the DNA splits open and the mRNA reads the code and "transcribes" the sequence onto a single strand of mRNA

TRANSLATION: the second phase of protein synthesis in which the assembly of the amino acids to build the protein occurs in the cytoplasm; the nucleotide sequence is translated to choose the correct amino acid sequence

This whole process is accomplished through the assistance of activating enzymes. Each of the twenty amino acids has its own enzyme that binds the amino acid to the tRNA. When the amino acids get close to each other on the ribosome, they bond together using peptide bonds. The start and stop codons are called nonsense codons. There is one start codon (AUG) and three stop codons. (UAA, UGA and UAG). Additional mutations cause the whole code to shift, thereby producing the wrong protein or, at times, no protein at all.

SKILL 16.3 Demonstrate understanding of the causes and results of mutation

MUTATIONS: an inheritable change in DNA

If the error occurs on an exon, it may be minor to lethal, depending on the severity of the mistake.

Usually the mutations on sex cells are more dangerous since they contain the basis of all information for the developing offspring.

Inheritable changes in DNA are called MUTATIONS. Mutations may be errors in replication or a spontaneous rearrangement of one or more segments by factors like radioactivity, drugs, or chemicals. The severity of the change is not as critical as where the change occurs. DNA contains large segments of noncoding areas called introns. The important coding areas are called exons. If an error occurs on an intron, there is no effect. If the error occurs on an exon, it may be minor to lethal, depending on the severity of the mistake. Mutations may occur on somatic or sex cells. Usually the mutations on sex cells are more dangerous since they contain the basis of all information for the developing offspring. But mutations are not always bad. They are the basis of evolution and if they make a more favorable variation that enhances the organism's survival, then they are beneficial. But mutations may also lead to abnormalities and birth defects and even death.

Types of Mutations

A point mutation is a mutation involving a single nucleotide or a few adjacent nucleotides.

TYPES OF POINT MUTATIONS	
Normal (the original strand)	A B C D E F
Duplication: One gene is repeated	A B **C C** D E F
Inversion: A segment of the sequence is flipped around	A **E D C B** F

Continued on next page

Deletion: A gene is left out	A B C E F (D is lost)
Insertion or Translocation: A segment from another place on the DNA is stuck in the wrong place	A B C **R S** D E F
Breakage: A piece is lost	A B C (DEF is lost)

Deletion and insertion mutations that shift the reading frame are frame shift mutations. A silent mutation makes no change in the amino acid sequence, therefore it does not alter the protein function. A missense mutation results in an alteration in the amino acid sequence.

A mutation's effect on protein function depends on which amino acid is involved and how many are involved. The structure of a protein usually determines its function. A mutation that does not alter the structure will probably have little or no effect on the protein's function. A mutation that does alter the structure of a protein can severely affect protein activity and thus is called a loss-of-function mutation. Sickle-cell anemia and cystic fibrosis are examples of loss-of-function mutations.

Sickle-cell anemia is characterized by weakness, heart failure, joint and muscular impairment, fatigue, abdominal pain and dysfunction, impaired mental function, and eventual death. The mutation that causes this genetic disorder is a point mutation in the sixth amino acid. A normal hemoglobin molecule has glutamic acid as the sixth amino acid and the sickle-cell hemoglobin has valine at the sixth position, which causes the chemical properties of hemoglobin to change. The hemoglobin of a sickle-cell person has a lower affinity for oxygen, and that causes red blood cells to have a sickle shape. The sickle shape of the red blood cell does not allow the cells to pass through capillaries well, forming clogs.

Cystic fibrosis, the most common genetic disorder of people with European ancestry, affects the exocrine system. A fibrous cyst forms on the pancreas that blocks the pancreatic ducts and causes sweat glands to release high levels of salt. Mucous glands secrete a thick mucous that accumulates in the lungs and may cause bacterial infections and possibly death. Cystic fibrosis cannot be cured but can be treated for a short while. Most children with the disorder die before adulthood. Scientists have identified a protein that transports chloride ions across cell membranes. Those with cystic fibrosis have a mutation in the gene coding for that protein. The majority of the mutant alleles have a deletion of the three nucleotides coding for phenylalanine at position 508. The other people with the disorder have mutant alleles caused by substitution, deletion, and frameshift mutations.

GREGOR MENDEL: the father of genetics, who realized that there were factors (now known as genes) that were transferred from parents to their offspring

ALLELES: a form of an inheritable trait or characteristic

GREGOR MENDEL is recognized as the father of genetics. His work in the late 1800s is the basis of our knowledge of genetics. Although unaware of the presence of DNA or genes, Mendel realized there were factors (now known as genes) that were transferred from parents to their offspring. Mendel worked with pea plants and fertilized the plants himself, keeping track of subsequent generations which led to the Mendelian laws of genetics. Mendel found that two "factors" governed each trait, one from each parent. Traits or characteristics came in several forms, known as **ALLELES**. For example, the trait of flower color had white alleles (*pp*) and purple alleles (*PP*).

Types and Expression of Alleles

- Homozygous: Having a pair of identical alleles. For example, PP and pp are homozygous pairs.

- Heterozygous: Having two different alleles. For example, Pp is a heterozygous pair.

- Phenotype: The organism's physical appearance.

- Genotype: The organism's genetic makeup. For example, PP and Pp have the same phenotype (purple in color), but different genotypes because the dominant P (purple) overrides the expression of the recessive p (white).

  – monohybrid cross: A cross using only one trait.

  – dihybrid cross: A cross using two traits. More combinations are possible.

- Punnet squares: These show the possible ways that genes combine or the probability of the occurrence of a certain genotype or phenotype. One parent's genes are noted at the top of the box and the other parent's are noted at the side of the box. Genes combine in the square just like numbers in addition tables. For example, a monohybrid cross generates four possible gene combinations. A dihybrid cross generates sixteen possible gene combinations.

LAW OF SEGREGATION: only one of the two possible alleles from each parent is passed on to the offspring

Mendel's Laws

The **LAW OF SEGREGATION** states that only one of the two possible alleles from each parent is passed on to the offspring. (During meiosis, the haploid division insures that half the sex cells get one allele, half get the other). If the two alleles differ, then one is fully expressed in the organism's appearance (the dominant allele) and the other has no noticeable effect on appearance (the recessive allele). The two alleles for each trait segregate into different gametes (sex cells). This Punnet square illustrates the law of segregation, showing the result of the cross of two first generation (F_1) hybrids.

	P	p
P	PP	Pp
p	Pp	pp

$P \quad PP \times pp$

$\downarrow$

$F_1 \quad Pp \times Pp$

$\downarrow$

$F_2 \quad \frac{1}{4} PP + \frac{1}{2} Pp + \frac{1}{4} pp$

This cross results in a 1:2:1 ratio of second generation (F_2) offspring. Here, the *P* is the dominant allele and the *p* is the recessive allele. The F_1 cross produces three offspring with the dominant allele expressed (two *PP* and one *Pp*) and one offspring with the recessive allele expressed (*pp*).

The **LAW OF INDEPENDENT ASSORTMENT** states that alleles sort independently of each other. (Many combinations are possible depending on which sperm ends up with which egg, just as many combinations of hands are possible when dealing a deck of cards). In a dihybrid cross, two characters are tested, with 16 possible gene combinations. Two of the seven characters Mendel studied were seed shape and color. Yellow is the dominant seed color (*Y*), and green is the recessive color (*y*). The dominant seed shape is round (*R*), and the recessive shape is wrinkled (*r*). A cross between a plant with yellow round seeds (*YYRR*) and a plant with green wrinkled seeds (*yyrr*) produces an F_1 generation with the genotype *YyRr*. The production of F_2 offspring results in a 9:3:3:1 phenotypic ratio.

> **LAW OF INDEPENDENT ASSORTMENT:** alleles sort independently of each other

	YR	Yr	yR	yr
YR	YYRR	YYRr	YyRR	YyRr
Yr	YYRr	YYrr	YyRr	Yyrr
yR	YyRR	YyRr	yyRR	yyRr
yr	YyRr	Yyrr	yyRr	yyrr

$P \quad YYRR \times yyrr$

$\downarrow$

$F_1 \quad YyRr$

$\downarrow$

$$
F_2 \quad
\left.
\begin{array}{ll}
YYRR & - \ 1 \\
YYRr & - \ 2 \\
YyRR & - \ 2 \\
YyRr & - \ 4
\end{array}
\right\} \quad \text{9 yellow round}
$$

$$
\left.
\begin{array}{ll}
yyRR & - \ 1 \\
yyRr & - \ 2
\end{array}
\right\} \quad \text{3 green round}
$$

$$
\left.
\begin{array}{ll}
YYrr & - \ 1 \\
Yyrr & - \ 2
\end{array}
\right\} \quad \text{3 yellow wrinkled}
$$

$$
\begin{array}{ll}
yyrr & - \ 1
\end{array}
\ \} \quad \text{1 green wrinkled}
$$

Dominance

COMPLETE DOMINANCE: one trait covers up the allele of the other trait

Based on Mendelian genetics, the more complex hereditary pattern of dominance was discovered. In Mendel's law of segregation, the F_1 generation of peas had either purple or white flowers. This is an example of **COMPLETE DOMINANCE**, where one trait covers up the allele of the other trait. **INCOMPLETE DOMINANCE** occurs when the F_1 generation produces an appearance somewhere between the two parents. For example, when red flowers are crossed with white flowers and result in an F_1 generation with pink flowers. The red and white traits are still carried by the F_1 generation, resulting in an F_2 generation with a phenotypic ratio of 1:2:1. In codominance, the genes may form new phenotypes. The ABO blood grouping is an example of codominance. A and B are of equal strength and O is recessive. Therefore, type A blood may have the genotypes of AA or AO, type B blood may have the genotypes of BB or BO, type AB blood has the genotype A and B, and type O blood has two recessive O genes.

INCOMPLETE DOMINANCE: when the F_1 generation produces an appearance somewhere between the two parents. For example, when red flowers are crossed with white flowers and result in an F_1 generation with pink flowers

Chromosome Theory

CHROMOSOME THEORY: genes are located on chromosomes

In the late 1800s, the processes of mitosis and meiosis and the role of chromosomes in cell division were understood. In the early 1900s, Walter Sutton saw how this explanation confirmed Mendel's "factors." The **CHROMOSOME THEORY** states that genes are located on chromosomes. The chromosomes undergo independent assortment and segregation.

Organelles have DNA-containing genes with their own patterns of inheritance that do not conform to Mendelian rules.

SKILL 16.5 Demonstrate understanding of some aspects of non-Mendelian inheritance *(for example, multiple alleles, multiple genes)*

NON-MENDELIAN INHERITANCE is a general term describing any patterns of genetic inheritance that do not conform to Mendel's laws or do not rely on a single chromosomal gene. Examples of non-Mendelian inheritance include complex traits, environmental influence, organelle DNA, transmission bias, and epigenetics.

Multiple genes determine the expression of many complex traits. For example, disorders arising from a defect in a single gene are rare compared to complex disorders like cancer, heart disease, and diabetes. The inheritance of such complex disorders does not follow Mendelian rules because they involve more than one gene.

While chromosomal DNA carries the majority of an organism's generic material, organelles, including mitochondria and chloroplasts, also have DNA-containing genes. Organelle genes have their own patterns of inheritance that do not conform to Mendelian rules. Such patterns of inheritance are often called maternal because offspring receive all of their organelle DNA from the mother.

TRANSMISSION BIAS describes a situation in which the alleles of the parent organisms are not equally represented in their offspring. Transmission bias often results from the failure of alleles to segregate properly during cell division. Mendelian genetics assumes equal representation of parent alleles in the offspring generation.

EPIGENETIC INHERITANCE involves changes not involving the DNA sequence. For example, the addition of methyl groups (methylation) to DNA molecules can influence the expression of genes and override Mendelian patterns of inheritance.

Finally, GENETIC LINKAGE, discussed in detail in the next section, is often considered a form of non-Mendelian inheritance because closely linked chromosomal genes tend to assort together, not separately. Linkage, however, is not entirely non-Mendelian because classical genetics can generally explain and predict patterns of inheritance of linked traits.

NON-MENDELIAN IN-HERITANCE: patterns of genetic inheritance that do not conform to Mendel's laws or do not rely on a single chromosomal gene

Multiple genes determine the expression of many complex traits.

TRANSMISSION BIAS: a situation in which the alleles of the parent organisms are not equally represented in their offspring

EPIGENETIC INHERITANCE: changes not involving the DNA sequence that can influence the expression of genes and override Mendelian patterns of inheritance

GENETIC LINKAGE: predicting patterns of inheritance of linked traits

Genetic engineering requires enzymes to cut DNA, a vector to insert the cut DNA into a host, and a host organism for the recombinant DNA.

SKILL 16.6 Demonstrate knowledge of how recombinant DNA is constructed

In its simplest form, genetic engineering requires enzymes to cut DNA, a vector to insert the cut DNA into a host, and a host organism for the recombinant DNA. A RESTRICTION ENZYME is a bacterial enzyme that cuts foreign DNA in specific

RESTRICTION ENZYME: a bacterial enzyme that cuts foreign DNA in specific locations

HOST CELL: the receptacle for a recombinant plasmid, which allows it to replicate

The use of recombinant DNA provides a means to transplant genes among species and opens the door for cloning specific genes of interest.

GEL ELECTROPHORE-SIS: another method for analyzing DNA by separating DNA or protein by size or electrical charge

POLYMERASE CHAIN REACTION (PCR: a technique in which a piece of DNA can be amplified into billions of copies within a few hours

locations. A vector, such as a virus or bacteriophage, inserts the restriction fragment that results into a bacterial plasmid. The splicing of restriction fragments into a plasmid results in a recombinant plasmid. This recombinant plasmid can now be placed in a **HOST CELL**, usually a bacterial cell, and replicate.

The use of recombinant DNA provides a means to transplant genes among species and opens the door for cloning specific genes of interest.

Finding and Isolating Genes of Interest

Hybridization can be used to find a gene of interest. A probe is a molecule complementary in sequence to the gene of interest. The probe, once it has bonded to the gene, can be detected by labeling with a radioactive isotope or a fluorescent tag.

GEL ELECTROPHORESIS is another method for analyzing DNA by separating DNA or protein by size or electrical charge. The DNA runs towards the positive charge as it separates the DNA fragments by size. The gel is treated with a DNA-binding dye that fluoresces under ultraviolet light. A picture of the gel can be taken and used for analysis.

One of the most widely used genetic engineering techniques is **POLYMERASE CHAIN REACTION (PCR)**. PCR is a technique in which a piece of DNA can be amplified into billions of copies within a few hours. This process requires a primer to specify the segment to be copied and an enzyme (usually taq polymerase) to amplify the DNA. PCR has allowed scientists to perform several procedures on the smallest amount of DNA.

SKILL 16.7 Identify uses of recombinant DNA *(for example, in the production of insulin)*

The insulin produced in genetically engineered bacteria is chemically identical to that made in the pancreas.

The applications of isolated genes through genetic engineering are varied. One major use is for diagnostic purposes. The gene that encodes for one type of hemophilia has been used for this purpose. This field of research is proving to be of invaluable help to people suffering from various diseases like cancer and diabetes, and research in this area holds great promise for future generations. Insulin and mammalian growth hormones have been produced in bacteria by gene-splicing techniques. Insulin treatment helps control diabetes for millions of people who suffer from the disease. The insulin produced in genetically engineered bacteria is chemically identical to that made in the pancreas. Human growth hormone

(HGH) has been genetically engineered for the treatment of dwarfism caused by insufficient amounts of HGH. HGH is being further researched for the possible treatment of broken bones and severe burns.

Biotechnology has advanced the techniques used to create vaccines. Genetic engineering allows for the modification of a pathogen to attenuate it for vaccine use. In fact, vaccines created by a pathogen attenuated by gene splicing may be safer than using the traditional mutants.

Vaccines created by a pathogen attenuated by gene splicing may be safer than using the traditional mutants.

Isolated genes can be used to isolate similar genes from other organisms, serving as probes. The nucleic acid sequence of a gene can be derived through genetic engineering techniques. For example, if a partial or complete sequence of the protein that it encodes is available, the gene can be confirmed in this manner. If a protein product is unknown, then comparing the sequence of the gene with those of the known genes can derive a function for that gene. Knowing the function of a gene is important in clinical diagnoses.

Isolated genes can be used to isolate similar genes from other organisms, serving as probes.

Aside from clinicaI uses, farmers use genetic engineering techniques, too. Isolating a gene that causes disease in a particular crop will help farmers deal with outbreaks and create healthier, sometimes disease-resistant and bountiful crops.

Though other factors have an influence, the genes provide the road map for the differentiation of tissues and the development of the organism.

SKILL 16.8 Demonstrate understanding of the interaction between heredity and environment

There are many, many factors that affect how an organism develops and how its tissues differentiate. Even when they are fully formed and mature, organisms continue to grow and change. Genetics is perhaps the single most important factor in determining the growth and development of an individual organism. Genes code for the proteins that determine all the traits of a creature. Though other factors have an influence, the genes provide the road map for the differentiation of tissues and the development of the organism.

Access to the proper nutrients, including food, water, and select inorganic compounds, is important for all organisms. These items provide important precursors for synthesis reactions and the energy for metabolic activities. Lack of nutrients is particularly likely to reduce the growth and survival of organisms.

Proper nutrients provide important precursors for synthesis reactions and the energy for metabolic activities.

Sunlight is especially important to the growth of plants, since they rely on it to manufacture the energy they require for all functions. Not only is it important to their development, mature plants bend toward sunlight to maximize their exposure. Access to sunlight is also important to animals, many of which need to synthesize important factors (i.e., vitamin D).

> Diseases and chemicals can interfere with or imitate growth factors and enzymes. They can also disrupt important signaling pathways or destroy cells and tissues.

EVOLUTION: a change in genotype over time

> Gene frequencies shift and change from generation to generation. Populations evolve, not individuals.

HARDY-WEINBERG THEORY OF GENE EQUILIBRIUM: a mathematical prediction to show shifting gene patterns

Diseases and chemicals can interfere with or imitate growth factors and enzymes. They can also disrupt important signaling pathways or destroy cells and tissues. Thus, diseases and these substances can be extremely damaging. Moreover, if exposure to these compounds occurs during development, they can prevent the proper differentiation of cells and deform the individual. Therefore, our environment is important to the expression of phenotype and the health of an organism. The organism's health will determine whether or not its genes are likely to be passed on to subsequent generations.

EVOLUTION currently is defined as a change in genotype over time. Gene frequencies shift and change from generation to generation. Populations evolve, not individuals.

Measuring Gene Frequency

The HARDY-WEINBERG THEORY OF GENE EQUILIBRIUM is a mathematical prediction to show shifting gene patterns. Let's use the letter "A" to represent the dominant condition of normal skin pigment. "a" would represent the recessive condition of albinism. In a population, there are three possible genotypes; *AA*, *Aa*, and *aa*. *AA* and *Aa* would have normal skin pigment and only aa would be albinos. According to the Hardy-Weinberg law, there are five requirements to keep a gene frequency stable, leading to no evolution:

1. There is no mutation in the population

2. There are no selection pressures; one gene is not more desirable in the environment

3. There is no mating preference; mating is random

4. The population is isolated; there is no immigration or emigration

5. The population is large (mathematical probability is more correct with a large sample)

The above conditions are extremely difficult to meet. If these five conditions are not met, then gene frequency can shift, leading to evolution.

Let's say in a population, 75% of the population has normal skin pigment (*AA* and *Aa*), and 25% are albino (*aa*). Using the following formula, which can be used over generations to determine if evolution is occurring, we can determine the frequency of the A allele and the "*a*" allele in a population:

$$1 = p^2 + 2pq + q^2$$

where 1 is the total population, p^2 is the number of *AA* individuals, $2pq$ is the number of *Aa* individuals, and q^2 is the number of *aa* individuals.

Since you cannot tell by looking if an individual is *AA* or *Aa*, you must use the *aa* individuals to find that frequency first. As stated above, aa is 25% of the population. Since aa $= q^2$, we can determine the value of *q* (or *a*) by finding the square root of 0.25, which is 0.5. Therefore, 0.5 of the population has the "*a*" gene. In order to find the value for *p*, use the following formula: $1 = p + q$. This would make the value of $p = 0.5$.

The gene pool is all the alleles at all gene loci in all individuals of a population. The Hardy-Weinberg theorem describes the gene pool in a nonevolving population. It states that the frequencies of alleles and genotypes in a population's gene pool are random unless acted on by something other than sexual recombination.

Now, to find the number of *AA*, plug it into the first formula;

$AA = p^2 = 0.5 \times 0.5 = 0.25$

$Aa = 2pq = 2(0.5 \times 0.5) = 0.5$

$aa = q^2 = 0.5 \times 0.5 = 0.25$

Any time you use the Hardy-Weinberg theorem, you will have an obvious squared number. The square of that number will be the frequency of the recessive gene, and you can figure anything else out knowing the formula and the frequency of *q*.

When frequencies vary from the Hardy-Weinberg equilibrium, the population is said to be evolving. The change to the gene pool is on such a small scale that it is called microevolution. Certain factors increase the chances of variability in a population, thus leading to evolution. Items that increase variability include mutations, sexual reproduction, immigration, large population, and variation in geographic local. Changes that decrease variation would be natural selection, emigration, small population, and random mating.

When frequencies vary from the Hardy-Weinberg equilibrium, the population is said to be evolving.

The environment can have an impact on phenotype. For example, a person living in a higher altitude will have a greater variation in the amount of red and white blood cells than those living at sea level.

In some cases, a particular trait is advantageous to the organism in a particular environment. Sickle-cell disease causes a low oxygen level in the blood which results in red blood cells having a sickle shape. About one in every ten African-Americans have the sickle-cell trait. These heterozygous carriers are usually healthy compared to homozygous individuals who can suffer severe detrimental effects. In the tropical Africa environment, a heterozygote is more resistant to malaria than those who do not carry any copies of the sickle-cell gene.

In the tropical Africa environment, a heterozygote is more resistant to malaria than those who do not carry any copies of the sickle-cell gene.

SKILL 16.9 Identify chromosomal and gene aberrations that lead to common human genetic disorders (for example, Down syndrome)

Thousands of genetic disorders are the result of inheriting a recessive trait.

Most people with recessive disorders are born to parents with normal phenotypes.

CARRIER: heterozygous parent that does not express a trait phenotypically but passes it on to its offspring

The same techniques of pedigree analysis apply when tracing inherited disorders. Thousands of genetic disorders are the result of inheriting a recessive trait. These disorders range from nonlethal traits (such as albinism) to life-threatening conditions (such as cystic fibrosis).

Most people with recessive disorders are born to parents with normal phenotypes. The mating of heterozygous parents would result in an offspring genotypic ratio of 1:2:1; thus 1 out of 4 offspring would express this recessive trait. The heterozygous parents are called **CARRIERS** because they do not express the trait phenotypically but pass the trait on to their offspring.

Lethal dominant alleles are much less common than lethal recessives. This is because lethal dominant alleles are not masked in heterozygotes. Mutations in a gene of the sperm or egg can result in a lethal dominant allele, usually killing the developing offspring.

- Sex-linked traits: The Y chromosome found only in males (XY) carries very little genetic information, whereas the X chromosome found in females (XX) carries important information. Since men have no second X chromosome to cover up a recessive gene, that recessive trait is expressed more often in men. Women need the recessive gene on both X chromosomes to show the trait. Examples of sex-linked traits include hemophilia and color-blindness.

- Sex-influenced traits: Traits are influenced by the sex hormones. Male pattern baldness, the primary expression of baldness in men, is an example of a sex-influenced trait. Testosterone influences the expression of the gene.

- Nondisjunction: During meiosis, some chromosomes may fail to separate properly. One sex cell may get both chromosomes and another may get none. Depending on the chromosomes involved, this may or may not be serious. Offspring end up with either an extra chromosome or are missing one. An example of nondisjunction is Down Syndrome, where three #21 chromosomes are present.

See also Skill 16.4

COMPETENCY 17
EVOLUTION

SKILL 17.1 **Identify evidence that supports the theory of evolution**

FOSSILS are the key to understanding biological history. They are the preserved remnants left by an organism that lived in the past. Scientists have established the geological time scale to determine the age of a fossil. The geological time scale is broken down into four eras: the Precambrian, Paleozoic, Mesozoic, and Cenozoic. The eras are further broken down into periods that represent a distinct age in the history of Earth and its life. Scientists use rock layers called strata to date fossils. Since the older layers of rock are at the bottom, scientists can correlate the dates of the rock layers with the era of the fossils.

> **FOSSILS:** the preserved remnants left by an organism that lived in the past

Dating Fossils

RADIOMETRIC DATING is a more precise method of dating fossils. Rocks and fossils contain isotopes of elements accumulated over time. The isotope's half-life is used to date older fossils by determining the amount of isotope remaining and comparing it to the half-life.

Dating fossils is helpful in constructing an EVOLUTIONARY TREE. Scientists can arrange the succession of animals based on their fossil record. The fossils of an animal's ancestors can be dated and placed on its evolutionary tree. For example, the branched evolution of horses shows the progression of the modern horse's ancestors to be larger, to have a reduced number of toes, and to have teeth modified for grazing.

> **RADIOMETRIC DATING:** a method of dating fossils by measuring accumulated amounts of isotopes and comparing that amount to the isotope's half life

> **EVOLUTIONARY TREE:** arrangement of the succession of organisms based on their fossil record

Classifying Organisms

Organization of life forms on Earth runs from the less complex to extremely complex life forms. Biological characteristics are used to classify organisms. Protein comparison, DNA comparison, and analysis of fossilized DNA are powerful comparative methods used to measure evolutionary relationships between species. Taxonomists consider the organism's life history, biochemical (DNA) makeup, behavior, and how the organisms are distributed geographically. The fossil record

> *Protein comparison, DNA comparison, and analysis of fossilized DNA are powerful comparative methods used to measure evolutionary relationships between species.*

is also used to show evolutionary relationships, for instance, using anatomy and embryology.

- **Homologous Structures:** Organs may have different functions, but are built from the same basic parts. Example: Skeletally, flippers, hands, and wings appear to be made from the same basic parts
- **Vestigial Structures:** Many parts still exist in organisms but are no longer used. Examples: Whale pelvis bone and human appendix.
- **Comparative Embryology:** Many organisms in the embryonic stage are virtually indistinguishable. Most amphibians and reptiles show tails during embryonic stage; however, many do not have tails when fully developed.

> **SKILL 17.2** Demonstrate understanding of the mechanisms of evolution

Variation

> *Heritable variation is responsible for the individuality of organisms. An individual's phenotype is based on inherited genotype and the surrounding environment.*

Heritable variation is responsible for the individuality of organisms. An individual's phenotype is based on inherited genotype and the surrounding environment. For example, people can alter their phenotypes by lifting weights or dieting and exercising.

> *Variation is generated by mutation and sexual recombination.*

Variation is generated by mutation and sexual recombination. Mutations may be errors in replication or a spontaneous rearrangement of one or more segments of DNA.

> *Mutations contribute a minimal amount of variation in a population. It is the unique recombination of existing alleles that causes the majority of genetic differences.*

Mutations contribute a minimal amount of variation in a population. It is the unique recombination of existing alleles that causes the majority of genetic differences. **RECOMBINATION** is caused when the parents' genes cross over during meiosis and result in a unique offspring. With all the possible mating combinations in the world, it is obvious that sexual reproduction is the primary cause of genetic variation.

> **RECOMBINATION:** when the parents' genes cross over during meiosis and result in a unique offspring

Natural Selection

> **NATURAL SELECTION:** the survival of certain traits in a population through the course of time

NATURAL SELECTION is based on the survival of certain traits in a population through the course of time. The phrase "survival of the fittest" often is associated with natural selection. **FITNESS** is the contribution an individual makes to the gene pool of the next generation.

> **FITNESS:** the contribution an individual makes to the gene pool of the next generation

Natural selection acts on phenotypes. An organism's phenotype is constantly exposed to its environment. Based on an organism's phenotype, selection indirectly adapts a population to its environment by maintaining favorable genotypes in the gene pool.

Modes of natural selection

Stabilizing selection favors the more common phenotypes, directional selection shifts the frequency of phenotypes in one direction, and diversifying selection occurs when individuals on both extremes of the phenotypic range are favored.

Sexual selection leads to the secondary sex characteristics of males and females. Animals that use mating behaviors may be successful or unsuccessful. A male animal that lacks attractive plumage or has a weak mating call will not attract a female, thereby eventually limiting his secondary sex genes in the gene pool.

Theories about the rate of evolution

The **THEORY OF GRADUALISM** states that minor evolutionary changes occur at a regular rate. Charles Darwin based his book *On the Origin of Species* on this theory. Darwin was born in 1809 and spent five years in his twenties on a ship called the *Beagle*. Of all the locations the *Beagle* sailed to, it was the Galapagos Islands that made the deepest impression on Darwin. There he collected 13 species of finches that were quite similar, but only later he determined that these finches were separate species. He reasoned that the finches' beak sizes evolved to accommodate different food sources. From this and other examples, Darwin hypothesized that a new species arose from its ancestors by the gradual collection of adaptations to a different environment. The beaks of the now-famous "Darwin's finches" provide the most popular proof of this hypothesis. Many people did not believe in Darwin's theories until recent field studies proved Darwin was right.

Although Darwin believed the origin of species was gradual, he was bewildered by the gaps in fossil records of living organisms. **PUNCTUATED EQUILIBRIUM** is an alternate model of evolution that states that organismal form diverges and species form rapidly over relatively short periods of geological history, and then progress through long stages of stasis with little or no change. Punctuationalists use fossil records to support their claim. It is probable that both theories are correct, depending on the particular lineage studied.

Selection indirectly adapts a population to its environment by maintaining favorable genotypes in the gene pool.

THEORY OF GRADUALISM: minor evolutionary changes occur at a regular rate

Although Darwin believed the origin of species was gradual, he was bewildered by the gaps in fossil records of living organisms.

PUNCTUATED EQUILIBRIUM: an alternate model of evolution that states that organismal form diverges and species form rapidly over relatively short periods of geological history, and then progress through long stages of stasis with little or no change

SKILL 17.3 Demonstrate knowledge of isolating mechanisms and speciation

BIOLOGICAL SPECIES CONCEPT (BSC): a species is a reproductive community of populations that occupy a specific niche in nature

The most commonly used concept of a species is the **BIOLOGICAL SPECIES CONCEPT (BSC)**, which states that a species is a reproductive community of populations that occupy a specific niche in nature. It focuses on reproductive isolation of populations as the primary criterion for recognition of species status. The biological species concept does not apply to organisms that are completely asexual in their reproduction, fossil organisms, or distinctive populations that hybridize.

Reproductive Isolation

PREZYGOTIC: any pre-mating factor that impedes two species from producing viable, fertile hybrids

Reproductive isolation is caused by any factor that impedes two species from producing viable, fertile hybrids. Reproductive barriers can be categorized as **PREZYGOTIC** (premating) or **POSTZYGOTIC** (postmating).

POSTZYGOTIC: any post-mating factor that impedes two species from producing viable, fertile hybrids

PREZYGOTIC BARRIERS	
Habitat Isolation	Species occupy different habitats in the same territory.
Temporal Isolation	Populations reach sexual maturity/flower at different times of the year.
Ethological Isolation	Behavioral differences (including those mediated by pheromones and other attractants) reduce or prevent interbreeding between individuals of different species.
Mechanical Isolation	Structural differences make gamete transfer difficult or impossible.
Gametic Isolation	Male and female gametes do not attract each other; no fertilization takes place.

POSTZYGOTIC BARRIERS	
Hybrid Inviability	Hybrids die before sexual maturity
Hybrid Sterility	Sterility disrupts gamete formation; no normal sex cells develop
Hybrid Breakdown	Genetic factors reduce viability or fertility in progeny of the F_2 backcross

Geographical isolation can also lead to the origin of species. **ALLOPATRIC SPECIATION** is speciation without geographic overlap. It is the accumulation of genetic differences through division of a species' range, either through a physical barrier separating the population or through expansion by dispersal such that gene flow is cut between portions of the population. In **SYMPATRIC SPECIATION**, new species arise within the range of parent populations. Populations are sympatric if their geographical range overlaps. This usually involves the rapid accumulation of genetic differences (usually chromosomal rearrangements) that prevent interbreeding with adjacent populations.

> **ALLOPATRIC SPECIATION:** speciation without geographic overlap; genetic differences accumulate through division of a species' range, either through a physical barrier separating the population or through expansion by dispersal

> **SYMPATRIC SPECIATION:** new species arise within the range of parent populations, usually through the rapid accumulation of genetic differences

---

SKILL 17.4 Demonstrate understanding of the scientific hypotheses for the origin of life on Earth

The hypothesis that life developed on Earth from nonliving materials is the most widely accepted theory on the origin of life. The transformation from nonliving materials to life had four stages.

- In the first stage, nonliving (abiotic) matter synthesized small monomers (molecules), such as amino acids and nucleotides

- In the second stage, these monomers combined to form polymers, such as proteins and nucleic acids

- In the third stage, the accumulation of these polymers accumulated into droplets called protobionts

- In the last stage, heredity originated, with RNA as the first genetic material

In the 1920s, A. I. Oparin and J. B. S. Haldane were the first to theorize that the primitive atmosphere was a reducing atmosphere with no oxygen present. The gases were rich in hydrogen, methane, water, and ammonia. In the 1950s, Stanley Miller proved Oparin's theory in the laboratory. By combining the above gases and giving the mixture an electrical spark, he was able to synthesize simple amino acids. It is commonly accepted that amino acids appeared before DNA. Further laboratory experiments have supported that the other stages in the origin of life theory could have happened.

Other scientists believe simpler hereditary systems originated before nucleic acids. In 1991, Julius Rebek was able to synthesize a simple organic molecule that replicates itself. According to his theory, this simple molecule may be the precursor to RNA.

COMPETENCY 18
DIVERSITY OF LIFE

SKILL 18.1	Demonstrate understanding of the levels of organization and characteristics of life

LIFE HAS DEFINING PROPERTIES	
Order	Organisms show complex organization
Reproduction	Life only comes from life (biogenesis)
Energy Utilization	Organisms use and make energy to do many kinds of work
Growth and Development	DNA directs growth and development
Adaptation to the Environment	Organisms exhibit homeostasis (ability to maintain a certain status), response to stimuli, and evolution

The organization of living systems builds on levels from small to increasingly larger and more complex. *Organelles* make up *cells* which make up *tissues* which make up *organs*. Groups of organs make up *organ systems*. Organ systems work together to provide life for the *organism*. Every living system, whether it be a cell or an ecosystem, has similar requirements to sustain life.

Several characteristics have been described to identify living versus nonliving substances.

- *Living things are made of cells.* They grow, are capable of reproduction, and respond to stimuli.

- *Living things must adapt to environmental changes or perish.*

- *Living things carry on metabolic processes.* They use and make energy.

It is believed that there are probably over ten million different species of living things. Of these, 1.5 million have been named and classified. Systems of classification show similarities and also assist scientists with a worldwide system of organization.

CAROLUS LINNAEUS is termed the father of taxonomy. **TAXONOMY** is the science of classification. Linnaeus based his system on morphology (study of structure). Later on, evolutionary relationships (phylogeny) were also used to sort and group species. The modern classification system uses binomial nomenclature, providing a two-word name for every species. The genus is the first part of the name and the species is the second part. For instance, homo sapiens is the scientific name for humans. Starting with the kingdom, the classification groups get progressively smaller and more alike as one moves down the levels in the classification of humans:

CAROLUS LINNAEUS:
the father of taxonomy

TAXONOMY: the science of classification

Kingdom: Animalia, Phylum: Chordata, Subphylum: Vertebrata, Class: Mammalia, Order: Primate, Family: Hominidae, Genus: *Homo*, Species: *sapiens*

Species are defined by the ability to successfully reproduce with members of their own kind.

MORPHOLOGICAL CRITERIA USED TO CLASSIFY ORGANISMS	
Ancestral Characters	Characteristics that remain unchanged even after millennia of evolution (i.e., five digits on the hand of an ape).
Derived Characters	characteristics that have evolved more recently (i.e., the absence of a tail on an ape).
Conservative Characters	Traits that change slowly.
Homologous Characters	Characteristics with the same genetic basis but used differently (i.e., wing of a bat, arm of a human. The bone structures have the same origin, but the limbs have different purposes.)
Analogous Characters	Structures that differ in their anatomical origins but are used for similar purposes (i.e., the wing of a bird and the wing of a butterfly).
Convergent Evolution	Development of similar adaptations by organisms that are unrelated.

Demonstrate knowledge of the characteristics of viruses, bacteria, protists, fungi, plants, and animals

Viruses, Prokaryotes, and Protists

MICROBIOLOGY includes the study of monera (prokaryotes), protists, and viruses.

MICROBIOLOGY: the study of monera (prokaryotes), protists, and viruses

Viruses

Although **VIRUSES** are not classified as living things, they greatly affect other living things by disrupting cell activity. They are considered to be obligate parasites because they rely on the host for their own reproduction. Viruses are composed of a protein coat and a nucleic acid, either DNA or RNA. A bacteriophage is a virus that infects a bacterium. Animal viruses are classified by the type of nucleic acid, presence of RNA replicase, and presence of a protein coat.

VIRUS: composed of a protein coat and a nucleic acid—either DNA or RNA, disrupt cell activity, are obligate parasites that rely on the host for their reproduction

There are two types of viral reproductive cycles:

1. Lytic cycle: The virus enters the host cell and makes copies of its nucleic acids and protein coats and reassembles. It then lyses or breaks out of the host cell and infects other nearby cells, repeating the process.

2. Lysogenic cycle: The virus may remain dormant within the cells until something initiates it to break out of the cell. Herpes is an example of a lysogenic virus.

Archaebacteria and eubacteria

Archaebacteria and eubacteria are the two main branches of prokaryotic (moneran) evolution.

PRINCIPAL CHARACTERISTICS OF ARCHAEBACTERIA AND EUBACTERIA
ARCHAEBACTERIA
Contain no peptidoglycan in the cell wall
Are not inhibited by antibiotics
Have several kinds of RNA polymerase
Lack a nuclear envelope

Continued on next page

EUBACTERIA (BACTERIA)
Have peptidoglycan in the cell wall
Are susceptible to antibiotics
Have one kind of RNA polymerase
Lack a nuclear envelope

ARCHAEBACTERIA evolved from the earliest cells, and most inhabit extreme environments. There are three main groups of archaebacteria: Methanogens are strict anaerobes, extreme halophiles live in high salt concentrations, and extreme thermophiles live in hot environments (hot springs).

Most prokaryotes fall into the **EUBACTERIA** (bacteria) domain. **BACTERIA** are divided according to their morphology (shape). Bacilli are rod-shaped bacteria, cocci are round bacteria, and spirilli are spiral shaped. Bacteria reproduce by binary fission, an asexual process that simply divides the bacterium in half. All new organisms are exact clones of the parent. Some bacteria have a sticky capsule that protects the cell wall and is also used for adhesion to surfaces. Pili are surface appendages for adhesion to other cells.

Bacteria locomotion is via flagella or taxis. **TAXIS** is the movement toward or away from a stimulus. Bacteria obtain nutrition by three methods:

- Photosynthetic organisms (producers) convert sunlight to chemical energy,
- Heterotrophs (consumers) consume other living organisms
- Saprophytes (consumers) live off dead or decaying material

Protists

PROTISTS are the earliest eukaryotic descendants of prokaryotes. Found almost anywhere there is water, protists can be broadly defined as the eukaryotic microorganisms and include the macroscopic algae with only a single tissue type. Protists are defined by exclusion of characteristics common to the other kingdoms.

- They are not prokaryotes because they (usually) have a true nucleus and organelles bound by a membrane (nuclear envelope).
- They are not fungi because fungi lack undulopidia (cilia) and develop from spores.
- They are not plants because plants develop from embryos
- They are not animals because animals develop from a blastula.

ARCHAEBACTERIA: evolved from the earliest cells, and most inhabit extreme environments

EUBACTERIA: most prokaryotes other than Archaebacteria

BACTERIUM: classified according to shape; reproduce by binary fission, an asexual process that simply divides the bacterium in half

TAXIS: the movement toward or away from a stimulus

PROTISTS: the earliest eukaryotic descendants of prokaryotes

Most protists have a true (membrane-bound) nucleus, complex organelles (mitochondria, chloroplasts, etc.), aerobic respiration in mitochondria, and undulipodiua in some life stage.

ARCHAEZOA: lack mitochondria, the Golgi apparatus, and have multiple nuclei

CHROMISTA: include diatoms, brown algae, and "golden" algae with chlorophyll c and have a different photosynthetic plastid from those of the green algae and plants

Most protists have a true (membrane-bound) nucleus, complex organelles (mitochondria, chloroplasts, etc.), aerobic respiration in mitochondria, and undulipodiua in some life stage.

Protist classification and nomenclature

The chaotic status of names and concepts of the higher classification of the protists reflects their great diversity of form, function, and life cycles. The protists are often grouped as algae (plant-like), protozoa (animal-like), or fungus-like, based on the similarity of their lifestyle and characteristics to these more derived groups. Two distinctive groups of protists are considered for separation as their own kingdoms. The **ARCHAEZOA** lack mitochondria, the Golgi apparatus, and have multiple nuclei. The **CHROMISTA**, including diatoms, brown algae, and "golden" algae with chlorophyll c, have a very different photosynthetic plastid from those found in the green algae and plants.

Fungi

The fungi are characterized by a short-lived diploid stage, which can be viewed only under a microscope. The structures that are visible to the naked eye are typically puffballs, mushrooms, and shelf fungi that represent the dikaryote form of the fungi. The haploid stages are commonly observed as the absorptive hyphae or as asexual reproductive sporangia.

The impact of viruses, bacteria, and fungi

Although bacteria and fungi may cause disease, they are also beneficial for use as medicines and food. Penicillin is derived from a fungus that is capable of destroying the cell wall of bacteria. Most antibiotics work in this way. Some antibiotics can interfere with bacterial DNA replication or can disrupt the bacterial ribosome without affecting the host cells. Viral diseases have been fought through the use of vaccination, where a small amount of the virus is introduced so the immune system is able to recognize it upon later infection. Antibodies are more quickly manufactured when the host has had prior exposure.

The majority of prokaryotes decompose material for use by the environment and other organisms. The eukaryotic fungi are the most important decomposers in the biosphere. They break down organic material to be used up by other living organisms.

The eukaryotic fungi are the most important decomposers in the biosphere

Nonvascular Plants

Small in size, the nonvascular plants do not require vascular tissue (**XYLEM AND PHLOEM**) since individual cells are close to their environment. The nonvascular plants have no true leaves, stems, or roots.

Division Bryophyta (mosses and liverworts): These plants have a dominant gametophyte generation. They possess rhizoids, which are rootlike structures and require moisture in their environment for reproduction and absorption.

> **XYLEM AND PHLOEM:** tubular structures that enable the transport of water and minerals to the top of the plant and food manufactured in the leaves to the bottom of the plant

Vascular Plants

The development of vascular tissue (xylem and phloem) enabled vascular plants to grow in size because they could transport water, minerals, and manufactured food throughout the plant. All vascular plants have a dominant sporophyte generation.

Division Lycophyta (club mosses): These plants reproduce with spores and require water for reproduction.

Division Sphenophyta (horsetails): These plants have small, needle-like leaves and rhizoids, also reproduce with spores, and require moisture for reproduction.

Division Pterophyta (ferns): These plants reproduce with spores and flagellated sperm, have a true stem, and need moisture for reproduction.

GYMNOSPERM means "naked seed." These were the first plants to evolve the use of seeds for reproduction, which made them less dependent on water to assist in reproduction. Their seeds, as well as pollen from the male, could travel by the wind. Gymnosperms have cones that protect the seeds.

Division Cycadophyta (cycads): These plants look like palms with cones.

Divison Ghetophyta: These plants are desert dwellers.

Division Coniferophyta (pines): These plants have needles and cones.

Divison Ginkgophyta: The Ginkgo is the only member of this division.

ANGIOSPERMS (Division Anthophyta) are the largest group in the plant kingdom. They are the flowering plants and produce true seeds for reproduction.

> **GYMNOSPERM:** means "naked seed"; the first plants to evolve the use of seeds for reproduction, which made them less dependent on water to assist in reproduction

> **ANGIOSPERMS:** the largest group in the plant kingdom, they are the flowering plants and produce true seeds for reproduction

Animals

DEVELOPMENT is defined as a change in form. Animals go through several stages of development after fertilization of the egg cell:

DEVELOPMENT: a change in form

- Cleavage: These first divisions of the fertilized egg continue until the egg forms a blastula.

- Blastula: The blastula is a hollow ball of undifferentiated cells.

- Gastrulation: During this stage, tissue differentiates into the separate germ layers: In general, the ectoderm (outer layer) becomes the epidermis or skin. The mesoderm (middle layer) becomes muscles and other organs beside the gut. The endoderm (inner layer) becomes the gut, also called the archenteron.

- Neuralation: The nervous system develops.

- Organogenesis: The various organs develop.

Diploblastic animals

Sponges are the simplest animals, lack true tissue, and exhibit no symmetry. **DIPLOBLASTIC ANIMALS** have only two germ layers, the ectoderm and endoderm, and lack a true digestive system. Diploblastic animals include the Cnideria (jellyfish), which exhibit radial symmetry.

DIPLOBLASTIC ANIMALS: have only two germ layers, the ectoderm and endoderm, and lack a true digestive system

Triploblastic animals

TRIPLOBLASTIC ANIMALS have all three germ layers and exhibit three basic structures:

TRIPLOBLASTIC ANIMALS: have all three germ layers

- Acoelomates have no defined body cavity. For example, the flatworm (Platyhelminthe) must absorb food from a host's digestive system.

- Pseudocoelomates have a body cavity, but it is not lined by tissue from the mesoderm. An example is the roundworm (*Nematoda*).

- Coelomates have a true, fluid-filled body cavity called a coelom, derived from the mesoderm. Coelomates can further be divided into protostomes and deuterostomes. In the development of *protostomes*, the first opening becomes the mouth and the second opening becomes the anus. The mesoderm splits to form the coelom. Protostomes include animals in phylums *Mollusca*, *Annelida* and *Arthropoda*. In the development of *deuterostomes*, the mouth develops from the second opening and the anus from the first opening. The mesoderm hollows out to become the coelom. Deuterostomes include animals in phylums *Echinodermata* and *Vertebrata*.

COMPETENCY 19
PLANTS

Demonstrate understanding of the characteristics of vascular and nonvascular plants

The **NONVASCULAR PLANTS** represent a grade of evolution characterized by several primitive features:

- Lack of roots and conducting tissues
- Reliance on random absorption of water or high humidity
- Lack of typical leaves (in ferns have microphylls)

Groups include the liverworts, hornworts, and mosses, each recognized as a separate division.

The characteristics of **VASCULAR PLANTS** are as follows:

- Synthesis of lignin to give rigidity and strength to cell walls for growing upright
- Evolution of tracheid cells for water transport and sieve cells for nutrient transport
- The use of underground stems (rhizomes) as a structure from which adventitious roots originate.

There are two kinds of vascular plants: nonseeded and seeded. (*See Skill 18.3 for divisions.*) The seeded vascular plants differ from the nonseeded plants by their method of reproduction.

The vascular seed plants are divided into two groups—the gymnosperms and the angiosperms. *Gymnosperms* were the first plants to evolve with the use of seeds for reproduction.

Angiosperms, the largest group in the plant kingdom, are the flowering plants and produce true seeds for reproduction. They arose about seventy million years ago when the dinosaurs were disappearing, and the environment was becoming drier. The plants' ability to produce seeds that could remain dormant until conditions became acceptable allowed for their success. Angiosperms also have more advanced vascular tissue and larger leaves for increased photosynthesis.

NONVASCULAR PLANTS: characterized by several primitive features: lack of roots, conducting tissues, and leaves; rely on absorption of water that falls on the plant or live in a zone of high humidity

VASCULAR PLANTS: characterized by lignin, which gives strength for growing upright, tracheid cells for water transport and sieve cells for nutrient transport, and underground root systems

MONOCOTS: have one cotelydon (seed leaf) with parallel veins on their leaves and flower petals in multiples of threes

Angiosperms consist of only one division, the Anthrophyta, but are divided into monocots and dicots. **MONOCOTS** have one cotelydon (seed leaf) with parallel veins on their leaves and flower petals in multiples of threes. **DICOTS** have two cotelydons with branching leaf veins and flower petals in multiples of fours or fives.

See also Skill 18.3

SKILL 19.2 **Demonstrate understanding of the structure and function of roots, stems, and leaves**

DICOTS: have two cotelydons with branching leaf veins and flower petals in multiples of fours or fives

Roots absorb water and minerals and exchange gases in the soil.

Roots

Roots absorb water and minerals and exchange gases in the soil. Like stems, roots contain *xylem* and *phloem*. The xylem transports water and minerals, called *xylem sap*, upwards. The sugar produced by photosynthesis travels down the phloem in the *phloem sap* to the roots and other nonphotosynthetic parts of the plant. In addition to water and mineral absorption, roots anchor plants in place, preventing erosion by environmental conditions.

Stems

Stems are the major support structure of plants, consisting primarily of three types of tissue: dermal tissue, ground tissue, and vascular tissue. Dermal tissue covers the outside surface of the stem to prevent excessive water loss and control gas exchange. Ground tissue consists mainly of parenchyma cells and surrounds the vascular tissue, providing support and protection. Finally, vascular tissue, xylem and phloem, provide long distance transport of nutrients and water.

Leaves

Stomata allow oxygen to move in or out of the plant and carbon dioxide to move in.

Leaves enable plants to capture light and carbon dioxide for photosynthesis. Photosynthesis occurs primarily in the leaves. Plants exchange gases through their leaves via stomata, small openings, on the underside of the leaves. Stomata allow oxygen to move in or out of the plant and carbon dioxide to move in. Leaf size and shape varies greatly between species of plants. Botanists often identify plants by their characteristic leaf patterns.

See also skill 19.5

SKILL 19.3 Demonstrate understanding of control mechanisms *(for example, hormones, photoperiods, and tropisms)*

PLANT HORMONES, or plant growth regulators, are chemicals, secreted internally by plants, that regulate growth and development. Plant hormones are present in low concentrations, produced in specific locations, and often act on cells at other locations. The mechanism of **HORMONAL SIGNALING** involves attachment of hormone molecules to protein receptors, transmission of the signal along a transduction pathway, and the activation of particular genes. The five major classes of plant growth regulators are: (1) auxins, (2) abscisic acid, (3) gibberellins, (4) ethylene, and (5) cytokinins.

Auxins play a major role in many growth and behavioral processes. Auxins promote cell elongation in growing shoot tips and cell expansion in swelling roots and fruits. In addition, auxins promote apical dominance, the tendency of the main stem of plants to grow more strongly than the side stems. Auxins induce **PHOTOTROPISM** (the tendency of plants to bend toward light), stimulation of ethylene synthesis and cell division, and inhibition of abscission (leaf shedding).

- Abscisic acid: (ABA) plays an important role in promoting dormancy, inhibiting growth, responding to water stress, and preventing fruit from ripening. High levels of ABA induce seed dormancy and inhibit germination. In addition, ABA build-up during water stress promotes closing of stomata (pores).

- Gibberellins: Have a wide range of effects, the most being stem elongation. Gibberellins also promote flower and fruit formation and stimulate the growth and development of seeds.

- Ethylene: Is the major hormone involved in fruit ripening and plant part abscission. Ethylene also induces seed germination, root hair growth, and flowering.

- Cytokinins: Play a key role in cell division. Cytokinins promote shoot development, chlorophyll production, and photosynthesis; inhibit root development; and delay senescence in flowers and fruits.

A **PHOTOPERIOD** is the duration of a plant's daily exposure to light. Variations in the length of photoperiods affect the growth, development, and physiological processes of plants. For example, plants adapt to seasonal changes in photoperiods by increasing or decreasing growth processes and changing patterns of photosynthesis and respiration. In addition, over time, species of plants develop traits that allow them to thrive in the characteristic photoperiods of their native environment.

PLANT HORMONES: chemicals, secreted internally by plants, that regulate growth and development

HORMONAL SIGNALING: involves attachment of hormone molecules to protein receptors, transmission of the signal along a transduction pathway, and the activation of particular genes

PHOTOTROPISM: the tendency of plants to bend toward light

PHOTOPERIOD: the duration of a plant's daily exposure to light

Variations in the length of photoperiods affect the growth, development, and physiological processes of plants.

Demonstrate understanding of water and nutrient uptake and transport systems

See Skill 19.2.

Demonstrate understanding of sexual and asexual reproduction in plants

> **ALTERNATION OF GENERATIONS:** a haploid stage in the plant's life history alternates with a diploid stage

Reproduction by plants is accomplished through **ALTERNATION OF GENERATIONS** in which a haploid stage in the plant's life history alternates with a diploid stage. The diploid sporophyte divides by meiosis to reduce the chromosome number to the haploid gametophyte generation. The haploid gametophytes undergo mitosis to produce gametes (sperm and eggs), and fertilized haploid gametes then return to the diploid sporophyte stage.

The diploid sporophyte divides by meiosis to reduce the chromosome number to the haploid gametophyte generation. The haploid gametophytes undergo mitosis to produce gametes (sperm and eggs), and fertilized haploid gametes then return to the diploid sporophyte stage.

Both the nonvascular plants and the vascular nonseeded plants need water to reproduce. Gymnosperms use seeds for reproduction and do not require water.

Angiosperms are the most numerous plants and therefore are the main focus of reproduction in this section. The sporophyte is the dominant phase in angiosperm reproduction. Angiosperm reproductive structures are the flowers.

Flower Reproductive Structure

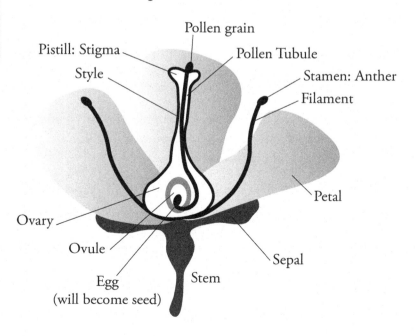

The male gametophytes are pollen grains, and the female gametophytes are embryo sacs that are inside of the ovules. The male pollen grains are formed in the anthers at the tips of the stamens. The female ovules are enclosed by the ovaries. The stamen is the reproductive organ of the male and the carpel is the reproductive organ of the female.

In a process called pollination, the pollen grains are released from the anthers, are carried by animals and the wind, and land on the carpels. The sperm is released to fertilize the eggs. Angiosperms reproduce through a method of double fertilization: An ovum is fertilized by two sperm. One sperm produces the new plant, and the other forms the food supply for the developing plant (endosperm). The ovule develops into a seed and the ovary develops into a fruit. The fruit is then carried by wind or animals and the seeds are dispersed to form new plants.

Angiosperms reproduce through a method of double fertilization: An ovum is fertilized by two sperm.

The development of the egg to form a plant occurs in three stages:

1. Growth

2. Morphogenesis: the development of form

3. Cellular differentiation: the acquisition of each cell's specific structure and function

Asexual reproduction, is simple cellular duplication in which no eggs or sperm are involved. Example: Bacteria reproduce by simply dividing in half.

In sexual reproduction, the process of meiosis producing gametes provides variability. Genetic variability is the key to survival of a species. Variability improves the offspring, making them more able to adapt to new environments.

Genetic variability is the key to survival of a species. Variability improves the offspring, making them more able to adapt to new environments.

COMPETENCY 20
ANIMALS

> **SKILL 20.1** Demonstrate understanding of the anatomy and physiology of structures associated with life functions of organisms in the animal kingdom: digestion; circulation; respiration; excretion; nervous control; musculo-skeletal system; immunity; the endocrine system; reproduction; and development

Skeletal System

The skeletal system functions to support the body. Vertebrates have an endoskeleton, with muscles attached to bones. Skeletal proportions are controlled by area to volume relationships: Body size and shape are limited due to the forces of gravity; surface area is increased to improve efficiency in all organ systems.

The axial skeleton consists of the bones of the skull and vertebrae. The appendicular skeleton consists of the bones of the legs, arms and tail and shoulder girdle.

Bone is a connective tissue. Parts of the bone include compact bone, which gives strength; spongy bone, which contains red marrow to make blood cells; yellow marrow in the center of long bones, which stores fat cells; and the periosteum, which is the protective covering on the outside of the bone.

A joint is defined as a place where two bones meet. Joints enable movement. Ligaments attach bone to bone. Tendons attach bones to muscles.

Muscular System

The muscular system enables the organism to move. There are three types of muscle tissue: Skeletal muscle, which attaches to bone, is voluntary, meaning the organism has conscious control over it. Smooth muscle, found in organs, is involuntary, meaning the organism has no conscious control over it, enables functions such as digestion and respiration. Cardiac muscle is a specialized type of smooth muscle found in the heart. Muscles can only contract; therefore they work in antagonistic pairs to allow back and forward movement. Muscle fibers are made of groups of myofibrils, which, in turn, are made of groups of sarcomeres. Actin and myosin are proteins, which make up the sarcomere.

Physiology of muscle contraction

When a nerve impulse strikes a muscle fiber, it causes calcium ions to flood the sarcomere. Calcium ions allow ATP to expend energy. The myosin fibers creep along the actin fibers causing the muscle to contract. Once the nerve impulse has passed, calcium is pumped out and the contraction ends.

Nervous System

The **NEURON** is the basic unit of the nervous system. It consists of an axon that carries impulses away from the cell body, the dendrite that carries impulses toward the cell body, and the cell body that contains the nucleus. **SYNAPSES** are spaces between neurons. Chemicals called neurotransmitters are found close to the synapse. The **MYELIN SHEATH**, composed of Schwann cells, covers the neurons and provides insulation.

Organization of the nervous system

The somatic nervous system is controlled consciously. It consists of the central nervous system (brain and spinal cord) and the peripheral nervous system (nerves that extend from the spinal cord to the muscles). The hypothalamus in the brain unconsciously controls the autonomic nervous system, which regulates, for instance, smooth muscles, the heart, and digestion. It is split into two systems: The sympathetic nervous system works in opposition to the parasympathetic nervous system. For example, if the sympathetic nervous system stimulates an action, the parasympathetic nervous system ends that action.

Physiology of a nerve impulse

Nerve action depends on depolarization and an imbalance of electrical charges across the neuron. A polarized nerve has a positive charge outside the neuron. A depolarized nerve has a negative charge outside the neuron. Neurotransmitters turn off the sodium pump, which results in depolarization of the membrane. This wave of depolarization (as it moves from neuron to neuron) carries an electrical impulse. This is actually a wave of opening and closing gates that allows for the flow of ions across the synapse. Nerves have an action potential. There is a threshold for the level of chemicals that must be met or exceeded in order for muscles to respond. This is called the "all-or-none" response.

The reflex arc is the simplest nerve response and bypasses the brain. When a stimulus (like touching a hot stove) occurs, sensors in the hand send the message directly to the spinal cord, which stimulates motor neurons that contract the muscles to move the hand.

NEURON: the basic unit of the nervous system consists of an axon that carries impulses away from the cell body, the dendrite that carries impulses toward the cell body, and the cell body that contains the nucleus

SYNAPSES: spaces between neurons

MYELIN SHEATH: composed of Schwann cells, covers the neurons and provides insulation

Nerve action depends on depolarization and an imbalance of electrical charges across the neuron.

Voluntary nerve responses involve the brain. Receptor cells send the message to sensory neurons, which lead to association neurons, which transport the message to the brain. Motor neurons are stimulated and the message is transmitted to effector cells, which cause the end effect.

Neurotransmitters

NEUROTRANSMITTERS are chemicals released by exocytosis that either stimulate or inhibit action.

- Acetylcholine, the most common neurotransmitter, controls muscle contraction and heartbeat. The enzyme acetylcholinesterase breaks it down to end the transmission.

- Epinephrine, also called adrenaline, is responsible for the "fight-or-flight" reaction. It causes an increase in heart rate and blood flow to prepare the body for action.

- Endorphins and enkephalins are natural pain killers and are released during serious injury and childbirth.

> **NEUROTRANSMITTER:** chemical that either stimulates or inhibits action

Digestive System

The function of the DIGESTIVE SYSTEM is to break food down and absorb it into the blood stream where it can be delivered to all the body's cells for use in cellular respiration. The teeth and saliva begin digestion by breaking food down into smaller pieces and lubricating it so it can be swallowed. The lips, cheeks, and tongue form a bolus or ball of food, which is carried down the pharynx by the process of PERISTALSIS (wavelike contractions). The bolus enters the stomach through the cardiac sphincter, which closes to keep food from going back up. In the stomach, pepsinogen and hydrochloric acid form pepsin, the enzyme that breaks down proteins. The food is broken down further by this chemical action and is churned into chyme. The pyloric sphincter muscle opens to allow the food to enter the small intestine. Most nutrient absorption occurs in the small intestine whose length and protrusions called villi and microvilli allow for a great absorptive surface into the bloodstream. Acidic chyme is neutralized to allow the enzymes found there to function. Any food left after the trip through the small intestine enters the large intestine. The large intestine reabsorbs water and produces vitamin K. The feces, or remaining waste, are passed out through the anus.

> **DIGESTIVE SYSTEM:** breaks food down and absorbs it into the blood stream where it can be delivered to all the body's cells for use in cellular respiration

> **PERISTALSIS:** wavelike contractions

Accessory organs

Although not part of the digestive tract, these organs function in the production of necessary enzymes and bile. The pancreas makes many enzymes to break down food in the small intestine. The liver makes bile, which breaks down and emulsifies fatty acids

Respiratory System

The RESPIRATORY SYSTEM delivers oxygen to the bloodstream and picks up carbon dioxide for release out of the body. Air enters the mouth and nose, where it is warmed, moistened, and filtered of dust and particles. Cilia in the trachea trap unwanted material in mucus, which can be expelled. The trachea splits into two bronchial tubes and the bronchial tubes divide into smaller and smaller bronchioles in the lungs. The internal surface of the lung is composed of alveoli, which are thin-walled air sacs, which provide a large surface area for gas exchange. The alveoli are lined with capillaries. Oxygen diffuses into the bloodstream, and carbon dioxide diffuses out to be exhaled by the lungs. The oxygenated blood is carried to the heart and delivered to all parts of the body.

The thoracic cavity holds the lungs. Below the lungs, the diaphragm, a muscle, makes inhalation possible. As the volume of the thoracic cavity increases, the diaphragm muscle flattens out and inhalation occurs. When the diaphragm relaxes, exhalation occurs.

> **RESPIRATORY SYSTEM** delivers oxygen to the bloodstream and picks up carbon dioxide for release out of the body

Circulatory System

The CIRCULATORY SYSTEM carries oxygenated blood and nutrients to all cells of the body and returns carbon dioxide waste to be expelled from the lungs. Unoxygenated blood enters the right atrium of the heart through the inferior and superior vena cava. The blood flows through the tricuspid valve to the right ventricle to the pulmonary arteries and then to the lungs where it is oxygenated. It returns to the heart through the pulmonary vein into the left atrium, travels through the bicuspid valve to the left ventricle from where it is pumped to all parts of the body through the aorta.

The sinoatrial node (SA node), located on the right atrium, is the heart's pacemaker, responsible for contraction of the right and left atrium. The atrioventricular node (AV node), located on the left ventricle, is responsible for contraction of the ventricles.

> **CIRCULATORY SYSTEM:** carries oxygenated blood and nutrients to all cells of the body and returns carbon dioxide waste to be expelled from the lungs

TYPES OF BLOOD VESSELS	
Arteries	Lead away from the heart. All arteries carry oxygenated blood except the pulmonary artery going to the lungs. Arteries are under high pressure.
Arterioles	Smaller vessels that branch off from arteries.
Capillaries	Tiniest vessels that branch off from arterioles and reach every cell. Because of the small size of the vessels, blood moves slowest here; only one red blood cell may pass at a time to allow for diffusion of gases into and out of cells and absorption of nutrients.
Venules	Larger vessels formed when capillaries combine. The vessels are now carrying waste products from the cells.
Veins	Larger vessels formed when venules combine and lead back to the heart. Veins and venules have thinner walls than arteries because they are not under as much pressure. Veins contain valves to prevent the backward flow of blood due to the force of gravity.

COMPONENTS OF BLOOD	
Plasma	60% of the blood is plasma, which contains salts called electrolytes, nutrients, and waste. Plasma is the liquid part of blood.
Erythrocytes	Also called red blood cells, they contain hemoglobin which carries oxygen molecules.
Leukocytes	Also called white blood cells, leukocytes are larger than red cells. They are phagocytic and can engulf invaders. White blood cells are not confined to the blood vessels and can enter the interstitial fluid between cells.
Platelets	Platelets are made in the bone marrow and assist in blood clotting.

The process of blood clotting

The neurotransmitter that initiates blood vessel constriction following an injury is called serotonin. A material called prothrombin is converted to thrombin with the help of thromboplastin. The thrombin is then used to convert fibrinogen to fibrin, which traps red blood cells to form a scab and stop blood flow.

Lymphatic System (Immune System)

IMMUNITY is the body's ability to recognize and destroy an antigen before it causes harm. Active immunity develops after recovery from an infectious disease (chicken pox) or after a vaccination (mumps, measles, rubella). Passive immunity may be passed from one individual to another but is not permanent. A good example is the immunities passed from mother to nursing child.

> **IMMUNITY:** the body's ability to recognize and destroy an antigen before it causes harm

NONSPECIFIC DEFENSE MECHANISMS do not target specific pathogens, but are a whole body response, seen as symptoms of an infection. These mechanisms include the skin, mucous membranes, and cells of the blood and lymph (i.e., white blood cells, macrophages). Fever is a result of an increase in white blood cells. Pyrogens are released by white blood cells, which set the body's thermostat to a higher temperature. This both inhibits the growth of microorganisms and increases metabolism to increase phagocytosis and body repair.

Specific defense mechanisms recognize foreign material, including individual pathogens, and respond by destroying the invader. An antigen is any foreign particle that invades the body. In response, the body manufactures antibodies that recognize and latch onto antigens, intent on destroying them. These mechanisms are specific and diverse. They also can recognize the self. Memory of the invaders provides immunity upon further exposure.

Excretory system

The EXCRETORY SYSTEM rids the body of nitrogenous wastes in the form of urea. The functional unit of excretion is the NEPHRON, which make up the kidneys. Antidiuretic hormone (ADH), which is made in the hypothalamus and stored in the pituitary, is released when differences in osmotic balance occur and causes more water to be reabsorbed. As the blood becomes more dilute, ADH release ends.

The Bowman's capsule contains the glomerulus, a tightly packed group of capillaries. The glomerulus is under high pressure, causing waste and fluids to leak out. Filtration is not selective in this area. Selective secretion by active and passive transport occur in the proximal convoluted tubule. Unwanted molecules are secreted into the filtrate. Selective secretion also occurs in the loop of Henle. Salt is actively pumped out of the tube and much water is lost due to the hyperosmosity of the inner part (medulla) of the kidney. As the fluid enters the distal convoluted tubule, more water is reabsorbed. Urine forms in the collecting duct, which leads to the ureter and then to the bladder where it is stored. Urine is passed from the bladder through the urethra. The amount of water reabsorbed back into the body is dependent upon how much water or fluids an individual has consumed. Urine can be very dilute or very concentrated if dehydration is present.

Endocrine System

The ENDOCRINE SYSTEM manufactures proteins called hormones that are released into the bloodstream and carried to a target tissue where they stimulate an action. Hormones may build up over time to cause their effect, as in puberty or the menstrual cycle.

NONSPECIFIC DEFENSE MECHANISMS: do not target specific pathogens, but are a whole body response, seen as symptoms of an infection

EXCRETORY SYSTEM: rids the body of nitrogenous wastes in the form of urea

NEPHRON: the functional unit of excretion that makes up the kidneys

ENDOCRINE SYSTEM: manufactures proteins called hormones that are released into the bloodstream and carried to a target tissue where they stimulate an action

Hormone activation

Hormones are specific and fit receptors on the target tissue cell surface. The receptor activates an enzyme that converts ATP to cyclic AMP. Cyclic AMP (cAMP) is a second messenger from the cell membrane to the nucleus. The genes found in the nucleus turn on or off to cause a specific response. Hormones work on a feedback system: The increase or decrease in one hormone may cause the increase or decrease in another.

> Hormones are specific and fit receptors on the target tissue cell surface.

Classes of hormones

There are two classes of hormones: Steroid hormones come from cholesterol. Steroid hormones, such as estrogen and progesterone in females and testosterone in males, cause sexual characteristics and mating behavior. Peptide hormones are made in the pituitary, adrenal glands on the kidneys, and the pancreas.

- Follicle stimulating hormone (FSH) assists in production of sperm or egg cells
- Luteinizing hormone (LH) functions in ovulation
- Luteotropic hormone (LTH) assists in production of progesterone
- Growth hormone (GH) stimulates growth
- Antidiuretic hormone (ADH) assists in retention of water
- Oxytocin stimulates labor contractions at birth and let-down of milk
- Melatonin regulates circadian rhythms and seasonal changes
- Epinephrine (adrenalin) causes fight-or-flight reaction of the nervous system
- Thyroxin increases metabolic rate
- Calcitonin removes calcium from the blood
- Insulin decreases glucose level in blood
- Glucagon increases glucose level in blood

Reproductive System

Sexual reproduction greatly increases diversity because of the many combinations possible through meiosis and fertilization. GAMETOGENESIS is the production of the sperm and egg cells. Spermatogenesis begins at puberty in the male. One spermatozoa produces four sperm, which mature in the seminiferous tubules located in the testes. Oogenesis, the production of egg cells, is usually complete by the birth of a female. Egg cells are not released until menstruation begins at puberty. Meiosis forms one ovum with all the cytoplasm and three polar bodies

> GAMETOGENESIS: the production of the sperm and egg cells

that are reabsorbed by the body. The ova are stored in the ovaries and released each month from puberty to menopause.

Path of the sperm
Sperm are stored in the seminiferous tubules in the testes where they mature. Mature sperm are found in the epididymis located on top of the testes. After ejaculation, the sperm travels up the vas deferens where they mix with semen made in the prostate and seminal vesicles and travel out the urethra.

Path of the egg
Ovulation releases the egg from the ovary into the fallopian tubes, which are ciliated to move the egg along. Fertilization normally occurs in the fallopian tube. If pregnancy does not occur, the egg passes through the uterus and is expelled through the vagina during menstruation. Levels of progesterone and estrogen stimulate menstruation and are affected by the implantation of a fertilized egg so menstruation does not occur.

Pregnancy
If fertilization occurs, the zygote implants in about two to three days in the uterus. Implantation promotes secretion of human chorionic gonadotrophin (HCG). This is what is detected in pregnancy tests. The HCG keeps the level of progesterone elevated to maintain the uterine lining to feed the developing embryo until the umbilical cord forms. Labor is initiated by oxytocin, which causes contractions and dilation of the cervix. Prolactin and oxytocin cause the production of milk.

Fertilization normally occurs in the fallopian tube.

The HCG keeps the level of progesterone elevated to maintain the uterine lining to feed the developing embryo until the umbilical cord forms.

Cell membranes are selectively permeable, which is the key to transport. Not all molecules may pass through easily. Some molecules require energy or carrier molecules and may only cross when needed.

SKILL 20.2 Demonstrate knowledge of homeostasis and how it is maintained

HOMEOSTASIS, or balance of the cell with its external environment, is made possible by cell transport. Cell membranes are selectively permeable, which is the key to transport. Not all molecules may pass through easily. Some molecules require energy or carrier molecules and may only cross when needed.

The molecular composition of the immediate environment outside of the organism is not the same as it is inside, and the temperature outside may not be optimal for metabolic activity within the organism. Homeostasis is the control of these

HOMEOSTASIS: the control of the differences between internal and external environments, is made possible by cell transport

OSMOREGULATION: the maintenance of the appropriate level of water and salts in body, fluids for optimum cellular functions

EXCRETION: the elimination of metabolic waste products from the body, including excess water

differences between internal and external environments. There are three homeostatic systems to regulate these differences:

OSMOREGULATION deals with maintenance of the appropriate level of water and salts in body fluids for optimum cellular functions. **EXCRETION** is the elimination of metabolic waste products from the body, including excess water. **THERMOREGULATION** maintains the internal, or core, body temperature of the organism within a tolerable range for metabolic and cellular processes.

The thyroid gland produces hormones that help maintain heart rate, blood pressure, muscle tone, digestion, and reproductive functions. The parathyroid glands maintain the calcium level in blood, and the pancreas maintains glucose homeostasis by secreting insulin and glucagon when necessary. The three gonadal steroids— androgen (testosterone), estrogen, and progesterone— regulate the development of the male and female reproductive organs.

SKILL 20.3 Demonstrate knowledge of how animals respond to stimuli

THERMOREGULATION: maintains the internal, or core, body temperature of the organism within a tolerable range for metabolic and cellular processes

Any detectable change in the internal or external environment (the stimulus) may trigger a response in an organism.

RESPONSES TO STIMULI: adaptations that allow organisms to better survive

Response to stimuli is one of the key characteristics of any living thing. Any detectable change in the internal or external environment (the stimulus) may trigger a response in an organism. Just like physical characteristics, organisms' **RESPONSES TO STIMULI** are adaptations that allow them to better survive. While these responses may be more noticeable in animals that can move quickly, all organisms are capable of responding to changes.

Lower members of the animal kingdom have responses similar to those seen in single-celled organisms. Higher animals, however, have developed complex systems to detect and respond to stimuli. The nervous system, sensory organs (eyes, ears, skin, etc.), and muscle tissue all allow animals to sense and quickly respond to changes in their environment.

As in other organisms, many responses to stimuli in animals are involuntary. For example, pupils dilate in response to the reduction of light. Such reactions are typically called reflexes. Many animals, however, also are capable of voluntary responses. In many animal species, voluntary reactions are instinctual. For instance, a zebra's response to a lion is a *voluntary* one, but, *instinctually*, it will flee quickly as soon as the lion's presence is sensed. Complex voluntary responses, which may or may not be instinctual, are typically termed behavior. An example is the annual migration of birds when seasons change. Even more complex social behavior is seen in animals that live in large groups.

168

COMPETENCY 21
ECOLOGY

Demonstrate understanding of population dynamics

BIOTIC FACTORS are living things in an ecosystem, such as plants, animals, bacteria, and fungi. If one population in a community increases, it affects the ability of another population to succeed by limiting the amount of available food, water, shelter, and space.

ABIOTIC FACTORS are nonliving aspects of an ecosystem, such as soil quality, rainfall, and temperature. Changes in climate and soil can cause effects at the beginning of the food chain, thus limiting or accelerating the growth of population.

A **POPULATION** is a group of individuals of one species that live in the same general area. Many factors can affect the population size and its growth rate. Population size can depend on the total amount of life a habitat can support. This is the **CARRYING CAPACITY** of the environment. Once the habitat runs out of food, water, shelter, or space, the carrying capacity decreases, and then stabilizes.

Limiting Factors on Populations

Limiting factors can affect population growth. As a population increases, the competition for resources becomes more intense, and the growth rate declines. This is a density-dependent growth factor. The carrying capacity can be determined by the density-dependent factor. Density-independent factors affect the individuals regardless of population size. The weather and climate are good examples. Too hot or too cold temperatures may kill many individuals from a population that has not reached its carrying capacity.

Population density is the number of individuals per unit area or volume. The spacing pattern of individuals in an area is dispersion. Dispersion patterns can be *clumped*, with individuals grouped in patches; *uniform*, where individuals are approximately equidistant from each other; or *random*.

Population densities usually are estimated based on a few representative plots. Aggregation of a population in a relatively small geographic area can have detrimental effects to the environment. Food, water, and other resources will be rapidly consumed, resulting in an unstable environment. A low population density is

BIOTIC FACTORS: living things in an ecosystem, such as plants, animals, bacteria, and fungi

If one population in a community increases, it affects the ability of another population to succeed by limiting the amount of available food, water, shelter, and space.

ABIOTIC FACTORS: nonliving aspects of an ecosystem, such as soil quality, rainfall, and temperature

POPULATION: a group of individuals of one species that live in the same general area

CARRYING CAPACITY: the total amount of life a habitat can support

Changes in climate and soil can cause effects at the beginning of the food chain, thus limiting or accelerating the growth of population.

less harmful to the environment. The use of natural resources will be more wide-spread, allowing for the environment to recover and continue growth.

The human population has been growing exponentially for centuries. People are living longer and healthier lives than ever before. Better health care and nutrition practices have helped in the survival of the population.

SKILL 21.2 **Demonstrate knowledge of social behaviors** *(for example, territoriality, dominance, altruism, threat display)*

There are many interactions that may occur between different species living together. Predation, parasitism, competition, commensalism, and mutualism are the different types of relationships populations have among each other.

Animal behavior is responsible for courtship leading to mating, communication between species, territoriality and aggression between animals, and dominance within a group. Behaviors may include body posture, mating calls, display of feathers or fur, coloration, or baring of teeth.

An **INNATE BEHAVIOR** is one that is inborn or instinctual. An environmental stimulus such as the length of day or temperature may cue an innate behavior, such as hibernation among some animals.

A **LEARNED BEHAVIOR** is one that is modified due to past experience.

In **ALTRUISM** an organism appears to act in a way that benefits others over itself. Altruistic behavior is often seen in more complex social groups.

Scientists have observed several groups of male turkeys that had an internal hierarchy. These groups fought for dominance in their mating ritual, spreading their wings, gobbling, and engaging in other courtship behaviors. Once one group gained dominance over the other groups, the leader of this group was the one who mated most frequently with the females.

> **INNATE BEHAVIOR:** one that is inborn or instinctual

> **LEARNED BEHAVIOR:** one that is modified due to past experience

> **ALTRUISM:** an organism appears to act in a way that benefits others over itself

---

SKILL 21.3 **Demonstrate understanding of intraspecific competition**

Competition is one of the many factors that affect the structure of ecologic communities. Competition among members of the same species is known as

INTRASPECIFIC COMPETITION, while competition between individuals of different species is known as INTERSPECIFIC COMPETITION.

Intraspecific competition plays a role in evolutionary change through its affect on a population's carrying capacity. Once populations reach high densities, density-dependent inhibition is exhibited through intraspecific competition. As resources become limited, the population size can no longer increase within the defined region. Competition between members of the same species may lead certain populations to move to new regions, eventually resulting in speciation.

Natural selection will favor individuals better suited for interspecific competition. For example, when a tree population becomes dense within a defined area, trees that grow higher will obtain more sunlight, prosper more, reproduce more, and thus contribute more to the population's gene pool. Over time, the taller trees' higher fitness will increase the general tree height of the entire population.

SKILL 21.4 Demonstrate understanding of interspecific relationships (for example, commensalism, mutualism, parasitism)

Predation and parasitism result in a benefit for one species and a detriment for the other. PREDATION occurs when a predator eats its prey. The common concept of predation is of a carnivore consuming other animals. This is one form of predation. Although not always resulting in the death of the plant, herbivory also is a form of predation. Some animals eat enough of a plant to cause death. PARASITISM involves a predator that lives on or in its hosts, causing detrimental effects to the host. An insect or a virus living off and reproducing in its host is an example of parasitism. Many plants and animals have defenses against predators. Some plants have poisonous chemicals that will harm the predator if ingested and some animals are camouflaged so they are harder to detect.

SYMBIOSIS occurs when two species live close together. Parasitism is one example of symbiosis described above. Another example of symbiosis is commensalism. COMMENSALISM occurs when one species benefits from the other without harmful effects to the other. MUTUALISM occurs when each species benefits from the other. Species involved in mutualistic relationships must coevolve to survive. As one species evolves, the other must as well if it is to be successful in life. The grouper and a species of shrimp live in a mutualistic relationship in which the shrimp feeds on parasites living on the grouper; thus the shrimp is fed, and the grouper stays healthy. Many microorganisms live in mutualistic relationships.

INTRASPECIFIC COMPETITION: competition among members of the same species

INTERSPECIFIC COMPETITION: competition between individuals of different species

Predation and parasitism result in a benefit for one species and a detriment for the other.

PREDATION: occurs when a predator eats its prey

PARASITISM: involves a predator that lives on or in its hosts, causing detrimental effects to the host

SYMBIOSIS: occurs when two species live close together; parasitism is one example

COMMENSALISM: occurs when one species benefits from the other without harmful effects to the other

MUTUALISM: occurs when each species benefits from the other

SKILL Demonstrate understanding of succession
21.5

SUCCESSION: an orderly process of replacing a community that has been damaged or has begun where no life previously existed

SUCCESSION is an orderly process of replacing a community that has been damaged or has begun where no life previously existed. Primary succession occurs where life never existed before, as in a flooded area or on a new volcanic island. Secondary succession takes place in communities that were once flourishing, then were disturbed but not totally stripped by some source, either human or nature. A climax community is one that is established and flourishing.

Abiotic factors have an impact on succession by affecting which species colonize an area. Certain species will or will not survive depending on the weather, climate, or soil makeup. Biotic factors such as competition between species may inhibit one species' population.

SKILL Demonstrate understanding of the concepts of stability of
21.6 ecosystems and the effects of disturbances

The environment is ever changing because of natural events and the actions of humans, animals, plants, and other organisms. Even the slightest changes in environmental conditions can greatly influence the function and balance of communities, ecosystems, and ecoregions. For example, subtle changes in salinity and temperature of ocean waters over time can greatly influence the range and population of certain species of fish. In addition, a slight increase in average atmospheric temperature can promote tree growth in a forest, but a corresponding increase in the viability of pathogenic bacteria can decrease the overall growth and productivity of the forest.

Human Threats Posed to the Stability of Ecosystems

- Ecological problems: Nonrenewable resources are fragile and must be conserved for use in the future. Human impact and knowledge of conservation will control our future.

- Biological magnification: Chemicals and pesticides accumulate along the food chain. Tertiary (top) consumers accumulate more toxins than animals at the bottom of the food chain, which threatens their survival.

- Simplification of the food web: Three major crops feed the world (rice, corn, wheat). The preferential planting of these foods wipes out other habitats and pushes their animals into other habitats, causing overpopulation or extinction.

- Dwindling fuel sources: Strip mining and the overuse of oil reserves have depleted these resources. At the current rate of consumption, only conservation or finding and using alternate fuel sources will guarantee our future as a species.

- Pollution: Although technology gives us many advances, pollution is a side effect of production. Waste disposal and the burning of fossil fuels have polluted our land, water, and air. Climate change and acid rain are two results of the burning of hydrocarbons and sulfur.

- Global warming: Rainforest depletion and the use of fossil fuels and aerosols have caused an increase in carbon dioxide production. This leads to a decrease in the amount of oxygen, which is directly proportional to the amount of ozone. As the ozone layer shrinks, more heat enters our atmosphere and is trapped, causing an overall warming effect that may eventually melt polar ice caps, raise ocean water levels, and change climate, which will affect weather systems.

- Endangered species: Construction to house our overpopulated world has caused a destruction of habitat for other animals and plants/other organisms, leading to the extinction of other species.

- Overpopulation: The human race is still growing at an exponential rate. Carrying capacity has not been met due to our ability to use technology to produce more food and housing. Space and water cannot be manufactured, and eventually our overuse will affect every living thing on this planet.

Stewardship

STEWARDSHIP is the responsible management of resources entrusted to one. Because human presence and activity has such a drastic impact on the environment, humans are the stewards of the earth. In other words, it is the responsibility of humans to balance their needs as a population with the needs of the environment and all of the earth's living creatures and resources. Stewardship requires the regulation of human activity to prevent, reduce, and mitigate environmental degradation. An important aspect of stewardship is the preservation of resources and ecosystems for future generations of humans. Finally, the concept of stewardship often, but not necessarily, draws from religious, theological, or spiritual thought and principles.

STEWARDSHIP: the responsible management of resources entrusted to one

Stewardship requires the regulation of human activity to prevent, reduce, and mitigate environmental degradation

Energy is lost as the trophic (nutritional) levels progress from producer to tertiary consumer. The amount of energy that is transferred between trophic levels is called the **ECOLOGICAL EFFICIENCY**. The visual of this energy flow is represented in a pyramid of productivity.

ECOLOGICAL EFFI-CIENCY: the amount of energy that is transferred between trophic levels

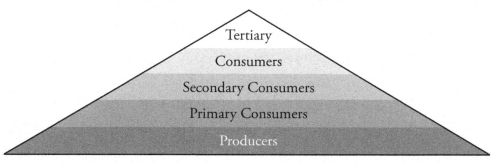

Pyramid of Productivity

Tertiary

Consumers

Secondary Consumers

Primary Consumers

Producers

BIOMASS PYRAMID: represents the total dry weight of organisms in each trophic level

The **BIOMASS PYRAMID** represents the total dry weight of organisms in each trophic level. A pyramid of numbers is a representation of the population size of each trophic level. The producers, being the most populous, are on the bottom of this pyramid with the tertiary consumers on the top with the fewest numbers.

Trophic levels are based on the feeding relationships that determine energy flow and chemical cycling.

Trophic levels are based on the feeding relationships that determine energy flow and chemical cycling.

Autotrophs are the primary producers of the ecosystem and mainly consist of plants. Primary consumers, the next trophic level, are the herbivores that eat plants or algae. Secondary consumers are the carnivores that eat the primary consumers. Tertiary consumers eat the secondary consumers. These trophic levels may go higher depending on the ecosystem. Decomposers are consumers that feed off animal waste and dead organisms. This pathway of food transfer is known as the **FOOD CHAIN**. Most food chains are more elaborate, becoming food webs.

FOOD CHAIN: a pathway of food transfer

The Food Chain

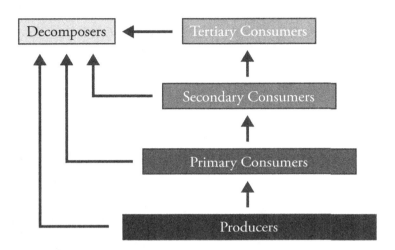

SKILL 21.8 **Demonstrate understanding of biogeochemical cycles** *(for example, nitrogen, carbon, water)*

Essential elements are recycled through an ecosystem. At times, the element needs to be "fixed" in a useable form. Cycles are dependent on plants, algae, and bacteria to fix nutrients for use by animals.

Biogeochemical Cycles

- **Water cycle:** Two percent of all the available water is fixed and unavailable in ice or the bodies of organisms. Available water includes surface water (lakes, oceans, and rivers) and ground water (aquifers, wells). 96% of all available fresh water is from ground water. Water is recycled through the processes of evaporation and precipitation. The water present now is the water that has been here since our atmosphere formed.

- **Carbon cycle:** Ten percent of all available carbon in the air (from carbon dioxide gas) is fixed by photosynthesis. Plants fix carbon in the form of glucose, animals eat the plants and are able to obtain their source of carbon. When animals release carbon dioxide through respiration, the plants again have a source of carbon to fix.

- **Nitrogen cycle:** Eighty percent of the atmosphere is in the form of nitrogen gas. Nitrogen must be fixed and taken out of the gaseous form to be

Water is recycled through the processes of evaporation and precipitation. The water present now is the water that has been here since our atmosphere formed.

Ten percent of all available carbon in the air (from carbon dioxide gas) is fixed by photosynthesis.

incorporated into an organism. Only a few genera of bacteria have the correct enzymes to break the triple bond between nitrogen atoms. These bacteria live within the roots of legumes (peas, beans, alfalfa) and add bacteria to the soil so plants may take it up. Nitrogen is necessary to make amino acids and the nitrogenous bases of DNA.

- **Phosphorus cycle:** Phosphorus exists as a mineral and is not found in the atmosphere. Fungi and plant roots have structures called mycorrhizae that are able to fix insoluble phosphates into useable phosphorus. Urine and decayed matter return phosphorus to the earth where it can be fixed in plants. Phosphorus is needed for the backbone of DNA and for ATP manufacture.

SKILL 21.9 Identify the types and characteristics of biomes

BIOMES are communities and ecosystems that are typical of broad geographic regions. Specific biomes include marine, freshwater, tropical forest, savanna, desert, temperate deciduous forest, taiga, tundra, polar/permafrost, chaparral, and temperate grasslands.

Common Biomes

- **Marine:** Covering 75% of the earth, this biome is classified by the depth of the water. The *intertidal zone* is from the tide line to the edge of the water. The *littoral zone* stretches from the water's edge to the open sea and includes coral reef habitats, the most densely populated area of the marine biome. The *open sea zone* is divided into the *epipelagic zone* and the *pelagic zone*. The epipelagic zone receives more sunlight and has a larger number of species. The ocean floor is called the *benthic zone* and is populated with bottom feeders.

- **Freshwater:** Lakes, rivers, streams, and swamplands are examples of freshwater biomes, which are closely linked to terrestrial biomes.

- **Tropical Forest:** Located around the area of the equator, the tropical forest features a near-constant temperature (25° C) and days and nights of approximately equal length of daylight in about 24 hours. In a tropical rainforest, rainfall exceeds 200 cm. per year and supports abundant, diverse species of plants and animals. A tropical dry forest gets scarce rainfall, and a tropical deciduous forest has wet and dry seasons.

- Savanna: Located in central South America, southern Africa, and parts of Australia, the savanna is a transitional biome between the rain forest and the desert. It is grassland with shrubs, grasses, and scattered individual trees. Depending on the location, temperatures range from 0 to 25° C, and rainfall is from 90 to 150 cm per year.

- Desert: Temperatures range from 10° to 38° C in hot deserts, and rainfall is under 25 cm per year. Plant species include xerophytes (plants adapted to survive with little water) and succulents (plants adapted to store water). Lizards, snakes, and small mammals are common animals. Hot deserts are located in northern Africa, southwestern United States, and the Middle East. Cold deserts are located in the Rocky Mountain region of the United States and much of central Asia.

- Temperate Deciduous Forest: Temperatures range from −24 to 38° C, and rainfall is between 65 to 150 cm per year. Deciduous trees are common, as well as deer, bears, and squirrels. This biome is located in most of eastern United States, middle Europe, and eastern Asia.

- Taiga: Taiga, the largest terrestrial biome, is coniferous forest located far north and far south of the equator, close to the poles. Temperatures range from −24 to 22° C, and rainfall is between 35 to 40 cm per year. Plant life includes conifers and plants that can withstand harsh winters. Animals include weasels, mink, and moose.

- Tundra: Temperatures range from −28 to 15° C, and rainfall is limited, ranging from 10 to 15 cm per year. The tundra is located even farther north and south than the taiga, closer to the poles. Common plants include lichens and mosses. Animals include polar bears and musk oxen.

- Polar or Permafrost: Temperature ranges from −40 to 0° C, rarely rising above freezing. Rainfall is below 10 cm per year. Most water is bound up as ice. Life is limited.

- Chaparral: The Mediterranean, the California coastline, and southwestern Australia feature this biome with mild, rainy winters and hot, long, dry summers. Trees do not grow as well here; spiny shrubs dominate.

- Temperate grasslands: Parts of Russia, Europe, and the prairie land of central United States are temperate grasslands, which are similar to savannas, but have cold winters.

DOMAIN V
EARTH/SPACE SCIENCES

PERSONALIZED STUDY PLAN

KNOWN MATERIAL/ SKIP IT

PAGE	COMPETENCY AND SKILL	KNOWN MATERIAL/ SKIP IT
183	**22: Physical geology**	☐
	22.1: Demonstrate understanding of the processes of mineral and rock formation	☐
	22.2: Demonstrate understanding of the methods used to identify and classify different types of minerals, rocks, and soils	☐
	22.3: Demonstrate knowledge of the structure of Earth and the physical characteristics of Earth's various layers	☐
	22.4: Demonstrate understanding of the internal processes and resulting features of Earth, including folding, faulting, earthquakes, and volcanoes	☐
	22.5: Demonstrate understanding of plate tectonic theory and the evidence that supports this theory	☐
	22.6: Demonstrate understanding of the hydrologic cycle and the processes by which water moves through the cycle	☐
	22.7: Demonstrate understanding of the processes of weathering, erosion, and deposition	☐
194	**23: Historical geology**	☐
	23.1: Demonstrate understanding of the principle of uniformitarianism	☐
	23.2: Demonstrate understanding of the basic principles of stratigraphy	☐
	23.3: Distinguish between relative and absolute time	☐
	23.4: Recognize the processes involved in the formation of fossils	☐
	23.5: Demonstrate understanding of the types of information fossils provide	☐
	23.6: Demonstrate understanding of the geologic timescale and how it was developed	☐
	23.7: Outline the sequence of important events in the Earth's history	☐
222	**24: Oceanography**	☐
	24.1: Demonstrate understanding of the geographic location of oceans and seas	☐
	24.2: Demonstrate understanding of the processes involved in the formation and movement of ocean waves	☐
	24.3: Demonstrate understanding of the primary causes and factors that influence tides	☐
	24.4: Demonstrate knowledge of the major surface and deepwater currents in the oceans and the causes of these currents	☐
	24.5: Demonstrate understanding of the processes that influence the topography and landforms of the ocean floor and shorelines	☐
	24.6: Demonstrate understanding of the factors that influence the physical and chemical properties of seawater and nutrient cycles of the ocean	☐

PERSONALIZED STUDY PLAN

✕✓
KNOWN MATERIAL/ SKIP IT

PAGE	COMPETENCY AND SKILL	
230	**25: Meteorology**	☐
	25.1: Demonstrate knowledge of the structure of the atmosphere	☐
	25.2: Demonstrate knowledge of the chemical composition of the atmosphere	☐
	25.3: Demonstrate understanding of the factors influencing seasonal and latitudinal variation of solar radiation	☐
	25.4: Demonstrate understanding of global wind belts	☐
	25.5: Identify the factors that contribute to small-scale atmospheric circulation	☐
	25.6: Distinguish among relative humidity, absolute humidity, dew point, and frost point	☐
	25.7: Demonstrate knowledge of cloud and precipitation types	☐
	25.8: Characterize air masses in terms of temperature, moisture content, and source areas	☐
	25.9: Demonstrate understanding of pressure systems	☐
	25.10: Demonstrate understanding of frontal systems and air circulation	☐
	25.11: Interpret information on weather maps	☐
	25.12: Demonstrate understanding of short-term weather forecasting and the methods used to perform long-term weather forecasting	☐
	25.13: Demonstrate understanding of factors that affect climate	☐
	25.14: Demonstrate understanding of how humans affect and are affected by climate	☐
255	**26: Astronomy**	☐
	26.1: Demonstrate knowledge of the major theories of origin and structure of the universe	☐
	26.2: Define and use large units of distance	☐
	26.3: Demonstrate understanding of the origin and life cycle of stars	☐
	26.4: Demonstrate understanding of the major theories involving the origin of the solar system	☐
	26.5: Identify the major features and characteristics of the Sun and the source of the Sun's energy	☐
	26.6: Identify the components of the solar system	☐
	26.7: Demonstrate understanding of the geometry of the Earth-moon-Sun system and the causes of eclipses	☐
	26.8: Demonstrate understanding of the causes of moon phases	☐
	26.9: Demonstrate understanding of the causes of Earth's seasons	☐
	26.10: Demonstrate knowledge of how units of time are based on Earth's motions	☐
	26.11: Demonstrate understanding of time zones on Earth	☐
	26.12: Demonstrate understanding of geosynchronous orbits	☐
	26.13: Recognize the contributions of space missions and the present limitations of space exploration	☐
	26.14: Recognize the scientific contribution of remote sensing	☐

COMPETENCY 22
PHYSICAL GEOLOGY

SKILL **Demonstrate understanding of the processes of mineral and rock**
22.1 **formation**

The three major subdivisions of rocks are sedimentary, metamorphic, and igneous.

Lithification of Sedimentary Rocks

When fluid sediments are transformed into solid sedimentary rocks, the process is known as LITHIFICATION. One common process affecting sediments is compaction where the weights of overlying materials compress and compact the deeper sediments. The compaction process leads to cementation. CEMENTATION is when sediments are converted to sedimentary rock.

Factors in Crystallization of Igneous Rocks

Igneous rocks can be classified according to their texture, their composition, and the way they formed.

Molten rock is called MAGMA. When molten rock pours out onto the surface of Earth, it is called LAVA.

As magma cools, the elements and compounds begin to form crystals. The slower the magma cools, the larger the crystals grow. Rocks with large crystals are said to have a coarse-grained texture. Granite is an example of a coarse-grained rock. Rocks that cool rapidly before any crystals can form have a glassy texture, such as obsidian, also commonly known as volcanic glass.

Metamorphic rocks are formed at high temperatures under great pressure. The process by which the rocks undergo these changes is called METAMORPHISM. The outcome of metamorphic changes include:

- Deformation by extreme heat and pressure

- Compaction

- Destruction of the original characteristics of the parent rock

LITHIFICATION: the process of transforming fluid sediments into solid sedimentary rocks

CEMENTATION: the process of converting sediments to sedimentary rock through compaction

MAGMA: molten rock

LAVA: molten rock that pours out onto the surface of Earth

METAMORPHISM: the process by which rocks are formed at high temperatures under great pressure

- Bending and folding while in a plastic stage
- The emergence of completely new and different minerals due to chemical reactions with heated water and dissolved minerals

Metamorphic rocks are classified into two groups, foliated (leaflike) rocks and unfoliated rocks. Foliated rocks consist of compressed, parallel bands of minerals, which give the rocks a striped appearance, such rocks as slate, schist, and gneiss. Unfoliated rocks, such as quartzite, marble, and anthracite rocks, are not banded.

MINERALS are natural, nonliving, naturally formed solids with a definite chemical composition and a crystalline structure. ORES are minerals or rock deposits that can be mined for a profit. ROCKS are Earth materials made of one or more minerals. A ROCK FACIES is a rock group that differs from comparable rocks (as in composition, age, or fossil content).

> **MINERALS:** natural, nonliving, naturally formed solids with a definite chemical composition and a crystalline structure

> **ORES:** minerals or rock deposits that can be mined for a profit

> **ROCKS:** Earth materials made of one or more minerals

SKILL 22.2 Demonstrate understanding of the methods used to identify and classify different types of minerals, rocks, and soils

> **ROCK FACIES:** a rock group that differs from comparable rocks (as in composition, age, or fossil content)

There are over 3,000 minerals in Earth's crust. Minerals are classified by composition. The major groups of minerals are silicates, carbonates, oxides, sulfides, sulfates, and halides with the largest group being the silicates. Silicates are made of silicon, oxygen, and one or more other elements.

SOILS are composed of particles of sand, clay, various minerals, tiny living organisms, and humus, plus the decayed remains of plants and animals.

> **SOILS:** composed of particles of sand, clay, various minerals, tiny living organisms, and humus, plus the decayed remains of plants and animals

SOIL CLASSES BASED ON TEXTURE	
Sandy soils	are gritty, and their particles do not bind together firmly. They are porous—water passes through them rapidly, so they do not hold much water.
Clay soils	are smooth and greasy with particles bound together firmly. Clay soils are moist and usually do not allow water to pass through easily.
Loamy soils	feel somewhat like velvet, and their particles of sand, clay, and silt clump together. Loamy soils hold water but some water can pass through.

SOILS TYPES BASED ON COMPOSITION	
Pedalfers	form in the humid, temperate climate of the eastern United States. Pedalfer soils contain large amounts of iron oxide and aluminum-rich clays, making the soil a brown to reddish-brown color, and supporting forest vegetation.
Pedocals	found in the western United States where the climate is dry and temperate. These soils are rich in calcium carbonate and support grasslands and brush vegetation.
Laterites	found where the climate is wet and tropical. Large amounts of water flow through this red-orange soil, rich in iron and aluminum oxides. There is little humus, and this soil is not very fertile.

For information on rocks see Skill 22.1

SKILL 22.3 Demonstrate knowledge of the structure of Earth and the physical characteristics of Earth's various layers

Although no one has ever drilled through the Earth's crust, geologists know the composition of the Earth through the study of seismic shock waves.

The composition and density of the materials in the Earth cause sound waves to either slow down or speed up. By measuring the speed of the seismic wave, scientists are able to determine the approximate location and composition of the material. The latest research indicates that the Earth's solid iron and nickel inner core actually is spinning around. The Earth has three layers surrounding its core.

LITHOSPHERE: The term lithosphere is Greek for "rock layer." Comprised of the crust and uppermost part of the mantle, the lithosphere consists of cool, rigid, and brittle materials. Most earthquakes originate in the lithosphere. Because the lithosphere is close to the surface, both temperatures and pressures are relatively low in comparison to the other layers.

LITHOSPHERE: the crust and uppermost part of the mantle, consisting of cool, rigid, and brittle materials

The lithosphere is divided into two different crusts:

1. Continental plates are very thick and composed of light (in density and color) materials.

2. Oceanic plates are very thin and composed of heavy (in density and color) materials.

ASTHENOSPHERE: the semi-plastic molten rock material located directly below the lithosphere

MESOSPHERE: the lower mantle is rigid, hard, and brittle and makes up 80% of the Earth's material

Since the lithosphere has a lower density than the layer below it, it "floats" on the asthenosphere similar to the way an iceberg or a block of wood floats on water.

ASTHENOSPHERE: The asthenosphere is the semi-plastic molten rock material located directly below the lithosphere. At the base of the asthenosphere, the mantle again becomes more rigid and less plastic, and it remains in that rigid state all the way to the core.

MESOSPHERE: The lower mantle is rigid, hard, and brittle and makes up 80% of the Earth's material.

THE COMPOSITIONAL LAYERS OF THE EARTH			
Layer	**Composition**	**Depth (km)**	**Properties**
LITHOSPHERE			
Lithosphere includes the crust and the uppermost portion of the mantle	Varies; the crust and mantle have different compositions	7 to about 100	Cool, rigid, and brittle
CRUST			
Oceanic Crust	Basalt	7-10	Cool, rigid, and brittle
Continental Crust	Granite	20-70	Cool, rigid, and brittle
Uppermost portion of the mantle	Ultramafic	70-100	1% to 2% melted, hot and plastic.
MANTLE			
Asthenosphere	Mineralogy varies with depth	100 to 350	Hot and plastic
Remainder of upper mantle	Ultramafic	350 to 670	Hot, rigid, and brittle
Mesosphere (Lower mantle)	Ultramafic	670 to 2900	Mostly hot, rigid, and brittle, some liquid.
CORE			
Outer core	Iron and nickel	2900 to 5150	Hot, liquid
Inner core	Iron and nickel	5150 to Earth center (6370)	Hot, solid

Note: Mafic *refers to minerals rich in magnesium and iron.*

SKILL 22.4 Demonstrate understanding of the internal processes and resulting features of Earth, including folding, faulting, earthquakes, and volcanoes

Continental Margins

There are three types of continental margins, and they are classified by tectonic setting.

- Passive margin: an area of little activity, no subduction, and no earthquakes. A spreading zone usually borders a passive margin, such as the Atlantic Coast of the U.S. A passive margin is typically characterized by large continental shelf/slope/rise and also has prominent features such as drowned river valleys.

- Drowned river valley: an area where, when the sea level was lower, river valleys were cut in the normal fashion. Later, the sea level rose, and the sea covered the valleys. Chesapeake Bay is a series of drowned river valleys, which accounts for the fingered look of meandering inlets, leading to a river mouth.

- Active margin: an area of active tectonics.

Shelf Boundaries

- Subduction Boundary: a narrow continental shelf bordered by a deep trench, such as the Pacific NW along the Washington & Oregon coastlines.

- Transform Boundary: a narrow continental shelf cut by a series of submarine canyons that run parallel to each other but perpendicular to the shoreline. Shaking along the earthquake fault lines causes the submarine canyons to form. For example, Monterey Bay is actually a large submarine canyon.

Plate Tectonics

Data obtained from many sources led scientists to develop the theory of plate tectonics. This theory is the most current model that explains not only the movement of the continents, but also the changes in the Earth's crust caused by internal forces.

The Earth's lithosphere is broken into nine, large moving slabs and several smaller ones, all called plates. The major plates are named after the continents they are "transporting." The plates float on and move with a layer of hot, plastic-like rock in the upper mantle. Geologists believe that the heat currents circulating within the mantle cause this plastic zone of rock to slowly flow, carrying along the overlying crustal plates.

Movement of these crustal plates creates areas where the plates diverge as well as areas where the plates converge. In the mid-Atlantic is a major area of divergence. Currents of hot mantle rock rise and separate at this point of divergence, creating new oceanic crust at the rate of 2 to 10 centimeters per year. Convergence is when the oceanic crust collides with either another oceanic plate or a continental plate. The oceanic crust sinks, forming an enormous trench and generating volcanic activity. Convergence also includes continent to continent plate collisions. When two plates slide past one another, a transform fault is created.

> Plate movements produce many major features of the Earth's surface, such as mountain ranges, volcanoes, and earthquake zones. Most of these features are located at plate boundaries, where the plates interact by spreading apart, pressing together, or sliding past each other.

These movements produce many major features of the Earth's surface, such as mountain ranges, volcanoes, and earthquake zones. Most of these features are located at plate boundaries, where the plates interact by spreading apart, pressing together, or sliding past each other. These movements are very slow, averaging only a few centimeters a year.

Boundaries form between spreading plates where the crust is forced apart in a process called **RIFTING**. Rifting generally occurs at mid-ocean ridges. Rifting can also take place within a continent, splitting the continent into smaller landmasses that drift away from each other, thereby forming an ocean basin (for instance, the Red Sea) between them. As the seafloor spreading takes place, new material is added to the inner edges of the separating plates. In this way, the plates grow larger, and the ocean basin widens. This is the process that broke up the super continent Pangaea and created the Atlantic Ocean.

> **RIFTING:** process in which boundaries form between spreading plates where the crust is forced apart

Boundaries between plates that are colliding are zones of intense crustal activity. When a plate of ocean crust collides with a plate of continental crust, the denser oceanic plate slides under the lighter continental plate and plunges into the mantle. This process is called **SUBDUCTION**, and the site where it takes place is called a subduction zone. A subduction zone is usually seen on the seafloor as a deep depression called a **TRENCH**.

> **SUBDUCTION:** the process when a plate of denser ocean crust collides with a plate of lighter continental crust, slides under the continental plate, and plunges into the mantle

The crustal movement characterized by plates sliding sideways past each other produces a plate boundary characterized by major faults that are capable of unleashing powerful earthquakes. The San Andreas Fault forms such a boundary between the Pacific plate and the North American plate.

> **TRENCH:** a deep depression in the seafloor

Mountain-Building Processes

OROGENY is the term given to natural mountain building.

A mountain is terrain that has been raised high above the surrounding landscape by volcanic action, or some form of tectonic plate collisions. The plate collisions could be intercontinental or ocean floor collisions with a continental crust (subduction). The physical composition of mountains includes igneous, metamorphic,

> **OROGENY:** the process of natural mountain building

or sedimentary rocks; some may have rock layers that are tilted or distorted by plate collision forces. There are many different types of mountains. The physical attributes of a mountain range depend on the angle at which plate movement thrusts layers of rock to the surface.

Most major mountain ranges are formed by the processes of folding and faulting.

FOLDED MOUNTAINS are produced by folding of rock layers. Crustal movements may press horizontal layers of sedimentary rock together from the sides, squeezing them into wavelike folds. Up-folded sections of rock are called anticlines; down-folded sections of rock are called synclines. The Appalachian Mountains are an example of folded mountains with long ridges and valleys in a series of anticlines and synclines formed by folded rock layers.

FAULTS are fractures in the Earth's crust that have been created by either tension or compression forces transmitted through the crust. These forces are produced by the movement of separate blocks of crust.

Faulting is categorized on the basis of the relative movement between the blocks on both sides of the fault plane. The movement can be horizontal, vertical, or oblique.

Volcanism

Volcanic mountains are built up by successive deposits of volcanic materials.

VOLCANISM is the term given to the movement of magma through the crust and its emergence as lava onto the Earth's surface. An active volcano is one that is presently erupting or building to an eruption. A dormant volcano is one that is between eruptions but still shows signs of internal activity that might lead to an eruption in the future. An extinct volcano is said to be no longer capable of erupting. When lava cools, igneous rock is formed. This formation can occur either above ground or below ground.

INTRUSIVE ROCK is any igneous rock that was formed below the Earth's surface. Batholiths are the largest structures of intrusive type-rock and are composed of near-granite materials; they are the core of the Sierra Nevada Mountains.

EXTRUSIVE ROCK is any igneous rock that was formed at the Earth's surface.

DIKES are old lava tubes formed when magma entered a vertical fracture and hardened. Sometimes magma squeezes between two rock layers and hardens into a thin horizontal sheet called a sill. A laccolith is formed in much the same way as a sill, but the magma that creates a laccolith is very thick and does not flow easily. It pools and forces the overlying stratum upward, creating an obvious surface dome.

FOLDED MOUNTAINS: mountains that are produced by folding of rock layers

FAULTS: fractures in the Earth's crust that have been created by either tension or compression forces transmitted through the crust

VOLCANISM: the movement of magma through the crust and its emergence as lava onto the Earth's surface

INTRUSIVE ROCK: any igneous rock that was formed below the Earth's surface

EXTRUSIVE ROCK: any igneous rock that was formed at the Earth's surface

DIKE: an old lava tube formed when magma entered a vertical fracture and hardened

The Theory of Continental Drift

At the beginning of the 20th century, most scientists accepted the view that the Earth's materials were largely fixed in their positions, because rock was thought to be too hard and brittle to permit much movement.

Alfred Wegener's postulations

In 1906, however, Alfred Wegener, a young meteorology student in Germany, became intrigued by how the shape of the continents seem to have fit together at one time. In 1910 he began a lifelong pursuit of supporting evidence for what eventually became known as his theory of Continental Drift.

Over the ensuing years of his research efforts, Wegener became convinced that the landmasses had—at one point in history—been connected, forming a giant supercontinent that he later dubbed **PANGEA**. As his research progressed, he collected data and offered evidence of this theory, most of which is still included in the proofs offered for modern tectonic theory.

Citing paleoclimatology, the close fit of the shape of the continents, and fossil and rock evidence, Wegener further subdivided Pangea into two giant areas he called **LAURASIA** and **GONDWANALAND**. Within these areas he placed the continents of North America and Eurasia, (Laurasia), and South America, India, Africa, Australia, and Antarctica (Gondwanaland).

A theory rejected

Not surprisingly, Wegener's controversial theory of moveable continents was not readily accepted. Although Wegener believed the continents had moved, he initially concentrated his efforts on supporting the possibility of movement and made no attempt to explain the "how" of movement.

For the mainline scientists of the time, this inability to explain "how" became the all-consuming barrier to acceptance. Finally, under severe academic criticism, a frustrated Wegener proposed two ill-thought-out mechanisms to explain the movement, both of which were readily disproved by physicists.

His credibility shattered, Wegener sought solace in his love of exploration—a love that eventually cost him his life. Wegener disappeared in a blinding snowstorm during an expedition to Greenland in 1930, and his frozen body was recovered the following summer.

PANGEA: according to the theory of Continental Drift, the original supercontinent that comprised all the Earth's landmasses

LAURASIA: according to the theory of Continental Drift, one of the main subdivisions of Pangea that contained the continents of North America and Eurasia

GONDWANALAND: according to the theory of Continental Drift, one of the main subdivisions of Pangea that contained South America, India, Africa, Australia, and Antarctica

A theory reinstated

Over the next 20 years or so, Wegener's theory of Continental Drift was largely ignored by science. As progress in scientific technology advanced, however, scientists were faced with a perplexing dilemma; new evidence collected did not fit the old model of an immovable Earth. Starting in the late 1950s and early 1960s, some scientists began to reexamine Wegener's impressive collection of data, and, much to their surprise, they discovered that Wegener's old data and the new data they had collected both supported the theory of Continental Drift.

Modern geology owes much to Alfred Wegener's initial postulations. The advent of new technologies has made it possible for science to verify most of his observations, and additional, new data has expanded Wegener's original concept into the widely accepted, modern theory of tectonics. (*For more on this theory, see Skill 22.4*)

Shape of the continents: When graphically displayed, the continents look as if they should fit together in a jigsaw puzzle.

Paleomagnetism: As igneous rock cools, iron minerals within the rock align much like a compass toward the magnetic pole. Scientific research has shown that the magnetic pole periodically—in cycles of hundreds of thousands of years—reverses polarity.

- Normal polarity: magnetic North

- Reverse polarity: magnetic South

Research also shows that the bands of rocks on either side of a spreading center are mirror images of each other in terms of magnetic polarity and that the alignment of minerals indicates a periodic shift in polarity. The reversals in polarity can be visualized as alternating "stripes" of magnetic oceanic materials.

Age of the rock: Besides being mirror images magnetically, dating research on rocks on either side of a spreading center also indicates a mirroring of age. The age of the rock on either side of a spreading center get progressively older as you move away from the center. The youngest rock is always found directly at the spreading center.

In comparison to continental rock materials, the youngest rock is found on the ocean floor, consistent with the tectonic theory of cyclic spreading and subduction. Overall, oceanic material is roughly 200 million years old, while most continental material is significantly older, with age measured in billions of years.

Climatology: Climatology offers one of the most compelling arguments supporting plate movement. Cold areas show evidence of once having been hot and vica-versa. For example, coal needs a hot and humid climate to form; it doesn't form in the areas of extreme cold, such as Antarctica. Yet Antarctica has huge coal deposits, which indicates that at one time in the past, Antarctica physically must have been much closer to the equator.

Evidence of identical rock units: Rock units can be traced across ocean basins. Many rocks are distinctive in feature, composition, etc. Identical rock units have been found on multiple continents, usually along the edges where plates once apparently joined. For example, a significant number of South American and African rock-unit formations are identical.

Topographic evidence: Topographic features can be traced across ocean basins. Some glacial deposits, stream channels, and mountain ranges terminate on one continent near the water's edge and resume on another continent in relatively the same position.

Fossil evidence: Limited-range fossils that couldn't swim or fly are found on either side of an ocean basin. For example, the fossilized remains of pandas, kangaroos, and the long-extinct Metesaurus are unique to only two areas of the world separated by ocean basin.

Sea turtle migration: The genetic instincts of sea turtles drive them to return to the islands where they hatched to lay eggs. The migration of the sea turtles over thousands of miles is well documented. The diverse location and number of islands to which the sea turtles migrate suggests that plate movement has changed the location of the islands from their original position—immediately off shore of major continental masses, forcing the turtles to make epic journeys.

SKILL 22.6 Demonstrate understanding of the hydrologic cycle and the processes by which water moves through the cycle

PRECIPITATION: water that falls to Earth in the form of rain and snow

Water that falls to Earth in the form of rain and snow is called **PRECIPITATION**. Precipitation is part of a continuous process in which water at the Earth's surface evaporates, condenses into clouds, and returns to Earth. This process is termed the **WATER OR HYDROLOGIC CYCLE**. The hydrologic cycle of water movement is driven by solar radiation from the Sun and maintains the water balance at any given location. The Earth constantly cycles water. It evaporates from the sea, falls as rain, and flows over the land as it returns to the ocean. The constant circulation of water through sea, land, and the atmosphere is called the hydrologic cycle.

WATER OR HYDRO-LOGIC CYCLE: the continuous process in which water at Earth's surface evaporates, condenses into clouds, and returns to Earth as precipitation

Evaporation

Water is constantly in motion on the Earth. As the water evaporates from the sea, it becomes water vapor in the atmosphere. Although a small amount of water evaporates from the land and inland waterways, the majority of evaporation occurs over the oceans. An additional small amount of evaporated water comes from plants as they breathe using the process of TRANSPIRATION.

Precipitation

The water vapor in the atmosphere that is returned to the earth in the form of precipitation falls as rain, hail, snow, and sleet. The amount of precipitation varies according to location, with some areas of Earth receiving plentiful moisture and others receiving little (the deserts). The overall proportional balance of evaporation and precipitation, however, remains relatively constant.

Runoff

Precipitation moves across the land according to the topology, with most of the water eventually flowing back into the oceans. Thus the cycle starts over: evaporation, precipitation, and runoff.

Changes of State and Energy Transfers

As water moves through each stage of the hydrologic cycle, it changes state (phase) and requires energy transfer. Based on the laws of physics and chemistry, this transfer involves either an exothermic or endothermic reaction. As the cycle begins over the oceans, solar radiation heats the water sufficiently to cause the liquid to change phase to a gas.

> *Precipitation is part of a continuous process in which water at the Earth's surface evaporates, condenses into clouds, and returns to Earth.*

> **TRANSPIRATION:** evaporated water that plants produce as they breathe

> *The overall proportional balance of evaporation and precipitation remains relatively constant*

SKILL 22.7 **Demonstrate understanding of the processes of weathering, erosion, and deposition**

EROSION is the inclusion and transportation of surface materials by another moveable material, usually water, wind, or ice. The most important agent of erosion is running water. Streams, rivers, tides and such are constantly at work removing weathered fragments of bedrock and carrying them away from their original location.

A stream erodes bedrock by the grinding action of the sand, pebbles, and other rock fragments in a process called ABRASION. Streams also erode rocks by dissolving or absorbing their minerals, for instance, limestone and marble.

> **EROSION:** the inclusion and transportation of surface materials by another moveable material, usually water, wind, or ice

> **ABRASION:** a process in which the grinding action of sand, pebbles, and other rock fragments causes erosion

> *The most important agent of erosion is running water.*

WEATHERING: the breaking down of rocks at or near to the Earth's surface by physical or chemical forces

The breaking down of rocks at or near to the Earth's surface is known as **WEATHERING**. Weathering breaks down these rocks into smaller and smaller pieces. There are two types of weathering, physical weathering and chemical weathering.

1. Physical weathering is the process by which rocks are broken down into smaller fragments without undergoing any change in chemical composition. Physical weathering is mainly caused by the freezing of water, the expansion of rock, and the activities of plants and animals.

   – Frost wedging is the cycle of daytime thawing and refreezing at night. This cycle causes large rock masses, especially those exposed on mountaintops, to break into smaller pieces.

   – The peeling away of the outer layers from a rock is called exfoliation. Rounded mountain tops are called exfoliation domes and have been formed in this way.

2. Chemical weathering is the breaking down of rocks through changes in their chemical composition. An example would be the change of feldspar in granite to clay. Water, oxygen, and carbon dioxide are the main agents of chemical weathering. When water and carbon dioxide combine chemically, they produce a weak acid that breaks down rocks.

DEPOSITION, OR SEDIMENTATION: the process by which material from one area is slowly deposited into another area, usually by the movement of wind, water, or ice containing particles of matter

DEPOSITION, also known as **SEDIMENTATION**, is the process by which material from one area is slowly deposited into another area, usually by the movement of wind, water, or ice containing particles of matter. When the rate of movement slows down, particles filter out and remain behind, causing a build up of matter. Note that this is a result of matter being eroded and removed from another site.

COMPETENCY 23
HISTORICAL GEOLOGY

SKILL 23.1 Demonstrate understanding of the principle of uniformitarianism

UNIFORMITARIANISM is a fundamental concept in modern geology. It simply states that the physical, chemical, and biological laws that operated in the geologic past operate in the same way today. The forces and processes that we observe presently shaping our planet have been at work for a very long time. This idea is commonly stated as "the present is the key to the past."

James Hutton, a Scottish gentleman farmer, medical doctor, and amateur geologist, first postulated in 1785 the primary principle upon which modern geology is based: the Principle of Uniformitarianism. Hutton's observations led him to conceptualize that there is a uniformity of geologic processes, past and present.

Hutton's simple but profound concept provided science with a dynamic tool with which to view the past. Suddenly, logical explanations were available for a wide variety of questions that had stymied geologists. By implication, the corollary to the principle of uniformitarianism is that, because the processes that modified our planet in the past continue to work at a slow pace today, an immense period of time must pass for the processes to accomplish the task. Thus by extension, Hutton's observations also introduced the concept of geologic time. For example, the period of time required to raise a mountain thousands of feet above the surface and then wear it down again had to have taken place over a truly impressive period of time, on the order of hundreds of thousands of human lifetimes.

UNIFORMITARIANISM: states that the physical, chemical, and biological laws that operated in the geologic past operate in the same way today

By extension, Hutton's observations also introduced the concept of geologic time.

Understanding the relative orientation and arrangement of the strata provides important information about the Earth's history and the ongoing sequence of events and processes that helped shape that history.

SKILL 23.2 Demonstrate understanding of the basic principles of stratigraphy

The Earth's materials—rocks, soils, and sediments—are piled on each other in layers called **STRATA**. Understanding the relative orientation and arrangement of the strata provides important information about the Earth's history and the ongoing sequence of events and processes that helped shape that history.

Certain assumptions come into play when determining the sequence of events and correlating stratigraphic layers. These assumptions are the basis for the principles of geology, often referred to as laws.

The determination of the age of rocks by cataloging their composition has been outmoded since the middle 1800s. Today a sequential history can be determined by the fossil content (principle of fossil succession) of a rock system as well as its superposition within a range of systems. This classification process was termed stratigraphy and permitted the construction of a **GEOLOGIC COLUMN** in which rock systems are arranged in their correct chronological order.

STRATIGRAPHY is the study of regional landforms to detail and understand the sequence of events and relative timeframe in which those events occurred within the regions.

STRATUM: one of many layers of the Earth's materials—rocks, soils, and sediments

GEOLOGIC COLUMN: a method for arranging rock systems in their correct chronological order

STRATIGRAPHY: the study of regional landforms to detail and understand the sequence of events and relative timeframe in which those events occurred within the regions

SKILL 23.3 Distinguish between relative and absolute time

There are two basic concepts involved in measuring time: relative and absolute time. Although both concepts are used in the Earth Sciences, absolute time provides the most accurate concept of describing the passage of time.

- **Relative time:** Comparison of the age of one object relative to another. Example: This object is older than that object.

- **Absolute time:** The exact age of an object. Example: This object is xxx years old.

In Earth Science, time is measured using relative and absolute dating techniques.

SKILL 23.4 Recognize the processes involved in the formation of fossils

> **FOSSIL:** the trace or remains of any once-living organism

A **FOSSIL** is the trace or remains of any once-living organism.

The preservation of fossils in the environment is not all that common an occurrence. Although there is no required age to be considered a fossil, the term usually is not applied to remains less than 100 years old. Although soft tissues can be fossilized, they are very rare. If preserved, the fossil is usually found as hard points. Bones and shells are the most frequently fossilized parts of the organism.

> *Rapid burial is a major factor in fossilization. It helps to keep scavengers at bay and bacterial decay at a minimum.*

Rapid burial is a major factor in fossilization. It helps to keep scavengers at bay and bacterial decay at a minimum. Ninety-nine percent of all fossils are found in sedimentary rock. The heat present in forming igneous and metamorphic rock generally obliterates organic remains.

> *Ninety-nine percent of all fossils are found in sedimentary rock.*

Methods of Fossilization

- **Direct fossilization:** May be unaltered or petrified.

- **Unaltered fossils:** This method of fossilization involves unaltered hard points: the original shell or bone material remains unchanged. Very uncommon if it occurs, it usually is found only in fossils less than 5 million years old.

- **Petrifaction:** This much more common method of fossilization involves altered hard points, the replacement, molecule by molecule, of the material in the organism, and takes two different paths.

- In replacement, the organism's material is replaced molecule by molecule, by rock material. Groundwater rich with silica or calcium carbonate runs over the buried material, and the original material is replaced very slowly by silica, which allows fine detail in both the interior and exterior of the fossil. For example, petrified wood appears to be stone because silica or other mineral material has replaced the original wood material.

- In permineralization, mineral material is deposited in the porous spaces of the organism. Some of the original material may be left as hard minerals—usually silica—in the groundwater, which fills in the porous spaces of the organism, leaving the original shell material largely untouched. This is commonly found in bone and shell fossils. Organisms that have permineralized look like bone on the outside, but actually are rock on the inside.

• Carbonization: This method of fossilization is a good way of preserving soft tissues. As sediments pile on, their weight causes compaction, flattening the organism. The pressure causes the gases to squeeze out of the material, leaving only a thin film of carbon impressed into the surrounding rock unit. The result is like a silhouette on stone that shows only the outline of the organism.

• Mold: A void left in the surrounding material after an object's original material is gone. This method occurs when an organism is buried or covered immediately after death, and the sediment around it hardens quickly, forming a mold. After it decays, an empty space or void in the shape of the organism is left. This method provides fine exterior detail.

• Cast: A filled-in mold. This commonly found method of fossilization occurs when a cast is formed after a small hole develops in a mold, and the interior of the mold fills in with silica, calcium carbonate, etc. The cast looks like the organism, but no original material remains. It appears to be a statue of the original organism. Geologists sometimes deliberately make a cast of a discovered mold, except they use plaster of Paris rather than silica. When the mold is removed, it leaves a cast of the organism's exterior.

Less common methods of direct fossilization

The preservation of the soft parts of an organism is rare, but the following fossilization processes often preserve an organism's soft parts, including skin and hair.

• Mummification: This process preserves an organism by desiccation (dying out of fluids) but does not refer to man-made mummies such as those discovered in Egypt. Instead, it refers to the natural processes that preserve an organism in an extremely hot and dry environment such as a desert. Preservation occurs because the body fluids dry up and prevent decay. The organism's skin, hair, and internal organs remain.

- **Freeze-drying:** Extreme cold can preserve an organism. As in mummification, the hair, skin, and internal organs do not decay and remain intact. Mastodons, wooly mammoths, and early humans have all been found preserved in this manner.

The meat of a wooly mammoth found in the late 1880s was edible.

- **Tar pits:** Tar pits trap any organisms and are a rich source of fossils. When thick tar material bubbles up to the Earth's surface and looks wet like a lake, organisms get fooled, stuck, and eventually sucked down. The hydrocarbons of the tar seal the organism, preventing decay and preserving some soft body parts.

- **Peat bogs:** More common in the northern climates, peat bogs are essentially dried-out swamps and muck. Little decay takes place because the material seals the organism. Fossils found in peat bogs generally are well preserved with skin, hair, and internal organs intact.

- **Amber:** Amber is tree sap that has solidified, hardened, and turned to stone. Small insects trapped in the amber are extremely well preserved with no decay.

Indirect fossilization

INDIRECT FOSSILIZATION is based on preservation of trace evidence of an organism's existence rather than preservation of the organism itself.

> **INDIRECT FOSSILIZA-TION:** preservation of trace evidence of an organism's existence rather than preservation of the organism itself

- **Trace fossils:** Preserved tracks, trails, footprints, and burrowing marks.
- **Gastroliths:** Stomach stones, similar to the gizzard stones in a chicken, only much, much larger.
- **Coprolith:** Fossilized dung. Coproliths provide dietary clues about organisms.

SKILL 23.5 **Demonstrate understanding of the types of information fossils provide**

The fossil record in conjunction with the correlation of rock units can provide scientists with important information about the organism and the area and climate in which it lived.

Fossil Study Types, Ranges, and Chronology

- Endemic fossil: A fossil that has a limited geographic area

- Cosmopolitan fossil: A fossil that has a wide geographic range

- Guide fossil: A fossil that has a short geologic range and is cosmopolitan (hence is geographically abundant) and is used to help pinpoint time periods and correlate those periods to rock units

- Geologic range: The time interval between first and last appearance of an organism

- Biozone (also called assemblage zone): A body of rock identified by the fossil groups within, for example, an oyster zone

- Concurrent range zone: Two fossils within different ranges that have a narrow overlap, which pinpoints a narrow time period

Environmental Clues

PALEOECOLOGY is the study of ancient ecosystems——the plants and animals of the past.

- Type of environment: By studying the fossil's records and surrounding sediments, we can reconstruct what type of environment was present. For example, the presence of fossilized coral indicates a reef, and of fossilized oysters indicates an estuary.

- Geographic feature change: Fossils are also used to indicate geographic feature changes. The absence or presence of certain organisms may suggest a once-present land bridge. For example, horses and elephants migrated from North America and South America to Africa and Europe. They then became extinct in the Americas once the land bridge was broken. Horses were reintroduced to North America by Spanish explorers.

- Climate traces: These show the approximate latitude of the land and environment at the time the fossil was laid down. 016 to 018 ratio in shells of carbonate organisms tell us about the climate changes in an area and provide clues about where the continents once were. Likewise, the types of fossils found in the arctic regions indicate that those regions at one time were equatorial.

> **PALEOECOLOGY:** the study of ancient ecosystems——the plants and animals of the past

SKILL 23.6 Demonstrate understanding of the geologic timescale and how it was developed

In the earth sciences, when you talk about time, you must think in terms of huge expanses of time.

Geological Timescale

The **GEOLOGICAL TIMESCALE** is the calendar/clock of events in geology based on the appearance and disappearance of fossil assemblages. The scale is divided into time units that are given distinctive names and approximate start and stop dates. These dates are based upon a reexamination of previously discovered fossils, using absolute dating techniques. Comprised of the Hadean, Archean, and Proterozoic eons, 87% of all geologic time is considered Pre-Cambrian.

> **GEOLOGICAL TIMESCALE:** the calendar/clock of events in geology, based on the appearance and disappearance of fossil assemblages

- **Eon:** The largest scale division

- **Era:** A subcategory of an eon based on profound differences in fossil life

- **Period:** Smaller division within an era based on less profound differences in the fossil record

- **Epoch:** A subcategory within a period that is specific to the types of fossils found within that period

MAJOR GEOLOGICAL TIMESCALE DIVISIONS	
Eon, Era, Period, or Epoch	Start Time (mya)
Hadean eon	4600
Archean eon	3800
Early era	3800
Middle era	3400
Late era	3000
Proterozoic eon	2500
Paleoproterozoic era	2500
Mesoproterozoic era	1600
Neoproterozoic era	1000

Continued on next page

Eon, Era, Period, or Epoch	Start Time (mya)
Phanerozoic eon	570
Paleozoic era	570
Cambrian period	570
Ordovician period	505
Silurian period	438
Devonian period	408
Carboniferous period	360
Mississippian period	360
Pennsylvanian period	320
Permian period	286
Mesozoic era	245
Triassic period	245
Jurassic period	208
Cretaceous period	144
Cenozoic era	66
Tertiary period	66
Paleogene period	66
Paleocene epoch	66
Eocene epoch	58
Oligocene epoch	37
Neogene period	24
Miocene epoch	24
Pliocene epoch	5
Quartenary period	2
Pleistocene epoch	2
Holocene epoch	10,000 years

SKILL 23.7 Outline the sequence of important events in the Earth's history

The Origins of Life

Life began in the oceans of the Archean eon (3.8 to 2.5 billion years ago). The oldest fossil found is approximately 3.4 – 3.5 billion years old.

By our present day standards, the early Earth was very hot with a warm, toxic ocean. Totally devoid of oxygen, Earth was composed of hydrogen sulfide, methane, ammonia, and carbon dioxide. Life began in the ocean. Simple logic proves this contention: There wasn't an ozone (O_3) layer because there wasn't any oxygen (O_2) to be altered into ozone. Without ozone, ultraviolet (UV) radiation from the

Sun scrambles the DNA in a cell. Therefore, no life could have existed because the earliest single-celled organism couldn't handle the UV rays.

This logic caused research scientists Stanley Miller and Harold Urey to investigate the development of life in a primordial oceanic environment. They simulated the primordial ocean atmosphere in laboratory tests, and although they didn't create life, they did create amino acids, which are the building blocks of life. Proteins form amino acids that are able to form complex organic molecules.

Between 4.6 and 3.6 billion years ago, something occurred that still isn't scientifically clear. We transition from an Earth that was uninhabited to the appearance of simple, single-celled bacteria. Around 2.5 billion years ago, the bacteria developed the ability to photosynthesize, which released oxygen as a by-product. As the bacteria multiplied, they released a massive amount of oxygen called the OXYGEN REVOLUTION. Concurrently, it marks the beginning of the Proterozoic eon.

> **OXYGEN REVOLUTION:** the massive release of oxygen around 2.5 billion years ago by bacteria that had just developed the ability to photosynthesize and subsequently multiplied exponentially

Life in the Early, Middle, and Late Proterozoic Eon

The Proterozoic eon: 2.5 billion years ago (bya) to 570 million years ago (mya), is divided into 3 periods.

1. Early: 2.5 to 1.6 bya.

2. Middle: 1.6 to 1.0 bya.

3. Late: 1.0 bya to 570 mya

Early Proterozoic

Formation of Red Beds: These Red Beds (3.8 to 2.5 billion years ago) are important because they herald the appearance of significant amounts of oxygen on Earth. Their red color is produced by rust and indicates the presence of oxygen acting upon ferrous material present in the ocean, and eventually, on land. The presence of significant amounts of oxygen allowed ozone to form, which in turn screened out the harmful ultraviolet (UV) rays and made life possible outside of the protective confines of the ocean.

STROMATOLITES are blue-green algae or cyanobacteria. Cyanobacteria produced oxygen by photosynthesis. Through the discovery of the Gunflint Chert, an assemblage of many different types of bacterial fossils, we know that around 1.9 billion years ago there was an abundance of primitive bacteria, which began to diversify.

> **STROMATOLITES:** blue-green algae or cyanobacteria that produce oxygen by photosynthesis and that had vastly multiplied and diversified by around 1.9 billion years ago

Prokaryotes	Eukaryotes
Bacteria	All others (except bacteria)
Small size	Large size
No nucleus	Has nucleus
DNA material is loose and floats around as a molecule in the cell	DNA material is on the chromosome in the nucleus
Reproduces by binary fission (asexual)	Reproduces sexually, which allows mixing of DNA between organisms and changes through the process of natural selection.

Middle Proterozoic

Development of eukaryotic fossils (fossils other than bacteria).

Late Proterozoic

First evidence of multicellular organisms called **EDICARAN FAUNA**: At 1.0 billion years ago, cells were starting to be organized into tissues, and tissues were being organized into organs. The early Edicaran fauna, however, didn't grow exterior cells. Three basic types of Edicaran fauna include:

- Circular or discordal: looked like jellyfish

- Frond life forms.

- Elongate forms: wormlike in appearance

> **EDICARAN FAUNA:** first evidence of multicellular organisms

The Edicaran fauna were three times larger than the fossils in the Gunflint Chert and gradually developed greater detail, including growing hard and exterior shells. At the end of the Proterozoic eon—approximately 540 million years ago—there was an abundance of shelled organisms. The first appearance of multicellular shelled organisms was approximately 4 billion years after the Earth's formation.

The Phanerozoic Eon

The Phanerozoic eon (570 mya to present time), is divided into 3 eras, the Paleozoic, the Mesozoic, and the Cenozoic. Because of the extent of life form diversity that occurred during this time frame, each era is addressed separately in regard to its respective evolutionary patterns.

Paleozoic era (570 to 245 million years ago)

PALEOZOIC PERIODS	
Cambrian	570 to 505 mya
Ordovician	505 to 438 mya
Silurian	438 to 408 mya
Devonian	408 to 360 mya
Mississippian	360 to 320 mya
Pennsylvanian	320 to 286 mya
Permian	286 to 245 mya

The Paleozoic era was a time of great evolutionary change and begins with the development of organisms' ability to secrete hard parts. Calcium phosphate shells appeared 570 mya; calcium carbonate shells appeared 540 mya.

The **BURGESS SHALE FORMATION** is a depository of very well-preserved Cambrian Age fossils that provides a snapshot of life in the Cambrian Age. It shows the great abundance of life forms during the time period, and the gradual development of capabilities and characteristics.

Paleozoic-era invertebrates

Arthropods

Characterized by an external skeleton, with segmented body, hair, and jointed appendages, most arthropods were somewhat similar in appearance to the modern-day lobster.

- Trilobites: With over 600 genera and thousands of species, trilobites were bottom-dwelling scavengers, found in shallow to deep water. For an extremely long period of time, trilobites were the dominant multicellular life form on the planet. Trilobites are very good guide fossils because they were extremely abundant and existed throughout the entire Paleozoic period. Their development underwent distinctive changes, and these differences are useful in subdividing the time period.

- Ostracodes: Similar in appearance to the modern oyster, Ostracodes were very small, 5-0.5 to 4 mm, and lived in a shell.

BURGESS SHALE FORMATION: a depository of very well-preserved Cambrian Age fossils that provides a snapshot of life in the Cambrian Age

- Euryptides: Similar in appearance to a giant scorpion, Euryptides were predators that grew up to 9 feet long (2.47 meters). They became extinct in the Permian period.

Brachiopods

Comprising roughly 30% of all Paleozoic life, brachiopods were the most abundant and diverse of all the skeletonized invertebrates, with well over 4,500 fossil genera known from the fossil record. Brachiopods are solitary, sessile (attached, cannot move about), simple filter feeders. Some 120 species of Brachiopods live today. They started out as inarticulate (not hinged), but later became articulate (hinged). Although they are shelled organisms, they are not oysters or clams. Oysters and clams have symmetrical shells; brachiopods have asymmetrical shells.

Bryozoans

Bryozoans are colonial marine animals with the individual bryozoan animal—the ZOOID—encased in calcium carbonate. Although the individual zooid is tiny, approximately 1 mm, the colony can grow to more than 2 meters wide. Bryozoans live in small holes in a twig-like structure. Bryozoans are incredibly diverse with over 15,000 fossils species and over 4,000 living species.

> **ZOOID:** the individual bryozoan animal encased in calcium carbonate

Archaeocyathids

Archaeocyathids were calcium-carbonate-shelled, reef-building cup organisms that became extinct in the Permian period.

Porifera (Sponges)

First appearing in the Cambrian Age, Porifera was a dead end group, never evolving into other forms. The sac-like body surrounds spicules of silica or $CaCO_3$, resembling a broken toothpick. A sponge feeds off of the plankton in the water that passes through its pores. Porifera are still much the same today as they were 500 million years ago. There are over 3,000 modern species of Porifera, and some float, while others stick to the bottom. Porifera are useful in estimating current strength and sediment load.

Cnidarians

Cnidarians have stinging cells and can, at various stages, either be a floater or a fixed (sessile) organism. Cnidarians are complex animals, but unlike higher animals, they do not have discrete organs. Basically, cnidarians are a membranous sac with a gut surrounded by stinging cells. There are three major types:

- Jellyfish: First appearing in the pre-Cambrian Age, jellyfish are soft and predacious.

- Sea anemones: Sea anemones are of modern, not Paleozoic origin.

- Coral: Live coral is fixed and builds up on top of dead coral. In a coral reef, only the top layer of animals is alive. Live coral is found only in shallow water since sunlight is needed to sustain the coral life. Columns of calcium carbonate tabula and septa hold the coral structure together. *Tabula* are the horizontal plates while *septa* are the vertical plates.

Molluscs

Molluscs are the most common group in the marine realm. Very diverse—occupying every marine environment—there are approximately 130,000 living species. Some live in shells, some are crawlers, and some are free floaters. They primarily occur in three forms: bivalve, gastropod, and cephalopod. All have a visceral mass, and with the exception of the bivalve, have a basic body structure of mantle, foot, and head.

- Bivalves (clams, oysters, scallops, and mussels): Symmetrically shelled, with a foot, but no head, bivalves were not abundant until the late Paleozoic era. There are still 8,000 to 15,000 living species. Bivalves are the most common burrowing shelled animals in marine environments.

- Gastropods (snails): Not truly abundant until the late Paleozoic era, gastropods are found in both marine and terrestrial ecosystems. Making up around 80% of all molluscs, there are about 40,000 to 100,000 species of gastropods. Although slow and limited in size, the gastropods have adapted remarkably to a diverse range of environments and diets, and in a marine environment, they are active predators, drilling through the shells of their prey.

- Cephalopods (squid, octopus, cuttlefish, and chambered nautilus): The largest, most active and intelligent of the molluscs, over 650 species still exist today. Through the late Cambrian to the end of the Devonian periods, the earliest cephalopods were the now-extinct Ammonites and several classes of giant, shelled Nautilus. The majority of the cephalopods are predatory animals with highly sophisticated defense mechanisms. Squid and octopus can instantly change color and they use a system of "jet power" for mobility that involves expulsing water, and/or changing pressure within the body cavity.

Echinoderms

In the early Paleozoic era, Echinoderms appeared in stalked forms called Crinoids and Blastoids. They feature a five-part body plan with radial symmetry, as in, for example, the sand dollar and starfish.

Graptolites

Colonial animals, graptolites look like a cup on a stem. Abundant in the early Paleozoic era, graptolites are good guide fossils. Although scientists originally believed that graptolites had gone extinct at the end of the Mississippian period, recently they believe they have discovered a species of graptolite.

Conodots

Although geologists are not quite sure what sort of animal the conodot is, (conodots are very small, with 1mm platelike shells), they make great guide fossils because their shape periodically changed. Conodots became extinct at the end of the Triassic period.

Paleozoic-era vertebrates

The first vertebrate fish appeared in the Paleozoic era and eventually dominated the marine environment. To be classified as a **VERTEBRATE** (chordate), the animal must have an internal skeleton and a single nerve cord or vertical column.

> **VERTEBRATE (CHOR-DATE):** an animal with an internal skeleton and a single nerve cord or vertical column

- Agnatha: Jawless fish. Although very abundant in the early Paleozoic, only a few genera survive today. Some modern examples are the lamprey and hagfish.

- Placodermy: Jawed fish. Although armored, they had inefficient fins and were not good swimmers.

- Acanthodii: Jawed fish. With only primitive fins and no armor, they became extinct in the Permian era.

- Chondrichthyes: Jawed fish. This includes sharks and other fish that have cartilage instead of bones. With paired, flexible fins, this type of fish first appeared in the Silurian period and is still around today.

- Osteichthyes: Jawed fish. This type of fish, with bones and modem fin structure, first appeared in the Devonian period and is still around today. Osteichthyes marks the start of the move into fresh water from an oceanic environment.

Evolution of Paleozoic-era plant life

The Beginning

Stromatolites: Algal plants. cynobacterical forms, Stromatolites were common at the beginning of the Cambrian Age.

Adaptations were required to make the move to land. To move into fresh water a plant must have:

- A watertight covering (keeping the plant from drying out)

- A support structure (no buoyancy since no longer in the water)

- Some way to get water (develop roots to hold fast and get nutrients)

- Develop a means of using O_2

After the transition to land

Psilophytes: The first undisputed land plant, it appeared in the Silurian-Devonian period. A psiIophyte had short, slender, primitive vascular tissue, with no roots or true leaves, and reproduced by shedding sperm and eggs into the water.

Lycopsids: These tall, fernlike, scaled trees had tops (crowns), primitive roots, and vascular tissue. They needed water for reproduction. Lycopsids were abundant during the wet Mississippian and Pennsylvanian periods that offered ideal wetland conditions for this type of pIant.

The rise of gymnosperms

During the late Pennsylvanian period the lands begin to dry out and new types of plants emerged.

Gymnosperms: Gymnosperms are nonflowering plants that reproduce by seeds dispersed by wind pollination so do not need water. Gymnosperms have thick bark (keeps the plants from drying out), well-developed root systems to get water and nutrients, and highly developed vascular tissue.

Evolution in the Late Paleozoic era

Geological changes in the Paleozoic environment spurred great evolutionary changes. Massive deformations caused by orogenies created massive erosion. The tons of sediment carried into the waters choked many brachiopod species out of existence. As the landscape changed, the habitats shrunk, forcing a higher degree of competition among species.

The byword for the late Paleozoic was "evolve or die." The changes created a tendency in evolution toward greater mobility, so most surviving organisms evolved from sessile to motile creatures. Slow-moving and with a weak shell for defense, trilobites did not successfully evolve and consequently went extinct. Other offensive and defensive mechanisms also improved. Brachiopods developed spines and heavy shells around the same time that sharks developed broad, flat, teeth, which improved their food-gathering techniques.

In response to the environmental changes, new species of organisms appeared in the late Paleozoic era.

- Middle Devonian: Insects and spiny brachiopods appear.

- Pennsylvanian: Land gastropods (snails) appear.

- Arthropods see a large increase in both number and diversity.

- Vertebrates diversify and become abundant.

The rise of the amphibians

The evolutionary path of fish leads in two directions: toward land organisms, or away from heavy armor to better jaws and fin structure. By the end of the

Devonian period, sharks and bony fish dominated. Some fish, however, were starting to develop a modest air-breathing capability.

- Dipnoi: These nostril-breathing lungfish were able to breathe in either water or on the surface. They are still around today.

- Crossopterygian: These lung-breathing fish were an important step in the transition to land animals. The CROSSOPTERYGIAN is the ancestor of the amphibians.

ADAPTATIONS WERE REQUIRED TO MAKE THE MOVE TO LAND
Eye coverings and tear ducts to keep eyes moist
Ears to hear prey and predators
A more efficient lung and circulatory system
Improved, 3-chambered heart
Strong skeleton that no longer was buoyant out of water
Rigid framework (backbone and ribs to support weight and legs)

The first land animal and earliest amphibian was ICTHYOSTEGIDES, which appeared in the late Devonian period. Although primarily a land animal, Icthyostegides—as all amphibians—was still dependent on water to keep its skin moist and to reproduce.

By the Mississippian and Pennsylvanian periods, the amphibians dominated, having become extremely abundant and diversified with many species, including predators.

As the landmass of Pangea formed (*see skill 22.5*), the land dried up and the swamps disappeared. The climate turned cooler and drier, which was not good news for the amphibians. The climactic changes caused by the formation of Pangea caused ninety percent of all species on Earth to become extinct. By the end of the Permian period, almost all the amphibians had disappeared. The only remaining amphibians today are the frogs, salamanders, toads, and newts.

The rise of the reptiles

The end of the Paleozoic era marks the rise of the reptiles. As is the nature of evolution, changes to reproductive, defensive, offensive, and dietary systems allowed the reptiles to become the dominant species. In comparison, reptiles enjoyed significant evolutionary advantages over the amphibians.

The evolutionary path of fish leads in two directions: toward land organisms, or away from heavy armor to better jaws and fin structure.

CROSSOPTERYGIAN: the ancestor of the amphibians

ICTHYOSTEGIDES: the first land animal and earliest amphibian, which appeared in the late Devonian period

Changes to reproductive, defensive, offensive, and dietary systems allowed the reptiles to become the dominant species.

The first true reptiles appear in the Pennsylvanian Epoch. They are:

- Pelycosaurs: Fin-backed reptiles
- Therapsids: Mammal-like reptiles

The therapsids were a more advanced class of reptile, in that their legs were placed *under* their bodies (rather than out to the sides) for greater mobility, their skull attachment scheme gave them greater flexibility of movement and range, and they had mammallike dentition, with a variety of differently shaped teeth to perform different functions.

The Mesozoic era: The age of reptiles (245 to 66 million years ago)

MESOZOIC PERIODS	
Triassic	245 to 208 mya
Jurassic	208 to 144 mya
Cretaceous	144 to 66 mya

Climate changes

The climate changed throughout the Mesozoic era, which started cool and dry because of the formation of Pangea. As Pangea broke up, however, the climate warmed throughout the Mesozoic era and was very warm by the Cretaceous period. Tropical conditions extended to 70 degrees north and south latitude.

At the end of the Cretaceous, there was a rapid cooling and, about 80 million years ago, a rapid decline in the temperature of the ocean water, precipitated by the sudden abundance of COCCOLITHOPHORES. These microscopic algae with calcium carbonate shells flourished in such abundance that they caused a "reverse greenhouse effect," by absorbing the carbon from the atmosphere and forcing a cooling of temperature.

Significant Mesozoic geological events

As the supercontinent of Pangea broke up, massive orogenies occurred in North America, salt domes and petrified forests formed, and the Atlantic Ocean opened up. Europe and North America underwent transgression and regression events as Africa, India, and North America moved northward. Additionally, Australia & Antarctica were connected, and South America split off from Africa and North America.

COCCOLITHOPHORES: microscopic, shelled algae that flourished in such abundance at the end of the Cretaceous that they caused a "reverse greenhouse effect," by absorbing the carbon from the atmosphere and cooling the temperature

Mesozoic-era life

The mass extinction in the late Permian period of the Paleozoic era left only ten percent of all life forms. New life forms and species evolved rapidly to fill the void left behind by the extinctions.

- The oyster became successful

- Brachiopods almost completely disappeared

- New organisms include: ScIeractinian coral, crabs, shrimp, starfish, sea urchins and belemnites (that later evolved into squid)

- Oceanic phytoplankton evolved and expanded

Plant evolution

As marine plants moved ashore, the first step of evolution had been developing spore-bearing plants and trees. The next step was developing nonflowering seed plants, and the final stage was development of plants with flowers and enclosed seeds. *See also Skills 18.3 and 19.1.*

At the beginning of the Mesozoic era, conifers dominated. Conifers are nonflowering, seed-bearing plants. In the middle Cretaceous period, Angiosperms—flowering plants with enclosed seeds—evolved.

Flowering plants had several advantages over the nonflowering species. Where nonflowering plants were solely dependent on the wind for pollination, the flowering species with their enclosed seeds had a greater potential to reproduce far away from the parent plant. The flowering plants were attractive to insects and other animals; their seeds were eaten and deposited via an animal's waste distances away.

The flourishing of the angiosperms encouraged insect pollination and forced insect evolution. The increased competition among insects caused evolution to push to take better advantage of the new food source. The insects became more efficient eaters.

Likewise, as the angiosperms evolved and nut- and fruit-bearing species appeared, the plant itself became a food source and caused it to develop defenses to ward off predators. Thorns, acidic sap, spines, etc., were mechanisms to ensure the continuation of the plant species.

Mesozoic-era vertebrate life

Vertebrate evolution during the Mesozoic era also accelerated as the reptiles became the dominant species. Four groups of reptiles emerged, classified by the number and positioning of temporal openings (holes in the skull). The first dinosaur was the **THECODONT**. Dinosaurs are divided by hip structure into two different orders.

> **THECODONT:** the first dinosaur

- Saurischia (lizard-hipped.) Ironically, these dinosaurs, and not the Ornithischia, evolved into birds.

- Ornithischia (bird-hipped)

Saurischia (lizard-hipped dinosaurs)

The first **SAURISCHIA** were small, had short forelimbs, had a much lighter bone structure than marine creatures, and often were bipedal. This is an important trait since bipedalism promotes speed and agility. Saurischia included both carnivores (theropods) and herbivores (sauropods). Eventually most members of both types evolved into giants in the latter part of the Mesozoic era.

- Theropods (carnivores): Theropods were bipedal, with three toes and a large claw on the middle toe. Some members also had claws on the digits of short forelimbs. Theropods were excellent predators, having a large head and serrated teeth. Although most members of this group eventually grew to gigantic sizes, smaller ones—like Coelophysis—were highly effective predators.

- Sauropods (herbivores): Sauropods began as bipedal dinosaurs in the Jurassic period, but as they evolved into larger species by the time of the late Jurassic and early Cretaceous periods, they became four-legged. Sauropods were not creatures of the swamp; they were grazing animals much like modern elephants, and they ranged through forests and grasslands.

The increasingly large size of the Sauropods was an evolutionary defense mechanism. Size became an intimidation defense and also regulated body temperature more efficiently since proportionately less surface area provided better retention of body heat.

EXAMPLES OF MESOZOIC DINOSAURS	
JURASSIC	**CRETACEOUS**
Theropods	
Allosaurus: 20-25 ft long	Tyrannasaurus rex: long, 42 ft long
Sauropods	
Apatosaurus: 30 meters high, > 3 tons	Ultrasaurus: 80 tons

SAURISCHIA: lizard-hipped dinosaurs, typically with short forelimbs, light bone structure, and bipedal mobility

Ornithischia (bird-hipped dinosaurs)

Evolving in the Triassic period, all **ORNITHISCHIA** were herbivores since their back teeth were arranged into grinding plates and they had a beak-like mouth for cropping vegetation. They evolved as both quadrupeds and bipeds, and the quadrupeds had shorter front legs, giving them a tilted appearance. Ornithischians are divided into four groups:

- **Ornithopods:** All ornithopods—like trachodons and hadrosaurs—were bipedal, some had large crests on their heads, and were duck-billed.

- **Stegasaurs:** Stegasaurs had two pairs of horny spikes on their tails and one or two rows of bony plates along their backs. They died out in the early Cretaceous period and were replaced by anklyosaurs.

- **Anklyosaurs:** Armadillo-like anklyosarus were about 1.5 meters (4 ft) high but about 6 meters long (18 ft), with a clubbed tail and heavy bone armor. They were very common in what is now the United States.

- **Ceretopsians:** Horned dinosaurs, the ceretopsians sported a horn located over the nostril, often with additional horns over the forehead, and a defensive neck frill. Ceretopsians like triceratops were common in the North American landmass, first appearing in the Cretaceous period.

> **ORNITHISCHIA:** herbivorous, bird-hipped dinosaurs with grinding teeth and beaklike mouths; they evolved as both quadrupeds and bipeds

Warm-blooded versus cold-blooded

There is a great deal of controversy among paleontologists about whether dinosaurs were warm-blooded or cold-blooded. The logical arguments in favor of warm blooded are:

1. Dinosaurs have limbs under their bodies like mammals. Reptile limbs are offset to the side of the body.

2. The microstructure of dinosaur bones is closer to that of mammals. As mammalian bones, dinosaur bones are richly vascular as compared to other reptile bones.

3. Oxygen isotope studies show that cold-blooded animals have more heat going to the body core than to the limbs. In warm-blooded organisms, like mammals, there is a homogenous blood flow between the core and the limbs. Some dinosaurs exhibit this homogenous flow.

4. The dinosaurs exhibit the same 1 to 7 ratio between predators and herbivores as do mammals.

Flying reptiles

Flying reptiles first appeared in the late Permian period of the Paleozoic era. The flying reptiles were not birds; instead, their aerodynamics were similar to that of the modern-day flying squirrel that glides.

The **PTEROSAURS** first appeared in the Triassic period. Most had teeth, and all were predators with hair and skin stretched between the body and the limbs. Some had tails while others were tailless. Some of the Pterosaurs became very big and grew claws on their limbs. The Pterandon had a 23-foot wingspan; Quetzalcoatlus had a 50-foot wingspan.

Marine dinosaurs

Marine dinosaurs evolved from land-based dinosaurs, not marine-based organisms. They had streamlined bodies, modified reproductive organs to allow for birth at sea, and paddle-shaped limbs. Significantly, the marine dinosaurs did not have gills, but were air-breathers with more efficient lungs. Some examples of the different types of marine dinosaurs are:

- Plesiosaur: Present in the late Jurassic and Cretaceous periods, the Plesiosaur had a long neck and sharp teeth and was similar in appearance to the mythical Loch Ness monster.

- Placodonts: Placodonts appeared in the Triassic period. The Mesozoic equivalent of the modern day walrus, they preyed on molluscs.

- Icthyosaurs: Fishlike in appearance, Icthyosaurs resembled dolphins. They were highly competitive predators with many sharp teeth.

- Mosasaurs: Mosasaurs were sharklike relatives of modern monitor lizards and were efficient, marine-adapted predators.

Mesozoic birds

Birds evolved from the small theropods. Unfortunately, because of the hollow bone structure of birds (less weight permitted flight), few ancient bird fossils have been found.

ARCHEOPTERYX was the first scientifically undisputed bird that appeared during the Jurassic period. Archeopteryx was about the size of a modern-day crow or pigeon, reptile-like skeleton, wings, claws, and a long tail. Significantly, it had feathers, which is a primary reason that paleontologists agree that it was a bird; it lacked a keeled breastbone like modern-day birds and any evidence of flight muscles. Archeopteryx is believed to be an intermediate step between reptiles and a true bird.

Mesozoic mammals

The first true mammal dates from the Triassic period. It was a small, rodent-like creature. During the Mesozoic, the mammal went through evolutionary change, experimentation, and development. Mammals ended up with improved nervous, circulatory, and reproductive systems, and developed warm-bloodedness. Mammals are differentiated in the fossil record by having

- One bone in the lower jaw, in contrast to the reptiles' many smaller bones in the jaw

- Several ear bones

- A larger skull cavity in relation to size, than reptiles

- Differentiated dentition

Mass extinction at the Cretaceous/Tertiary (KT) boundary

This massive extinction ended the dominance of the reptiles as a wide range of life disappeared. At sea, the extinction event claimed all large marine dinosaurs and reptiles with the exception of the sea turtles and signaled the end of significant numbers of marine invertebrates and species of plankton. On land, all dinosaurs, flying reptiles, and many plants disappeared. Only mammals, snakes, turtles, lizards, and crocodiles survived.

The Cenozoic era: The age of mammals (66 million years ago to present)

CENOZOIC TIMELINE	
Tertiary period	66 to 2 mya
Paleogene subperiod	66 to 24 mya
Paleocene epoch	66 to 58 mya
Eocene epoch	58 to 37 mya
Oligocene epoch	27 to 24 mya
Neogene sub-period	24 to 2 mya
Miocene epoch	24 to 5 mya
Pliocene epoch	5 to 2 mya
Quaternary period	2 mya to present
Pleistocene epoch	2 mya to 10,000 years ago
Holocene epoch	10,000 years ago to present

The mass extinction of almost all reptiles at the end of the Mesozoic era left a void in the biosphere that precipitated an explosion in the diversity and number of mammals. From this point on to the present day, mammals became the dominant species.

Cenozoic-era plant life

Angiosperms evolved and spread significantly during the Cenozoic era. Grasses appeared in the Miocene epoch of the Tertiary period. Adapted and suited to the dry climate of the interior, they spread over the continents, becoming dominant on the steppes of Russia, the pampas of South America, the African veldt, and the great plains of the United States. The grasslands put enormous environmental pressure on the animals, because there are problems associated with living in the grasslands.

- Grass has silica secretions on and within the plant. Quartz silica is destructive to the animals' teeth, and the dirt on the grass is also an abrasive, which further wears down teeth.

- Grass is hard to digest.

- Grasslands present visibility issues: if the animal is large, it's hard to hide in the grass. If the animal is small, it can't see over the grass.

The environmental pressure the grasslands presented spurred diversity as animals adapted to fit the new environment.

CENOZOIC ADAPTATIONS TO GRASSLANDS	
New, improved dentition	Teeth grew continuously from roots to replace worn-down teeth. Teeth evolved complex infolding (both within the teeth and on the surface) and enameled surfaces, both to make the teeth wear resistant.
Elongated faces	They needed to accommodate continuously growing teeth.
Taller animals	Greater height allowed them to be able to see over the tall grasses.
Improved foot design	The original flat-footed design evolved into a new, hoofed foot designed to facilitate running away from predators
Improved digestive system	A four-chambered stomach evolved, allowing the animals to digest tough grasses.

Cenozoic-era animal life

- **Marine invertebrates:** The massive numbers of marine phytoplankton species that became extinct during the K/T boundary period were replaced by new species such as coccolithophores and diatoms.

- **Fish:** Fish, especially sharks, continued to diversify and evolve and become abundant. Sharks went through a giant phase, but eventually returned to their modern size.

- **Amphibians:** The few remaining amphibians remain virtually unchanged.

- **Reptiles:** Poisonous snakes appeared during the Miocene epoch of the Tertiary period in direct response to the corresponding evolution in mammal species. The poisons are either neurotoxins or hemotoxins. A neurotoxin, such as that from an African puff adder, affects the nervous system and kills the victim within minutes. A hemotoxin, such as that from a diamondback rattlesnake, affects the blood and is slower acting.

- Birds: Birds had just started to appear in the late Mesozoic era. During the Cenozoic era, the birds underwent an explosion of evolution as they diversified and multiplied. In the Eocene epoch, large, flightless birds were abundant. Some, similar to a giant parrot at nine feet tall, used their powerful beaks to crush their victims. Some flightless species, like the now-extinct dodo, survived until the 16th and 17th centuries of modern times.

Cenozoic-era mammals

CHARACTERISTICS OF MAMMALS
Two hard palates (allows eating and breathing at the same time)
Warm-blooded (maintains constant body temperature)
Mammary glands
Lower jawbone a single bone
Three bones in the middle ear
Seven neck vertebrae
Expanded brain case inside the skull
Differentiated dentition
Hair

Types of mammals

- MONOTREME: Lays eggs but still suckles the young with mammary glands. Only two species are still alive: the platypus and the spiny anteater.

- MARSUPIAL: Pouched animals, with young not viable when born, which develop in the mother's pouch. Marsupials like the kangaroo, koala, and wombat were highly successful in the isolated landmass of Australia. Placental animals dominated in North and South America. The marsupials became totally extinct in South America and are virtually extinct in North America. The only remaining marsupial in North America is the opossum.

- PLACENTAL: The most common type of mammal, whose young are gestated longer, but are also born viable. Placental mammals first appeared in the Cretaceous period, and evolved into many different groups.

MONOTREME: lays eggs but still suckles the young with mammary glands

MARSUPIAL: pouched animals, with young not viable when born, which develop in the mother's pouch

PLACENTAL: the most common type of mammal, whose young are gestated longer, but are also born viable

The evolutionary design of both carnivores and herbivores diversified during the Cenozoic.

- **Pinnipeds** (marine carnivores): Although pinnipeds like seals, sea lions, and walruses developed special adaptations to live in the ocean, they actually spend much of their time on land.

- **Cetaceans** (whales): Cetaceans underwent a complete marine adaptation from a terrestrial predator. They still have lungs, need to breathe air, and have skeletal vestiges of limbs and a pelvic bone.

- **Ungulates** (hoofed herbivores): The ungulates started out flat-footed, but as the grasslands developed, so did the ungulates: they developed hoofs. See "Cenozoic adaptations to grasslands," above.

Primate evolution

Primates first appeared in the fossil record around 48 million years ago.

PRIMATE CHARACTERISTICS
Generalized form: No special features such as hooves or a trunk
Flatter face and binocular vision
Postorbital ridge that protects the eyes
Opposable thumb on a grasping hand
More upright posture
Increased brain size

Primate classification

Classified as order Primata, with two suborders: prosimian and anthropoid

Prosimian (more primitive): The prosimians that remain today are small, nocturnal creatures.

Anthropoid (apes, monkeys, and humans): The split between prosimian and anthropoid occurred around 33 to 34 million years ago. Anthropoids are divided into three groups:

- **Cebidae:** New world monkeys. Prehensile tail (one that grasps)

- **Cercopithecidae:** Old world monkeys. Nonprehensile tail. Example: baboon.

- **Hominoidea:** Includes orangutans, chimpanzees, gorillas, and humans.

Evolution of Hominoidea

Hominoidea first appeared around 25 million years ago and shared a common history until around 8-6 million years ago, when Hominoidea split into Pongidae and Hominidae.

- **Pongidae:** More apelike. Includes orangutans, chimpanzees, and gorillas.
- **Hominidae:** More humanlike. Includes humans and their ancestors.

Although the fossil record is incomplete, the earliest of the Hominoidea appears to be Proconsol, which appeared around 25 million years ago. This marked the transition point from monkey to hominoid. Around 12 million years ago, Ramapithecus—the common ancestor to both human and ape—appeared. Ramapithecus lived closer to the ground, in the woodlands. Short in stature, Ramapithecus developed big teeth.

Around 10 million years ago, orangutans appear in the fossil record.

Approximately 8 to 6 million years ago, hominids (humans), split from the hominoids (apes). This is the missing link. Because very few rock units have been found that date from 4 to 8 million years ago, no fossil record has been found. Scientists used DNA protein structural studies to project a biological clock of change. They counted the differences in DNA structures between chimpanzees and humans to postulate a common ancestry.

Approximately 8 to 6 million years ago, hominids (humans), split from the hominoids (apes). This is the missing link.

Why did humans evolve?

The traditional view is egocentric. Hominids began to walk upright, use tools, lose the canine teeth, and evolve an expanded brain. The modern view approaches the study of hominds as it would any other animal by looking primarily at primate feeding habits. A climate change around 8 to 6 mya occurred as the grasslands expanded. Bipedalism developed in response to the problems posed by the new environment.

Hominid fossils

Ardipithecus ramidus ("Ardi"): Discovered in Ethiopia in1994, this fossil of a female hominid dates from approximately 4 million years ago. The fossilized remains consist of almost half a complete skeleton (skull, pelvis, hands, feet, and multiple limb bones) and reveal much about the Ardipithecus ramidus species.

This species had a small skull and brain, similar to a chimpanzee. The teeth lacked specialization, which suggests that the species was an omnivore. The fossils also indicated that the species was bipedal on land and quadrupedal in trees.

Australopithecus afarensis ("Lucy"): Discovered in 1974, the fossil was only a partial skeleton, but between that and preserved footprints, we know that Lucy was bipedal and walked upright. Most fossil skeletons are found in the Far East and in the South Africa Rift Valley. "Lucy," however, was discovered in Ethiopia.

The fossil record shows that a split occurred in the hominid evolutionary lines. Scientists generally believe that Australopithecus afarensis is the common ancestor to both the Homo and Australopithecus evolutionary lines. Newer evidence shows that members of both lines existed simultaneously for a period of time.

GENUS AUSTRALOPITHECUS	
Australopithecus Afarensis ("Lucy")	• Appeared 3.5 million years ago. • Cranial capacity: estimated to be about the size of a modem chimpanzee's (from fossilized skull fragments only.) • 3-4 ft. tall, with long arms and an ape-like jaw (jutting forward). • Bipedal, A. afarensis lived in the grasslands, used (but did not make) primitive tools, such as sticks, broken bones, rocks, etc.
Australopithecus Africanus	• Appeared 3 – 2 million years ago. • Cranial capacity: 450 cc. • A. africanus still was unable to have articulated speech, primarily because of skull and neck construction.
Australopithecus Robustus	• Appeared 2 – 1.5 million years ago. • Cranial capacity: 530 cc. • Flat face and forehead. Very heavily built. Had a sagital crest (bony ridge on top of head). This crest is believed to have been an anchor point for the muscles needed for the extremely heavy and powerful jaw. Still used (but did not make) primitive tools.
Australopithecus Bosei	• Appeared 2 – 1.5 million years ago. • Cranial capacity: 530 cc. • Contemporary to Australopithecus robustus. Large build but slightly smaller than robustus. • Paleontologists suspect that robustus and bosei are the same species, and the differences between them are simply sexual dimorphism (one was male and the other female). • The Australopithecus genus became extinct around 1.5 million years ago.

GENUS HOMO	
Homo Habilis	• Appeared around 2 million years ago. • Cranial capacity: 680cc. • Contemporary of Australopithecus robustus and bosei, but habilis was more advanced than the Australopithecus line. Face very ape-like, but hand and foot structure more modern. Scientists believe that rudimentary speech was possible, but not advanced speech because of head and shoulder physical constraints. H. habilis walked upright, used (but did not make) primitive tools. Evidence suggests that there was more meat in the habilis diet.
Homo Erectus ("Peking Man and Java Man")	• Appeared around 1.5 million years ago, just as the Australopithecus line disappeared. • Cranial capacity: 775cc to 1300cc. • Homo erectus is considered to be the first true species of humans. • H. erectus was the first of the Homo genus to leave Africa, becoming widely dispersed in both Africa and Eurasia. Although H. erectus had a heavy brow ridge, the lower anatomy was similar to modern humans'. Scientists believe H. erectus had speech, used fire, were good hunters, made and used more advanced tools such as flint and chert axes and scrapers with wooden handles.
Homo Sapiens (Archaic)	• Appeared between 500,000 and 250,000 years ago. • Cranial capacity: 1200cc. • H. sapiens (Archaic) represents a transition between Homo erectus and Homo Sapiens neanderthalensis. Scientists are not sure if this fossil represents an advanced erectus or an early neanderthalensis.
Homo Sapiens Neanderthalensis (Neanderthal)	• Appears after 250,000 to 125,000 years ago. • Cranial capacity: That of modern humans, 1500 cc. • The skull has a big brow and a sloping forehead. Neanderthals were short in height, but bigboned and heavyset. They made and used specialized stone and bone tools. There is significant evidence that they buried their dead.

Continued on next page

Homo Sapiens Sapiens (Cro-Magnon)	• First appeared after 35,000 years ago.
	• Cranial capacity: That of modern humans, 1500 cc.
	• H. sapiens sapiens had modern human features. Although they coexisted for a short period with neanderthalensis, H. sapiens sapiens eventually emerged as the sole surviving species of the Homo genus. There are two main theories why Cro-Magnon outlasted the Neanderthals:
	• Cro-Magnon humans interbred with the Neanderthals and eventually absorbed the line through genetics, or,
	• The Cro-Magnons were victorious in a long-term war and simply killed off the Neanderthals.
	• H. sapiens sapiens had the leisure time to create a highly developed culture as evidenced by cave paintings and sculptures. They both created and used well-developed stone and bone tools and had sophisticated food-gathering and hunting skills. There is evidence that Cro-Magnon humans domesticated animals around 15,000 years ago. H. sapiens sapiens practiced burial of the dead and included the deceased's possessions, suggesting some belief in an afterlife. H. sapiens sapiens has been popularly personified as the "Cave Man." The species disappeared 30,000 to 40,000 years ago.

COMPETENCY 24
OCEANOGRAPHY

SKILL 24.1 Demonstrate understanding of the geographic location of oceans and seas

Approximately 70 percent of the Earth's surface is covered by oceans

Approximately 70 percent of the Earth's surface is covered by oceans (large bodies of saline water). They are divided into five principal oceans and thirteen smaller seas.

1. Arctic Ocean: Smallest ocean, located in the Arctic, the polar region of the Northern Hemisphere.

2. Atlantic Ocean: Second largest ocean, located between the Americas on the west and Eurasia and Africa to the east. Connected in the north to the Arctic Ocean, in the southwest to the Pacific Ocean, in the southeast to the Indian Ocean, and in the south to the Southern Ocean.

3. Indian Ocean: Third largest ocean, located between Asia to the north, Africa to the west, the Malay Peninsula, Sunda Islands, and Australia to the east, and the Southern Ocean to the south.

4. Pacific Ocean: Largest ocean, extending from the Arctic Ocean in the north to the Southern Ocean in the south. Bounded by Asia and Australia to the west and the Americas to the east.

5. Southern Ocean: Fourth largest ocean consisting of the southernmost portions of the Pacific, Atlantic, and Indian Oceans.

There are thirteen seas, listed here from largest to smallest:

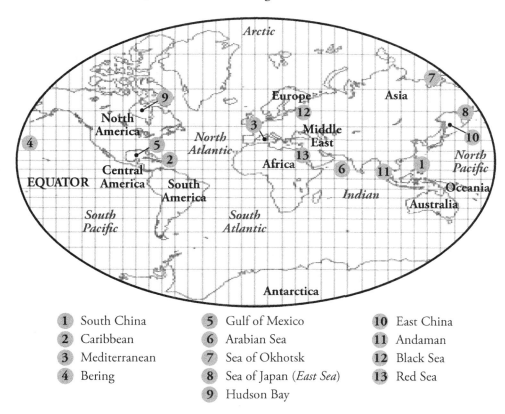

1	South China	5	Gulf of Mexico	10	East China
2	Caribbean	6	Arabian Sea	11	Andaman
3	Mediterranean	7	Sea of Okhotsk	12	Black Sea
4	Bering	8	Sea of Japan (*East Sea*)	13	Red Sea
		9	Hudson Bay		

SKILL 24.2 Demonstrate understanding of the processes involved in the formation and movement of ocean waves

The movement of ocean water is caused by the wind, the Sun's heat energy, the Earth's rotation, the moon's gravitational pull on Earth, and by underwater earthquakes.

SEISMIC SEA WAVE: a wave formed by an earthquake

The depth of the waveform where the energy is felt is equal to $\frac{1}{2}$ of the wavelength.

CURRENTS: caused by changes in water density, salinity, and pressure

The movement of ocean water is caused by the wind, the Sun's heat energy, the earth's rotation, the moon's gravitational pull on Earth, and by underwater earthquakes. Most ocean waves are caused by the impact of winds. Wind blowing over the surface of the ocean transfers energy (friction) to the water and causes waves to form. Waves are also formed by a seismic activity on the ocean floor. A wave formed by an earthquake is called a **SEISMIC SEA WAVE**. These powerful waves can be very destructive, with wave heights increasing to 30 meters or more near the shore. The crest of a wave is its highest point. The trough of a wave is its lowest point. The distance from wave top to wave top is the wavelength. The wave period is the time between the passing of two successive waves. (*See also skill 9.1*)

A transfer of energy from currents can also cause waves. Water will remain in place unless moved by the current or tide. **CURRENTS** are caused by changes in water density, salinity, and pressure.

Waves move in an orbital pattern, causing an up-and-down motion. They have a forward or lateral motion only if moved by the wind, current, or tides.

The depth of the waveform where the energy is felt is equal to $\frac{1}{2}$ of the wavelength. Below that depth, the water remains relatively calm.

When a wave approaches the shore, the circular orbit action flattens out and becomes more elliptical. As the wavelength shortens, the wave steepens until it finally breaks, creating surf. The waves break at a distance of $\frac{1}{20}$ of the wavelength.

SKILL 24.3 Demonstrate understanding of the primary causes and factors that influence tides

The periodic rise and fall of the liquid bodies on Earth are the direct result of the gravitational influence of the moon and, to a much lesser extent, the Sun.

The periodic rise and fall of the liquid bodies on Earth are the direct result of the gravitational influence of the moon and, to a much lesser extent, the Sun. Tides are produced by the differences between gravitational forces acting on parts of an object. As shown in **NEWTON'S UNIVERSAL LAW OF GRAVITATION**, the gravitational effect of two bodies is mutually constant and depends largely on the distance and mass between the objects.

The side of the Earth that faces the moon is roughly 4,000 miles (6,400 km) closer to the moon than is the Earth's center. This has the effect of increasing the moon's gravitational attraction on Earth's oceans and landforms. Although the effect is so small on the mass of the landforms as to be invisible, the effect on the liquid parts is greater.

If we were able to view such subtle change from outer space, the affected waters would create an elliptical shape, compressing downward at the top and bottom of the planet and extending outward on the sides. This double-bulge effect causes the tides to fall and rise twice a day. The time of the high and low tides is dependent on the phase of the moon.

Yet not all locations are uniformly affected. The tidal cycle at a particular location is actually a very complicated interaction of the location's latitude, shape of the shore, etc. For example, the Bay of Fundy has a twice-daily tide that exceeds 12 meters, while the northern coast of the Gulf of Mexico has only one tidal cycle that seldom exceeds 30 centimeters' rise and fall.

Because of its distance from the Earth, the Sun's gravitational effect on tides is only half that of the moon's. When the gravitational effects of both the Sun and moon join together during a new moon and a full-moon phase, however, the tidal effects can be extreme. Then the tidal bulges join together to produce very high and very low tides. These pronounced tides are known as spring tides. During the first and third quarters of the moon phases, the Sun's effect is negligible and consequently, the tides are lower. These are neap tides.

> **NEWTON'S UNIVERSAL LAW OF GRAVITATION:** the gravitational effect of two bodies is mutually constant and depends largely on the distance and mass between the objects

> The moon's gravitational effect causes a bulge to form on both sides of the Earth.

SKILL 24.4 Demonstrate knowledge of the major surface and deepwater currents in the oceans and the causes of these currents

World weather patterns are greatly influenced by ocean **SURFACE CURRENTS** in the upper layer of the ocean. These currents continuously move along the ocean surface in specific directions. Ocean currents that flow deep below the surface are called **SUBSURFACE CURRENTS**. These currents are influenced by such factors as the location of landmasses in the current's path and the Earth's rotation.

Surface currents are caused by winds and classified by temperature. Cold currents originate in the polar regions and flow through surrounding water that is measurably warmer. Those currents with a higher temperature than the surrounding water are called warm currents and can be found near the equator. These currents follow swirling routes around the ocean basins and the equator.

The Gulf Stream and the California Current are the two main surface currents that flow along the coastlines of the United States. The Gulf Stream is a warm current in the Atlantic Ocean that carries warm water from the equator to

> **SURFACE CURRENTS:** currents in the upper layer of the ocean that continuously move along the ocean surface in specific directions and influence world weather patterns

> **SUBSURFACE CURRENTS:** ocean currents that flow deep below the surface

> Surface currents are caused by winds and classified by temperature.

DENSITY CURRENTS: currents that flow because of a difference in the density or salinity of the ocean water

EQUATORIAL COUNTER CURRENTS: the primary currents in both hemispheres

the northern parts of the Atlantic Ocean. The California Current is a cold current that originates in the Arctic regions and flows southward along the west coast of the United States.

Differences in water density also create ocean currents. Water found near the bottom of oceans is the coldest and the densest. Water tends to flow from a denser area to a less dense area. Currents that flow because of a difference in the density of the ocean water are called **DENSITY CURRENTS**. Water with a higher salinity is denser than water with a lower salinity. Water that has salinity different from the surrounding water may form a density current.

The pressure gradient is a major player in determining ocean circulation. For example, the Gulf Stream is one of the strongest, most consistent ocean currents.

The primary currents in both hemispheres are the **EQUATORIAL COUNTER CURRENTS**. These currents are located slightly above the equator in the Northern Hemisphere and slightly below the equator in the Southern Hemisphere. They are offset from the equator because of the Intertropical Convergence Zone (ITCZ).

Western Boundary Currents

All six of the major western boundary currents flow north.

1. Gulf Stream (also called the Florida Current)—Atlantic Ocean: The Gulf Stream receives more water than it theoretically should because the Brazil Current supplements it. This extra water is present because of the shape of Brazil; it forces the water up into the lower part of the Gulf Stream in the Caribbean.

2. Brazil Current—Atlantic Ocean: The Southern Hemisphere equivalent of the Gulf Stream

3. Japan Current (Kuroshio Current)—Pacific Ocean

4. East Australian Current—Pacific Ocean

5. Agulhas Current—Indian Ocean

6. Somalia Current—Indian Ocean: The Somalia current is present only half of the year. The rest of the time it flows south.

Because the Pacific Ocean is so large, the western boundary currents in the north and south Pacific (Kuroshio Current and East Australian Current) each have two gyres. Additionally, the Kuroshio Current is a big player in the El Niño effect.

Antarctic water freely circulates, causing the Southern Ocean to remain fairly constant in temperature. The West Wind Drift causes the Antarctic flow.

In the Indian Ocean, the South Equatorial Current is affected by the southwest monsoon winds. When the southwest monsoon winds blow, it reverses the current of the northern leg of the South Equatorial Current. That leg is renamed and becomes the Southwest Monsoon Current.

Direction of ocean circulation: The direction indicated in the current's name is the direction the current is heading in. For example, the Northwest Current flows northwest. Rule of thumb: fly from, sail to.

Rule of thumb: fly from, sail to.

SKILL 24.5 **Demonstrate understanding of the processes that influence the topography and landforms of the ocean floor and shorelines**

The ocean floor starts at the end of the continental rise and has an extensive **ABYSSAL PLAIN**, a flat, featureless landscape, broken only by ridges or trenches. Covered with deep deposits of sediment, the ocean floor is the flattest topography on Earth.

ABYSSAL PLAIN: a flat, featureless landscape, broken only by ridges or trenches

Ocean Floor Sediment Deposits

- Terrigenous: Deposits derived from the land, including very fine sediments from runoff and erosion, as well as some sand, ash, and sediment carried by the wind in sandstorms and volcanic events.

- Glacial: Material dropped out of an iceberg as it melts, an uncommon event.

- Biogenous: The predominant sediment of the abyssal plain. Derived from biologic organisms, mainly carbonate and silica shells of microscopic plankton which drop to the bottom and build up when the plankton die.

- Hydrogenous: Material that precipitates out of the seawater. The two most common chemical nodules formed from solution are manganese and phosphate nodules. Both are a viable commercial ore source found in localized deposits.

Ridges

There are two types of ridges:

1. Mid-ocean ridge: Characterized by great length and steep slopes, this is the site of seafloor spreading.

2. Aseismic ridge: Formed by hot spots, islands, seamounts, and guyots.

Seamount

A volcano that never reached the ocean surface. A seamount is a pointy-topped, undersea mountain, usually formed by a hot spot as part of a ridge or chain.

Guyot

A flat-topped undersea mountain. Originally the mountain was above the surface, but, when the tectonic plate moved off a hot spot, either erosion and/or subsidence of seafloor bulging caused the mountain to sink beneath the ocean's surface. A chain of aseismic guyots links Midway Island to Hawaii.

Trench

One of the deepest parts of the ocean. It breaks the abyssal plain, has steep slopes, and is found at the sites of subduction zones.

Shoreline erosional features

Erosional features are most evident on rocky shorelines such as those found in parts of California or New England.

- **Sea cave:** Erosive effects gradually hollow out cliff faces where the water strikes. This erosion continues until the water can no longer reach the back of the cave.

- **Wave-cut Platform (wave-cut terrace):** After a sea cave is dug by erosion, sometimes the face of the cliff collapses and forms a plateau-type platform that is smoothed by further erosion.

- **Sea arch:** The erosive effects of the waves have the greatest effect against the material of a headland. The erosion literally digs sea caves in from both sides of the headland. Eventually, these caves join together, forming a sea arch.

- **Sea stack:** When the top of a sea arch collapses, it leaves a vertical column of land. A sea stack can be quite huge, resembling a small island. The California coastline has thousands of sea stacks.

Coastline deposition and beaches

Deposition along the coastline affects mostly unconsolidated particles, sand sized or smaller, and occurs whenever the longshore current slows. The main feature of this deposition is the building of beaches.

Beach: A large accumulation of sand and sand-sized particles along a body of water. A beach is in equilibrium with the distinct forces that create it. Unless changes occur to disturb the equilibrium, the beach will remain constant in composition and size.

A beach is in equilibrium with the distinct forces that create it. Unless changes occur to disturb the equilibrium, the beach will remain constant in composition and size.

The beach actually extends outward to a depth of 30 feet. After 30 feet, the sand is lost to the ocean bottom. The 30-foot depth can be as much as a mile offshore.

The longshore current runs parallel to the coastline, and there is literally a river of sand carried down the beach shoreline by the current. This is not necessarily negative, because the sand is mostly redeposited further down the beach. Overall, the transportation effect merely moves the sand with no net loss or gain, but problems can arise when the longshore drift is disturbed by storms or severe rip tides. Then the sand is carried out to sea and lost to the process of building up the beach.

Because beaches attempt to remain in equilibrium, as they adjust, black material can be found on some beaches. The material is not oil spill, but it is muck from the swampy area behind the original berms. The beach moved inland, exposing the dried muck from the bottom of the swampy area.

SKILL 24.6 Demonstrate understanding of the factors that influence the physical and chemical properties of seawater and nutrient cycles of the ocean

Seventy percent of the Earth's surface is covered with salt water, which is termed the HYDROSPHERE. The mass of this salt water is about 1.4×10^{24} grams. The ocean waters continuously circulate among different parts of the hydrosphere.

Pure water is a combination of the elements hydrogen and oxygen. These two elements make up about 96.5% of the ocean water. The remaining portion is made up of dissolved solids whose concentration determines the water's salinity.

SALINITY is the number of grams of dissolved salts in 1,000 grams of sea water. The average salinity of ocean water is about 3.5 percent. In other words, one kilogram of seawater contains about 35 grams of salt (sodium chloride). Salt (NaCl) is the most abundant of the dissolved salts, which also include smaller quantities of magnesium chloride, magnesium and calcium sulfates, and traces of several other salt elements. Salinity varies throughout the world's oceans and varies with depth. Salinity is low near river mouths where the ocean mixes with fresh water, and salinity is high in areas of high evaporation rates.

The temperature of ocean water varies with different latitudes and with ocean depths. Ocean water temperature is about constant to depths of 90 meters. The temperature of surface water drops rapidly from 28°C at the equator to -2°C at the poles. The freezing point of seawater is lower than the freezing point of pure

HYDROSPHERE: the seventy percent of the Earth's surface that is covered with salt water

SALINITY: the number of grams of dissolved salts in 1,000 grams of sea water

The temperature of ocean water varies with different latitudes and with ocean depths.

water. Pure water freezes at 0°C while the dissolved salts in the seawater keep it at a freezing point of -2°C. The freezing point of seawater may vary depending on its salinity in a particular location.

The ocean can be divided into three temperature zones. The surface layer consists of relatively warm water and exhibits most of the wave action present. The area where the wind and waves churn and mix the water is called the mixed layer. This is the layer where most living creatures are found because of abundant sunlight and warmth. The second layer is called the thermocline, which becomes increasingly cold as its depth increases. This change is due to the lack of energy from sunlight. The layer below the thermocline continues to the deep dark, very cold, and semibarren ocean floor.

Deepwater upwelling replaces the displaced surface water and brings up rich nutrients for the marine food chain. This results in good fishing areas, for example, along the coasts of Oregon and Peru/Chile.

COMPETENCY 25
METEOROLOGY

SKILL 25.1 Demonstrate knowledge of the structure of the atmosphere and thermal and chemical properties of atmospheric layers

The atmosphere makes up only 0.25% of what we call the Earth, and like the fluids of the ocean, our atmosphere is driven by heat, primarily solar radiation

The Earth's atmosphere is very similar to a fluid. The atmosphere makes up only 0.25% of what we call the Earth, and like the fluids of the ocean, our atmosphere is driven by heat, primarily solar radiation. Having an atmosphere is not unique for a planet. To a degree, most of the planets in our solar system have an atmosphere, but the presence of significant oxygen in Earth's atmosphere is unique and makes life possible on our planet.

Earth's atmosphere is composed of 78 percent nitrogen, 21 percent oxygen, and 1 percent other gasses.

Components of the Atmosphere

- **Water vapor:** Along with carbon dioxide (CO_2) and methane, water vapor (H_2O) is considered a **GREENHOUSE GAS**: a gas that absorbs heat energy. Water vapor is the most prevalent of the greenhouse gasses and is especially good at collecting heat energy, as evidenced by the Earth's ability to retain heat at night when solar radiation is lowest.

- **Dust and aerosols:** These are natural components of the atmosphere, and their presence produces optical phenomena such as making the sky appear blue, rainbows, and the northern and southern lights. *See also Skill 9.3*

- **Pollutants:** Some are human produced, including industrial waste, chemical refrigerants, and hydrocarbons released from burning fossil fuels. Some are natural such as terpene released from trees, Saharan dust, and CO_2 released by volcanoes.

> **GREENHOUSE GAS:**
> a gas that absorbs heat energy

Layers of the atmosphere

Troposphere (ground level to 11 Km, 0 to 17.6 miles): The troposphere varies in height according to the temperature. It is lower at the poles and higher at the equator. Because the pressure decreases, it gets colder as you go up in the troposphere. Only very rarely do you have a mixing between the troposphere and the next layer, the stratosphere. All storms, weather fronts, and weather occur in the troposphere.

Stratosphere (11 Km to 50 Km, 17.6 to 80 miles): The stratosphere is characterized by weak vertical air motion, and strong horizontal air motion. There is very little lifting or sinking air in the stratosphere. Temperatures warm as you go up due to the presence of the ozone layer.

Mesosphere (50 to 85 Km, 80 to 136 miles): It is bitterly cold in the mesosphere.

Thermosphere (85 to 600 Km, 136 to 960 miles): This is the hottest portion of the atmosphere with rapid warming accompanying a rise in altitude. There are very few molecules left to block out the incoming solar radiation. The outer reaches of the thermosphere are also sometimes referred to as the exosphere.

Ionosphere (located within the upper portion of the mesosphere at 80Km and goes into the thermosphere): The ionosphere is an area of free ions, positively charged ions, produced as a result of solar radiation striking the atmosphere. The solar wind strikes the ionosphere at the polar dips in the magnetosphere. The ions are excited to a higher energy state and this energy is released into the visible spectrum to form the aurora borealis (northern lights).

The ionosphere varies with the time of day, season, and sunspot cycles:

When the Sun sets at night, fewer ions strike, extending radio-wave communications. There is more radiation during sunspot cycles, which hypercharge the atmosphere and can disrupt radio waves during the daytime.

Ozone layer (O_3): Contained within the stratosphere, ozone is essential to life on Earth and is continually formed and destroyed within the atmosphere. Only a very thin layer of ozone protects against ultraviolet (UV) radiation. Ultraviolet radiation scrambles the DNA codes in human cells, and can kill the cells or, at a minimum, cause cancer.

Much concern is made in the press about a hole in the ozone layer. This is a misnomer. In reality, there is not a hole, but a possible thinning of the layer, which many scientists believe is due to the presence of carbon fluorocarbons (CFCs). The chlorine (CI) in CFCs and from other sources steals an oxygen atom from ozone (O_3) molecules, leaving only plain oxygen (O_2), which does not effectively screen out UV radiation ($Cl + O_3 = ClO + O_2$). The resultant ClO molecule is very unstable, and UV radiation can easily break it apart. The released chlorine then attacks another ozone molecule, and the process repeats itself.

CFCs were thought to be the primary culprit, but this theory has problems. CFCs were only invented in the 1920s for use in aerosol spray cans, industrial processes, and refrigerants. Although CFCs may be a contributor in the depletion of the ozone layer, not all scientists believe that CFCs are solely responsible. Why does the thinning occur only over Antarctica? The greatest use of CFCs occurred in the industrialized nations of the Northern Hemisphere. Additionally, the hole varies in size from year to year, appearing during the Antarctic spring in October and disappearing by mid-November or December.

Since scientists only started collecting data on thinning of the ozone layer in 1979, there is a lack of data. There is a possibility that the "ozone hole" may have existed before the introduction of CFCs.

An alternate theory to explain the cause of ozone thinning is the circumpolar vortex theory. Because there is a great deal of open ocean in Antarctica, it is a very cold place during the winter. The cold, in effect, isolates the Antarctic atmosphere from the rest of the warmer atmosphere. This extreme cold forms ice crystals in the atmosphere, and chlorine is locked into the crystals. When the Antarctic spring comes, the atmosphere thaws out, releasing the chlorine into the atmosphere. The chlorine attacks the ozone layer, decreasing its density.

As spring progresses, the circumpolar vortex weakens, allowing the air to mix with the normally ozone-rich air. Thus, the "hole" disappears.

SKILL 25.2 Demonstrate knowledge of the chemical composition of the atmosphere

See Skill 25.1

SKILL 25.3 Demonstrate understanding of the factors influencing seasonal and latitudinal variation of solar radiation

The distribution of solar energy is called INSOLATION. Solar radiation isn't distributed evenly across the Earth, because of the Earth's curvature, axial tilt, and orbit. This results in uneven heating of the atmosphere, and is why the temperature is warmer at the equator and colder at the poles.

Because of the curvature and tilt, the energy striking the polar areas is spread over a larger area, which dilutes the energy received by a particular area. At the equator the energy is more concentrated.

The effect of insolation is important to life on Earth. The absence of solar radiation would cause the creation of very cold air masses and the thermal blanket of the atmosphere would not have heat to hold and reradiate. In short order, the world would become an icy rock.

Externalists put forth the concept that the axial tilt of the Earth is responsible for the ice ages. This tilt does vary over time relative to the Earth's orbital plane. Although these changes do not change the total amount of sunlight striking the planet, they do affect the distribution of the solar radiation.

MILANKOVITCH CYCLES: Based on the Earth's relationship to the Sun, this theory proposes that the axial tilt and wobble of the Earth's orbit is responsible for warming or cooling. Technically, the theory deals with these terms:

- Precession: the wobble of the Earth on its axis.

- Obliquity: the tilt of the Earth's axis. This ranges between 22.5 to 25.5 degrees. Today the tilt is 23.5 degrees.

- Eccentricity: the shape of an orbit. The Earth's orbital shape changes periodically from elliptical to circular.

If there is a change in the tilt and orbit, then the amount of incoming solar radiation will change over time. The tilt of the axis is key in determining where most of the solar radiation strikes. It causes either longer or shorter summers and winters. A shorter summer increases the snow pack in the mountains. As this builds over time, it causes an interglacial or glacial period.

INSOLATION: the distribution of solar energy

Solar radiation isn't distributed evenly across the Earth, because of the Earth's curvature, axial tilt, and orbit.

MILANKOVITCH CYCLES: theory proposing that the axial tilt and wobble of the Earth's orbit is responsible for warming or cooling

The cycle is between 18,000 to 100,000 years. With the exception of one period, ice core O_{18} ratio data correlates with this cycle and also shows a possible correlation between the Milankovitch Cycles and the oceans as a CO_2 sink.

SKILL 25.4 Demonstrate understanding of the causes of global wind belts

WIND BELTS: one of three convection cells that encircle Earth like belts

On a weather map, closely spaced isobars indicate high winds.

GEOSTROPHIC OR GRADIENT WINDS: winds at high altitudes that, with no friction present, form an undulating, surface-like topography and easily flow to low-pressure areas

CORIOLIS EFFECT: causes the winds to move in either a clockwise motion (high-pressure areas), or a counter-clockwise motion (low-pressure area)

ZONAL WINDS: blow in a west-to-east pattern roughly parallel to the lines of latitude

MERIDONAL WINDS: blow north to south and cross the line of latitude

The **WIND BELTS** in each hemisphere consist of convection cells that encircle Earth like belts. There are three major wind belts on Earth: (1) trade winds, (2) prevailing westerlies, and (3) polar easterlies. Wind-belt formation depends on the differences in air pressures that develop in the doldrums, the horse latitudes, and the polar regions. The doldrums surround the equator. Within this belt heated air usually rises straight up into Earth's atmosphere. The horse latitudes are regions of high barometric pressure with calm and light winds, and the polar regions contain cold dense air that sinks to the Earth's surface.

Temperature differences cause the pressure differences that cause wind. The pressure moves the wind from high- to low-pressure areas. The greater the difference in pressure, the larger the gradient, and the faster the wind will move. On a weather map, closely spaced isobars indicate high winds. The winds at altitudes, with no friction present, form an undulating, surface-like topography and easily flow to low-pressure areas. These winds at altitude are called **GEOSTROPHIC** or **GRADIENT WINDS**. Geostrophic winds are affected by the pressure gradient force (PGF) and the **CORIOLIS EFFECT**, which causes the winds to move in either a clockwise motion (high-pressure areas), or a counter-clockwise motion (low-pressure area). The winds blow parallel to the isobars because of the Coriolis effect, and upper-level winds always follow the isobars.

ZONAL WINDS blow in a west-to-east pattern roughly parallel to the lines of latitude, while **MERIDONAL WINDS** blow north to south and cross the line of latitude.

SURFACE WINDS are found at less than 1,000 meters altitude. These winds are no longer balanced because the terrain introduces friction, which in turn, reduces the Coriolis effect and causes a 30° deflection of the wind from the PGF.

The rise and fall of heat at the 0°, 30°, 60°, and 90° latitudes drives convection cells by causing the pressure gradients to speed up or slow down. The **JET STREAMS** are zones of strong, moving air confined to narrow columns that mark the zones where the cold polar air and warmer air meet, producing the greatest pressure gradients. The jet streams can be either straight or can dramatically dip, creating ridges and troughs on the 500-300 mb pressure surface.

The **INTERTROPICAL CONVERGENCE ZONE (ITCZ)**, controls the weather in the tropics, and it moves north and south of the equator. The ITCZ is responsible for the formation of monsoon rains.

The **DOLDRUMS**, an area of no wind, are located at 0°. The **HORSE LATITUDES** are located between 0° and 30° north and south latitudes. The **TRADE WINDS** are very strong winds that blow all the time in the horse latitudes and provide direct heating to the coastal climate in this zone.

The **PREVAILING WESTERLIES** west-to-east winds found between 30°–60° north and south latitude, causing storms.

POLAR WINDS are the product of the presence or absence of sunlight, not polar cells.

MONSOONS are huge wind systems that cover large geographic areas and that reverse direction seasonally. The monsoons of India and Asia are examples of these seasonal winds. They alternate wet and dry seasons. As denser cooler air over the ocean moves inland, a steady seasonal wind called a summer or wet monsoon is produced.

SKILL 25.5 **Identify the factors that contribute to small-scale atmospheric circulation**

Small-Scale Wind Systems

Small-scale wind systems are found in the area of surface winds (<1,000 m altitude), and are affected by surface friction caused by the topography.

Turbulence is caused by surface heating and the effect of the topography on the wind movement. An increase in surface heating creates greater turbulence.

Eddies are formed when surface winds hit an obstruction and cause an air pocket to form that diminishes or changes the direction of the trapped wind. Pilots refer to eddies as windshear.

Wind direction refers to the direction from which the wind is flowing and is measured with a wind vane. Prevailing wind is the term used to describe the dominant direction from which the wind is blowing.

During the day, the land is hot and the water is cool. At night the situation is reversed; the land is cool while the water is warmer. Sea breezes are caused by the temperature differentials between the land and oceans. Land breezes

SURFACE WINDS: winds found at less than 1,000 meters altitude and that are no longer balanced because the terrain introduces friction, which in turn, reduces the Coriolis effect

JET STREAMS: zones of strong, moving air that mark the zones where the cold polar air and warmer air meet

INTERTROPICAL CONVERGENCE ZONE (ITCZ): moving north and south of the equator, controls the weather in the tropics

DOLDRUMS: an area of no wind

HORSE LATITUDES: located between 0° and 30° north and south latitudes

TRADE WINDS: strong winds that blow all the time provide direct heating to the coastal climate

PREVAILING WESTERLIES: found between 30° and 60° north and south latitude and cause storms and winds to move in a west-to-east pattern

MONSOONS: huge wind systems that cover large geographic areas and that reverse direction seasonally

POLAR WINDS: the product of the presence or absence of sunlight

An increase in surface heating creates greater turbulence.

follow the reverse pattern of sea breezes, with daytime causing airflow from the land to the sea and from the sea to land at night.

Mountain and valley breezes are the result of thermal differences and topography. During the day the thermal currents rise up from the valley floor and move up the sides of the mountains. At night, the mountains act as a lingering heat source, retaining the heat in the valleys.

A chinook breeze occurs when the prevailing westerlies get squeezed between the bottom of the stratosphere and the top of large mountain ranges. This causes a heating and expansion of the air as it moves over the mountains, drying the area and melting snow. This effect can be intensified by the presence of high- and low-pressure systems. The chinook breeze is concentrated on the eastern edge of the Rocky Mountains where it can cause early snowmelt, increasing the likelihood of flooding downstream. *Santa Ana winds* are a specialized form of the chinook breeze, formed when air moves down the valleys to the coast when a high-pressure area is present. The wind is very warm and dry, creating dangerous fire conditions.

A haboob is seen in the deserts and is a dynamic of thunderstorms that do not have enough condensation to precipitate. It is characterized by violent up and down drafts that pick up sand and carry it far up into the atmosphere. This sand rains down thousands of miles away.

URBAN HEAT ISLANDS: the result of concentrated masses of buildings and concrete and asphalt paving that absorb more heat than grass and fields in the countryside

URBAN HEAT ISLANDS are the result of concentrated masses of buildings and concrete and asphalt paving that absorb more heat than grass and fields in the countryside. The heat produced in and reradiated by urban areas forms a rising thermal zone over the urban area, making it usually 10 degrees or more hotter in the city than in the countryside.

LAKE EFFECT SNOW/RAIN is caused by air moving over a large body of water, absorbing large amounts of moisture, and then releasing it as snow or rain over urban heat islands. Situated close to large lakes, Chicago, Illinois, and Buffalo, New York, often experience unexpected precipitation or early snowfall during the fall months because of the lake effect. This usually ceases when the lakes freeze over during the winter months.

LAKE EFFECT SNOW/ RAIN: caused by air moving over a large body of water, absorbing large amounts of moisture, and then releasing it as snow or rain over urban heat islands

El Niño is a reverse of the normal weather patterns in the Pacific that affects wind patterns (especially the jet stream and trade winds) as well as, for instance, wildlife, agriculture, commercial fishing. La Niña is the opposite of El Nino, with a lesser effect. (*For more on these phenomena, see Skill 25.14*)

SKILL 25.6 Distinguish among the terms relative humidity, absolute humidity, dew point, and frost point

As the temperature changes, the capacity of the air to hold water changes: as air cools, water condenses; as air warms, water evaporates. The air is constantly changing temperature as it is heated by the Sun or cooled by altitude.

ABSOLUTE HUMIDITY: the mass of the water vapor divided by the volume of air. The resulting number in calculating absolute humidity is actually meaningless because the mass of water vapor may stay the same as volume changes.

RELATIVE HUMIDITY: the actual water vapor content divided by the water vapor capacity multiplied by 100. Relative humidity looks at the total amount of water vapor a mass of area could hold (capacity), in relation to how much it actually holds. Relative humidity is used in weather prediction and is expressed as a percentage.

100% humidity: The air is saturated with water vapor and can't hold any more without upsetting the equilibrium between water vapor and liquid water.

50% humidity: There is only one-half as much water vapor in the air as it could actually hold, or at 50% humidity the air could evaporate two times the water vapor if you increase the air's temperature. In this case, the capacity increases, but the relative humidity actually decreases.

If the temperature drops, the amount of water vapor present is not altered, but the water vapor capacity decreases and the relative humidity increases.

Another way to look at humidity is by how much evaporation could occur. If there is 100% relative humidity, then the air is saturated and no more evaporation can occur. But, if there is 50% relative humidity, then evaporation is more likely to occur.

The air temperature at which water vapor begins to condense is called the **DEW POINT**. If there is a large difference between the dew point and the temperature, then you have low humidity. If there is a small difference between the dew point and the temperature, then you have a higher humidity. Remember: Colder air has a lower water vapor capacity than warm air does. That is why you can have high humidity in cold air and medium humidity in warm air. Ironically, the warm air actually has more water vapor present (specific humidity).

ABSOLUTE HUMIDITY: the mass of the water vapor divided by the volume of air

RELATIVE HUMIDITY: measures the total amount of water vapor a mass of area could hold (capacity), in relation to how much it actually holds

DEW POINT: the air temperature at which water vapor begins to condense

If there is a large difference between the dew point and the temperature, then you have low humidity. If there is a small difference between the dew point and the temperature, then you have a higher humidity.

FROST POINT: the temperature, always below 0°C (32°F), at which moisture in the air will condense as a layer of frost on any exposed surface

The **FROST POINT** is the temperature, always below 0°C (32°F), at which moisture in the air will condense as a layer of frost on any exposed surface. Like the dew point, the frost point is dependent upon the relative humidity of the air. Because it is more difficult for water molecules to escape a frozen surface than a liquid surface (ice has stronger bonding between neighboring water molecules), the frost point is greater in temperature than the dew point. The frost point is located between the temperature and dewpoint.

> SKILL 25.7 **Demonstrate knowledge of various cloud and precipitation types and their formation**

Forms of Precipitation

All forms of precipitation start from an interaction of water vapor and other particulate matter in the atmosphere. These particulates act as a nucleus for raindrops.

All forms of precipitation start from an interaction of water vapor and other particulate matter in the atmosphere. These particulates act as a nucleus for raindrops, as the water vapor particles attach themselves to the other airborne particles. Because one of water's major properties is that its water particles attract other water particles, the raindrop grows as water vapor particles accrete around the nuclei.

Drizzle: any form of liquid precipitation where the drops are less than 0.02 inches in diameter.

Rain: any form of liquid precipitation where the drops are greater than 0.02 inches in diameter.

Virga: the meteorological condition in which rain evaporates before touching the ground. You see it rain, but raindrops never hit the ground.

The shape of the snowflakes depend on the temperature at which they formed.

Snow: water molecules that form into ice crystals through freezing. The shape of the snowflakes depends on the temperature at which they formed:

- Needles = 0°C to -10°C
- Dendrites = -10°C to -20°C
- Plates = -20°C to -30°C
- Columns = -30°C to -40°C

Freezing rain or ice storm: drops fall as rain but immediately depose (freeze) upon hitting an extremely cold surface such as power lines, roofs, or the ground.

Rime Ice: ice droplets that have tiny air bubbles trapped within the ice, producing an opaque whitish layer of granular ice.

Sleet: officially called ice pellets, these are drops of rain 5 mm or less in diameter. Sleet freezes before hitting the ground and bounces when it strikes a surface.

Hail: precipitation in the form of balls or lumps of ice. Hail forms when an ice pellet is transported through a cloud that contains varied concentrations of super-cooled water droplets. The pellet may descend slowly through the entire cloud, or it may be caught in a cycle of updraft and downdraft. The ice pellet grows by accreting (adding) freezing water droplets. Eventually, the weight of the hail grows too heavy to be supported by the air column and hailstone falls to the ground. The size of the stone depends on the amount of time it spent in the cloud.

Fog: a cloud that touches the ground. Fog forms when cold air moves over a warmer surface. Fog is common along shorelines because the specific heat of water retains heat and is consequently much warmer than the overlying air. Fog can also form inland where the same basic conditions exist.

Clouds are classified by their physical appearance and are given special Latin names corresponding to the cloud's appearance and the altitude where they occur. Classification by appearance results in three simple categories: cirrus, stratus, and cumulus clouds. Cirrus clouds appear fibrous. Stratus clouds appear layered. Cumulus clouds appear as heaps or puffs, similar to cotton balls in a pile. Classification by altitude results in four groupings: high, middle, low, and clouds that show vertical development. Other adjectives are added to the names of the clouds to show specific characteristics.

Causes of Precipitation

- Collision and coalescence: In warm clouds the water vapor moves, merges, and collides to form bigger drops. Generally, the darker a cloud is, the bigger the drops formed. Eventually, the drops get too heavy for the supporting updrafts and drop out of the clouds as rain.

- Bergeron process: In a cold cloud (below freezing), ice begins to form into crystals and attracts other water droplets. Eventually the crystals get too heavy and drop out of the cloud.

Generally, the darker a cloud is, the bigger the drops formed.

CLOUD CLASSIFICATIONS
HIGH CLOUDS -13 °F (-25 °C); >23,000 FT (7,000 M): COMPOSED ALMOST EXCLUSIVELY OF ICE CRYSTALS
• **Cirrus:** Nearly transparent; delicate, silky strands (mare's tails), or patches • **Cirrostratus:** A thin veil or sheet that partially or totally covers the sky; Nearly transparent, so the Sun or moon readily shines through • **Cirrocumulus:** Small, white, rounded patches arranged in a wave or spotted mackerel pattern
MIDDLE CLOUDS 32 – -13°F (0 – -25 °C); 6600 – 23,000 FT (2000 – 7000 M): COMPOSED OF SUPERCOOLED WATER DROPLETS OR A MIXTURE OF DROPLETS AND ICE CRYSTALS
• **Altostratus:** Uniform white or bluish-gray layers that partially or totally obscure the sky layer • **Altocumulus:** Roll-like puffs or patches that form into parallel bands or waves
LOW CLOUDS > 23 °F (-5 °C): COMPOSED MOSTLY OF WATER DROPLETS
• **Stratocumulus:** 0–6,600 ft (0–2000 m) Large, irregularly shaped puffs or rolls separated by bands of clear sky • **Stratus:** 0–6600 ft (0–2000 m) Uniform gray layer that stretches from horizon to horizon from which drizzle may fall • **Nimbostratus:** 0–13,120 ft (0–4000 m) Thick, uniform, gray layer from which precipitation (significant rain or snow) is falling
CLOUDS WITH VERTICAL DEVELOPMENT 0-9840 FT (0-3000 M): WATER DROPLETS BUILD UPWARD AND SPREAD LATERALLY
• **Cumulus:** Resemble cotton balls dotting the sky • **Cumulonimbus:** Often associated with thunderstorms; large puffy, clouds that have smooth or flattened tops and can produce heavy rain and thunder

Characterize major types of air masses in terms of temperature, moisture content, and source areas

An **AIR MASS (PARCEL OF AIR)** is a large body of air that assumes a characteristic temperature, pressure, and humidity from sitting over a landmass. Horizontally, the parcel has relatively uniform temperature, pressure, and humidity. Vertically, the parcel may have widely differing temperatures, pressures, and humidity. When you think of air parcels, think in the horizontal plane.

The characteristics of the world's air masses are largely determined by where they are formed, as shown in the chart below:

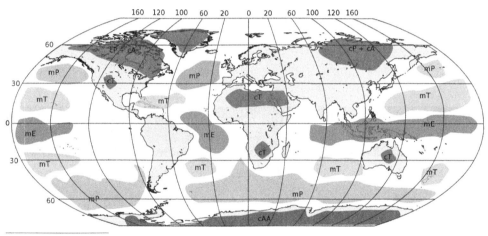

Courtesy of NASA, http://rst.gsfc.nasa.gov/Sect14/air_masses_2.jpg

Warmer air masses are formed near the tropics ("T"), both over the ocean (maritime "m"), and over the continents ("c"). Cold air masses are formed in polar regions (polar "p" and the Arctic or Antarctica "A"). Dryer air masses are formed over continents, while moisture-laden air masses are formed over the ocean. As an air mass moves, it may gain moisture if it moves over the water, or lose moisture as it moves over land.

As with ocean currents, warm air masses tend to move toward the poles, losing heat as they go. Cold, polar air masses will move down toward the equator. Because of Coriolis forces, air masses move in a circular manner, and also circulate upward from the Earth and back down again, in cells as shown below.

Areas where hot air masses are rising away from the Earth create **LOW-PRESSURE ZONES**, and areas where cold air masses are sinking down create **HIGH-PRESSURE ZONES**. Surface air masses generally move toward latitudes of low pressure and away from latitudes of high pressure. These latitudes of high and low pressure are known as pressure belts. Locally, the movement of air masses may also be affected by continental landforms, such as mountains.

AIR MASS (PARCEL OF AIR): large body of air that assumes a characteristic temperature, pressure, and humidity from sitting over a landmass

When you think of air parcels, think in the horizontal plane.

As an air mass moves, it may gain moisture if it moves over the water, or lose moisture as it moves over land.

As with ocean currents, warm air masses tend to move toward the poles, losing heat as they go. Cold, polar air masses will move down toward the equator.

LOW-PRESSURE ZONE: an area where hot air masses are rising

HIGH-PRESSURE ZONE: an area where cold air masses are sinking

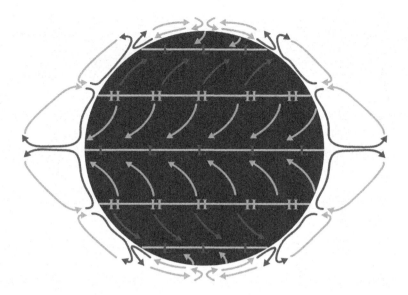

SKILL 25.9 Demonstrate understanding of high- and low-pressure systems

Atmospheric pressure is affected by temperature and reflects what is happening in the air.

PRESSURE is the force exerted by the molecules in the air. If you take two columns of air (A and B) with the same temperature and same density, and raise the temperature of B and lower the temperature of A, then you will cause an expansion or contraction of the columns of air.

> **PRESSURE:** the force exerted by the molecules in the air

- Column A contracts because you are lowering the temperature. The molecules become less energetic and are packed closer together, hence, denser.

- Column B expands because you've raised the temperature. The molecules become more active and are packed more loosely, hence, less dense.

- Although the columns now are of physically differing sizes (volume), the pressure is identical in both columns because the density has adjusted for the difference in volume.

- However, the atmosphere is not neatly isolated into columns. So another way to consider this pressure change is to visualize two columns of air not isolated from each other.

- Columns A and B both have the same temperature, density, and pressure throughout. Now cool the air in column A and heat the air in column B. Overlay these two columns of air with a scale calibrated in millibars. When both columns are at the same altitude, the air in column B now has a higher pressure than the air in column A.

Meteorogically, the air in column A represents an area of low pressure, and the air in column B represents an area of high pressure. Since nature abhors a vacuum, the air tries to move from the area of high pressure to the area of low pressure. Surface pressure in column A starts to rise because the air is moving in. Surface pressure in column B starts to drop because the air is moving out.

Since nature abhors a vacuum, the air tries to move from the area of high pressure to the area of low pressure.

For use in weather prediction, the effect of temperature is more important to changes in upper atmosphere air pressure than to changes in the surface pressure. Temperature has the biggest effect on air pressure in the atmosphere.

The Effect of Water on Pressure

The moisture in the air affects pressure, and the effect is more prevalent in the surface pressure. Water vapor in the air makes the air less dense. Example: The atomic weight of an air molecule is 29 atomic mass units (amu). The atomic weight of a water molecule is 18 amu. For every molecule of air displaced by water, the density of the air decreases by 7 amu.

A change in density affects the pressure of the air and all the factors of the gas law come into play since temperature and density both affect pressure. Dry, cold air has the highest pressure, while warm, moist air has the lowest pressure.

Dry, cold air has the highest pressure, while warm, moist air has the lowest pressure.

SKILL 25.10 Demonstrate understanding of the structure and movement of frontal systems (cold, warm, stationary, occluded) and the air circulation around and weather associated with frontal systems

---

Atmospheric Stability

Warm air rises and will continue to rise until it meets air that is as cold, or colder, than the rising air. When rising air cools to the dew point, clouds form because of condensation. Air can rise even if it is only a few degrees warmer than the surrounding air.

Warm air rises and will continue to rise until it meets air that is as cold, or colder, than the rising air.

ATMOSPHERIC STABILITY is determined by comparing the temperature change of an ascending or descending air parcel with the temperature profile of the ambient air layer in which the parcel ascends or descends. Air is considered either stable or unstable.

ATMOSPHERIC STABILITY: determined by comparing the temperature change of an ascending or descending air parcel with the temperature profile of the ambient air layer in which the parcel ascends or descends

An air layer becomes more stable when it descends, and less stable when it ascends. Unstable air will remain unstable until it encounters air of the same temperature or colder. In **STABLE AIR**, there is no vertical movement. In **UNSTABLE AIR**, there is a great deal of vertical movement.

Stable air

Stable air exists when there is no vertical movement of the air. An ascending air parcel becomes cooler (denser) than the ambient air, and a descending air parcel becomes warmer (less dense) than the ambient air. Any upward or downward displacement of an air parcel in stable air gives rise to forces that tend to return the parcel to its original altitude.

Once stable air becomes colder than the surrounding air, it sinks. It will sink to the altitude at which the temperature of the ambient air equals that of the sinking air. If a warm air mass is over a cold air mass, the air is very stable.

During the nighttime, radiational cooling of the ground tends to stabilize the overlying air. During the daytime, however, solar heating of the ground tends to destabilize the overlying air masses.

Unstable air

Stable air can easily become unstable through radiational heating. As the ground heats up, the air also heats up, becomes unstable, and will continue to rise until it encounters air as cold, or colder, than it is. Air tends to stabilize over a colder surface and destabilize over a warmer surface.

The stability of air is affected by the relative humidity of the air mass, which can cause conditional stability. The air mass is considered stable if the environment is dry but is unstable if the air becomes saturated.

Stability is an everchanging situation throughout the day because of heating of the Earth's surface and atmosphere. Sometimes a layer of stable air can become trapped between two layers of unstable air. This is called an **INVERSION** and is the result of the fact that stability can change with altitude.

Fronts

A **FRONT** is a narrow zone of transition between air masses of different densities that is usually due to temperature differences. Because they are associated with temperature, fronts are usually referred to as either warm or cold.

An air layer becomes more stable when it descends, and less stable when it ascends.

STABLE AIR: air layer in which there is no vertical movement, which is the same temperature as the ambient air

UNSTABLE AIR: air layer in which there is much vertical movement as it seeks to encounter air of the same temperature or colder

If a warm air mass is over a cold air mass, the air is very stable

Nighttime radiational cooling of the ground tends to stabilize the overlying air. Daytime radiational heating of the ground tends to destabilize the overlying air masses.

INVERSION: a layer of stable air that is trapped between two layers of unstable air

FRONT: a narrow zone of transition between air masses of different densities that is usually due to temperature differences

---

- Warm front: A front whose movement causes the lighter warm air to advance, while the denser cold air retreats. A warm front usually triggers a cloud development sequence of cirrus, cirrostratus, altostratus, nimbostratus, and stratus. It may result in an onset of light rain or snowfall immediately ahead of the front, which gives way, as the cloud sequence forms, to steady precipitation (light to moderate), until the front passes, a time frame that may exceed 24 hours.

  The gentle rains associated with a warm front are normally welcomed by farmers. However, if it is cold enough for snow to fall, the snow may significantly accumulate. If the air is unstable, cumulonimbus clouds may develop, and brief, intense thunderstorms may punctuate the otherwise gentler rain or snowfall.

- Cold front: A front whose movement causes the denser cold air to displace the lighter warm air. The results of cold front situations depend on the stability of the air. If the air is stable, nimbostratus and altostratus clouds may form, and brief showers may immediately precede the front.

  If the air is unstable, there is greater uplift. Cumulonimbus clouds may tower over nimbostratus, and cirrus clouds may be blown downstream from the cumulonimbus by high-altitude winds. Thunderstorms may occur, accompanied by gusty surface winds and hail, as well as other, more violent weather. If the cold front moves quickly (roughly 28 mph or greater), a squall line of thunderstorms may form either right ahead of the front or up to 180 miles ahead of it.

- Occluded front: A front formed when a cold front has caught up to a warm front and has intermingled, usually by sliding under the warmer air. Cold fronts generally move faster than warm fronts and occasionally overrun slower-moving warm fronts. The weather ahead of an occluded front is similar to that of a warm front during its advance but switches to that of a cold front as the cold front passes through.

- Stationary front: A front that shows no overall movement. The weather produced by this front can vary widely and depends on the amount of moisture present and the relative motions of the air pockets along the front. Most of the precipitation falls on the cold side of the front.

SKILL 25.11 Interpret information on weather maps

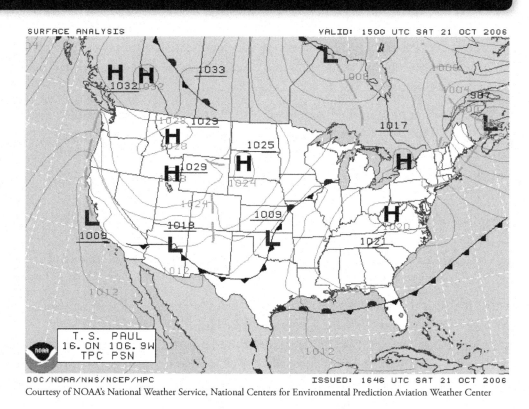

SURFACE ANALYSIS   VALID: 1500 UTC SAT 21 OCT 2006

T.S. PAUL
16.0N 106.9W
TPC PSN

DOC/NOAA/NWS/NCEP/HPC   ISSUED: 1646 UTC SAT 21 OCT 2006

Courtesy of NOAA's National Weather Service, National Centers for Environmental Prediction Aviation Weather Center

See Skill 25.9 for information on the weather associated with various pressure systems and Skill 25.10 for information on the weather associated with various front systems.

Meteorological map symbology

Meteorology uses an extensively defined set of alphanumeric notations and iconology to graphically display the collected data elements. Depending on the extent of detail desired in the presented map, the symbology conveys information about cloud types, coverage, and base heights, visibility, precipitation, wind speed, air pressure tendency, temperature, and isobaric fronts.

The most common weather map is called a surface analysis map. It displays contour lines which connect areas of equal or near equal conditions, as reported from various weather stations.

> *Meteorological maps can convey information about cloud types, coverage and base heights, visibility, precipitation, wind speed, air pressure tendency, temperature, and isobaric fronts.*

Contour lines

- Isobars: Lines connecting areas of equal pressure. When these lines form closed, concentric circles, the smallest inner circle represents the pressure center. This pressure center can represent either a center of high pressure (indicated by a capital H) or a center of low pressure (indicated by a capital L). Numbers placed near these isobars indicate the pressure (in millibars) along that contour line.

- Isotherms: Lines connecting areas of equal temperature.

- Isotachs: Lines connecting areas of equal wind speed.

Movement of fronts

- Cold fronts: Indicated by blue lines with triangles on one side of the line. The triangles face the direction the cold front is moving.

- Warm fronts: Indicated by red lines with semicircles on one side of the line. The semicircles face the direction the warm front is moving.

- Occluded fronts: Indicated by a purple line with triangles and semicircles next to each other on the same side of the line. The triangles and semicircles face the direction the front is moving.

- Stationary fronts: Indicated by a line with red semicircles on one side of the line and blue triangles on the opposite side, indicating that the front is stationary.

SKILL 25.12 **Demonstrate understanding of the analyses needed to perform short-term weather forecasting and recognize some of the methods used to perform long-term weather forecasting**

METEOROLOGY is the scientific study of the atmosphere and the atmospheric processes.

> **METEOROLOGY:** the scientific study of the atmosphere and the atmospheric processes

Weather Stations

The National Weather Service runs the 500 active weather stations used for national forecasting. However, there are thousands of local weather stations that contribute observations. They collect temperature, precipitation, and humidity data and provide remarks about local conditions.

The data is collected four times daily, every six hours, around the clock, and sent to the National Weather Bureau. The bureau in turn provides the data to the World Meteorological Association, which uses it for making long-term predictions, not immediate forecasting.

Meteorological data is collected on the basis of GREENWICH MEAN TIME (GMT OR ZULU TIME). Greenwich, England, is located on the prime meridian, or 0 degrees. Time is measured as either plus or minus the current GMT. Each line of longitude is equal to 4 minutes of time, and 15 degrees of longitude is equal to 1 hour of time. You subtract hours as you go west, and add hours as you go east. Example: 8 a.m. Zulu is equal to 6 a.m. at 30° west longitude.

Collection Devices

- Weather balloons: Launched twice a day at 1200 and 2400 Zulu, weather balloons carry a RADIOSONDE, an electronic device that measures temperature, pressure, and humidity.

Measurements are taken throughout the ascent of the balloons and this real-time data is radioed back to the surface during the ascent. Weather stations use radars to track the balloons to gather wind speed and direction information.

When the balloon reaches its maximum height, an altimeter releases the radiosonde package via parachute for recovery and reuse, but only 20 percent of radiosondes are recovered. These balloons can also be launched from a plane to gather special data on immediate meteorological disturbances (i.e., hurricanes, storms).

- Ground-based radar: Doppler-effect radar is the primary type used for meteorological data collection because it is accurate, sensing motion as well as range and direction, which allows for pinpoint accuracy over an area. This is the type of radar you see on television. Next Generation Doppler Radar (NEXRAD) emits beams of energy that are reflected by water droplets in the atmosphere. This type of radar is useful for tracking and predicting rain but less useful for predicting snow or sleet.

- Satellites: The National Weather Service depends heavily on its network of weather satellites to provide wide-area coverage of the Earth. These satellites primarily provide infrared, water vapor, and photographic data and are used to track the formation, development, and motion of major meteorological events such as hurricanes and tropical storms.

In terms of orbit, there are two types of satellites: geostationary and polar orbiting. GEOSTATIONARY SATELLITES move with the Earth's rotation, always looking at the

---

GREENWICH MEAN TIME (GMT OR ZULU TIME): the point located on the prime meridian, or 0 degrees, from which time is measured as either plus or minus the current GMT

Each line of longitude is equal to 4 minutes of time, and 15 degrees of longitude is equal to 1 hour of time.

RADIOSONDE: electronic device that measures temperature, pressure, and humidity

GEOSTATIONARY SATELLITES: move with the Earth's rotation, always looking at the same point, which allows for a view showing changes over time

same point, which allows for a view showing changes over time. **POLAR ORBITING SATELLITES** follow an orbit from pole to pole. The Earth rotates underneath the satellite and gives a view of different areas, in effect, producing slices of the Earth.

The GOES Satellite—a geostationary satellite that primarily scans the Atlantic Ocean and U.S. East Coast— has four detection bands:

1. Visible spectrum: takes photographic surveys during daylight hours of light reflecting off the tops of clouds.

2. Near IR: looks at heat to detect naturally emitted and reflected infrared radiation.

3. Enhanced IR: adds colors to the tops of the clouds; uses an enhanced IR receiver/detector to look at reflected or emitted heat. Hotter areas show up as red/yellow/orange, while colder areas appear as blue/green/violet.

4. Water vapor: Uses radar to detect water vapor in the atmosphere and looks for uplifts that provide an indicator of weather change. Swirls produced by this type of satellite show air rising, which can indicate thunderstorms, and high, well-developed clouds can signal the advance of a storm formation.

Using the collected data

The collected data is sent to the National Meteorological Center in Maryland where it is plotted and then sent to other weather centers throughout the world. The collected data helps in developing mathematical models that are used to predict the weather. These models have been used since the late 1950s and place differing emphasis on various aspects of the equational factors involved. A typical model will consist of six to eight different equational factors.

In turn, the data elements are disseminated to the National Weather Service, which uses them to calculate model results based on 12-, 24-, 36-, 48-, and 72-hour predictions. The further out you extend the predictions, however, the less accurate they are likely to be. This is because of the wide variation in the data elements that can occur between the time of prediction and the realization of the prediction time.

The data model is also disseminated to local meteorological offices and radio and television stations for local interpretation. The resulting local forecast often includes a great deal of "*Kentucky windage*," experience-based guesses by local meteorologists, and can vary considerably from the forecasts of the National Weather Service. The accuracy of local forecasting is dependent on the experience and expertise of the local meteorologist. Forecasting is only as good as the data collected and local intuition (experience) modifications. Four main types of forecast are developed:

1. **Persistence:** This doesn't really change much and is very inaccurate

2. **Steady state (trend):** This is a guesstimate as to what the system will do based on the assumption that there will be no change in the data parameters

3. **Analog (numerical forecasting):** The best type of forecast basis, it takes the data numbers and plugs them into equations, equations into models, and uses the models for forecasting

4. **Climatological:** This type of forecast is often vague and is based on long-standing trends, for instance, the weather predictions in the Old Farmer's Almanac

> **SKILL 25.13** **Demonstrate understanding of the regional and local natural factors that affect climate**

KÖPPEN CLIMATE SYSTEM: explains that the origin of climate is based on the average monthly and yearly temperatures, location of the land-mass, precipitation rates, and seasonality of the precipitation

The **KÖPPEN CLIMATE SYSTEM** explains that the origin of climate is based on the average monthly and yearly temperatures, location of the landmass, precipitation rates, and seasonality of the precipitation. When Wladimir Köppen, a climatologist, created his classification system, he determined that one of the best indicators for climate is native plant life. He created the Köppen climate system map with native vegetation in mind.

Types of Climate

1. **Tropical/megathermal climate:** The temperature is constantly high—over 18°C or 64.4°F. There are three subcategories: tropical rain forest, tropical monsoon, and tropical savanna.

   - The *tropical rain forest climate* has no seasons and more than 60 mm of rain each month of the year.

   - The *tropical monsoon climate* has more than 100 mm of rain total in the year, but may have some months that fall below 60 mm because of seasonal changes in wind direction.

   - The *tropical savanna climate* has a prominent dry season and less than 100 mm of rain each year.

2. Arid and semiarid climate: The precipitation of the region is less than the evapotranspiration of the region.

3. Temperate/mesothermal climate: The average temperature is above 10°C for the warmest months and between -3°C and 18°C in the coldest months. There are four subcategories: Mediterranean, humid subtropical, maritime temperate, and maritime subarctic.

   - The *Mediterranean climate* is found on the western sides of continents. It has moderate temperatures and experiences a polar front in the winter and a tropical front in the hot and dry summer.

   - The *humid subtropical climate* is found in the interior or on the east coast of the continents. The summers are usually very humid because the trade winds bring moisture to the region.

   - The *maritime temperate climate*, usually found on the continents between 45° and 55° latitude, experiences a polar front all year and usually is overcast year round.

   - The *maritime subarctic climate* lies closer to the poles than the maritime temperate climates and is usually limited to thin strips of land or islands off the western coast of the continents.

4. Continental/microthermal climate: Temperatures are above 10°C in the summer months and below -3°C in the winter months. There are three subcategories: hot summer continental, warm summer continental, and continental subarctic.

   - The *hot summer continental climate*, occurring inland around 30° to 40° latitude, can be affected by monsoons.

   - The *warm summer continental climate* is found inland between 40° to 50° latitude in North America, and up to 60° latitude in Eastern Europe due to wind patterns.

   - The *continental subarctic climate* exists inland in the 50° to 60° latitude.

5. Polar Climates: Temperatures are below 10°C all year. There are two subcategories: the tundra and the ice cap.

   - The *tundra climate* is dry and has an average temperature between 0° and 10°C in the warmest months.

   - The *ice cap climate* has temperatures below 0°C year round.

Variation in climate

Climate varies over time. The diurnal cycle indicates how the weather has changed in the last 24 hours. Over a year, regions experience changes in seasons. The climate of a region may vary due to changes in atmospheric dust from large dust storms and volcanic eruptions. Over the course of 10 years, changes in climate may take place due to the El Niño and La Niña cycles in Earth's oceans. Climate change over the course of 100 years can be attributed to solar variability and changes within ocean temperature. Over the last 100 years, significant climate changes have been noted in some regions due to deforestation and increased carbon dioxide output. Climate variability over 1,000 years can be linked to thermocline circulation (between surface and deepwater layers) in the oceans and changes in the carbon cycle.

Paleoclimatology indicates that climate variation on the 100,000 year time frame can be attributed to the Milankovitch cycles, solar variability, precession, and orbit eccentricity (*see also Skill 25.3*). By studying variations in climate, paleoclimatologists can determine how current changes in climate are related to long-term trends. This can help scientists to further understand humanity's effect on climate change.

SKILL **Demonstrate understanding of how humans affect and are affected**
25.14 **by climate** (*for example, desertification, greenhouse effect, volcanic ash effect, El Niño*)

Long-Distance Transport of Matter

Much of the world's long-distance transport is caused by particulate material being caught in the jet streams, high-altitude, very strong winds that form narrow belts (*see also skill 25.4*). Volcanic ash has been particularly susceptible to such transport, and over the past years, scientists have observed materials carried distances in excess of 3,000 miles (5,000 km). For example, ash from the 1815 eruption of Mount Tambora in Indonesia was carried by the jet streams over a wide area. It marked 1816 as the "Year without Summer" in Europe and caused famine and crop failure in New England.

Climate Change

One of the major environmental issues of today is the controversy over global climate change. Many scientists forcefully contend that we are experiencing a period of global warming, and that our dependence on modern technology is the major reason behind the warming. Not surprisingly, other scientists equally oppose this theory. Much of the controversy depends on the source of information as to whether humankind is at fault. (*For a further discussion of this topic, see skill 21.6.*)

In the 1970s the scientific issue was if there was going to be another ice age. As we approached the new millennium, however, the issue shifted to concern about warming. The controversy is based on interpretations of historical records. For the past century, temperatures have been recorded based on four temperature readings per day from each collection location. The collected readings are sent to the World Metrological Organization where the readings are correlated and averaged. That data indicates a rise in average temperature.

The most accurate method to measure global temperature is to use space satellite technology. Since 1979, the GOES satellite (*see Skill 25.12*) has collected temperature readings. Instead of sampling only the cities, the GOES samples all areas in blocks of data, including the oceans. Data taken during the period of 1979-1998 showed no net warming. However, from a scientific method point of view, this is not a long enough period of sampling to be fully conclusive.

El Niño and La Niña

EL NIÑO is a reverse of the normal weather patterns in the Pacific. A low-pressure area normally sits in the Pacific Ocean west of Hawaii and a high-pressure area normally sits off of the California coast. When an El Niño forms, these pressure areas shift eastward, causing the low-pressure area to be situated below Hawaii and the high-pressure area to move inland over California. Because of the shift in pressure areas, an El Niño affects the wind patterns (especially the jet stream and trade winds), and creates a wide variety of effects, including a direct impact on commercial fishing.

> **EL NIÑO:** a reverse of the normal weather patterns in the Pacific that affects wind patterns (especially the jet stream and trade winds) and creates a wide variety of other impacts

Normally, there is a shallow warm water layer over the colder, deeper waters along the coastlines. The temperature disparity causes an upwelling of rich nutrients from the lower layers of the cold water, creating a feeding zone that attracts a variety of marine life forms that make for productive fisheries. During an El Niño event, the warm water layer increases in both area and depth. It extends downward, blocking the nutrient-rich upwelling from reaching the feeding zone. Although many species can migrate to more friendly waters, some have limited mobility and die. In any event, depending on the intensity, duration, and repetition of El Niño events, a fishery area can become permanently barren. Other effects of El Niño are both direct and indirect.

Direct effects of El Niño:

- In the west, fires and drought
- In the east, rain, landslides, and fish migration

Indirect effects of El Niño:

- Greater chance of hurricanes in Hawaii
- Lesser chance of hurricanes in Virginia because of weakened trade winds
- Less rain during September and October
- Coastal erosion in the western states
- Fewer storms that deposit snow in the Cascades in Washington and Oregon
- Altered jet streams as the high-pressure areas move

LA NIÑA: the opposite of El Nino, with a lesser effect

LA NIÑA is the opposite of El Nino, with a lesser effect. It causes the east to be wetter and the west to be drier. Many scientists believe that both of these conditions are caused by a change in the surface temperature of the water of the Pacific Ocean.

Desertification

DESERT: any region with low rainfall

A **DESERT** is any region with low rainfall. A region is normally classified as having a dry or arid climate if less than 25 centimeters (10 inches) of rain falls during the year. Deserts typically have little rain, high evaporation, plentiful sunshine, and clear skies. Technically, despite the presence of vast ice sheets, the continent of Antarctica is the driest region on Earth, since it averages less than 1 inch (2.5 cm) of rain per year.

The location of a desert is a direct result of global air circulatory patterns. The equator receives more solar radiation than the rest of the planet. As the heated air rises, it moves both northward and southward where it cools and sinks near the 30° north and south latitudes. The great deserts of the world lie between these boundaries.

These conditions exist primarily because the air, as it sinks down from the atmosphere, compresses and is able to hold more water vapor that seldom falls back to the surface as rain. The opposite conditions exist at the equator, where rainfall is abundant.

COMPETENCY 26
ASTRONOMY

> **SKILL 26.1** Demonstrate knowledge of the major theories of origin and structure of the universe

The early models of the universe were primarily products of philosophical musings combined with religious and social tenets and observable phenomena. As civilizations continued to advance so did our understanding of the physical processes affecting the universe. The early scientific models still blended elements of philosophy and religious thought with measurable data, but as our technological base improved, models reflected less and less of those influences to the point that today, it's a commonly accepted practice to totally discount them in modeling the universe.

Two main theories that explain the origins of the universe are: The Steady State theory and the Big Bang theory.

Steady State Theory

This theory held that the universe was static and that it did not evolve, having always maintained a balance of the same general properties through replacement of dying stars and galaxies by new stars and galaxies. This theory was simultaneously both a popular and controversial explanation of the universe during its heyday in the 1950s and 1960s, but astronomers have not found any evidence to prove it.

All astronomers, however, did not accept the concept of a static universe, and they proposed an alternate theory centered on a nonstatic, expanding universe. Steady-state supporter, American astronomer Fred Hoyle sarcastically dubbed this theory the "Big Bang."

The controversy between supporters and opponents of the steady state theory continued until the late 1960s when detection of primordial background radiation dealt a decisive blow to the steady state theory. In a static state the background radiation should be uniform. Since it clearly was not, however, this indicated that something had occurred to cause it to "clump" together. The logical explanation was a massive explosion that disordered the radiation.

Big Bang Theory

BIG BANG THEORY: a massive explosion that scattered mass, matter, and energy throughout the universe, which then formed galaxies as matter cooled during the next half-billion years

BIG BANG THEORY proposes that all the mass and energy of the universe originally was concentrated at a single geometric point, which, for unknown reasons, experienced a massive explosion that scattered mass, matter, and energy throughout the universe that then formed galaxies as matter cooled during the next half-billion years.

The concept of a massive explosion is supported by the distribution of background radiation and the measurable fact that the galaxies are moving away from each other at great speed.

The universe originated around 15 billion years ago with the "Big Bang," and continued to expand for the first 10 billion years. The universe originally was unimaginably hot, but around 1 million years after the Big Bang, it cooled enough to allow for the formation of atoms from the energy and particles.

Most of these atoms were hydrogen, and they comprise the most abundant form of matter in the universe. Around a billion years after the Big Bang, the matter had cooled enough to begin congealing into the first stars and galaxies.

The Big Bang theory has been widely accepted by many astronomers.

OSCILLATING UNIVERSE HYPOTHESIS: as the universe oscillates galaxies will move away from one another and will in time slow down and stop; then a gradual moving toward each other will activate another Big Bang

The future of the universe is hypothesized with the **OSCILLATING UNIVERSE HYPOTHESIS**, which states that the universe will oscillate or expand and contract. Galaxies will move away from one another and will in time slow down and stop. Then a gradual moving toward each other will again activate another explosion or Big Bang.

SKILL 26.2 **Define and use large units of distance** *(for example, astronomical unit, lightyear, parsec)*

Astronomical distances represent mind-boggling amounts of distance. Because our standard units of distance measurement (i.e., kilometers) would result in such huge numbers as to become almost incomprehensible, physicists use different units of measurement to reference the vast distances involved in astronomy.

ASTRONOMICAL UNIT (AU): within our solar system, the standard unit of distance measurement, the mean distance between the Sun and the Earth or 1 AU = 1.495979×10^{11}m

Within our solar system, the standard unit of distance measurement is the **ASTRONOMICAL UNIT (AU)**. The AU is the mean distance between the Sun and the Earth. 1 AU = 1.495979×10^{11}m. Outside of our solar system, the standard unit of distance measurement is the Parsec. 1 Parsec = 206,265 AU or 3.26 light years.

A light year (LY) is the distance light travels in one year because the speed of light is 3.00×108 m/sec, one light year represents a distance of 9.5×10^{12} km, or 63,000 AU.

SKILL 26.3 Demonstrate understanding of the origin and life cycle of stars

Stars form in **PLANETARY NEBULAE**, cold clouds of dust and gas within a galaxy, and go through different stages of development in a specific sequence. This theory of star development is called the condensation theory.

> **PLANETARY NEBULAE:** cold clouds of dust and gas within a galaxy

Stellar Sequence of Development

In the initial stage, the diffuse, cloudlike spheres of the nebula begin to shrink under the influence of its own weak gravity into a knot of gasses called a **PROTOSTAR**. The original diameter of the protostar is many times greater than the diameter of our solar system, but gravitational forces cause it to continue to contract. This compression raises the internal temperature of the protostar.

> **PROTOSTAR:** the initial stage of star formation

When the protostar reaches a temperature of around 10 million °C (18 million °F), nuclear fusion starts, which stops the contraction of the proto star and changes its status to a star. **NUCLEAR FUSION** is the process in which hydrogen atoms fuse together to form helium atoms, releasing massive amounts of energy. It's the fusion of atoms, not combustion, which causes stars to shine.

> **NUCLEAR FUSION:** the process by which hydrogen atoms fuse together to form helium atoms, releasing massive amounts of energy

Red stars have a small mass. Yellow stars have a medium mass. Blue stars have a large mass. Large-mass stars consume their hydrogen at a faster rate and have a shorter life cycle in comparison to small-mass stars that consume their hydrogen at a much slower rate. All stars eventually convert a large percentage of their hydrogen to heavier atoms and begin to die. Just as a star's mass determines its length of life, however, it also determines the pattern it follows in the last stages of its existence.

> *A star's life cycle depends on its initial mass. Just as a star's mass determines its length of life, however, it also determines the pattern it follows in the last stages of its existence.*

Lower Main Sequence Stars

When small and medium mass stars (such as the Sun) consume all of their hydrogen, their inner cores begin to cool. The stars begin to consume the heavier elements produced by fusion (carbon and oxygen) and the star's shell expands tremendously outward, causing the star to become a giant star. A **GIANT STAR** is a large, cool, extremely luminous body, 10 to 100 times the diameter of the Sun.

> **GIANT STAR:** 10 to 100 times the diameter of the Sun, created when hydrogen-depleted stars begin to consume the heavier elements produced by fusion

In roughly 4.6 billion years from now our Sun will become a giant star. As it expands, its outer layers will reach halfway to Venus.

The dying giant gives off thermal pulses approximately every 200,000 years, throwing off concentric shells of light gasses enriched with heavy elements. As it enters its last phases of the life cycle, its depleted inner core begins to contract, and the giant becomes a **WHITE DWARF STAR**, a small, slowly cooling, extremely dense star, no larger than 10,000 km in diameter.

The final phase of a lower main sequence star life cycle can take two paths: after a few billion years, most main sequence white dwarfs completely burn out to become **BLACK DWARFS**, cold, dead stars.

The path is different, however, if a white dwarf is part of a **BINARY STAR**, one of two suns in the same solar system. Instead of slowly cooling to become a black dwarf, it may capture hydrogen from its companion star. If this happens, the temperature of the white dwarf soars, and when it reaches approximately 10 million° C, a nuclear explosion occurs, creating a nova. A nova is the sudden brightening of a lower main sequence star to approximately 10,000 times its normal luminosity caused by the explosion of the star. A **NOVA** reaches its maximum brightness in a short time (one or two days) and then gradually dims as the gasses and cosmic dust cool.

Upper Main Sequence Stars

The initial sequence of the high-mass, upper main sequence stars is identical to the lower-mass stars: planetary nebula to protostar. If the protostar accretes enough material, however, it forms as a blue star. When a blue star has consumed all of its hydrogen it, too, expands outward, but on a much larger scale than a lower-mass star. It becomes a **SUPERGIANT STAR**, an exceptionally bright star, 10 to 1,000 times the diameter of the Sun.

The supergiant's now-depleted core cannot support such a vast weight and collapses inward, causing its temperature to soar. When it reaches roughly 599 million° C, it implodes and then explodes, creating a **SUPERNOVA**, the massive explosion of an upper main sequence supergiant star caused by the detonation of carbon within the star.

A supernova releases more energy than Earth's Sun will produce in its entire life cycle. The luminosity of a supernova is as bright as 500 million suns. Chinese astronomers in 1054 recorded the sudden appearance of a new star in what is now known as the Taurus constellation. Bright enough to be seen during daytime for over a month, it remained visible for over two years.

WHITE DWARF STAR: a small, slowly cooling, extremely dense star, no larger than 10,000 km in diameter

BLACK DWARFS: a dead star

BINARY STAR: one of two suns in the same solar system

NOVA: the sudden brightening of a lower main sequence star caused by the explosion of the star

SUPERGIANT STAR: an exceptionally bright star, 10 to 1,000 times the diameter of the Sun

SUPERNOVA: the massive explosion of an upper main sequence supergiant star caused by the detonation of carbon within the star.

A supernova releases more energy than Earth's Sun will produce in its entire life cycle.

The explosive release of energy in a supernova is so great (1,028 megatons of TNT) as to literally blow the atomic nuclei of the carbon to bits. The shattered mass is accelerated outward at nearly the speed of light (300,000 km/sec. or 186,000 mph).

Ninety percent of the shattered mass scatters into space, becoming planetary nebulae from which the life cycle may begin anew. The other ten percent, the core of the star, is blown inward, becoming a **NEUTRON STAR**, the very small—10 km diameter—imploded core of a collapsed supergiant star that rotates at a high speed (60,000 rpm) and has a strong magnetic field (1012 gauss).

A neutron star may capture gas from space, a companion star, or a nearby star and become a **PULSAR**, a neutron star that emits a sweeping beam of ionized-gas radiation. As the pulsar rotates, the beams of light sweep into space similarly to a beacon from a lighthouse. Since first discovered in 1967, over 350 pulsars have been catalogued.

The alternate product of a supernova is a **BLACK HOLE**, a volume of space from which no form of radiation can escape. Black holes are created when a supergiant star with a mass roughly three times that of the Sun implodes. The inner core of the star is compacted by the supernova into a **SINGULARITY**, an object of zero radius and infinite density.

A singularity is difficult to picture. Zero radiuses imply objects with size less than an electron, but also possessing a density that precludes the escape of all radiation including light. Although a singularity has yet to be detected, theoretically, they exist in and cause the effects exhibited by black holes.

NEUTRON STAR: the very small imploded core of a collapsed supergiant star that rotates at a high speed and has a strong magnetic field

PULSAR: a neutron star that has captured gas from space or other stars and emits a sweeping beam of ionized-gas radiation

BLACK HOLE: a volume of space created by an imploded supergiant from which no form of radiation can escape

SINGULARITY: the inner core of an imploded supergiant, compacted by a supernova into an object of zero radius and infinite density

SKILL 26.4 Demonstrate understanding of the major theories involving the origin of the solar system

Most cosmologists believe that the Earth is the indirect result of a supernova. The thin cloud (planetary nebula) of gas and dust from which the Sun and its planets are formed was struck by the shock wave and remnant matter from an exploded star, or stars, outside of our galaxy. In fact, the stars manufactured every chemical element heavier than hydrogen. The turbulence caused by the shock wave caused our solar system to begin forming as it absorbed some of the heavy atoms flung outward in the supernova.

Around five billion years ago our planetary nebula spun faster as it condensed, and material near the center contracted inward forming a protosun. As more

Most cosmologists believe that the Earth is the indirect result of a supernova.

Our solar system is composed mostly of matter assembled from a star or stars that disappeared billions of years ago.

materials came together, mass and consequently gravitational attraction increased, pulling in more mass. This cycle continued until the mass reached the point that nuclear fusion occurred, and the Sun was born.

Concurrently, the protosun's gravitational mass pulled heavier, denser elements inward from the clouds of cosmic material surrounding it. These elements eventually coalesced through the process of ACCRETION, the clumping together of small particles into larger masses, into the planets of our solar system.

ACCRETION: the clumping together of small particles into larger masses

The period of accretion lasted approximately 50 to 70 million years, ceasing when the protosun experienced nuclear fusion to become the Sun. The violence associated with this nuclear reaction swept through the inner planets, clearing the system of particles, ending the period of rapid accretion.

The closest planets (Mercury, Venus, and Mars) received too much heat and consequently did not develop the planetary characteristics to support life as we know it. The farthest planets did not receive enough heat to sufficiently coalesce the gasses into solid form. Earth was the only planet in the perfect position to develop the conditions necessary to maintain life.

SKILL 26.5 Identify the major features and characteristics of the Sun and the source of the Sun's energy

SUN: the nearest star to Earth that produces solar energy by the process of nuclear fusion, converting hydrogen to helium

The SUN is the nearest star to Earth that produces solar energy by the process of nuclear fusion, converting hydrogen to helium. Energy flows out of the core to the surface, and radiation then escapes into space.

Parts of the Sun include:

- Core: The inner portion of the Sun where fusion takes place
- Photosphere: Considered the surface of the Sun, which produces sunspots (cool, dark areas that can be seen on its surface)
- Chromosphere: Colored red by hydrogen gas
- Solar flares: Produce excited protons and electrons that shoot outward from the chromosphere at great speeds reaching Earth, disturb radio reception, and affect the magnetic field on Earth
- Solar prominences: Gases that shoot outward from the chromosphere
- Corona: The transparent area of Sun visible only during a total eclipse

SOLAR RADIATION: energy traveling from the Sun that radiates into space

SOLAR RADIATION is energy traveling from the Sun that radiates into space.

SKILL 26.6 Identify the components of the solar system and characterize the physical features and movements of the planets, asteroids, comets, and other solar system components

There are eight planets in our solar system: Mercury, Venus, Earth, Mars, Jupiter, Saturn, Uranus, and Neptune. Pluto is no longer called a planet. These eight planets are divided into two groups based on distance from the Sun. The inner planets include: Mercury, Venus, Earth, and Mars. The outer planets include Jupiter, Saturn, Uranus, and Neptune. Recent proposals for altering the definition of a planet have reduced Pluto to a celestial body, not a planet.

The planets

Mercury is the closest planet to the Sun, named after the Roman messenger god. Mercury's surface has craters and rocks, and its atmosphere is composed of hydrogen, helium, and sodium.

Venus has a slow rotation when compared to Earth's. Venus and Uranus rotate in opposite directions from the other planets, called retrograde rotation. The surface of Venus is not visible due to extensive cloud cover whose sulfuric acid droplets give Venus a yellow appearance. The atmosphere is composed mostly of carbon dioxide, which, combined with the dense cloud cover, traps heat. Thus Venus has a greater greenhouse effect than observed on Earth. Venus was named after the Roman goddess of love.

Earth is considered a water planet, with seventy percent of its surface covered with water. Gravity holds the masses of water in place. The different temperatures observed on Earth allow for the different states of water to exist: solid, liquid or gas. The atmosphere is composed mainly of oxygen and nitrogen. Earth is the only planet that is known to support life.

Mars has a surface that contains numerous craters, active and extinct volcanoes, and ridges and valleys with extremely deep fractures. Iron oxide found in the dusty soil makes the surface seem rust colored and the skies seem pink. The atmosphere is composed of carbon dioxide, nitrogen, argon, oxygen, and water vapor. Mars has polar regions with ice caps composed of water. Mars has two satellites. Mars was named after the Roman war god.

Jupiter is largest planet in the solar system. Jupiter has 16 moons. The atmosphere is composed of hydrogen, helium, methane, and ammonia. White-colored bands of clouds indicate rising gases, and dark-colored bands of clouds indicate descending gases, caused by heat Jupiter's core. Jupiter's Great Red Spot is thought to be a hurricane-type cloud. Jupiter has a strong magnetic field. Jupiter was named after Roman king of the gods.

Saturn is the second largest planet in the solar system. Saturn has beautiful rings of ice, rock, and dust particles circling it. Saturn's atmosphere is composed of hydrogen, helium, methane, and ammonia. Saturn has 20-plus satellites. Saturn was named after the Roman god of agriculture.

Uranus is a gaseous planet with 10 dark rings, 15 satellites, and retrograde revolution. Its atmosphere is composed of hydrogen, helium, and methane. Uranus was named after the Greek god of the heavens.

Neptune is another gaseous planet with an atmosphere consisting of hydrogen, helium, and methane. Neptune has 3 rings and 2 satellites. Neptune was named after the Roman sea god because its atmosphere is the color of the seas.

Pluto was once the smallest planet in the solar system. It is now considered to be a celestial body, with one satellite. Pluto's atmosphere probably contains methane, ammonia, and frozen water. Pluto revolves around the Sun every 250 years. Pluto was named after the Roman god of the underworld.

All the planets revolve around the Sun, and all the planets, except Venus and Uranus, rotate on their axes in the same direction. Except for Pluto, all the planets follow roughly the same elliptical orbital planes around the Sun. Neptune and Pluto occasionally change places in the order. Pluto's orbit is so erratic compared to the other planets that sometimes it carries Pluto inside of Neptune's orbit.

The asteroid belt is located between Mars and Jupiter and may be the remnants a planet crushed by the massive gravitational force of Jupiter. Astronomers believe that **ASTEROIDS** are the rocky fragments that may have been the remains of the birth of the solar system and that never formed into a planet.

COMETS are masses of frozen gases, cosmic dust, and small rocky particles. Astronomers think that most comets originate in a dense comet cloud beyond Pluto. A comet consists of a nucleus, a coma, and a tail that always points away from the Sun. The most famous comet, now known as Halley's Comet, was first discovered in 240 BCE. It returns to the skies near Earth every 75 to 76 years, as predicted by Edmund Halley (1656–1742), for whom it has been named.

METEOROIDS are composed of particles of rock and metal of various sizes floating in space. When a meteoroid travels through the Earth's atmosphere, friction causes its surface to heat up and it begins to burn. The burning meteoroid falling through the Earth's atmosphere then is called a **METEOR** or a "shooting star."

METEORITES are meteors that strike the Earth's surface. A physical example of the impact of a meteorite—the Barringer Crater—can be seen in Arizona.

ASTEROIDS: rocky fragments that may be the remains of the birth of the solar system and that never formed into a planet

COMETS: masses of frozen gases, cosmic dust, and small rocky particles

METEOROIDS: particles of rock and metal of various sizes floating in space

METEOR: a burning meteoroid falling through the Earth's atmosphere; also called a "shooting star"

METEORITES: meteors that strike the Earth's surface

SKILL 26.7 Demonstrate understanding of the geometry of the Earth-moon-Sun system and the causes of lunar and solar eclipses

According to the nebular theory, the solar system was formed by a gravitational collapse of a giant molecular cloud approximately 4.6 billion years ago. From the time of its formation, the solar system has undergone constant change, often as a result of planetary impacts and collisions.

Formation of Earth's Moon

The Sun, Mercury, Venus, Earth, and Mars currently make up the inner solar system, but at the formation of the solar system, it is believed that five planets existed in this inner orbit of the Sun. According to the **GIANT IMPACT HYPOTHESIS**, the current inner solar system was established when Earth collided with a fifth planet, or Mars-sized body, shortly after Earth's solidification (approximately 4.5 billion years ago). The fragments of this collision —some scientists estimate as much as one-third of Earth's original matter—were blasted outward into space where much of the ejected mass continued onward, but some of it was held in close proximity by the Earth's gravitational attraction. These fragments began orbiting the Earth and through the process of accretion, eventually coalesced into the moon. Following this impact, the fifth planet is said to have drifted out of the orbit of the inner solar system, leaving the current four planets.

> **GIANT IMPACT HYPOTHESIS:** explains the origin of Earth's moon as part of the residue of a collision with another body that Earth's gravitation pulled into orbit

Eclipses

An **ECLIPSE** is a phenomenon that occurs when a stellar body is shadowed by another and, as a result, is rendered invisible.

> **ECLIPSE:** occurs when a stellar body is shadowed by another and, as a result, is rendered invisible

The Earth, moon, and Sun must be in perfect alignment with each other to produce an eclipse. The Sun never moves in between the Earth and the moon. The orbits of the Earth and moon cause them to move in and out of the shadow areas. The **UMBRA** is the central region of the shadow caused by an eclipse that receives no light from the Sun. The **PENUMBRA** is the lighter outer edges of the shadow created during a partial eclipse where some light hits.

> **UMBRA:** the central region of the shadow caused by an eclipse, which receives no light from the Sun

There are two types of eclipses:

- Lunar eclipse: The Earth is between the Sun and the moon. The moon is in the Earth's shadow, making the moon invisible.

- Solar eclipse: The moon is between the Sun and the Earth. The Earth is in the moon's shadow, making the Sun invisible.

> **PENUMBRA:** the lighter outer edges of the shadow created during a partial eclipse where some light hits

Both types of eclipses have two forms: partial and full.

- A total eclipse can be seen only in the equatorial regions. Most total eclipses are spaced six months apart and normally last only two to ten minutes. During a total solar eclipse, the moon covers most of the Sun, usually only showing a flaming corona around the Sun's edges.

- A partial lunar eclipse occurs when the moon does not completely enter the Earth's shadow, so part of the moon is visible.

- A partial solar eclipse (or annular eclipse) occurs when the moon appears as a small, dark spot in the center of the Sun.

SKILL 26.8 **Demonstrate understanding of the causes of moon phases**

Just as the Earth follows an orbit around the Sun, the moon follows an eastward-moving orbit around the Earth.

Because the moon's rotational period matches the Earth's and its period of revolution is 27.3 days (called the sidereal period), this keeps one side of the moon always facing Earth. The side always facing us is called the near side, and the darkened side we never see is called the far side.

The **PHASES OF THE MOON** are the apparent changes in the shape of the moon caused by the absence or presence of reflected sunlight as the moon orbits around the Earth. The orbital pattern of the moon in relation to the Sun and Earth determines the extent of lunar illumination, and, consequently, what illuminated shape is presented to the Earth.

When the moon is between the Sun and the Earth, the side facing us is darkened, and we refer to this as a new moon. The opposite pattern occurs in the second half of the complete lunar cycle, when the moon is fully illuminated and bright in the night sky. This is called a full moon. The other phases between these extremes reflect the orbital point of the moon as it completes its journey around the Earth.

PHASES OF THE MOON: the apparent changes in the shape of the moon caused by the absence or presence of reflected sunlight as the moon orbits around the Earth

The orbital pattern of the moon in relation to the Sun and Earth determines the extent of lunar illumination, and, consequently, what illuminated shape is presented to the Earth.

SKILL 26.9 Demonstrate understanding of the causes of Earth's seasons

Seasonal change on Earth is caused by the orbit and axial tilt of the planet in relation to the Sun's ecliptic, the rotational path of the Sun. These factors combine to vary the degree of insolation at a particular location and thereby change the seasons.

Equinox and Solstice

There are four key points on the ecliptic whose dates vary slightly in relation to leap years.

- Winter solstice (December 21): the shortest day of the year in the Northern Hemisphere.

- Summer solstice (June 21): the longest day of the year in the Northern Hemisphere.

- Vernal equinox (March 21): marks the beginning of spring.

- Autumnal equinox (Sept 21): marks the beginning of autumn

During the summer solstice, insolation is at a maximum in the northern hemisphere, and at a minimum in the Southern Hemisphere. Because of the tilt and curvature of the Earth, to get the Sun directly overhead, you must be between 23.5°N latitude and 23.5°S latitude. This is between the Tropic of Cancer and the Tropic of Capricorn.

During the summer months in the Northern Hemisphere, the far northern latitudes receive 24 hours of daylight. This situation is reversed during the winter months, when there are 24 hours of darkness.

SKILL 26.10 Demonstrate knowledge of how units of time (for example, year, day, hour) are based on Earth's motions

A day is a unit of time equivalent to 24 hours on Earth. This is because it takes Earth one sidereal day, or 23.934 solar hours, to complete a single rotation around the Sun. The day is then further divided into equal periods of hours and seconds.

See also Skill 26.9

SKILL 26.11 Demonstrate understanding of time zones on Earth

Time zones are determined by longitudinal lines. Each time zone represents one hour. Since there are 24 hours in one complete rotation of the Earth, there are 24 international time zones. Each time zone is roughly 15° wide. While time zones are based on meridians, they do not strictly follow lines of longitude. Time-zone boundaries are subject to political decisions and have been moved around cities and other areas at the whim of the electorate.

The International Date Line is the 180° meridian, and it is on the opposite side of the world from the prime meridian. The International Date Line is one-half of one day or 12 time zones from the prime meridian. If you were traveling west across the International Date Line, you would lose one day. If you were traveling east across the International Date Line, you would gain one day.

SKILL 26.12 Demonstrate understanding of geosynchronous orbits and recognize how satellites have contributed to science and technology

Satellites have improved our ability to communicate and transmit radio and television signals. Navigational abilities have been greatly improved through the use of satellite signals. Sonar uses sound waves to locate objects, especially underwater. The sound waves bounce off the object and are picked up to assist in location. Seismographs record vibrations in the Earth and allow us to measure earthquake activity.

GEOSYNCHRONOUS ORBIT: an orbit around the Earth that has an orbital period matching the Earth's sidereal rotation period

A GEOSYNCHRONOUS ORBIT is an orbit around the Earth that has an orbital period matching the Earth's sidereal rotation period. This means that for an observer at a fixed location on Earth, a satellite placed in a geosynchronous orbit returns to exactly the same place in the sky at exactly the same time each day, making measurements easy and predictable.

For further discussion of satellites, see Skill 25.23 about meteorological data collection and Skill 25.14 about measuring global climate change.

SKILL 26.13 Recognize the contributions of manned and unmanned space missions and the present limitations of space exploration

One of the primary means of learning more about the planetary bodies of the solar system is through space exploration. Beginning in the 1960s, when the first probes journeyed toward Earth's Moon, a planned sequence of spacecraft has visited some of the planetary objects in our solar system.

Mercury was visited in the early 1970s. Launched in November 1973, the Mariner 10 probe reached Mercury in 1974. It orbited the planet three times, collecting basic photographic data. Since the initial visit, no other probes have been sent there.

Venus has been explored by twelve probes, primarily during the 1960s and 1970s:

- Mariner 4, 5, and 10 conducted orbital reconnaissance.
- Venera 4, 7, 12, 15, and 16 (Soviet Union) conducted mostly orbital reconnaissance. Venera 7 actually landed on the surface.
- Pioneer conducted orbital reconnaissance.
- Magellan conducted orbital reconnaissance, providing the most recent and most accurate data. Venus's surface is very hot! Electronics have trouble surviving the heat and this limits attempts to land.

Mars was visited in the late 1960s, early 1970s, and then again in the 1990s.

- Viking 1 and 2: Viking 1, the first probe to Mars, actually landed on the surface.
- Pathfinder and Sojourner: Sojourner actually probed the surface with a small, remote-controlled, robotic, all-terrain vehicle.

Jupiter was visited in the early 1970s:

- Pioneer 10 and 11 visited Jupiter in the early 1970s.
- Voyager 1 visited Jupiter and Titan (a moon of Saturn) and conducted orbital reconnaissance
- Voyager 2 visited Jupiter, Saturn, Uranus, Neptune, and then exited the solar system. It is the only probe to visit all 4 of the Jovian planets.

Recent Explorations

- **Galileo:** Launched in 1989, Galileo is currently orbiting Jupiter.

- **Cassini-Huygens:** Launched in 1997, it was scheduled to reach Saturn in 2004. Cassini is the spacecraft; Huygens is the probe to be sent down to Titan. Titan was chosen because it has an atmosphere, and other probes have detected possible water phases. Additionally, Titan's density indicates it's more Earthlike than gaseous Saturn is. Given the possibility of water and a solid surface, conditions may exist to support some form of life.

- **Stardust:** Launched in 1998, it is currently orbiting the Sun for the second time. After it finishes the second solar orbit, it will go to a comet, collect material from its tail, and return to Earth. This will mark the first time (except for the moon) that collected physical specimens will be returned to Earth.

Efforts in the 20th century to more fully explore space have taught us much about our solar system and conditions in outer space. Additionally, these programs have yielded advances in robotics, material science, electronics, optics, packaging, and communications. Through the process of technology transfer, these advances have improved our everyday lives. Manned space missions, of course, carry a risk to human life. Most space programs are governmentally funded and some citizens and politicians object to the high cost of space research. In fact, space exploration accounts for a very small portion of the US federal budget. Moreover, many supporters maintain that space programs are a source of national pride and can be a focal point for international cooperation (for example, the International Space Station).

SKILL 26.14 Recognize the scientific contribution of remote sensing

---

Remote sensing is the acquisition of information about an object or phenomenon by the use of a recording device(s) that is not in physical or intimate contact with the object. Remote sensing is especially helpful in discerning weather via satellites and reconnaissance aircraft, and in outer-space exploration. Remote sensing is made possible by sensors that either detect radiation emitted by the object being studied, or the sensors emit energy that is then used to scan the object under study. Radars help us to detect storms and prepare for them. Space probes with remote sensing capabilities aboard the Magellan spacecraft provided detailed maps of Venus, and the 2001 Mars Odyssey Spacecraft used similar devices to hunt for evidence of past or present water and volcanic activity on Mars.

DOMAIN VI
SCIENCE, TECHNOLOGY, AND SOCIETY

PERSONALIZED STUDY PLAN

KNOWN MATERIAL/ SKIP IT

PAGE	COMPETENCY AND SKILL	
271	**27: SCIENCE, TECHNOLOGY, AND SOCIETY**	☐
	27.1: Demonstrate an understanding of the uses and applications of science and technology in daily life	☐
	27.2: Demonstrate understanding of the issues certain technologies have on the environment and human affairs	☐

COMPETENCY 27
SCIENCE, TECHNOLOGY, AND SOCIETY

> **SKILL 27.1** **Demonstrate an understanding of the uses and applications of science and technology in daily life** *(e.g., production, transmission, and use of energy; production, storage, use, management, and disposal of consumer products; management of natural resources; nutrition and public health issues, agricultural practices, etc.)*

Management of Natural Resources

How long our natural resources will last depends on future demand and willingness on the part of governments to efficiently manage their energy needs and resources. Likewise, industry must get much more deeply involved by modifying existing or developing new techniques and procedures to effectively use our natural materials.

Unfortunately, natural resources are not evenly distributed throughout the earth, and political considerations, to date, have hampered cooperation in conservation efforts and development of alternative energy sources on a global scale.

As grim as the projected shortfalls may seem, there is some hope. There is a growing awareness of the problems we face, and although not usually coordinated on a global scale, some countries are taking steps to address the issues.

Better agricultural techniques to prevent soil depletion, reclamation of waterways, banning use of chemicals damaging to the atmosphere, recycling plastics and metals, and seeking alternative energy sources are all examples of ongoing initiatives to ensure resources for future generations.

Water Conservation

We have a watery planet. Unfortunately, a large percentage (97 percent) of the water is not fit for human consumption or agricultural use because of its high salinity.

Plants and animals (including humans) require water for survival. In fact, statistics show that every person in the United States uses 300 liters of water per day, and when industrial uses are included, that number soars to roughly 5,000 liters per day, per person. Groundwater provides drinking water for 53 percent of the

Statistics show that every person in the United States uses 300 liters of water per day, and when industrial uses are included, that number soars to roughly 5,000 liters per day, per person.

population in the United States. Much groundwater is clean enough to drink without any type of treatment. Impurities in the water are filtered out by the rocks and soil through which it flows.

Contamination and Pollution of Natural Resources

Many groundwater sources, however, are becoming contaminated. Septic tanks, broken pipes, agriculture fertilizers, garbage dumps, rainwater runoff, leaking underground tanks—all pollute groundwater. Toxic chemicals from farmland mix with groundwater. Removal of large volumes of groundwater can cause collapse of soil and rock underground, causing the ground to sink. Along shorelines, excessive depletion of underground water supplies allows the intrusion of salt water into the freshwater field, making the groundwater supply undrinkable.

Organic wastes—sewage—are produced by both humans and animals. Left untreated, these wastes, and the wastes from food treatment plants can enter the waterways and upset the ecological balance. As the wastes decay, they consume oxygen in the water, depriving aquatic life forms of oxygen, or causing algal blooms that further deplete the oxygen supply, and eventually turning some water anoxic (without oxygen).

Another danger to the ecology is the poisoning of the food chain through pesticides and fertilizers, or with high concentrations of heavy metals carried into the water supply through runoff from farmlands, factories, and mine tailings.

Pollution also affects our air. The uncontrolled burning of fossil fuel hydrocarbons and high-sulfur content coals pose severe health risks, especially to the very young and the very old. Smog alerts are routine in many of the major metropolitan areas, and in Mexico City, air pollution is reaching a critical level.

The Fallout from Urbanization

Forestry management is another area of concern. As our population grows, the demand for lumber and wood products has grown exponentially. The increased urbanization has claimed once-vast tracts of forests, replacing them with concrete paving and closely packed structures.

This same drive to urbanization also affects our soil. Arable farmland is shrinking as the press to develop home and commercial sites increases. Of the approximately 15 billion hectares of dry land on the earth, only 2 billion are suitable for agriculture. If the same land is used year after year, there is a definite danger of soil exhaustion as vital nutrients are depleted.

Along shorelines, excessive depletion of underground water supplies allows the intrusion of salt water into the freshwater field, making the groundwater supply undrinkable.

Of the approximately 15 billion hectares of dry land on the earth, only 2 billion are suitable for agriculture.

Farmland is not the only victim of urbanization. Grazing lands for our cattle and other domesticated animals are also shrinking, and as a consequence, many of the remaining areas are being overgrazed. Overgrazing leads to the loss of the grassland's topsoil cover, leaving it vulnerable to erosion.

Nonrenewable Resource Concerns

The focus in nonrenewable resources is the ever-increasing demand for energy. The key concern about nonrenewable resources is that once they are depleted, they are permanently gone.

Despite a finite supply of fossil fuels and radioactive fuels such as uranium, at our present rate of consumption, there are only an estimated 28 years of petroleum reserves and 40 years of uranium reserves left. To try to alleviate this predictable energy gap, scientists are exploring new methods of recovering additional fuels from once economically unfeasible sites and are researching alternative energy sources.

At our present rate of consumption, there are only an estimated 28 years of petroleum reserves and 40 years of uranium reserves left.

Alternative Energy Resources

The research efforts into alternative energy sources are directed at producing viable renewable energy sources.

- Hydroelectric power: Producing power from falling water is not a new idea because waterwheels have been in use for centuries. The drawback to this energy source lies in the availability of suitable locations for dams and the expense of construction.

- Wind power: Windmills are another ancient technology being revisited by engineers, but wind generators produce very little electricity for the expense involved, and suitable locations (with steady, high winds) for windfields are limited.

- Tidal power: Another concept in use in some areas of the world is the generation of the electricity by deflecting and diverting strong tidal currents through offshore turbines that drive electric generators. Again, the presence of proper conditions (strong tidal power) is necessary, and suitable locations are limited.

- Geothermal energy: In some areas of the world, such as New Zealand, Iceland, and Italy, energy is produced from hot, igneous rocks within the earth. Rainwater percolates porous strata near an active magma chamber and flashes to steam. Some of the steam returns to the surface through natural fissures or is extracted through drilled vents. The steam is captured and routed to turbine-powered electrical generators to produce geothermal power or may be used to directly heat buildings. For example, Reykjavik, Iceland, uses the captured steam to directly heat buildings. The limitations of this alternative energy source are obvious: the majority of metropolitan locations are not situated near an active magma chamber; but New Zealand does manage to gather enough geothermal power to meet approximately 5% of its electrical needs.

- Solar energy: Solar power can be used directly as a source of heat or indirectly to produce electricity. The most common use is to heat water. An array of dark colored piping is placed on the roof of a structure and, as water circulates through the piping, it heats.

- Solar cells: Solar cells produce electricity from solar radiation. Photons striking the junction between two semiconductors (usually selenium) induce an electrical current that is stored in batteries. Although this source of power is pollution free, there are two main limitations:

  - First, the production of power is limited by the distribution and periods of insolation, and atmospheric conditions can easily interfere with collection efforts (i.e., winter months, cloud cover, pollution, and storms).

  - Second, the solar cells individually produce small amounts of electricity (trickle changes) and must be arrayed in large banks. For example, a solar power plant with a capacity of 100 MW would cover a surface area of approximately 4 km^2.

Solar cells have been used successfully in outer space where atmospheric conditions and cell-size restraints are of less concern. Spacecraft and satellites use solar cells to charge batteries that provide electrical power for communications equipment and operating power.

Biomass: Plant and animal wastes (decaying or decayed) can be burned to produce heat for steam turbine electrical generators. In most highly developed countries, the biomass is first converted to either methane gas (given off by decaying biomass) or alcohol, but in some underdeveloped countries, the biomass is still burned directly as a fuel source. For example, for centuries, peat bogs have been exploited as a traditional source of home heating and cooking fuel.

Fusion power: Although the technology does not currently exist, researchers are actively pursuing the means to make fusion power a reality. Unlike fission, the other form of nuclear energy currently in use, fusion does not rely on splitting atoms of uranium or other potentially deadly radioactive elements. Instead, fusion energy mimics the same process that produces the energy of the sun.

Energy is produced when small atomic nuclei fuse together to form new atoms. In a fusion reaction, two isotopes of hydrogen, deuterium, and tritium combine to make helium. The most significant advantage offered by fusion power as compared to fission power is that no dangerous radioactive isotopes are produced. The reaction produces only harmless helium that easily diffuses into the atmosphere and escapes into outer space. Additionally, the elements required for a fusion reaction are abundant on Earth (i.e., deuterium and tritium are extracted from seawater), and readily renew themselves through natural processes.

SKILL Demonstrate understanding of the social, political, ethical, and 27.2 economic issues arising from the use of certain technologies *(e.g., cloning, prolonging life, prenatal testing, etc.)* **and the impact of science and technology on the environment and human affairs**

Society as a whole impacts biological research. The pressure from the majority of society has led to bans and restrictions on human cloning research in the United States and many other countries. The U.S. legislature has banned the use of federal funds for the development of human cloning techniques. Some individual states have banned human cloning regardless of where the funds originate.

The demand for genetically modified crops by society and industry has steadily increased over the years. Genetic engineering in the agricultural field has led to improved crops for human use and consumption. Crops are genetically modified for increased growth and insect resistance because of the demand for larger and greater quantities of produce.

With advances in biotechnology come those in society who oppose it. Ethical questions come into play when discussing animal and human research. Does it need to be done? What are the effects on humans and animals? There are no right or wrong answers to these questions. There are governmental agencies in place to regulate the use of humans and animals for research.

Science and technology are often referred to as a "double-edged sword." Although advances in medicine have greatly improved the quality and length of life, certain moral and ethical controversies have arisen. Unforeseen environmental problems may result from technological advances. Advances in science have led to an improved economy through the application of biotechnology to agriculture, yet it has put our health care system at risk and has caused the cost of medical care to skyrocket. Society depends on science, yet the public needs to be scientifically literate and informed in order to prevent potentially unethical procedures from occuring. Especially vulnerable are the areas of genetic research and fertility. It is important for science teachers to stay abreast of current research and to involve students in critical thinking and ethics discussions whenever possible.

DOMAIN VII
SHORT CONTENT ESSAYS

This part of the test contains three constructed-response questions taken from the following content areas: Physical Sciences (Chemistry/Physics), Life Sciences, and Earth/Space Sciences. For example:

Formulate Scientific Concepts Correctly and Identify and Correct Improperly Formulated Concepts

There are many common misconceptions about science. The following are a few scientific misconceptions that are, or have been, common among students in the past:

- The earth is the center of the solar system.

- The earth is the largest object in the solar system

- Rain comes from the holes in the clouds

- Acquired characteristics can be inherited

- The eye receives upright images

- Energy is a thing

- Heat is not energy

Science can be supported by research, observation, experiment, and/or data analysis. When creating or assessing a scientific concept, students should be encouraged to have an inquiring mind. They should search out mistakes, double-check work, secure variables and controls, make sure the experiment addresses the hypothesis, and that the conclusion makes sense. Some strategies to uncover and dispel misconceptions include:

- Planning appropriate activities, so that the students will see for themselves where there are misconceptions.

- Web research is a useful tool to dispel misconceptions. Students need to be guided in how to look for answers on the Web, and, if necessary, the teacher should explain scientific literature to help the students understand it.

- Science journals are a great source of information. Recent research is highly beneficial for the science student.

- Critical thinking and reasoning are two important skills that the students should be encouraged to use to discover facts—for example, that heat is a form of energy. Here, the students have to be challenged to use their critical thinking skills to reason that heat can cause change—for example, by causing water to boil—so students understand that it is not an object but a form of energy, since only energy can cause change.

Use Models (Defined as Ideas or Constructs Created as Tentative Descriptions of Structures or Processes in Nature) to Communicate Concepts and to Explain Natural Phenomena

Students will be asked to relate the process of scientific inquiry and understand the variety of natural phenomena that take place in the science world. Science is a way of learning about the natural world. Students must know how science has built a model for increasing knowledge by understanding physical, mathematical, and conceptual models. Students must also understand that these concepts don't answer all scientific questions. Students must understand that investigations are used to depict the events of the natural world. Methods and models are used to build, explain, and attempt to investigate. They help us to draw conclusions that serve as observations and increase our understanding of how the systems of the natural world work.

Analyze and Interpret Data Obtained from an Experiment or Investigation, Including Graphical Data

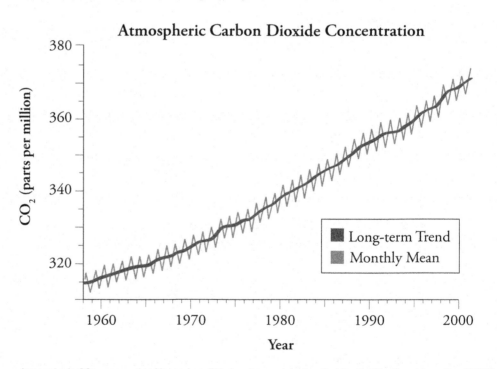

Atmospheric CO_2 measured at Mauna Loa. This is a famous graph called the Keeling Curve (courtesy NASA).

In the preceding graph the x-axis represents time in units of years and the y-axis represents CO_2 concentration in units of parts per million (ppm). The best-fit line (solid dark line) shows the trend in CO_2 concentration during the time period shown. This steady, upward-sloping line indicates an overall trend of increasing CO_2 concentration between 1958 and 2002. The light blue line, which indicates monthly mean CO_2 levels, shows the periodic variation in CO_2 concentrations during each year. The graph can be used to predict future trends in the data.

Example: If CO_2 emission trends continue roughly as they have over the last 40 years, what will be the estimated CO_2 concentration in the atmosphere in 2020?

Solution: The average concentration of CO_2 in 2002 is listed in the table in the right-hand column, and is 372.95 ppm. 18 yrs × an average increase of about 1.3 ppm/yr = 23.4 ppm increase by 2020, for a total concentration of about 396.4 ppm CO_2.

Design an Experiment or Investigation That Tests a Simple Hypothesis

Let's consider several identical potted African violets and suppose we have lights of different color, fertilizer, water, and a variety of common household items. Below are some possible questions, phrased as hypotheses, and a bit about why they are or are not valid.

- African violets will grow taller in blue light than they will in red light: This hypothesis is valid because it could easily be tested by growing one violet in blue light and another in red. The results are easily observed by measuring the height of the violets.

- Invisible microbes cause the leaves of African violets to turn yellow: This hypothesis is not valid because we cannot know whether a given violet is infected with the microbe. This hypothesis could be tested if we had appropriate technology to detect the presence of the microbe.

- Lack of water will stop the growth of African violets: This hypothesis is also valid because it could be tested by denying water to one violet while continuing to water another. The hypothesis may need to be refined to more specifically define how growth will be measured, but presumably this could be easily done.

- African violets will not grow well in swamps: This hypothesis is not valid in our specific situation because we have only potted plants. It could be tested by actually attempting to grow African violets in a swamp, but that is not within this scenario.

Describe a Laboratory or Field Demonstration That Would Illustrate a Fundamental Scientific Concept

In field studies it is sometimes difficult to isolate a single variable. In the laboratory we can manipulate our surroundings to truly study just one thing. For instance, let's consider water. When matter changes in size, shape, or state, it undergoes a physical change. Boiling, melting, evaporation, and freezing are changes in the state of matter.

Experiment: Fill a beaker about $\frac{1}{3}$ full of water. Place the beaker over a flame such as a Bunsen burner, to bring the water to a boil. (Alternatively, the water could be boiled in a microwave oven.) Place an ice cube in the beaker of hot water. Put a watch glass on top of the beaker. Place an ice cube on the watch glass.

Questions: What change of state occurs at the surface of the water in the beaker? [*evaporation of liquid to gas: water to steam*] What change of state is occurring on the underside of the watch glass? [*condensation of gas to liquid: steam to water*] What change of state is occurring in the ice cubes? [*melting of solid to liquid: ice to water*]

The boiling point of a substance is the temperature at which that substance changes from liquid (water in this case) to gas such as steam. That process is called evaporation. If the steam cools below the boiling point, it will undergo condensation and change back into liquid water.

The freezing point of a substance is the temperature at which that substance changes from liquid (water) to a solid (ice). The process is called solidification. As the solid ice is warmed to the freezing point, the freezing point becomes the melting point, which is the temperature at which the substance changes from a solid to a liquid.

Analyze Relationships among the Interacting Parts of a Natural System

While the hydrosphere, lithosphere, and atmosphere can be described and considered separately, they are actually constantly interacting with one another. Energy and matter flows freely between these different spheres. For instance, in the water cycle, water beneath the earth's surface and in rocks (in the lithosphere) is exchanged with vapor in the atmosphere and liquid water in lakes and the ocean (the hydrosphere). Similarly, significant events in one sphere almost always have effects in the other spheres. The recent increase in greenhouse gases provides an example of this ripple effect. Additional greenhouse gases produced by human activities were released into the atmosphere where they built up and caused global warming and widening holes in certain areas of the atmosphere. These increasing temperatures have had many effects on the hydrosphere: rising sea levels, increasing water temperature, and climate changes. These have led to even more changes in the lithosphere, such as glacier retreat and alterations in the patterns of water-rock interaction (run-off, erosion, etc).

Identify and Explain the Processes That Follow Patterns and Cycles in Natural Systems

Two of the clearest examples of patterns in natural systems are the hydrologic cycle and the rock cycle. Each consists of a constant recycling of material. The hydrologic cycle of water movement is driven by solar radiation from the sun. The cycle of evaporation from the oceans and precipitation over land is the methodology employed by nature to maintain the water balance at any given location. The Earth constantly cycles water. It evaporates from the sea, falls as rain, and flows over the land as it returns to the ocean. The constant circulation of water among sea, land, and the atmosphere is called the hydrologic cycle.

The rock cycle is a dynamic process of ongoing change that reflects the recycling of the Earth's materials. Although the processes involved in the rock cycle are dynamic, they follow a geological, rather than human, time scale, and consequently, changes occur so slowly that they are not readily observable.

To help understand the recycling processes, the rock cycle is often graphically presented in the form of a circle with one process following another until the cycle is complete. The formation and decomposition of the Earth's materials, however, often do not happen in a neatly fixed pattern of events. Depending on the circumstances involved in any specific event, the recycling sequence may be interrupted, and the material may go directly from one stage to another, skipping stages in between.

There are three major subdivisions of rocks: sedimentary, metamorphic and igneous. Igneous rock is formed when either sedimentary or metamorphic rock buried deep underground succumbs to heat and pressure and is melted into magma. When the magma cools and hardens, the remaining material is igneous rock. Sedimentary rock is formed when exposed igneous or metamorphic rock erodes away and collects in water. Over time, the eroded particles are fused together by pressure, resulting in sedimentary rock. An example of sedimentary rock is sandstone. Metamorphic rock is commonly called marble. Metamorphic rock is formed when either sedimentary or basalt rock buried deep in the earth is surrounded by heat and pressure. These extreme conditions cause the rock to change; hence the new rock is called metamorphic rock.

SAMPLE TEST

SAMPLE TEST

(Skill 1.1) (Easy)

1. **When is a hypothesis formed?**

    A. Before the data is taken

    B. After the data is taken

    C. After the data is analyzed

    D. While the data is being graphed

(Skill 1.1) (Average)

2. **Which is the correct order of methodology?**

    1. **Collecting data**

    2. **Planning a controlled experiment**

    3. **Drawing a conclusion**

    4. **Hypothesizing a result**

    5. **Revisiting a hypothesis to answer a question**

    A. 1,2,3,4,5

    B. 4,2,1,3,5

    C. 4,5,1,3,2

    D. 1,3,4,5,2

(Skill 1.2) (Easy)

3. **A hypothesis is _____**

    A. a simplification of or substitute for what is being studied.

    B. the raw data collected from an experiment.

    C. an unproven theory or educated guess to explain a phenomenon.

    D. the independent variable in an experiment.

(Skill 1.3) (Rigorous)

4. **Identify the control in the following experiment: A student had four corn plants and was measuring photosynthetic rate (by measuring growth mass). Half of the plants were exposed to full (constant) sunlight, and the other half were kept in 50% (constant) sunlight.**

    A. The control is a set of plants grown in full (constant) sunlight

    B. The control is a set of plants grown in 50% (constant) sunlight

    C. The control is a set of plants grown in the dark

    D. The control is a set of plants grown in a mixture of natural levels of sunlight

(Skill 1.3) (Easy)

5. **In a laboratory report, what is the abstract?**

    A. The abstract is a summary of the report, and is the first section of the report

    B. The abstract is a summary of the report, and is the last section of the report

    C. The abstract is predictions for future experiments, and is the first section of the report

    D. The abstract is predictions for future experiments, and is the last section of the report

(Skill 1.4) (Easy)

6. **In an experiment measuring the growth of bacteria at different temperatures, what is the independent variable?**

    A. Number of bacteria

    B. Growth rate of bacteria

    C. Temperature

    D. Light intensity

(Skill 1.4) (Average)

7. When designing a scientific experiment, a student considers all the factors that may influence the results. The process goal is to _____

    A. recognize and manipulate independent variables.

    B. recognize and record independent variables.

    C. recognize and manipulate dependent variables.

    D. recognize and record dependent variables.

(Skill 2.1) (Easy)

8. When measuring the volume of water in a graduated cylinder, where does one read the measurement?

    A. At the highest point of the liquid

    B. At the bottom of the meniscus curve

    C. At the closest mark to the top of the liquid

    D. At the top of the plastic safety ring

(Skill 2.1) (Easy)

9. Why is the metric system the standard measuring system used in science?

    A. It is the most accurate measuring system available to scientists

    B. It has the highest degree of accuracy

    C. It is the measuring system taught in most school systems

    D. It allows for easy comparison of experiments done by scientists around the world

(Skill 2.1) (Average)

10. A laboratory balance is most appropriately used to measure the mass of which of the following?

    A. Seven paper clips

    B. Three oranges

    C. Two hundred cells

    D. One student's elbow

(Skill 2.2) (Average)

11. Which of the following data sets is properly represented by a line graph?

    A. The activity of different enzymes at varying temperatures

    B. The ages of children in a classroom

    C. The percent of time students spend on various after-school activities

    D. The concentrations of bacteria colonies on a petri dish

(Skill 2.4) (Average)

12. Which of the following is NOT a likely source of error in an experiment?

    A. Using different sources of materials for the same experiment

    B. Using different calculators to perform the calculations required to analyze data

    C. Using different instruments in the course of one experiment

    D. Using different methods in the course of one experiment

(Skill 3.1) (Easy)

13. Chloroform should NOT be used in school laboratories for the following reason:

    A. It smells unpleasant

    B. It is a potential carcinogen

    C. It is expensive to obtain

    D. It is an explosive

(Skill 3.1) (Rigorous)

14. Chemicals should be stored _____

    A. in the principal's office.

    B. in a dark room.

    C. in an off-site research facility.

    D. according to their reactivity with other substances.

(Skill 3.1) (Average)

15. Prepared laboratory solutions should be made with:

    A. Alcohol

    B. Hydrochloric acid

    C. Distilled water

    D. Tap water

(Skill 3.2) (Average)

16. Separating blood into blood cells and plasma involves the process of:

    A. Electrophoresis

    B. Spectrophotometry

    C. Centrifugation

    D. Chromatography

(Skill 3.2) (Rigorous)

17. In a science experiment, a student needs to dispense very small measured amounts of liquid into a well-mixed solution. Which of the following is the best choice of equipment to use?

    A. Buret with buret stand, stir-plate, stirring rod, beaker

    B. Buret with buret stand, stir-plate, beaker

    C. Volumetric flask, dropper, graduated cylinder, stirring rod

    D. Beaker, graduated cylinder, stir-plate

(Skill 3.2) (Average)

18. Blue litmus paper turns pink when exposed to which of the following?

    A. An acid

    B. A base

    C. An indicator substance

    D. Light

(Skill 3.3) (Rigorous)

19. Which of these is the best example of "negligence"?

    A. A teacher fails to give oral instructions to those with reading disabilities

    B. A teacher fails to exercise ordinary care to ensure safety in the classroom

    C. A teacher displays inability to supervise a large group of students

    D. A teacher reasonably anticipates that an event may occur, and plans accordingly

(Skill 3.3) (Average)

20. **Who should be notified in the case of a serious chemical spill?**

    A. The custodian

    B. The fire department or other municipal authority

    C. The science department chair

    D. The School Board

(Skill 4.1) (Easy)

21. **Which of the following is most accurate?**

    A. Mass is always constant; weight may vary by location

    B. Mass and weight are both always constant

    C. Weight is always constant; mass may vary by location

    D. Mass and weight may both vary by location

(Skill 4.1) (Average)

22. **What is specific gravity?**

    A. The mass of an object

    B. The ratio of the density of a substance to the density of water

    C. Density

    D. The pull of the Earth's gravity on an object

(Skill 4.1) (Easy)

23. **The measure of the pull of Earth's gravity on an object is called**

    A. Mass number

    B. Atomic number

    C. Mass

    D. Weight

(Skill 4.4) (Average)

24. **The Law of Conservation of Energy states that:**

    A. There must be the same number of products and reactants in any chemical equation

    B. Objects always fall toward large masses such as planets

    C. Energy is neither created nor destroyed, but may change form

    D. Lights must be turned off when not in use, by state regulation

(Skill 4.5) (Easy)

25. **Energy is measured with the same units as _____**

    A. force.

    B. momentum.

    C. work.

    D. power.

(Skill 5.2) (Rigorous)

26. **A long silver bar has a temperature of 50 degrees Celsius at one end and 0 degrees Celsius at the other end. The bar will reach thermal equilibrium (barring outside influence) by the process of heat _____**

    A. conduction.

    B. convection.

    C. radiation.

    D. phase change.

(Skills 5.2, 5.3) (Rigorous)

27. **When you step out of the shower, the floor feels colder on your feet than the bathmat. Which of the following is the correct explanation for this phenomenon?**

    A. The floor is colder than the bathmat

    B. Your feet have a chemical reaction with the floor, but not with the bathmat

    C. Heat is conducted more easily into the floor

    D. Water is absorbed from your feet into the bathmat

(Skill 5.4) (Average)

28. **Which of the following statements is NOT true?**

    A. Heat cannot pass spontaneously from a colder to a hotter object

    B. Systems that are nearly always in a state of equilibrium are called reversible systems

    C. Some machines can absorb heat from a heat source and do an equal amount of work without losing any heat to the environment; these are known as perfect machines

    D. Work occurs when heat is transferred from hotter to cooler objects

(Skill 6.1) (Rigorous)

29. **When heat is added to most solids, they expand. Why is this the case?**

    A. The molecules get bigger

    B. The faster molecular motion leads to greater distance between the molecules

    C. The molecules develop greater repelling electric forces

    D. The molecules form a more rigid structure

(Skill 6.2) (Easy)

30. **Which parts of an atom are located inside the nucleus?**

    A. Protons and electrons

    B. Protons and neutrons

    C. Protons only

    D. Neutrons only

(Skill 6.3) (Average)

31. **Which of the following accurately describes an ionic bond?**

    A. A bond formed by the sharing of electrons

    B. A bond formed when one electronegative atom shares a hydrogen atom with another electronegative atom

    C. A bond formed by the transfer of electrons

    D. A bond formed between nonmetals

(Skill 6.5) (Average)

32. **In a fission reactor, "heavy water" is used to _____**

    A. terminate fission reactions.

    B. slow down neutrons and moderate reactions.

    C. rehydrate the chemicals.

    D. initiate a chain reaction.

(Skill 6.5) (Rigorous)

33. **What is the main obstacle to using nuclear fusion for obtaining electricity?**

   A. Nuclear fusion produces much more pollution than nuclear fission

   B. There is no obstacle; most power plants use nuclear fusion today

   C. Nuclear fusion requires very high temperature and activation energy

   D. The fuel for nuclear fusion is extremely expensive

(Skill 7.2) (Average)

34. **Newton's Laws are taught in science classes because _____**

   A. they are the correct analysis of inertia, gravity, and forces.

   B. they are a close approximation to correct physics for usual Earth conditions.

   C. they accurately incorporate Relativity into studies of forces.

   D. Newton was a well-respected scientist in his time.

(Skill 7.2) (Rigorous)

35. **Which of the following is a correct explanation for astronaut "weightlessness"?**

   A. Astronauts continue to feel the pull of gravity in space, but they are so far from planets that the force is small

   B. Astronauts continue to feel the pull of gravity in space, but spacecraft have such powerful engines that those forces dominate, reducing effective weight

   C. Astronauts do not feel the pull of gravity in space, because space is a vacuum

   D. Astronauts do not feel the pull of gravity in space, because black hole forces dominate the force field, reducing their masses

(Skill 7.2) (Easy)

36. **All of the following are considered Newton's Laws except for:**

   A. An object in motion will continue in motion unless acted upon by an outside force

   B. For every action force, there is an equal and opposite reaction force

   C. Nature abhors a vacuum

   D. Mass can be considered the ratio of force to acceleration

(Skill 7.5) (Average)

37. **A Newton is fundamentally a measure of _____**

   A. force.

   B. momentum.

   C. energy.

   D. gravity.

(Skill 7.8) (Rigorous)

38. **A ball rolls down a smooth hill. You may ignore air resistance. Which of the following is a true statement?**

   A. The ball has more energy at the start of its descent than just before it hits the bottom of the hill, because it is higher up at the beginning

   B. The ball has less energy at the start of its descent than just before it hits the bottom of the hill, because it is moving more quickly at the end

   C. The ball has the same energy throughout its descent, because positional energy is converted to energy of motion

   D. The ball has the same energy throughout its descent, because a single object (such as a ball) cannot gain or lose energy

(Skill 8.2) (Average)

39. **Resistance is measured in units called:**

   A. Watts

   B. Volts

   C. Ohms

   D. Current

(Skill 9.1) (Easy)

40. **Sound can be transmitted in all of the following except:**

   A. Air

   B. Water

   C. Diamond

   D. A vacuum

(Skill 9.3) (Average)

41. **The speed of light is different in different materials. This is responsible for** _____

   A. interference.

   B. refraction.

   C. reflection.

   D. relativity.

(Skill 9.5) (Rigorous)

42. **As a train approaches, the whistle sounds:**

   A. Higher, because it has a higher apparent frequency

   B. Lower, because it has a lower apparent frequency

   C. Higher, because it has a lower apparent frequency

   D. Lower, because it has a higher apparent frequency

(Skill 9.5) (Rigorous)

43. **The Doppler effect is associated most closely with which property of waves?**

   A. Amplitude

   B. Wavelength

   C. Frequency

   D. Intensity

(Skill 9.8) (Average)

44. **Sound waves are produced by** _____

   A. pitch.

   B. noise.

   C. vibrations.

   D. sonar.

(Skill 9.9) (Rigorous)

45. **The electromagnetic radiation with the longest wave length is** _____

   A. radio waves.

   B. red light.

   C. X-rays.

   D. ultraviolet light.

(Skill 10.1) (Easy)

46. **The elements in the modern Periodic Table are arranged:**

   A. In numerical order by atomic number

   B. Randomly

   C. In alphabetical order by chemical symbol

   D. In numerical order by atomic mass

(Skill 10.2) (Average)

47. **Which of the following is NOT a property of metalloids?**

    A. Metalloids are solids at standard temperature and pressure

    B. Metalloids can conduct electricity to a limited extent

    C. Metalloids are found in groups 13 through 17

    D. Metalloids all favor ionic bonding

(Skill 11.2) (Rigorous)

48. **The chemical equation for water formation is: $2H_2 + O_2 \rightarrow 2H_2O$. Which of the following is an incorrect interpretation of this equation?**

    A. Two moles of hydrogen gas and one mole of oxygen gas combine to make two moles of water

    B. Two grams of hydrogen gas and one gram of oxygen gas combine to make two grams of water

    C. Two molecules of hydrogen gas and one molecule of oxygen gas combine to make two molecules of water

    D. Four atoms of hydrogen (combined as a diatomic gas) and two atoms of oxygen (combined as a diatomic gas) combine to make two molecules of water

(Skill 11.2) (Average)

49. **Which of the following will not change in a chemical reaction?**

    A. Number of moles of products

    B. Atomic number of one of the reactants

    C. Mass (in grams) of one of the reactants

    D. Rate of reaction

(Skill 11.2) (Average)

50. **Which of the following is a correct definition for "chemical equilibrium"?**

    A. Chemical equilibrium is when the forward and backward reaction rates are equal; the reaction may continue to proceed forward and backward

    B. Chemical equilibrium is when the forward and backward reaction rates are equal, and equal to zero; the reaction does not continue

    C. Chemical equilibrium is when there are equal quantities of reactants and products

    D. Chemical equilibrium is when acids and bases neutralize each other fully

(Skill 11.6) (Average)

51. **What is the purpose of Lewis dot structures?**

    A. They show the three-dimensional shape of the molecule

    B. They are a super-simplified representation of the molecule with lines representing bonds

    C. They provide a method for keeping track of each atom's valence electrons in a molecule

    D. They provide a method for keeping track of each atom's non-valence electrons in a molecule

(Skill 12.1) (Rigorous)

52. **Which of the following is NOT true about phase change in matter?**

    A. Solid water and liquid ice can coexist at water's freezing point

    B. At 7 degrees Celsius, water is always in liquid phase

    C. Matter changes phase when enough energy is gained or lost

    D. Different phases of matter are characterized by differences in molecular motion

(Skill 13.2) (Average)

53. **Which reaction below is a decomposition reaction?**

    A. $HCl + NaOH \rightarrow NaCl + H_2O$

    B. $C + O_2 \rightarrow CO_2$

    C. $2H_2O \rightarrow 2H_2 + O_2$

    D. $CuSO_4 + Fe \rightarrow FeSO_4 + Cu$

(Skill 13.4) (Average)

54. **Enzymes speed up reactions by** _____

    A. utilizing ATP.

    B. lowering pH, allowing reaction speed to increase.

    C. increasing volume of substrate.

    D. lowering energy of activation.

(Skill 13.4) (Average)

55. **Catalysts assist reactions by** _____

    A. lowering effective activation energy.

    B. maintaining precise pH levels.

    C. keeping systems at equilibrium.

    D. adjusting reaction speed.

(Skill 14.4) (Easy)

56. **Vinegar is an example of a** _____

    A. strong acid.

    B. strong base.

    C. weak acid.

    D. weak base.

(Skill 15.1) (Average)

57. **What cell organelle contains the cell's stored food?**

    A. Vacuoles

    B. Golgi Apparatus

    C. Ribosomes

    D. Lysosomes

(Skill 15.5) (Rigorous)

58. **Which process(es) result(s) in a haploid chromosome number?**

    A. Mitosis

    B. Meiosis

    C. Both mitosis and meiosis

    D. Neither mitosis nor meiosis

(Skill 15.5) (Easy)

59. **The first stage of mitosis is called** _____

    A. telophase.

    B. anaphase.

    C. prophase.

    D. mitophase.

(Skill 16.1) (Rigorous)

60. Which of the following is not a nucleotide?

    A. Adenine

    B. Alanine

    C. Cytosine

    D. Guanine

(Skill 16.2) (Average)

61. Amino acids are carried to the ribosome in protein synthesis by:

    A. transfer RNA (tRNA)

    B. messenger RNA (mRNA)

    C. ribosomal RNA (rRNA)

    D. transformation RNA (trRNA)

(Skill 16.4) (Rigorous)

62. A series of experiments on pea plants performed by _____ showed that two invisible markers existed for each trait, and one marker dominated the other.

    A. Pasteur

    B. Watson and Crick

    C. Mendel

    D. Mendeleev

(Skill 16.4) (Rigorous)

63. A white flower is crossed with a red flower. Which of the following is a sign of incomplete dominance?

    A. Pink flowers

    B. Red flowers

    C. White flowers

    D. No flowers

(Skill 16.4) (Average)

64. A child has type O blood. Her father has type A blood, and her mother has type B blood. What are the genotypes of the father and mother, respectively?

    A. AO and BO

    B. AA and AB

    C. OO and BO

    D. AO and BB

(Skill 16.8) (Rigorous)

65. Which of the following is a correct explanation for scientific evolution?

    A. Giraffes need to reach higher for leaves to eat, so their necks stretch. The giraffe babies are then born with longer necks. Eventually, there are more long-necked giraffes in the population.

    B. Giraffes with longer necks are able to reach more leaves, so they eat more and have more babies than other giraffes. Eventually, there are more long-necked giraffes in the population.

    C. Giraffes want to reach higher for leaves to eat, so they release enzymes into their bloodstream, which in turn causes fetal development of longer-necked giraffes. Eventually, there are more long-necked giraffes in the population.

    D. Giraffes with long necks are more attractive to other giraffes, so they get the best mating partners and have more babies. Eventually, there are more long-necked giraffes in the population.

(Skill 17.2) (Rigorous)

66. Extensive use of antibacterial soap has been found to increase the virulence of certain infections in hospitals. Which of the following might be an explanation for this phenomenon?

    A. Antibacterial soaps do not kill viruses

    B. Antibacterial soaps do not incorporate the same antibiotics used in medicine

    C. Antibacterial soaps kill a lot of bacteria, and only the hardiest ones survive to reproduce

    D. Antibacterial soaps can be very drying to the skin

(Skill 18.1) (Rigorous)

67. Which of the following is NOT a necessary characteristic of living things?

    A. Movement

    B. Reduction of local entropy

    C. Ability to cause local energy form changes

    D. Reproduction

(Skill 18.1) (Average)

68. Identify the correct sequence of organization of living things from lower to higher order:

    A. Cell, Organelle, Organ, Tissue, System, Organism

    B. Cell, Tissue, Organ, Organelle, System, Organism

    C. Organelle, Cell, Tissue, Organ, System, Organism

    D. Organelle, Tissue, Cell, Organ, System, Organism

(Skill 18.2) (Rigorous)

69. The scientific name *Canis familiaris* refers to the animal's _____

    A. kingdom and phylum.

    B. genus and species.

    C. class and species.

    D. type and family.

(Skill 18.2) (Rigorous)

70. Animals with a notochord or a backbone are in the phylum:

    A. Arthropoda

    B. Chordata

    C. Mollusca

    D. Mammalia

(Skill 18.3) (Rigorous)

71. Which of the following organisms use spores to reproduce?

    A. Fish

    B. Flowering plants

    C. Conifers

    D. Ferns

(Skill 18.3) (Rigorous)

72. Why are viruses considered obligate parasites?

    A. Because once they enter the host, they are obligated to infect the host

    B. Because the immune system of the host is obligated to combat the effects of the virus

    C. Because they are not reliant on the host for any of the means of their own survival or reproduction

    D. Because they rely on the host for their own reproduction

(Skill 21.4) (Average)

73. A wrasse (fish) cleans the teeth of other fish by eating away plaque. This is an example of _____ between the fish.

   A. parasitism

   B. symbiosis (mutualism)

   C. competition

   D. predation

(Skill 21.8) (Rigorous)

74. What is the most accurate description of the Water Cycle?

   A. Rain comes from clouds, filling the ocean. The water then evaporates and becomes clouds again.

   B. Water circulates from rivers into groundwater and back, while water vapor circulates in the atmosphere.

   C. Water is conserved except for chemical or nuclear reactions, and any drop of water could circulate through clouds, rain, ground-water, and surface-water.

   D. Weather systems cause chemical reactions to break water into its atoms.

(Skill 21.9) (Rigorous)

75. Which of the following animals are most likely to live in a tropical rain forest?

   A. Reindeer

   B. Monkeys

   C. Puffins

   D. Bears

(Skill 22.1) (Average)

76. Lithification refers to the process by which unconsolidated sediments are transformed into _____

   A. metamorphic rocks.

   B. sedimentary rocks.

   C. igneous rocks.

   D. lithium oxide.

(Skill 22.1) (Average)

77. Igneous rocks can be classified according to which of the following?

   A. Texture

   B. Composition

   C. Formation process

   D. All of the above

(Skill 22.1) (Average)

78. Which of the following types of rock are made from magma?

   A. Fossils

   B. Sedimentary

   C. Metamorphic

   D. Igneous

(Skill 22.2) (Rigorous)

79. Which of these is a true statement about loamy soil?

   A. Loamy soil is gritty and porous

   B. Loamy soil is smooth and a good barrier to water

   C. Loamy soil is hostile to microorganisms

   D. Loamy soil is velvety and clumpy

(Skill 22.4) (Rigorous)

80. _____ are cracks in the plates of the Earth's crust, along which the plates move.

   A. Faults

   B. Ridges

   C. Earthquakes

   D. Volcanoes

(Skill 22.5) (Average)

81. The theory of "continental drift" is supported by which of the following?

   A. The way the shapes of South America and Europe fit together

   B. The way the shapes of Europe and Asia fit together

   C. The way the shapes of South America and Africa fit together

   D. The way the shapes of North America and Antarctica fit together

(Skill 23.4) (Average)

82. Fossils are usually found in _____ rock.

   A. igneous

   B. sedimentary

   C. metamorphic

   D. cumulus

(Skill 23.6) (Easy)

83. Which of the following is the longest (largest) unit of geological time?

   A. Solar Year

   B. Epoch

   C. Period

   D. Era

(Skill 24.6) (Rigorous)

84. The salinity of ocean water is closest to _____

   A. 0.035%.

   B. 0.35%.

   C. 3.5%.

   D. 35%.

(Skill 25.7) (Rigorous)

85. A cup of hot liquid and a cup of cold liquid are both sitting in a room at comfortable room temperature and humidity. Both cups are made of thin plastic. Which of the following is a true statement?

   A. There will be fog on the outside of the hot liquid cup, and also fog on the outside of the cold liquid cup

   B. There will be fog on the outside of the hot liquid cup, but not on the cold liquid cup

   C. There will be fog on the outside of the cold liquid cup, but not on the hot liquid cup

   D. There will not be fog on the outside of either cup

(Skill 26.4) (Rigorous)

86. What is the main difference between the "condensation hypothesis" and the "tidal hypothesis" for the origin of the solar system?

A. The tidal hypothesis can be tested, but the condensation hypothesis cannot

B. The tidal hypothesis proposes a near collision of two stars pulling on each other, but the condensation hypothesis proposes condensation of rotating clouds of dust and gas

C. The tidal hypothesis explains how tides began on planets such as Earth, but the condensation hypothesis explains how water vapor became liquid on Earth

D. The tidal hypothesis is based on Aristotelian physics, but the condensation hypothesis is based on Newtonian mechanics

(Skill 26.6) (Average)

87. Which of the following is the best definition for "meteorite"?

A. A meteorite is a mineral composed of mica and feldspar

B. A meteorite is material from outer space that has struck the Earth's surface

C. A meteorite is an element that has properties of both metals and nonmetals

D. A meteorite is a very small unit of length measurement

(Skill 26.6) (Rigorous)

88. The Earth's atmosphere is composed mainly of which of the following?

A. Oxygen and nitrogen

B. Carbon and hydrogen

C. Carbon and oxygen

D. Nitrogen and carbon

(Skill 26.12) (Average)

89. Sonar works by _____

A. timing how long it takes sound to reach a certain speed.

B. bouncing sound waves between two metal plates.

C. bouncing sound waves off an object and timing how long it takes for the sound to return.

D. evaluating the motion and amplitude of sound.

(Skill 27.1) (Easy)

90. What is the source for most of the United States' drinking water?

A. Desalinated ocean water

B. Surface water (lakes, streams, mountain runoff)

C. Rainfall into municipal reservoirs

D. Groundwater

Answer Key

ANSWER KEY								
1. A	11. A	21. A	31. C	41. B	51. C	61. A	71. D	81. C
2. B	12. B	22. B	32. B	42. A	52. B	62. C	72. D	82. B
3. C	13. B	23. D	33. C	43. C	53. C	63. A	73. B	83. D
4. A	14. D	24. C	34. B	44. C	54. D	64. A	74. C	84. C
5. A	15. C	25. C	35. A	45. A	55. A	65. B	75. B	85. C
6. C	16. C	26. A	36. C	46. A	56. C	66. C	76. B	86. B
7. A	17. B	27. C	37. A	47. D	57. A	67. A	77. D	87. B
8. B	18. A	28. C	38. C	48. B	58. B	68. C	78. D	88. A
9. D	19. B	29. B	39. C	49. B	59. C	69. B	79. D	89. C
10. A	20. B	30. B	40. D	50. A	60. B	70. B	80. A	90. D

Rigor Table

RIGOR TABLE	
Rigor level	**Questions**
Easy 20%	1, 3, 5, 6, 8, 9, 13, 21, 23, 25, 30, 36, 40, 46, 56, 59, 83, 90
Average 40%	2, 7, 10, 11, 12, 15, 16, 18, 20, 22, 24, 28, 31, 32, 34, 37, 39, 41, 44, 47, 49, 50, 51, 53, 54, 55, 57, 61, 64, 68, 73, 76, 77, 78, 81, 82, 87, 89
Rigorous 40%	4, 14, 17, 19, 26, 27, 29, 33, 35, 38, 42, 43, 45, 48, 52, 58, 60, 62, 63, 65, 66, 67, 69, 70, 71, 72, 74, 75, 79, 80, 84, 85, 86, 88

Sample Test with Rationales:

(Skill 1.1) (Easy)

1. **When is a hypothesis formed?**

    A. Before the data is taken

    B. After the data is taken

    C. After the data is analyzed

    D. While the data is being graphed

    Answer: A. Before the data is taken

    A hypothesis is an educated guess, made before undertaking an experiment. The hypothesis is then evaluated based on the observed data. Therefore, the hypothesis must be formed before the data is taken, not during or after the experiment.

(Skill 1.1) (Average)

2. **Which is the correct order of methodology?**

    1. **Collecting data**

    2. **Planning a controlled experiment**

    3. **Drawing a conclusion**

    4. **Hypothesizing a result**

    5. **Revisiting a hypothesis to answer a question**

    A. 1,2,3,4,5

    B. 4,2,1,3,5

    C. 4,5,1,3,2

    D. 1,3,4,5,2

Answer: B. 4,2,1,3,5

The correct methodology for the scientific method is first to make a meaningful hypothesis (educated guess), then plan and execute a controlled experiment to test that hypothesis. Using the data collected in that experiment, the scientist then draws conclusions and attempts to answer the original question related to the hypothesis.

(Skill 1.2) (Easy)

3. **A hypothesis is _____**

    A. a simplification of or substitute for what is being studied.

    B. the raw data collected from an experiment.

    C. an unproven theory or educated guess to explain a phenomenon.

    D. the independent variable in an experiment.

Answer: C. an unproven theory or educated guess to explain a phenomenon.

A hypothesis is an unproven theory or educated guess that attempts to explain an observed phenomenon. After forming a hypothesis, the researcher designs an experiment to test the hypothesis. The research and testing either prove or disprove the hypothesis.

(Skill 1.3) (Rigorous)

4. Identify the control in the following experiment: A student had four corn plants and was measuring photosynthetic rate (by measuring growth mass). Half of the plants were exposed to full (constant) sunlight, and the other half were kept in 50% (constant) sunlight.

    A. The control is a set of plants grown in full (constant) sunlight

    B. The control is a set of plants grown in 50% (constant) sunlight

    C. The control is a set of plants grown in the dark

    D. The control is a set of plants grown in a mixture of natural levels of sunlight

    Answer: A. The control is a set of plants grown in full (constant) sunlight

    In this experiment, the goal was to measure how two different amounts of sunlight affected plant growth. The control in any experiment is the "base case," or the usual situation without a change in variable. Because the control must be studied alongside the variable, answers (C) and (D) are omitted (because they were not in the experiment). The better answer of (A) and (B) is (A), because plants' usual growing circumstances are in full sunlight. This is particularly true for crops like the corn plants in this question.

(Skill 1.3) (Easy)

5. In a laboratory report, what is the abstract?

    A. The abstract is a summary of the report, and is the first section of the report

    B. The abstract is a summary of the report, and is the last section of the report

    C. The abstract is predictions for future experiments, and is the first section of the report

    D. The abstract is predictions for future experiments, and is the last section of the report

    Answer: A. The abstract is a summary of the report, and is the first section of the report

    In a laboratory report, the abstract is the section that summarizes the entire report (often containing one representative sentence from each section). It appears at the very beginning of the report, even before the introduction, often on its own page (instead of a title page). This format is consistent with articles in scientific journals.

(Skill 1.4) (Easy)

6. In an experiment measuring the growth of bacteria at different temperatures, what is the independent variable?

    A. Number of bacteria

    B. Growth rate of bacteria

    C. Temperature

    D. Light intensity

Answer: C. Temperature

To answer this question, recall that the independent variable in an experiment is the entity that is changed by the scientist in order to observe the effects (the dependent variable(s)). In this experiment, temperature is changed in order to measure growth of bacteria, so (C) is the answer. Note that answer (A) is the dependent variable, and neither (B) nor (D) is directly relevant to the question.

(Skill 1.4) (Average)

7. **When designing a scientific experiment, a student considers all the factors that may influence the results. The process goal is to _____**

   A. recognize and manipulate independent variables.

   B. recognize and record independent variables.

   C. recognize and manipulate dependent variables.

   D. recognize and record dependent variables.

Answer: A. recognize and manipulate independent variables.

When a student designs a scientific experiment, she must decide what to measure, and what independent variables will play a role in the experiment. She must determine how to manipulate these independent variables to refine her procedure and to prepare for meaningful observations. Although she will eventually record dependent variables (D), this does not take place during the experimental design phase. Although the student will likely recognize and record the independent variables (B), this is not the process goal, but a helpful step in manipulating the variables. It is unlikely that the student will manipulate dependent variables directly in her experiment (C), or the data would be suspect.

(Skill 2.1) (Easy)

8. **When measuring the volume of water in a graduated cylinder, where does one read the measurement?**

   A. At the highest point of the liquid

   B. At the bottom of the meniscus curve

   C. At the closest mark to the top of the liquid

   D. At the top of the plastic safety ring

Answer: B. At the bottom of the meniscus curve

To measure water in glass, you must look at the top surface at eye-level, and ascertain the location of the bottom of the meniscus (the curved surface at the top of the water). The meniscus forms because water molecules adhere to the sides of the glass, which is a slightly stronger force than their cohesion to each other. This leads to a U-shaped top of the liquid column, the bottom of which gives the most accurate volume measurement. (Other liquids have different forces, e.g., mercury in glass, which has a convex meniscus.)

(Skill 2.1) (Easy)

9. **Why is the metric system the standard measuring system used in science?**

    A. It is the most accurate measuring system available to scientists

    B. It has the highest degree of accuracy

    C. It is the measuring system taught in most school systems

    D. It allows for easy comparison of experiments done by scientists around the world

Answer: D. It allows for easy comparison of experiments done by scientists around the world

The metric system is like a universal language in science, allowing scientists from every corner of the world to easily understand and analyze results of experiments performed by others.

(Skill 2.1) (Average)

10. **A laboratory balance is most appropriately used to measure the mass of which of the following?**

    A. Seven paper clips

    B. Three oranges

    C. Two hundred cells

    D. One student's elbow

Answer: A. Seven paper clips

Usually, laboratory/classroom balances can measure masses between approximately 0.01 gram and 1 kilogram. Therefore, answer (B) is too heavy and answer (C) is too light. Answer (D) is silly, but it is a reminder to instruct students not to lean on the balances or put their things near them. Answer (A), which is likely to have a mass of a few grams, is correct in this case.

(Skill 2.2) (Average)

11. **Which of the following data sets is properly represented by a line graph?**

    A. The activity of different enzymes at varying temperatures

    B. The ages of children in a classroom

    C. The percent of time students spend on various after-school activities

    D. The concentrations of bacteria colonies on a petri dish

Answer: A. The activity of different enzymes at varying temperatures

The ages of children in a classroom or the concentrations of bacteria colonies in a petri dish would be best represented by a bar graph or histograph, which are used to compare different items and make comparisons among them. The percent of time students spend on various after-school activities would be best displayed by a pie chart, which is used to organize data as part of a whole. Line graphs should be used to compare different sets of related data or predict data that have not yet been measured.

(Skill 2.4) (Average)

12. **Which of the following is NOT a likely source of error in an experiment?**

    A. Using different sources of materials for the same experiment

    B. Using different calculators to perform the calculations required to analyze data

    C. Using different instruments in the course of one experiment

    D. Using different methods in the course of one experiment

Answer: B. Using different calculators to perform the calculations required to analyze data

Using different sources of materials can lead to experimental error because of potential variations in the composition of the compounds used. Using different instruments can lead to experimental errors because slight variations between instruments can lead to an error in measured values. Using different methods can lead to experimental error because the results obtained from one method cannot be directly compared to the results obtained from another method. Using different calculators to perform your calculations is not a likely source of error.

(Skill 3.1) (Easy)

13. **Chloroform should NOT be used in school laboratories for the following reason:**

    A. It smells unpleasant

    B. It is a potential carcinogen

    C. It is expensive to obtain

    D. It is an explosive

Answer: B. It is a potential carcinogen

Chloroform is a potential carcinogen, so it is too dangerous for use in schools. In general, teachers should not use carcinogens in school laboratories. Although chloroform also smells unpleasant, a smell alone is not a definitive marker of danger. For example, many people find the smell of vinegar to be unpleasant, but vinegar is considered a very safe classroom/laboratory chemical. Furthermore, some odorless materials are toxic. Chloroform is neither particularly expensive nor explosive.

(Skill 3.1) (Rigorous)

14. **Chemicals should be stored _____**

    A. in the principal's office.

    B. in a dark room.

    C. in an off-site research facility.

    D. according to their reactivity with other substances.

Answer: D. according to their reactivity with other substances.

Chemicals should be stored with other chemicals of similar properties (e.g., acids with other acids), to reduce the potential for either hazardous reactions in the store-room, or mistakes in reagent use. Certainly, chemicals should not be stored in anyone's office, and the light intensity of the room is not very important because light-sensitive chemicals are usually stored in dark containers. In fact, good lighting is desirable in a store-room, so that labels can be read easily. Chemicals may be stored off-site, but that makes their use inconvenient.

(Skill 3.1) (Average)

15. **Prepared laboratory solutions should be made with:**

    A. Alcohol

    B. Hydrochloric acid

    C. Distilled water

    D. Tap water

Answer: C. Distilled water

Alcohol and hydrochloric acid should never be used to make solutions unless that is necessary for the experiment. All solutions should be made with distilled water as tap water contains dissolved particles which may affect the results of an experiment.

(Skill 3.2) (Average)

16. **Separating blood into blood cells and plasma involves the process of:**

    A. Electrophoresis

    B. Spectrophotometry

    C. Centrifugation

    D. Chromatography

Answer: C. Centrifugation

Electrophoresis uses electrical charges of molecules to separate them according to their size. Spectrophotometry uses percent light absorbance to measure a color change, thus giving qualitative data a quantitative value. Chromatography uses the principles of capillarity to separate substances. Centrifugation involves spinning substances at a high speed. The more dense part of a solution will settle to the bottom of the test tube and the lighter material will stay on top.

(Skill 3.2) (Rigorous)

17. **In a science experiment, a student needs to dispense very small measured amounts of liquid into a well-mixed solution. Which of the following is the best choice of equipment to use?**

    A. Buret with buret stand, stir-plate, stirring rod, beaker

    B. Buret with buret stand, stir-plate, beaker

    C. Volumetric flask, dropper, graduated cylinder, stirring rod

    D. Beaker, graduated cylinder, stir-plate

    Answer: B. Buret with buret stand, stir-plate, beaker

    The most accurate and convenient way to dispense small measured amounts of liquid in the laboratory is with a buret, on a buret stand. To keep a solution well-mixed, a magnetic stir-plate is the most sensible choice, and the solution will usually be mixed in a beaker. Although other combinations of materials could be used for this experiment, choice (B) is the simplest and best.

(Skill 3.2) (Average)

18. **Blue litmus paper turns pink when exposed to which of the following?**

    A. An acid

    B. A base

    C. An indicator substance

    D. Light

    Answer: A. An acid

    An indicator is any substance used to assist in the classification of another substance. An example of an indicator is litmus paper that measures whether a substance is acidic or basic. Blue litmus turns pink when placed in an acid, and pink litmus turns blue when placed in a base.

(Skill 3.3) (Rigorous)

19. **Which of these is the best example of "negligence"?**

    A. A teacher fails to give oral instructions to those with reading disabilities

    B. A teacher fails to exercise ordinary care to ensure safety in the classroom

    C. A teacher displays inability to supervise a large group of students

    D. A teacher reasonably anticipates that an event may occur, and plans accordingly

    Answer: B. A teacher fails to exercise ordinary care to ensure safety in the classroom

    "Negligence" is the failure to "exercise ordinary care" to ensure an appropriate and safe classroom environment. It is best for a teacher to meet all special requirements for disabled students, and to be good at supervising large groups. However, if a teacher can prove that he has done a reasonable job to ensure a safe and effective learning environment, then it is unlikely that he would be found negligent.

(Skill 3.3) (Average)

20. **Who should be notified in the case of a serious chemical spill?**

    A. The custodian

    B. The fire department or other municipal authority

    C. The science department chair

    D. The School Board

Answer: B. The fire department or other municipal authority

Although the custodian may help to clean up laboratory messes, and the science department chair should be involved in discussions of ways to avoid spills, a serious chemical spill may require action by the fire department or other trained emergency personnel. It is best to be safe by notifying them in case of a serious chemical accident.

(Skill 4.1) (Easy)

21. **Which of the following is most accurate?**

    A. Mass is always constant; weight may vary by location

    B. Mass and weight are both always constant

    C. Weight is always constant; mass may vary by location

    D. Mass and weight may both vary by location

Answer: A. Mass is always constant; weight may vary by location

When considering situations exclusive of nuclear reactions, mass is constant (mass, the amount of matter in a system, is conserved). Weight, on the other hand, is the force of gravity on an object, which is subject to change due to changes in the gravitational field and/or the location of the object.

(Skill 4.1) (Average)

22. **What is specific gravity?**

    A. The mass of an object

    B. The ratio of the density of a substance to the density of water

    C. Density

    D. The pull of the Earth's gravity on an object

Answer: B. The ratio of the density of a substance to the density of water

Mass is a measure of the amount of matter in an object. Density is the mass of a substance contained per unit of volume. Weight is the measure of the Earth's pull of gravity on an object. The only option here is the ratio of the density of a substance to the density of water.

(Skill 4.1) (Easy)

23. **The measure of the pull of Earth's gravity on an object is called**

    A. Mass number

    B. Atomic number

    C. Mass

    D. Weight

Answer: D. Weight

To answer this question, recall that mass number is the total number of protons and neutrons in an atom, atomic number is the number of protons in an atom, and mass is the amount of matter in an object. The only remaining choice is (D), weight, which is correct because weight is the force of gravity on an object.

(Skill 4.4) (Average)

24. **The Law of Conservation of Energy states that:**

    A. There must be the same number of products and reactants in any chemical equation

    B. Objects always fall toward large masses such as planets

    C. Energy is neither created nor destroyed, but may change form

    D. Lights must be turned off when not in use, by state regulation

    Answer: C. Energy is neither created nor destroyed, but may change form

    Answer (C) is a summary of the Law of Conservation of Energy (for non-nuclear reactions). In other words, energy can be transformed into various forms such as kinetic, potential, electric, or heat energy, but the total amount of energy remains constant. Answer (A) is untrue, as demonstrated by many synthesis and decomposition reactions. Answers (B) and (D) may be sensible, but they are not relevant in this case.

(Skill 4.5) (Easy)

25. **Energy is measured with the same units as _____**

    A. force.

    B. momentum.

    C. work.

    D. power.

    Answer: C. work.

    In SI units, energy is measured in Joules, i.e., (mass) (length squared)/(time squared). This is the same unit that is used for work. You can verify this by calculating that since work is force times distance, the units work out to be the same. Force is measured in Newtons in SI; momentum is measured in (mass) (length)/(time); power is measured in Watts (which equal Joules/second).

(Skill 5.2) (Rigorous)

26. **A long silver bar has a temperature of 50 degrees Celsius at one end and 0 degrees Celsius at the other end. The bar will reach thermal equilibrium (barring outside influence) by the process of heat _____**

    A. conduction.

    B. convection.

    C. radiation.

    D. phase change.

Answer: A. conduction.

Heat conduction is the process of heat transfer via solid contact. The molecules in a warmer region vibrate more rapidly, jostling neighboring molecules and accelerating them. This is the dominant heat transfer process in a solid with no outside influences. Recall, also, that convection is heat transfer by way of fluid currents; radiation is heat transfer via electromagnetic waves; and phase change can account for heat transfer in the form of shifts in matter phase.

(Skills 5.2, 5.3) (Rigorous)

27. **When you step out of the shower, the floor feels colder on your feet than the bathmat. Which of the following is the correct explanation for this phenomenon?**

    A. The floor is colder than the bathmat

    B. Your feet have a chemical reaction with the floor, but not with the bathmat

    C. Heat is conducted more easily into the floor

    D. Water is absorbed from your feet into the bathmat

Answer: C. Heat is conducted more easily into the floor

When you step out of the shower and onto a surface, the surface is most likely at room temperature, regardless of its composition (eliminating answer (A)). Your feet feel cold when heat is transferred from them to the surface, which happens more easily on a hard floor than a soft bathmat. This is because of differences in specific heat (the energy required to change temperature, which varies according to material). Therefore, the answer must be (C), i.e., heat is conducted more easily into the floor from your feet.

(Skill 5.4) (Average)

28. **Which of the following statements is NOT true?**

    A. Heat cannot pass spontaneously from a colder to a hotter object

    B. Systems that are nearly always in a state of equilibrium are called reversible systems

    C. Some machines can absorb heat from a heat source and do an equal amount of work without losing any heat to the environment; these are known as perfect machines

    D. Work occurs when heat is transferred from hotter to cooler objects

Answer: C. Some machines can absorb heat from a heat source and do an equal amount of work without losing any heat to the environment; these are known as perfect machines

The first part of the second law of thermodynamics tells us that no machine is 100% efficient. It is impossible to construct a machine that only absorbs heat from a heat source and performs an equal amount of work because some heat will always be lost to the environment.

(Skill 6.1) (Rigorous)

29. **When heat is added to most solids, they expand. Why is this the case?**

    A. The molecules get bigger

    B. The faster molecular motion leads to greater distance between the molecules

    C. The molecules develop greater repelling electric forces

    D. The molecules form a more rigid structure

Answer: B. The faster molecular motion leads to greater distance between the molecules

The atomic theory of matter states that matter is made up of tiny, rapidly moving particles. These particles move more quickly when warmer, because temperature is a measure of average kinetic energy of the particles. Warmer molecules therefore move further away from each other, because they have enough energy to separate from each other more often and for greater distances. The individual molecules do not get bigger, by conservation of mass, eliminating answer (A). The molecules do not develop greater repelling electric forces, eliminating answer (C). Occasionally, molecules form a more rigid structure when becoming colder and freezing (such as water)—but this gives rise to the exceptions to heat expansion, so it is not relevant here, eliminating answer (D).

(Skill 6.2) (Easy)

30. **Which parts of an atom are located inside the nucleus?**

    A. Protons and electrons

    B. Protons and neutrons

    C. Protons only

    D. Neutrons only

Answer: B. Protons and neutrons

Protons and neutrons are located in the nucleus, while electrons move around outside the nucleus.

(Skill 6.3) (Average)

31. **Which of the following accurately describes an ionic bond?**

    A. A bond formed by the sharing of electrons

    B. A bond formed when one electro-negative atom shares a hydrogen atom with another electronegative atom

    C. A bond formed by the transfer of electrons

    D. A bond formed between nonmetals

    Answer: C. A bond formed by the transfer of electrons

    An ionic bond is a bond formed by the transfer of electrons. It happens when metals and nonmetals bond. Before chlorine and sodium combine, for instance, the sodium has one valence electron and chlorine has seven. Neither valence shell is filled, but the chlorine's valence shell is almost full. During the reaction, the sodium gives one electron to the chlorine atom so both atoms then have filled shells and are stable.

(Skill 6.5) (Average)

32. **In a fission reactor, "heavy water" is used to _____**

    A. terminate fission reactions.

    B. slow down neutrons and moderate reactions.

    C. rehydrate the chemicals.

    D. initiate a chain reaction.

Answer: B. slow down neutrons and moderate reactions.

"Heavy water" is used in a nuclear [fission] reactor to slow down neutrons, controlling and moderating the nuclear reactions. It does not terminate the reactions, and it does not initiate the reactions. Also, although the reactor takes advantage of water's other properties (e.g., high specific heat for cooling), the water does not "rehydrate" the chemicals.

(Skill 6.5) (Rigorous)

33. **What is the main obstacle to using nuclear fusion for obtaining electricity?**

    A. Nuclear fusion produces much more pollution than nuclear fission

    B. There is no obstacle; most power plants use nuclear fusion today

    C. Nuclear fusion requires very high temperature and activation energy

    D. The fuel for nuclear fusion is extremely expensive

    Answer: C. Nuclear fusion requires very high temperature and activation energy

    Nuclear fission is the usual process for power generation in nuclear power plants. This is carried out by splitting nuclei to release energy. The sun's energy is generated by nuclear fusion, i.e., combination of smaller nuclei into a larger nucleus. Fusion creates much less radioactive waste, but it requires extremely high temperature and activation energy, so it is not yet feasible for electricity generation.

(Skill 7.2) (Average)

34. Newton's Laws are taught in science classes because _____

    A. they are the correct analysis of inertia, gravity, and forces.

    B. they are a close approximation to correct physics for usual Earth conditions.

    C. they accurately incorporate Relativity into studies of forces.

    D. Newton was a well-respected scientist in his time.

Answer: B. they are a close approximation to correct physics for usual Earth conditions.

Although Newton's Laws are often taught as fully correct for inertia, gravity, and forces, it is important to realize that Einstein's work (and that of others) has indicated that Newton's Laws are reliable only at speeds much lower than that of light. This is reasonable, though, for most middle- and high-school applications. At speeds close to the speed of light, Relativity considerations must be used.

(Skill 7.2) (Rigorous)

35. Which of the following is a correct explanation for astronaut "weightlessness"?

    A. Astronauts continue to feel the pull of gravity in space, but they are so far from planets that the force is small

    B. Astronauts continue to feel the pull of gravity in space, but spacecraft have such powerful engines that those forces dominate, reducing effective weight

    C. Astronauts do not feel the pull of gravity in space, because space is a vacuum

    D. Astronauts do not feel the pull of gravity in space, because black hole forces dominate the force field, reducing their masses

Answer: A. Astronauts continue to feel the pull of gravity in space, but they are so far from planets that the force is small

Gravity acts over tremendous distances in space (theoretically, infinite distance, though certainly at least as far as any astronaut has traveled). However, gravitational force is inversely proportional to distance squared from a massive body. This means that when an astronaut is in space, he is far enough from the center of mass of any planet that the gravitational force is very small, and he feels "weightless." Space is mostly empty (i.e., vacuum), and there are some black holes, and spacecraft do have powerful engines. However, none of these has the effect attributed to it in the incorrect answer choices (B), (C), and (D).

(Skill 7.2) (Easy)

36. **All of the following are considered Newton's Laws except for:**

    A. An object in motion will continue in motion unless acted upon by an outside force

    B. For every action force, there is an equal and opposite reaction force

    C. Nature abhors a vacuum

    D. Mass can be considered the ratio of force to acceleration

    Answer: C. Nature abhors a vacuum

    Newton's Laws include his law of inertia (an object in motion (or at rest) will stay in motion (or at rest) until acted upon by an outside force) (A), his law that (Force)=(Mass) (Acceleration) (D), and his equal and opposite reaction force law (B). Therefore, the answer to this question is (C), because "Nature abhors a vacuum" is not one of these.

(Skill 7.5) (Average)

37. **A Newton is fundamentally a measure of _____**

    A. force.

    B. momentum.

    C. energy.

    D. gravity.

Answer: A. force.

In SI units, force is measured in Newtons. Momentum and energy each have different units, without equivalent dimensions. A Newton is one (kilogram) (meter)/(second squared), while momentum is measured in (kilogram) (meter)/(second) and energy, in Joules, is (kilogram) (meter squared)/(second squared). Although "gravity" can be interpreted as the force of gravity, i.e., measured in Newtons, fundamentally it is not required.

(Skill 7.8) (Rigorous)

38. **A ball rolls down a smooth hill. You may ignore air resistance. Which of the following is a true statement?**

    A. The ball has more energy at the start of its descent than just before it hits the bottom of the hill, because it is higher up at the beginning

    B. The ball has less energy at the start of its descent than just before it hits the bottom of the hill, because it is moving more quickly at the end

    C. The ball has the same energy throughout its descent, because positional energy is converted to energy of motion

    D. The ball has the same energy throughout its descent, because a single object (such as a ball) cannot gain or lose energy

Answer: C. The ball has the same energy throughout its descent, because positional energy is converted to energy of motion

The principle of Conservation of Energy states that (except in cases of nuclear reaction, when energy may be created or destroyed by conversion to mass), "Energy is neither created nor destroyed, but may be transformed." Answers (A) and (B) give you a hint in this question—it is true that the ball has more Potential Energy when it is higher, and that it has more Kinetic Energy when it is moving quickly at the bottom of its descent. However, the total sum of all kinds of energy in the ball remains constant, if we neglect "losses" to heat/friction. Note that a single object can and does gain or lose energy when the energy is transferred to or from a different object. Conservation of Energy applies to systems, not to individual objects unless they are isolated.

(Skill 8.2) (Average)

39. **Resistance is measured in units called:**

    A. Watts

    B. Volts

    C. Ohms

    D. Current

Answer: C. Ohms

A watt is a unit of energy. Potential difference is measured in a unit called the volt. Current is the number of electrons per second that flow past a point in a circuit. An ohm is the unit for resistance.

(Skill 9.1) (Easy)

40. **Sound can be transmitted in all of the following except:**

    A. Air

    B. Water

    C. Diamond

    D. A vacuum

Answer: D. A vacuum

Sound, a longitudinal wave, is transmitted by vibrations of molecules.

Therefore, it can be transmitted through any gas, liquid, or solid. However, it cannot be transmitted through a vacuum, because there are no particles present to vibrate and bump into their adjacent particles to transmit the waves. This is consistent only with answer (D). (It is interesting to note that sound is actually faster in solids and liquids than in air.)

(Skill 9.3) (Average)

41. **The speed of light is different in different materials. This is responsible for**

    _____

    A. interference.

    B. refraction.

    C. reflection.

    D. relativity.

Answer: B. refraction.

Refraction (B) is the bending of light when it hits a material at an angle in which it has a different speed. (This is analogous to a cart rolling on a smooth road. If it hits a rough patch at an angle, the wheel on the rough patch slows down first, leading to a change in direction.) Interference (A) is when light waves interfere with each other to form brighter or dimmer patterns; reflection (C) is when light bounces off a surface; relativity (D) is a general topic related to light speed and its implications, but not specifically indicated here.

(Skill 9.5) (Rigorous)

42. **As a train approaches, the whistle sounds:**

    A. Higher, because it has a higher apparent frequency

    B. Lower, because it has a lower apparent frequency

    C. Higher, because it has a lower apparent frequency

    D. Lower, because it has a higher apparent frequency

    Answer: A. Higher, because it has a higher apparent frequency

    By the Doppler effect, when a source of sound is moving toward an observer, the wave fronts are released closer together, i.e., with a greater apparent frequency. Higher frequency sounds are higher in pitch.

(Skill 9.5) (Rigorous)

43. **The Doppler effect is associated most closely with which property of waves?**

    A. Amplitude

    B. Wavelength

    C. Frequency

    D. Intensity

    Answer: C. Frequency

    The Doppler effect accounts for an apparent increase in frequency when a wave source moves toward a wave receiver or apparent decrease in frequency when a wave source moves away from a wave receiver. (Note that the receiver could also be moving toward or away from the source.) As the wave fronts are released, motion toward the receiver mimics more frequent wave fronts, while motion away from the receiver mimics less frequent wave fronts. Meanwhile, the amplitude, wavelength, and intensity of the wave are not as relevant to this process (although moving closer to a wave source makes it seem more intense).

(Skill 9.8) (Average)

44. **Sound waves are produced by**

    _____

    A. pitch.

    B. noise.

    C. vibrations.

    D. sonar.

Answer: C. vibrations.

Sound waves are produced by a vibrating body. The vibrating object moves forward and compresses the air in front of it, then reverses direction so that the pressure on the air is lessened and expansion of the air molecules occurs. The vibrating air molecules move back and forth parallel to the direction of motion of the wave as they pass the energy from adjacent air molecules closer to the source to air molecules farther away from the source.

(Skill 9.9) (Rigorous)

45. **The electromagnetic radiation with the longest wave length is _____**

   A. radio waves.

   B. red light.

   C. X-rays.

   D. ultraviolet light.

Answer: A. radio waves.

As one can see on a diagram of the electromagnetic spectrum, radio waves have longer wave lengths (and smaller frequencies) than visible light, which in turn has longer wave lengths than ultraviolet or X-ray radiation. If you did not remember this sequence, you might recall that wave length is inversely proportional to frequency, and that radio waves are considered much less harmful (less energetic, i.e., lower frequency) than ultraviolet or X-ray radiation.

(Skill 10.1) (Easy)

46. **The elements in the modern Periodic Table are arranged:**

   A. In numerical order by atomic number

   B. Randomly

   C. In alphabetical order by chemical symbol

   D. In numerical order by atomic mass

Answer: A. In numerical order by atomic number

Although the first periodic tables were arranged by atomic mass, the modern table is arranged by atomic number, i.e., the number of protons in each element. (This allows the element list to be complete and unique.) The elements are not arranged either randomly or in alphabetical order.

(Skill 10.2) (Average)

47. **Which of the following is NOT a property of metalloids?**

   A. Metalloids are solids at standard temperature and pressure

   B. Metalloids can conduct electricity to a limited extent

   C. Metalloids are found in groups 13 through 17

   D. Metalloids all favor ionic bonding

Answer: D. Metalloids all favor ionic bonding

Metalloids are substances that have characteristics of both metals and nonmetals, including limited conduction of electricity and solid phase at standard temperature and pressure. Metalloids are found in a "stair-step" pattern from Boron in group 13 through Astatine in group 17. Some metalloids, e.g., Silicon, favor covalent bonding. Others, e.g., Astatine, can bond ionically. Therefore, the answer is (D). Recall that metals/nonmetals/metalloids are not strictly defined by Periodic Table group, so their bonding is unlikely to be consistent with one another.

(Skill 11.2) (Rigorous)

48. **The chemical equation for water formation is: $2H_2 + O_2 \rightarrow 2H_2O$. Which of the following is an incorrect interpretation of this equation?**

    A. Two moles of hydrogen gas and one mole of oxygen gas combine to make two moles of water

    B. Two grams of hydrogen gas and one gram of oxygen gas combine to make two grams of water

    C. Two molecules of hydrogen gas and one molecule of oxygen gas combine to make two molecules of water

    D. Four atoms of hydrogen (combined as a diatomic gas) and two atoms of oxygen (combined as a diatomic gas) combine to make two molecules of water

Answer: B. Two grams of hydrogen gas and one gram of oxygen gas combine to make two grams of water

In any chemical equation, the coefficients indicate the relative proportions of molecules (or atoms), or of moles of molecules. They do not refer to mass, because chemicals combine in repeatable combinations of molar ratio (i.e., number of moles), but vary in mass per mole of material. Therefore, the answer must be the only choice that does not refer to numbers of particles, i.e., answer (B), which refers to grams, a unit of mass.

(Skill 11.2) (Average)

49. **Which of the following will not change in a chemical reaction?**

    A. Number of moles of products

    B. Atomic number of one of the reactants

    C. Mass (in grams) of one of the reactants

    D. Rate of reaction

Answer: B. Atomic number of one of the reactants

Atomic number, i.e., the number of protons in a given element, is constant unless involved in a nuclear reaction. Meanwhile, the amounts (measured in moles (A) or in grams(C)) of reactants and products change over the course of a chemical reaction, and the rate of a chemical reaction (D) may change due to internal or external processes.

(Skill 11.2) (Average)

50. **Which of the following is a correct definition for "chemical equilibrium"?**

    A. Chemical equilibrium is when the forward and backward reaction rates are equal; the reaction may continue to proceed forward and backward

    B. Chemical equilibrium is when the forward and backward reaction rates are equal, and equal to zero; the reaction does not continue

    C. Chemical equilibrium is when there are equal quantities of reactants and products

    D. Chemical equilibrium is when acids and bases neutralize each other fully

    Answer: A. Chemical equilibrium is when the forward and backward reaction rates are equal; the reaction may continue to proceed forward and backward

    Chemical equilibrium is defined as when the quantities of reactants and products are at a "steady state" and are no longer shifting, but the reaction may still proceed forward and backward. The rate of forward reaction must equal the rate of backward reaction. Note that there may or may not be equal amounts of chemicals, and that this is not restricted to a completed reaction or to an acid-base reaction.

(Skill 11.6) (Average)

51. **What is the purpose of Lewis dot structures?**

    A. They show the three-dimensional shape of the molecule

    B. They are a super-simplified representation of the molecule with lines representing bonds

    C. They provide a method for keeping track of each atom's valence electrons in a molecule

    D. They provide a method for keeping track of each atom's non-valence electrons in a molecule

    Answer: C. They provide a method for keeping track of each atom's valence electrons in a molecule

    Lewis dot structures are like electron accounting. They provide a method for keeping track of each atom's valence electrons in a molecule. Dot structures help to demonstrate how the bonds are formed; whether they are single, double, or triple bonds; and whether there are any non-bonded electron pairs.

(Skill 12.1) (Rigorous)

52. **Which of the following is NOT true about phase change in matter?**

    A. Solid water and liquid ice can coexist at water's freezing point

    B. At 7 degrees Celsius, water is always in liquid phase

    C. Matter changes phase when enough energy is gained or lost

    D. Different phases of matter are characterized by differences in molecular motion

Answer: B. At 7 degrees Celsius, water is always in liquid phase

According to the molecular theory of matter, molecular motion determines the "phase" of the matter, and the energy in the matter determines the speed of molecular motion. Solids have vibrating molecules that are in fixed relative positions; liquids have faster molecular motion than their solid forms, and the molecules may move more freely but must still be in contact with one another; gases have even more energy and more molecular motion. (Other phases, such as plasma, are even more energetic.) At the "freezing point" or "boiling point" of a substance, both relevant phases may be present. For instance, water at zero degrees Celsius may be composed of some liquid and some solid, all liquid, or all solid. Pressure changes, in addition to temperature changes, can cause phase changes. For example, nitrogen can be liquefied under high pressure, even though its boiling temperature is very low. Therefore, the correct answer must be (B). Water may be a liquid at that temperature, but it may also be a solid, depending on ambient pressure.

(Skill 13.2) (Average)

53. **Which reaction below is a decomposition reaction?**

    A. $HCl + NaOH \rightarrow NaCl + H_2O$

    B. $C + O_2 \rightarrow CO_2$

    C. $2H_2O \rightarrow 2H_2 + O_2$

    D. $CuSO_4 + Fe \rightarrow FeSO_4 + Cu$

Answer: C. $2H_2O \rightarrow 2H_2 + O_2$

To answer this question, recall that a decomposition reaction is one in which there are fewer reactants (on the left) than products (on the right). This is consistent only with answer (C). Meanwhile, note that answer (A) shows a double-replacement reaction (in which two sets of ions switch bonds), answer (B) shows a synthesis reaction (in which there are fewer products than reactants), and answer (D) shows a single-replacement reaction (in which one substance replaces another in its bond, but the other does not get a new bond).

(Skill 13.4) (Average)

54. **Enzymes speed up reactions by**

    _____

    A. utilizing ATP.

    B. lowering pH, allowing reaction speed to increase.

    C. increasing volume of substrate.

    D. lowering energy of activation.

Answer: D. lowering energy of activation.

Because enzymes are catalysts, they work the same way—they cause the formation of activated chemical complexes, which require a lower activation energy. Therefore, the answer is (D). ATP is an energy source for cells, and pH or volume changes may or may not affect reaction rate, so these answers can be eliminated.

(Skill 13.4) (Average)

55. **Catalysts assist reactions by _____**

   A. lowering effective activation energy.

   B. maintaining precise pH levels.

   C. keeping systems at equilibrium.

   D. adjusting reaction speed.

   Answer: A. lowering effective activation energy.

   Chemical reactions can be enhanced or accelerated by catalysts, which are present with both reactants and products. They induce the formation of activated complexes, thereby lowering the effective activation energy so that less energy is necessary for the reaction to begin. Although this often makes reactions faster, answer (D) is not as good a choice as the more generally applicable answer (A), which is correct.

(Skill 14.4) (Easy)

56. **Vinegar is an example of a _____**

   A. strong acid.

   B. strong base.

   C. weak acid.

   D. weak base.

   Answer: C. weak acid.

   The main ingredient in vinegar is acetic acid, a weak acid. Vinegar is a useful acid in science classes, because it makes a frothy reaction with bases such as baking soda (e.g., in the quintessential volcano model). Vinegar is not a strong acid, such as hydrochloric acid, because it does not dissociate as fully or cause as much corrosion. It is not a base.

(Skill 15.1) (Average)

57. **What cell organelle contains the cell's stored food?**

   A. Vacuoles

   B. Golgi Apparatus

   C. Ribosomes

   D. Lysosomes

   Answer: A. Vacuoles

   In a cell, the sub-parts are called organelles. Of these, the vacuoles hold stored food (and water and pigments). The Golgi Apparatus sorts molecules from other parts of the cell; the ribosomes are sites of protein synthesis; and the lysosomes contain digestive enzymes.

(Skill 15.5) (Rigorous)

58. **Which process(es) result(s) in a haploid chromosome number?**

   A. Mitosis

   B. Meiosis

   C. Both mitosis and meiosis

   D. Neither mitosis nor meiosis

   Answer: B. Meiosis

   Meiosis is the division of sex cells. The resulting chromosome number is half the number of parent cells, i.e., a "haploid chromosome number." Mitosis, however, is the division of other cells, in which the chromosome number is the same as the parent cell chromosome number.

(Skill 15.5) (Easy)

59. The first stage of mitosis is called

_____

A. telophase.

B. anaphase.

C. prophase.

D. mitophase.

Answer: C. prophase.

In mitosis, the division of somatic cells, prophase is the stage where the cell enters mitosis. The four stages of mitosis, in order, are: prophase, metaphase, anaphase, and telophase. ("Mitophase" is not one of the steps.) During prophase, the cell begins the nonstop process of division. Its chromatin condenses, its nucleolus disappears, the nuclear membrane breaks apart, mitotic spindles form, its cytoskeleton breaks down, and centrioles push the spindles apart. Note that interphase—the stage where chromatin is loose, chromosomes are replicated, and cell metabolism is occurring—is technically not a stage of mitosis; it is a precursor to cell division.

(Skill 16.1) (Rigorous)

60. Which of the following is not a nucleotide?

A. Adenine

B. Alanine

C. Cytosine

D. Guanine

Answer: B. Alanine

Alanine is an amino acid. Adenine, cytosine, guanine, thymine, and uracil are nucleotides.

(Skill 16.2) (Average)

61. Amino acids are carried to the ribosome in protein synthesis by:

A. transfer RNA (tRNA)

B. messenger RNA (mRNA)

C. ribosomal RNA (rRNA)

D. transformation RNA (trRNA)

Answer: A. transfer RNA (tRNA)

The job of tRNA is to carry and position amino acids to/on the ribosomes. mRNA copies DNA code and brings it to the ribosomes; rRNA is in the ribosome itself. There is no such thing as trRNA.

(Skill 16.4) (Rigorous)

62. A series of experiments on pea plants performed by _____ showed that two invisible markers existed for each trait, and one marker dominated the other.

A. Pasteur

B. Watson and Crick

C. Mendel

D. Mendeleev

Answer: C. Mendel

Gregor Mendel was a ninteenth-century Austrian botanist, who derived "laws" governing inherited traits. His work led to the understanding of dominant and recessive traits, carried by biological markers. Mendel cross-bred different kinds of pea plants with varying features and observed the resulting new plants. He showed that genetic characteristics are not passed identically from one generation to the next. (Pasteur, Watson, Crick, and Mendeleev were other scientists with different specialties.)

(Skill 16.4) (Rigorous)

63. **A white flower is crossed with a red flower. Which of the following is a sign of incomplete dominance?**

    A. Pink flowers

    B. Red flowers

    C. White flowers

    D. No flowers

Answer: A. Pink flowers

Incomplete dominance means that neither the red nor the white gene is strong enough to suppress the other. Therefore both are expressed, leading in this case to the formation of pink flowers.

(Skill 16.4) (Average)

64. **A child has type O blood. Her father has type A blood, and her mother has type B blood. What are the genotypes of the father and mother, respectively?**

    A. AO and BO

    B. AA and AB

    C. OO and BO

    D. AO and BB

Answer: A. AO and BO

Because O blood is recessive, the child must have inherited two O's—one from each of her parents. Since her father has type A blood, his genotype must be AO; likewise, her mother's blood must be BO.

(Skill 16.8) (Rigorous)

65. **Which of the following is a correct explanation for scientific evolution?**

    A. Giraffes need to reach higher for leaves to eat, so their necks stretch. The giraffe babies are then born with longer necks. Eventually, there are more long-necked giraffes in the population.

    B. Giraffes with longer necks are able to reach more leaves, so they eat more and have more babies than other giraffes. Eventually, there are more long-necked giraffes in the population.

    C. Giraffes want to reach higher for leaves to eat, so they release enzymes into their bloodstream, which in turn causes fetal development of longer-necked giraffes. Eventually, there are more long-necked giraffes in the population.

    D. Giraffes with long necks are more attractive to other giraffes, so they get the best mating partners and have more babies. Eventually, there are more long-necked giraffes in the population.

Answer: B. Giraffes with longer necks are able to reach more leaves, so they eat more and have more babies than other giraffes. Eventually, there are more long-necked giraffes in the population.

Although evolution is often misunderstood, it occurs via natural selection. Organisms with a life/reproductive advantage will produce more offspring.

Over many generations, this changes the proportions of the population. In any case, it is impossible for a stretched neck (A) or a fervent desire (C) to result in a biologically mutated baby. Although there are traits that are naturally selected because of mate attractiveness and fitness (D), this is not the primary situation here, so answer (B) is the best choice.

(Skill 17.2) (Rigorous)

66. **Extensive use of antibacterial soap has been found to increase the virulence of certain infections in hospitals. Which of the following might be an explanation for this phenomenon?**

   A. Antibacterial soaps do not kill viruses

   B. Antibacterial soaps do not incorporate the same antibiotics used in medicine

   C. Antibacterial soaps kill a lot of bacteria, and only the hardiest ones survive to reproduce

   D. Antibacterial soaps can be very drying to the skin

Answer: C. Antibacterial soaps kill a lot of bacteria, and only the hardiest ones survive to reproduce

All of the answer choices in this question are true statements, but the question specifically asks for a cause of increased disease virulence in hospitals. This phenomenon is due to natural selection. The bacteria that can survive contact with antibacterial soap are the strongest ones, and without other bacteria competing for resources, they have more opportunity to flourish. This problem has led to several antibiotic-resistant bacterial diseases in hospitals nationwide. Therefore, the answer is (C). However, note that answers (A) and (D) may be additional problems with over-reliance on antibacterial products.

(Skill 18.1) (Rigorous)

67. **Which of the following is NOT a necessary characteristic of living things?**

   A. Movement

   B. Reduction of local entropy

   C. Ability to cause local energy form changes

   D. Reproduction

Answer: A. Movement

There are many definitions of "life," but in all cases, a living organism reduces local entropy, changes chemical energy into other forms, and reproduces.

Not all living things move, however, so the correct answer is (A).

(Skill 18.1) (Average)

68. **Identify the correct sequence of organization of living things from lower to higher order:**

    A. Cell, Organelle, Organ, Tissue, System, Organism

    B. Cell, Tissue, Organ, Organelle, System, Organism

    C. Organelle, Cell, Tissue, Organ, System, Organism

    D. Organelle, Tissue, Cell, Organ, System, Organism

    Answer: C. Organelle, Cell, Tissue, Organ, System, Organism

    Organelles are parts of the cell; cells make up tissue, which makes up organs. Organs work together in systems (e.g., the respiratory system), and the organism is the living thing as a whole.

(Skill 18.2) (Rigorous)

69. **The scientific name *Canis familiaris* refers to the animal's _____**

    A. kingdom and phylum.

    B. genus and species.

    C. class and species.

    D. type and family.

Answer: B. genus and species.

To answer this question, you must be aware that genus and species are the most specific way to identify an organism, and that usually the genus is capitalized and the species, immediately following, is not. Furthermore, it helps to recall that "Canis" is the genus for dogs, or canines. Therefore, the answer must be (B). If you did not remember these details, you might recall that there is no such kingdom as "Canis," and that there isn't a category "type" in official taxonomy. This could eliminate answers (A) and (D).

(Skill 18.2) (Rigorous)

70. **Animals with a notochord or a backbone are in the phylum:**

    A. Arthropoda

    B. Chordata

    C. Mollusca

    D. Mammalia

Answer: B. Chordata

The phylum arthropoda contains spiders and insects, and phylum mollusca contains snails and squid. Mammalia is a class in the phylum chordata.

(Skill 18.3) (Rigorous)

71. **Which of the following organisms use spores to reproduce?**

    A. Fish

    B. Flowering plants

    C. Conifers

    D. Ferns

Answer: D. Ferns

Ferns, in Division Pterophyta, reproduce with spores and flagellated sperm.

Flowering plants reproduce via seeds, and conifers reproduce via seeds protected in cones (e.g., pinecones). Fish, of course, reproduce sexually.

(Skill 18.3) (Rigorous)

72. **Why are viruses considered obligate parasites?**

    A. Because once they enter the host, they are obligated to infect the host

    B. Because the immune system of the host is obligated to combat the effects of the virus

    C. Because they are not reliant on the host for any of the means of their own survival or reproduction

    D. Because they rely on the host for their own reproduction

    Answer: D. Because they rely on the host for their own reproduction

    Although viruses are not classified as living things, they greatly affect other living things by disrupting cell activity. They are considered to be obligate parasites because they rely on the host for their own reproduction.

(Skill 21.4) (Average)

73. **A wrasse (fish) cleans the teeth of other fish by eating away plaque. This is an example of _____ between the fish.**

    A. parasitism

    B. symbiosis (mutualism)

    C. competition

    D. predation

    Answer: B. symbiosis (mutualism)

    When both species benefit from their interaction in their habitat, this is called "symbiosis," or "mutualism." In this example, the wrasse benefits from having a source of food, and the other fish benefit by having healthier teeth. Note that "parasitism" is when one species benefits at the expense of the other, "competition" is when two species compete with one another for the same habitat or food, and "predation" is when one species feeds on another.

(Skill 21.8) (Rigorous)

74. **What is the most accurate description of the Water Cycle?**

    A. Rain comes from clouds, filling the ocean. The water then evaporates and becomes clouds again.

    B. Water circulates from rivers into groundwater and back, while water vapor circulates in the atmosphere.

    C. Water is conserved except for chemical or nuclear reactions, and any drop of water could circulate through clouds, rain, ground-water, and surface-water.

    D. Weather systems cause chemical reactions to break water into its atoms.

Answer: C. Water is conserved except for chemical or nuclear reactions, and any drop of water could circulate through clouds, rain, ground-water, and surface-water.

All natural chemical cycles, including the Water Cycle, depend on the principle of Conservation of Mass. (For water, unlike for elements such as Nitrogen, chemical reactions may cause sources or sinks of water molecules.) Any drop of water may circulate through the hydrologic system, ending up in a cloud, as rain, or as surface- or ground-water. Although answers (A) and (B) describe parts of the water cycle, the most comprehensive and correct answer is (C).

(Skill 21.9) (Rigorous)

75. **Which of the following animals are most likely to live in a tropical rain forest?**

A. Reindeer

B. Monkeys

C. Puffins

D. Bears

Answer: B. Monkeys

The tropical rain forest biome is hot and zumid, and is very fertile—it is thought to contain almost half of the world's species. Reindeer (A), puffins (C), and bears (D), however, are usually found in much colder climates. There are several species of monkeys that thrive in hot, humid climates, so answer (B) is correct.

(Skill 22.1) (Average)

76. **Lithification refers to the process by which unconsolidated sediments are transformed into _____**

A. metamorphic rocks.

B. sedimentary rocks.

C. igneous rocks.

D. lithium oxide.

Answer: B. sedimentary rocks.

Lithification is the process of sediments coming together to form rocks, i.e., sedimentary rock formation. Metamorphic and igneous rocks are formed via other processes (heat and pressure or volcano activity, respectively). Lithium oxide shares a word root with "lithification," but is otherwise unrelated to this question.

(Skill 22.1) (Average)

77. **Igneous rocks can be classified according to which of the following?**

A. Texture

B. Composition

C. Formation process

D. All of the above

Answer: D. All of the above

Igneous rocks, which form from the crystallization of molten lava, are classified according to many of their characteristics, including texture, composition, and how they were formed.

(Skill 22.1) (Average)

78. **Which of the following types of rock are made from magma?**

   A. Fossils

   B. Sedimentary

   C. Metamorphic

   D. Igneous

   Answer: D. Igneous

   Few fossils are found in metamorphic rock and virtually none are found in igneous rocks. Igneous rocks are formed from magma, and magma is so hot that any organisms trapped by it are destroyed. Metamorphic rocks are formed by high temperatures and great pressures. When fluid sediments are transformed into solid sedimentary rocks, the process is known as lithification.

(Skill 22.2) (Rigorous)

79. **Which of these is a true statement about loamy soil?**

   A. Loamy soil is gritty and porous

   B. Loamy soil is smooth and a good barrier to water

   C. Loamy soil is hostile to microorganisms

   D. Loamy soil is velvety and clumpy

   Answer: D. Loamy soil is velvety and clumpy

   The three classes of soil, by texture are: sandy (gritty and porous), clay (smooth, greasy, and most impervious to water), and loamy (velvety, clumpy, and able to hold water and let water flow through). In addition, loamy soils are often the most fertile soils.

(Skill 22.4) (Rigorous)

80. _____ are cracks in the plates of the Earth's crust, along which the plates move.

   A. Faults

   B. Ridges

   C. Earthquakes

   D. Volcanoes

   Answer: A. Faults

   Faults are cracks in the Earth's crust, and when the Earth moves, an earthquake results. Faults may lead to mismatched edges of ground, forming ridges, and ground shape may also be determined by volcanoes.

(Skill 22.5) (Average)

81. **The theory of "continental drift" is supported by which of the following?**

   A. The way the shapes of South America and Europe fit together

   B. The way the shapes of Europe and Asia fit together

   C. The way the shapes of South America and Africa fit together

   D. The way the shapes of North America and Antarctica fit together

Answer: C. The way the shapes of South America and Africa fit together

The theory of "continental drift" states that many years ago, there was one land mass on the Earth (Pangea). This land mass broke apart via Earth crust motion, and the continents drifted apart as separate pieces. This is supported by the shapes of South America and Africa, which seem to fit together like puzzle pieces if you look at a globe. Note that answer choices (A), (B), and (D) give either land masses that do not fit together, or those that are still attached to each other.

(Skill 23.4) (Average)

82. **Fossils are usually found in _____ rock.**

    A. igneous

    B. sedimentary

    C. metamorphic

    D. cumulus

Answer: B. sedimentary

Fossils are formed by layers of dirt and sand settling around organisms, hardening, and taking an imprint of the organisms. When the organism decays, the hardened imprint is left behind. This is most likely to happen in rocks that form from layers of settling dirt and sand, i.e., sedimentary rock. Note that igneous rock is formed from molten rock from volcanoes (lava), while metamorphic rock can be formed from any rock under very high temperature and pressure changes. "Cumulus" is a descriptor for clouds, not rocks.

(Skill 23.6) (Easy)

83. **Which of the following is the longest (largest) unit of geological time?**

    A. Solar Year

    B. Epoch

    C. Period

    D. Era

Answer: D. Era

Geological time is measured by many units, but the longest unit listed here (and indeed the longest used to describe the biological development of the planet) is the Era. Eras are subdivided into Periods, which are further divided into Epochs.

(Skill 24.6) (Rigorous)

84. **The salinity of ocean water is closest to _____**

    A. 0.035%.

    B. 0.35%.

    C. 3.5%.

    D. 35%.

Answer: C. 3.5%.

Salinity, or concentration of dissolved salt, can be measured in mass ratio (i.e., mass of salt divided by mass of sea water). For Earth's oceans, the salinity is approximately 3.5%, or 35 parts per thousand. Note that answers (A) and (D) can be eliminated, because (A) is so dilute as to be hardly saline, while (D) is so concentrated that it would not support ocean life.

(Skill 25.7) (Rigorous)

85. A cup of hot liquid and a cup of cold liquid are both sitting in a room at comfortable room temperature and humidity. Both cups are made of thin plastic. Which of the following is a true statement?

    A. There will be fog on the outside of the hot liquid cup, and also fog on the outside of the cold liquid cup

    B. There will be fog on the outside of the hot liquid cup, but not on the cold liquid cup

    C. There will be fog on the outside of the cold liquid cup, but not on the hot liquid cup

    D. There will not be fog on the outside of either cup

Answer: C. There will be fog on the outside of the cold liquid cup, but not on the hot liquid cup

Fog forms on the outside of a cup when the contents of the cup are colder than the surrounding air, and the cup material is not a perfect insulator. This happens because the air surrounding the cup is cooled to a lower temperature than the ambient room, so it has a lower saturation point for water vapor. Although the humidity had been reasonable in the warmer air, when that air circulates near the colder region and cools, water condenses onto the cup's outside surface. This phenomenon is also visible when someone takes a hot shower, and the mirror gets foggy. The mirror surface is cooler than the ambient air, and provides a surface for water condensation. Furthermore, the same phenomenon is why defrosters on car windows send heat to the windows—the warmer window does not permit as much condensation.

(Skill 26.4) (Rigorous)

86. What is the main difference between the "condensation hypothesis" and the "tidal hypothesis" for the origin of the solar system?

   A. The tidal hypothesis can be tested, but the condensation hypothesis cannot

   B. The tidal hypothesis proposes a near collision of two stars pulling on each other, but the condensation hypothesis proposes condensation of rotating clouds of dust and gas

   C. The tidal hypothesis explains how tides began on planets such as Earth, but the condensation hypothesis explains how water vapor became liquid on Earth

   D. The tidal hypothesis is based on Aristotelian physics, but the condensation hypothesis is based on Newtonian mechanics

Answer: B. The tidal hypothesis proposes a near collision of two stars pulling on each other, but the condensation hypothesis proposes condensation of rotating clouds of dust and gas

Most scientists believe the "condensation hypothesis," i.e., that the solar system began when rotating clouds of dust and gas condensed into the sun and planets. A minority opinion is the "tidal hypothesis," i.e., that the sun almost collided with a large star. The large star's gravitational field would have then pulled gases out of the sun; these gases are thought to have begun to orbit the sun and condense into planets. Because both of these hypotheses deal with ancient, unrepeatable events, neither can be tested, eliminating answer (A). Note that both "tidal" and "condensation" have additional meanings in physics, but those are not relevant here, eliminating answer (C). Both hypotheses are based on best guesses using modern physics, eliminating answer (D).

(Skill 26.6) (Average)

87. Which of the following is the best definition for "meteorite"?

   A. A meteorite is a mineral composed of mica and feldspar

   B. A meteorite is material from outer space that has struck the Earth's surface

   C. A meteorite is an element that has properties of both metals and nonmetals

   D. A meteorite is a very small unit of length measurement

Answer: B. A meteorite is material from outer space that has struck the Earth's surface

Meteoroids are pieces of matter in space, composed of particles of rock and metal. If a meteoroid travels through the Earth's atmosphere, friction causes burning and a "shooting star"—i.e., a meteor. If the meteor strikes the Earth's surface, it is known as a meterorite. Note that although the suffix –ite often indicates a mineral, answer (A) is incorrect. Answer (C) refers to a "metalloid" rather than a "meteorite," and answer (D) is simply a misleading pun on "meter."

(Skill 26.6) (Rigorous)

88. **The Earth's atmosphere is composed mainly of which of the following?**

    A. Oxygen and nitrogen

    B. Carbon and hydrogen

    C. Carbon and oxygen

    D. Nitrogen and carbon

    Answer: A. Oxygen and nitrogen

    The atmosphere is composed mainly of oxygen and nitrogen. Earth is the only planet that is known to support life.

(Skill 26.12) (Average)

89. **Sonar works by _____**

    A. timing how long it takes sound to reach a certain speed.

    B. bouncing sound waves between two metal plates.

    C. bouncing sound waves off an object and timing how long it takes for the sound to return.

    D. evaluating the motion and amplitude of sound.

    Answer: C. bouncing sound waves off an object and timing how long it takes for the sound to return.

    Sonar is used to measure distances. Sound waves are sent out, and the time for the sound to hit an obstacle and bounce back is measured. By using the known speed of sound, observers (or machines) can calculate the distance to the obstacle.

(Skill 27.1) (Easy)

90. **What is the source for most of the United States' drinking water?**

    A. Desalinated ocean water

    B. Surface water (lakes, streams, mountain runoff)

    C. Rainfall into municipal reservoirs

    D. Groundwater

Answer: D. Groundwater

Groundwater currently provides drinking water for 53% of the population of the United States. (Although groundwater is often less polluted than surface water, it can be contaminated and it is very hard to clean once it is polluted. If too much groundwater is used from one area, then the ground may sink or shift, or local salt water may intrude from ocean boundaries.) The other answer choices can be used for drinking water, but they are not the most widely used.

CPSIA information can be obtained
at www.ICGtesting.com
Printed in the USA
BVOW04s1152061217
502110BV00012B/993/P